Gower Handbook of Management Development

FOURTH EDITION

GOWER HANDBOOK OF MANAGEMENT DEVELOPMENT

FOURTH EDITION

Edited by
Alan Mumford

Gower

First published 1973 as *Handbook of Management Development*
Second edition 1986
Third edition 1991
Fourth edition published by
Gower Publishing Limited
Gower House
Croft Road
Aldershot
Hampshire GU11 3HR
England

Gower
Old Post Road
Brookfield
Vermont 05036
USA

British Library Cataloguing in Publication Data
Handbook of Management Development. –
4Rev.ed
  I. Mumford, Alan
  658.4
  ISBN 0–566–07445–1

Library of Congress Cataloging-in-Publication Data
Gower handbook of management development/edited by Alan Mumford. –
  4th ed.
     p. cm.
  Includes index.
  ISBN 0–566–07445–1
  1. Executives--Training of. I. Mumford, Alan.
HD38.2.H36 1994
658.4'07124--dc20

94–9668
CIP

Typeset in Great Britain by Poole Typesetting (Wessex) Limited, Bournemouth, Dorset and printed in Great Britain by Hartnolls Ltd, Bodmin

Contents

PART I   SETTING THE SCENE

1. Effectiveness in management development   3
Alan Mumford
The threefold nature of effectiveness in management
development – Effective managerial behaviour – Development
processes emphasizing effectiveness – Effective learning
processes – Successful management development – References

PART II   PLANNING FOR MANAGEMENT DEVELOPMENT

2. Planning management development   23
Tony Vineall
The basic disciplines – Management resource planning
meetings at company or unit level – Review of resources at
higher levels – Planning of individual careers – Conclusions
– References

List of illustrations

Preface

In this fourth edition of the *Handbook* I have continued the approach adopted in the previous two editions. My own research and experience have been increasingly concerned with an expansion of the meaning of 'management development' so that we can incorporate the relatively accidental processes, not even always recognized as a development or a learning process, which managers call 'learning by experience'. It is still true, however, that the propositions I have offered about the nature of management development, based on this incorporation of formal and informal processes, have not yet been widely accepted, or at least written about. So although readers will be introduced to the concepts and my model of management development in Chapter 1 (and can follow the argument in more detail in my other books), much of the attention in this *Handbook* is to formal management development processes. Thus, most chapters focus on the kind of planned and deliberate processes used by most management development advisers and personnel directors.

I have also retained a number of chapters which are largely unchanged. Some features of the formal management development systems do not change significantly in the space of three or four years. And some of the more personal chapters have also become classics of their kind. The new authors I have recruited for this edition have enabled me to give even greater emphasis to issues of organization and national culture, and to what the management development specialist actually does.

A final comment about the nature of a handbook of this kind might be helpful to some readers. My concern as editor has been that each chapter should be self-sustaining, because I expect few readers will want to go through every chapter in one long sitting. They are more likely to choose chapters which relate to immediate needs. In a book essentially aimed at practitioners, while I think it desirable to avoid duplication, I do not find it necessary to provide *xv* elaborate cross-referencing, nor have I attempted to impose a theme running through all the contributions.

Chapter 1 discusses learning from, and about, the reality of management, compared with attempting to learn from simulations or descriptions of reality. It also emphasizes the significance of understanding and working on learning processes themselves. It provides therefore a statement – both conceptual and practical – about what I believe management development encompasses. It also covers a great deal of the ground which otherwise might have been covered in Part III which deals with learning processes.

In Part II the chapters by Tony Vineall and Andrew Stewart (Chapters 2, 3 and 4) respond to the needs for 'planned and deliberate' processes. The relatively small number of chapters I have allocated to this subject reflects my priorities – by implication those that I am suggesting to readers. I do not regard the mechanics as unimportant, but in past years too much attention was paid to formal management development systems and not enough to questions such as, 'Management Development for What?', and 'How Do Managers Learn More Effectively?' The chapter by Charles Margerison (Chapter 5) offers some innovative ideas on managing careers, as well as including some of the more traditional processes of career management. Wendy Hirsh and Marie Strebler in Chapter 6 extend the issues initially identified in Chapters 3 and 4, and discuss the issues involved in defining managerial skills or competences – and indeed what the differences are between these two words. A particular application of the competence process is given in Chapter 18 by Mike Stringfellow.

Part III illustrates a different aspect of the priorities I have adopted. The learning process itself is still given far too little weight in books or articles about management development. For many years, management developers, trainers and educators have based their activities either on a single management development process regarded as the only way to develop managers, or on a catholic menu through which managers are exposed to a variety of processes. In the latter case there was at least a recognition that some managers learn better from one process than from another, but there was no attempt to identify what processes suited which managers.

Part III offers, too, exciting insights into the characteristics of the individual learner by Peter Honey and Ian Cunningham (Chapters 7 and 8). John Morris in Chapter 9 looks at the same kind of issue from a slightly different perspective, by discussing it as an organizational as well as an individually determined process. Readers who want to refer to issues about organizational learning will find additional comments in my own Chapter 1, in Graham Robinson (Chapter 24), and in Tony Pont (Chapter 25).

In new chapters George Boak (Chapter 10) discusses Management Learning Contracts, the idea of a formal agreement specifying learning goals, plans and methods of assessment, and David Clutterbuck and Bernard Wynne (Chapter 11) detail the processes involved in mentoring and coaching, and very importantly discuss some of the obstacles to achieving these processes. While this chapter may be seen to discuss relatively old processes with new disciplines attached, Chapter 12 by Don Binsted and Sue Armitage is at the other end of a continuum. They discuss the issues involved in using a particular aspect of technology, clearly representing a field of growing significance.

Part IV provides a number of specific cases of applying management development. Bruce Nixon in Chapter 13 gives a fascinating insight into the development of improved answers to management development problems over a period of time. Jean Lawrence, writing about the process known as action learning which is increasingly being used in management development, is stimulating not only in content, but in the form of her chapter. Jim Butler in Chapter 15 describes with both conceptual clarity and specific detail the design of some senior management courses; again readers will notice the emphasis on how managers are helped to understand how they are learning, as well as what they are learning. John Teire (Chapter 16) gives an admirable statement of the process of learning in the 'outdoors', which certainly avoids the dangers revealed in 1993 by a notorious television programme on this subject. In Chapter 17 Andrew Mayo comments on the specific application of some of the issues of organizational and national culture discussed from a wider perspective in Chapters 20, 21 and 22. In the other specific company case Mike Stringfellow discusses the development of competences at Safeway (a chapter which should be read in association with the earlier chapters by Stewart and Hirsh/Strebler).

Finally in Part IV, in another very unusual chapter, Ed Moorby uses his personal diary as a means of commenting on the reality of applying management development concepts. In discussing the reality of the adviser's daily life, he reveals from a different perspective some of the points about informal and accidental learning discussed in Chapter 1.

Part V deals with a number of issues which do not readily fit into any of the first four parts of the book. Bob Garratt in Chapter 20 discusses organizational culture and its impact on the development of managers. The chapters by David Ashton and Irene Rodgers take up again from slightly different perspectives the perennial issues of handling multi-cultural management development. Irene's chapter is particularly significant, since she is not writing from the perspective of a Briton looking at other cultures, but from the perspective of a French-based consultancy often dealing with Continental cultures not involving Britons at all. Specific issues of differences are also dealt with by Judi Marshall with her challenging views on the development of women managers.

Graham Robinson in Chapter 24 brings together issues of management development and organization development, and comments on what might be the newest theme or at worst newest fad – organizational learning.

Chapter 25 by Tony Pont discusses what management development specialists should be attempting to do – and not do. The not do question is also discussed in relation to the specific question of team building by Bill Critchley and David Casey. Not only did they discuss whether it is necessary to develop a 'team', but also whether the development of particular skills may be good management development but not very effective in terms of *xvii* managerial priorities. The next but last chapter by Peter Bramley on evaluation could by some logical choices have been placed at the forefront of the book, since evaluation should really be seen as the start of management development rather than the conclusion. His chapter reveals both the potential and the difficulties involved. Finally in Chapter 28, Mike Abrahams discusses how to choose resources; at my request he has done so from the perspective of a consumer rather than as a provider.

The only theme I can recognize in management development during the period for which I have been responsible for this *Handbook* (since 1985) has been a continuing move towards the greater use of reality. This has led logically to an increase in more specific tailored management development, certainly in terms of courses. I hope it is not wishful thinking to perceive that this reality has been expressed also through the increased attention to Action Learning, and to the learning process itself – with the greater use of diagnostic instruments about learning. On this latter subject I have deliberately edited the book in a way which will, I hope, provide something different for Theorists, Reflectors and Pragmatists. Nor do I regard Activists as a lost cause – they are most likely to want to pursue a theme of immediate interest, and I hope this Preface will enable them to do this. (See Peter Honey's chapter for an explanation of these terms.) The Management Charter Initiative was set up in the UK in 1988 to encourage the development of more professional management, and has sponsored the identification of competences for different levels of manager. Although in this fourth edition I have put greater emphasis on competences, my own view is that the future is more likely to be with organization-specific competences rather than national competences. Management development driven by the priorities associated with the requirements for national competences in order to achieve a 'professional' qualification seems to me neither the most practical nor the most desirable route to improved management development.

Wherever appropriate, he/she or she/he have been used. Where this is not the case, the reference is to a particular group of all-male managers.

Alan Mumford

Acknowledgements

The editor and publishers wish to thank the following for permission to reproduce copyright material.

British Postgraduate Medical Federation for Figure 8.1, from an idea in J. Heron, *Dimensions of Facilitator Style* (1977).

Economist Publications for Figure 20.1, from A. Campbell and M. Devine, *A Sense of Mission* (1990).

Management Education and Development (1984) for the original version of Chapter 26.

Notes on the Contributors

Michael Abrahams (*Choosing resources*) is a consultant to national and international companies and a founding partner in the management development consultancy which publishes the Brind Register. For fifteen years he managed the Marks & Spencer management development and training programme. He is an academic adviser to the City University MBA programme and lectures at leading British business schools. Michael Abrahams has also written articles for a number of professional journals and is a Fellow of the IPD.

Susan Armitage (*Facilitating management learning with interactive video*) was educated as a computer scientist, obtaining an MPhil. in Computer Science. She worked in industry as a systems analyst/programmer, where she developed an interest in training non-technical computer users. She now teaches at the University of Lancaster where she is a Fellow in the Department of Management Learning. Her research and teaching work has been concentrated on the use of new technology, especially in the use of interactive video and computer-based management simulations.

David Ashton (*Handling cultural diversity*) is the Chief Executive of The Cable & Wireless College in Warwickshire. His career reflects a balance of business and academic experience. From 1978 to 1986 he worked for BAT Industries Group where he held a senior corporate management position. At Durham University Business School he was a senior lecturer and director of the Management Development Unit, and in the USA was McKinsey Foundation Fellow, Graduate School of Business, University of California at Berkeley. In 1990 Professor Ashton was elected chairman of the Council of University Management Schools and, in 1992, co-chairman of the Association of Business Schools. He is a council member of the National Forum for Management Education and Development and acts as consultant to a wide range of businesses. He has published seven books, and serves on the editorial board of an international management publishing house.

Don Binsted (*Facilitating management learning with interactive video*) had an industrial career with ICI. In his twenty-one years with the company he held posts in line and staff management, training and organizational development. In 1974 he became founder/director of the Management Teacher Development Unit at the University of Lancaster, where, as Director of Distance Learning, he has researched the use of technology to facilitate learning. In 1987 he accepted the honorary post of Senior Fellow in Lancaster's Centre for the Study of Management Learning, and has since retired.

George Boak (*Management learning contracts*) is a senior consultant at the Northern Regional Management Centre (NRMC). From 1989 to 1992 he was the course director for an MBA competence programme at Durham University. He has had extensive experience in researching and developing training and development programmes for managers, including the use of flexible learning systems. In recent years he has worked on competence models for management development. He is the editor of NRMC's eight-volume series, *The Competent Manager*.

Peter Bramley (*Evaluation*) is a lecturer in the Department of Organizational Psychology at Birkbeck College, London. His responsibilities include teaching of masters' degree courses and direction of modules on training and development and organizational change. As the director of the Centre for Training and Evaluation, a consultancy group, he has worked on the evaluation of change initiatives based on management development activities. Peter Bramley is the author of *Evaluating Training Effectiveness* and has also published a number of papers on evaluation issues.

Jim Butler (*Learning design for effective programmes*) is Director of the Training and Development Group, Post Office. In both private and public industry he has held senior management positions. He was responsible for management planning at Burmah Oil, and for management development at the National Water Council, UK. He also directed management education for some years at BAT Industries Group. He is a member of the British Psychological Society, the Association of Management Education and Development, and a Fellow of IPM (now the Institute of Personnel and Development (IPD)). He has special interests and expertise in management and organization learning and has published papers in these fields.

David Casey (*Team-building*) started his working life as a teacher. From those early days, a deep interest in creating learning environments has been a continuing theme in his work. His interest in management began when he left teaching to manage the R & D laboratories at Berger Paints, and later the training function for part of Reed International. He then combined his managerial expertise with his initial teaching experience and started creating learning environments for managers. Since 1971 this work has widened to encompass full management teams and whole organizations in both the private and public sectors in the United Kingdom. As well as working independently, he is an associate at Ashridge Management College.

David Clutterbuck (*Mentoring and coaching*) is an entrepreneur and management author. He worked for the Home Office before becoming editor of the *Journal of the British Nuclear Energy Society*, news editor of *New Scientist*, and editor-in-chief of *International Management*. Since 1982 he has been chairman of the communications consultancy, ITEM Group plc. His special interests are in training, corporate communications and in-house periodicals. He is senior partner in Clutterbuck Associates, an editorial-based management company and director of the European Mentoring Centre. He holds academic appointments at Stirling, IMC, Sheffield and Puttridge Bury.

Bill Critchley (*Team-building*) joined Ashridge Consulting Group in 1987 as a business director. His particular interest is in working with the deep cultural level of organizations. He obtained an MBA at Cranfield School of Management and was a marketing director within the Bowring Group, a product manager at Lever Brothers and a retail area manager for K Shoes Ltd. He has led a number of large-scale change projects for organizations in both public and private organizations. He has worked as a consultant for Hay Management Consultants, Sheppard Moscow, and Marketing Improvements Ltd. His research interests include the new forms and processes which are now emerging in response to the radical shift in traditional organizational theory. He lectures, and has written for a number of management development and learning publications.

Ian Cunningham (*Self-Managed Learning*) is Chairman of the Centre for Self Managed Learning and is Chairman of Metacommunications Ltd. He has worked as a manager, research chemist, trainer in local government and head of division in a regional management centre; he has also taught in the USA and India as a visiting professor. He was Chief Executive of Roffey Park from 1987 to 1992. Dr Cunningham has published some eighty articles and papers on strategic management, leadership, organizational change, management development and learning, and cross-cultural management. His book, *The Wisdom of Strategic Learning*, was published in June 1994 by McGraw Hill.

Bob Garratt (*The cultural contexts*) is an international strategy consultant, director and academic. He has a long-established practice in London and Hong Kong, and is well known for his work in developing competences of boards of directors, senior executives and organizations, particularly through the use of action-learning processes. He is a member of the Professional Development Committee of the Institute of Directors and a former Chairman of the Association for Management Education and Development. His consultancy *xxiii* work is national and international and includes advising the City of Bradford Metropolitan Council and management development work in the Far East. In East and South-East Asia he has been involved in the development of management education; he is an EC adviser to Brunei. His academic interests include the Judge Institute, Cambridge University, and he is a Visiting Fellow at the Management School, Imperial College, London. Bob Garratt is the author of *Learning to Lead*, *Breaking Down Barriers* and *The Learning Organization*. He also wrote, with Sally Garratt, *China Business Briefing* and, with John Stopford, *Priorities and Practice in International Management Education*. He has also contributed many articles to professional journals.

Wendy Hirsh (*Defining managerial skills and competences*) is a consultant and researcher specializing in career development and human resources planning. Her interest in defining managerial skills and competences arose from her Institute of Manpower Studies research which, later, resulted in publication of her books *What Makes a Manager?* and *Defining Managerial Skills*. At the Institute for Employment Studies (formerly IMS) she now heads a multi-disciplinary team working in the field of human resources development.

Peter Honey (*Styles of learning*) is a British Psychological Association chartered psychologist and a member of the Association for Management Education and Development. He has worked for the Ford Motor Company and British Airways and became a freelance in 1969. A specialist in the study of people's behaviour, Peter Honey designs and runs training programmes, writes and acts as a consultant in this field. He is also Professor of Managerial Learning at the International Management Centres and a Fellow of both the Institute of Management Consultants and the Institute of Training and Development. His books are well known and include *Developing Interactive Skills*, *Face to Face Skills*, *The Manual of Learning Styles, Solving People Problems*, *Improve Your People Skills* and the *Manual of Learning Opportunities*. He appears in the VideoArts production, 'Talking About Behaviour'.

Jean Lawrence (*Action learning*) left Manchester Business School in 1982 to set up the Development Consortium. As a managing partner in this consultancy she works in action learning programmes in and between organizations. These activities develop both managers and their organizations and support them in the management of change. A visiting staff member at Henley and Templeton College, Jean also works regularly overseas. She was a production manager at Cadbury Bros and was a senior consultant with Anne Shaw before joining Manchester Business School in 1967. Her topic there was project management, and she developed skills in providing learning opportunities in small groups, particularly in association with Tavistock Institute. She has directed their conferences and continues to work as a member of staff in the USA as well as in the UK. In the 1970s she was Chairman of AMED (then ATM) and worked with GEC in the first UK management development programme based in action learning. Extensive experience in many forms of action learning followed, and led to her current chairmanship of the International Foundation for Action Learning. Her recent book *Managing the Unknown*, edited with Richard Boot and John Morris (McGraw Hill, 1994), grew out of the 1990 AMED Conference, 'Creating New Futures'.

Charles Margerison (*Managing career choices*) is a graduate of the London School of Economics, Liverpool University and Bradford University where he obtained his doctorate. The co-creator of the Margerison McCann Team Management Systems, he has worked with Mobil Oil, Shell, Citibank and, in Australia, ICI, ACI, Australian Airlines and other leading industrial companies. As a management eductor in three business schools his work is recognized internationally. Charles Margerison is currently an international vice-president of International Management Centres and editor of the *Journal of Management Development*. He writes for professional journals and is author of several books on management.

Judi Marshall (*Developing women managers*) is Reader in Organizational Behaviour at the School of Management, University of Bath. Earlier in her academic career she studied managerial job stress, publishing several books with Cary Cooper, including *Understanding Executive Stress*. She is presently researching women in management, developing feminist contributions to organizational theory and exploring post-positivist approaches to research. She writes extensively in these areas, and has also published *Women Managers: Travellers in a Male World*.

Andrew Mayo (*Business strategy and international people development*) is currently responsible for human resources development for all the ICL Group. He obtained degrees in Chemical Engineering and Management Science, before serving his management apprenticeship with Proctor & Gamble in several line and staff management positions. He later worked in personnel, marketing and general management with companies engaged in chemical processing and electronic manufactures. He is a member of the European Foundation for Management Development, where he sits on the board and the executive committee, and a fellow of the IPM. Andrew Mayo has published several articles and is author of *Managing Careers: Strategies for Organizations*.

Ed Moorby (*Making it happen*) is a consultant with over twenty-five years' experience in management development. In 1991 he was appointed Chief Examiner in Employee Development for the IPM. He has worked for the Ford Motor Company, the Prudential Corporation, and the TSB Retail Bank where he was director of Training and Development. His executive responsibilities include Industry Training Board appointments in the engineering, air transport and travel industries. He has a strong interest in Europe, and was president of the European Institute for Vocational Training from 1988 to 1993. Ed Moorby is the author of *How to Succeed in Employee Development*.

John Morris (*Development work and the learning spiral*) is Emeritus Professor of Management Development at the Manchester Business School; there, between 1965 and 1982, he developed initiatives in project-based work which led to the award of the British Institute of Management's Burnham Medal. He is now a managing partner in the Development Consortium consultancy where he specializes in action-learning and the management of change for clients in financial services, engineering, IT, music, transport, industrial products and large utilities. He has also worked with public sector organizations in the health service, education, local authorities and development agencies.

Alan Mumford (*Effectiveness in management development*) has exceptional experience in management development, including employment with John Laing & Sons, IPC Magazines, International Computers and the Chloride Group. He was also Deputy Chief Training Adviser at the Department of Employment. In 1993 he was appointed Professor of Management Development at International Management Centres, and is now a Visiting Professor there. He has worked with organizations in Australia, the USA and South Africa and, in the UK, with Pilkington Glass, Ford Europe, Brooke Bond and Unison (now the largest trade union in the UK). He has published numerous articles and books on management development.

Bruce Nixon (*An in-house senior managers' programme for organizational change*) is an independent management consultant. He has worked abroad and in the UK and was Training and Development Manager with Sun Alliance. As a consultant he helps clients create development programmes in the management of change; his special interest is helping develop an empowering culture in their organizations. Bruce Nixon has published numerous articles and is a member of AMED.

Tony Pont (*The role of the management development specialist*) is a consultant and a director of Heyford Associates, human resources development consultancy in Northamptonshire. He has degrees in the behavioural sciences and in management development. In 1982 he obtained a Fulbright Exchange Award, working in the USA as director of continuing education at a college in Maine. He has taught at educational institutes in the UK and also at several European business schools, latterly on MBA and post-degree courses. In the UK he worked for one of the world's leading healthcare companies as a management development trainer. His consultancy work has included assignments in the public sector, and work for clients in pharmaceuticals, oil and gas, construction, insurance, automobiles and retailing. Dr Pont has published widely and is a consultant to the Institute of Management.

Graham Robinson (*Management development and organization development*) is a founder-director of the consultancy, Kennedy Robinson Business Development. His career has been spent almost entirely in management and organization research and development, both as provider and purchaser. He has worked as a personnel director in the computer industry and as a researcher at Ashridge Management College. As a consultant he specializes in the design and development of senior management organization structures, development of interdisciplinary project teams and enhancement of senior managers' potential. Clients have included the Standard Chartered Group, British Aerospace, CMB, the Department of Employment, the International Atomic Energy Agency, the Civil Service College, the Granada Group, and the States of Guernsey Civil Service. Graham Robinson is a Fellow of the Institute of Directors and author of a number of publications on business and management development.

Irene Rodgers (*Cultural pitfalls of international alliances and culture-bridging strategies*) is an American with degrees in language and linguistics from both French and American universities. She has been Managing Director of Inter Cultural Management Associates since its creation in 1983. Earlier, she taught in the USA and Europe and directed the management training programme for the American Chamber of Commerce in France and the New York University Business School. In West Africa she has led several long-term missions recruiting, training and managing teams of African technical trainers. At ICM her work includes steering international companies through the turmoils of change, large climate surveys, personal coaching and leadership training for senior executives. Irene Rodgers is the author of articles on change management and the impact of cultural differences on business organizations; she co-authored (with F. Gauthey, I. Ratiun and D. Xardel) *Leaders Sans Frontières*.

The late Andrew Stewart (*Diagnosing needs, performance appraisal*) was the Managing Director of Informed Choice, an industrial psychology consultancy. He had lectured at the universities of Aberdeen and Surrey and was responsible for personnel and management development at IBM (UK). He was a Senior Fellow at the Institute of Manpower Studies and was co-author (with Valerie Stewart) of *Practical Performance Appraisal*, *Managing the Manager's Growth*, and *Managing the Poor Performer*.

Marie Strebler (*Defining management skills and competences*) is a consultant and researcher in human resources management. She has worked with many organizations developing her interests in skill and competence analysis, training and its application, graduate recruitment and early career development. Her publications include *Skill Mix and Working Practices in Hospital Pharmacy* and *Shortlisting the Best Graduates*.

Michael Stringfellow (*Assessing for competence at Safeway Stores plc*) is Career Development Controller for Safeway Group plc. He is a member of the National Endorsement Board for the Management Charter Initiative (MCI), a Fellow of the IPM and Board Director of CTC Gateshead.

John Teire (*Using the outdoors*) has been a training and development consultant since 1975. He makes use of the outdoors to complement other learning activities which include company workshops, residential courses and business simulations. He is a member of the Business Graduates Association, the Group Relations Training Association, and AMED.

Tony Vineall (*Planning management development*) is a consultant in human resources development. He read Philosophy, Politics and Economics at New College, Oxford. He was responsible for worldwide human resources development in Unilever. His interest in this field has been further developed in his consultancy work at the Conference Board Europe, the Aegon N.V. Insurance Group and other companies. Tony Vineall is Chairman of the Centre for International Briefing at Farnham Castle and of the Careers Advisory Centre at Cambridge. He is a Fellow of the IPM.

Bernard Wynne (*Mentoring and coaching*) is a director of Bernard Wynne Associates. An experienced trainer and management development practitioner, he was formerly responsible for management development at the Woolwich Building Society. Bernard Wynne currently advises businesses throughout the UK on aspects of management development. He is a director of the European Mentoring Centre.

Part I
SETTING THE SCENE

1 Effectiveness in management development

Alan Mumford

This chapter presents the view that effective management development is based first on awareness of effective managerial behaviour. Secondly, it proposes that awareness of effective learning processes must also be a prime constituent. Thirdly, it suggests that development is most likely to arise from real work rather than from abstract knowledge or even simulations of real work.

In the mid-1980s I was still defining management development as 'an attempt to improve managerial effectiveness through a planned and deliberate learning process'. I later came to the view that a great deal of management development is not 'planned and deliberate', and probably never can be. In two books (1988, 1993a) I have developed and illustrated the idea that management development must be considered to include *formal* and *accidental* processes, as well as those defined as planned and deliberate. Of course, most personnel directors and management development advisers reading this book have operated to a planned and deliberate definition, and advised formal planned and deliberate processes which they have understood to be, uniquely, 'management development'. While in this chapter I shall be giving much more emphasis to formal processes of management development, the additional material I have given on effective learning processes particularly brings out the point that a great deal of the development of managers is brought about by activities which have not been influenced at all by planned and deliberate interventions in the traditional sense.

The question of our definition of management development, and of the areas in which we as advisers choose to intervene, is of course vital in considering issues of effectiveness: however effective our interventions may be on formal processes, if (as has largely been the case) we do not intervene in those informal accidental day-by-day activities through which managers learn, their effectiveness is both reduced and partial. Reduced because we may succumb to the temptation of dealing only with those managerial issues which we can *understand* and *influence*; partial because we are acting only on a small and often *highly untypical* part of the manager's life – a big decision about a job move, or the occasion of attendance on a course. So part of the case made in this chapter revolves around the idea that we must embrace a wider vision of what we understand 'management development' to be, in order to expand our contribution to the manager's learning and development capacity. That wider vision is expressed in the following definition:

> An attempt to improve managerial effectiveness through a learning process.

THE THREEFOLD NATURE OF EFFECTIVENESS IN MANAGEMENT DEVELOPMENT

Effectiveness in management development is best achieved when we bring together three different aspects of effectiveness:

- A contingent definition of effective *managerial behaviour*
- A developmental process which emphasizes *activities* in which managers are required to be effective, rather than emphasizing the *knowledge* necessary for action
- The identification of learning processes which are effective for the *individual or group*, rather than economical and convenient for tutors or trainers.

It should be noted that in 'the effectiveness triangle' shown in Figure 1.1, the triangle is *equilateral*: this means that all three aspects are equally important. Moreover, the particular presentation offered in Figure 1.1, which could be interpreted as showing two contributors to 'effective managerial behaviour', is

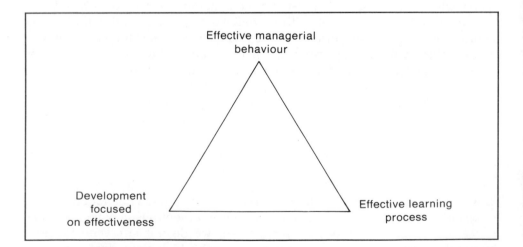

4   **Figure 1.1   Effectiveness triangle in management development**

not the only way of representing the triangle. In some situations, the triangle could be moved round so that effectiveness was seen as depending on a triangle resting on a single point – effective learning processes. As presented in Figure 1.1, the triangle gives emphasis to the desired end conclusion – effective managerial behaviour.

EFFECTIVE MANAGERIAL BEHAVIOUR

It is, of course, absolutely fundamental to recognize that the prime purpose of management development is effective managerial behaviour: it is not just knowledge, or attitudes, although these clearly can often be significant contributors to effective behaviour. As anyone with experience of management knows, there are managers who have been extremely knowledgeable who have not been effective, and managers with appropriate attitudes who have not been effective. An 'effective manager' is one who does the right things in the right way – and it is the emphasis on 'doing' which is the key requirement for a manager, as distinct from a researcher, writer or academic. Unless we also recognize the necessary features of what effective managers *do*, and what proportions of emphasis are appropriate in different situations, then the purposes of management development will be as badly aligned as they will be if we give too much emphasis to issues of knowledge and attitude.

For many years the formal process of management development followed what might be called the 'classical view' of the nature of management. A familiar version of this could be summarized under five heads:

- Forecast/Plan
- Organize
- Motivate
- Coordinate
- Control

These terms, and the concepts and misunderstandings underpinning them, still survive in some formal courses. Rosemary Stewart (1976), Henry Mintzberg (1980) and John Kotter (1982) have provided research which shows that the basis of these concepts is unscientific. All three authors have also argued strongly that these inappropriate statements have led to structures for developing managers which have been unrealistic, and therefore unhelpful. Since each has then proceeded to his or her own statement of key managerial activities, it might be argued that their demolition of one list of managerial tasks and its replacement by another is simply due to differing perceptions and personal preferences when describing those managerial activities.

In fact, for management development purposes an even more significant common theme is that any generalized statement about managerial activities, including their own, is likely to be at least partially (and possibly substantially) incorrect for any particular manager or group of managers. The authors found substantial variations in required managerial behaviour in different organizations; the managerial activities in which any individual had to be effective were seen to depend on the specific kind of function and job, or the   5 manager's interpretation of that job or role, and others' interpretation of the manager's role and responsibilities within that job. The main features of their analyses are conveniently spelled out in Mumford (1988).

It still seems to be the case that these discoveries have not had the impact on management development processes that they ought to have done; the more intellectual courses probably include such analyses as important and thought-provoking contributions to the debate about what managers do. The consequences of their discoveries do not, however, seem generally to have been used to develop the course itself. Take as an example the importance given by Kotter and Mintzberg to the way in which *networks*, and their *effective use*, can contribute to effective managerial performance. Many courses will include sessions about interpersonal relationships; how many include sessions on the effective use of networks? Even more important, as we shall see later in this chapter, how many include practical work on the effective use of networks?

While the generation of more appropriate generalizations, and their incorporation into appropriate management training, seems not to have been fully carried through, some improvement does seem to have been made in producing more organization-specific training. It is still unfortunately true that in many (probably most) organizations needs analysis is relatively superficial and leads to the facile adoption of training courses whose content differs remarkably little from one organization to another.

There have been two problems in adopting a more rigorously analytical approach. Even where the professional management development adviser knows what he or she ought to do, there can be considerable obstacles in terms of actually engaging line managers in the analytical process. The definition, and interpretation, of what is meant by 'effective behaviour' takes time and energy, which managers on the whole would rather give to some other activity. This is most obviously true for a demanding process such as the repertory grid; although well-used by some organizations, it has not been adopted as an appropriate approach by most of them.

The alternative approach receiving most attention in recent years has been that of management competences. Originating with the work of Boyatzis (1982) and being more widely aimed through the revived national management development debate in the UK in the late 1980s, this is an approach found helpful by a large number of organizations. It has the advantage of not requiring managers to start totally from scratch, as with the repertory grid; it is possible to start with the list produced by Boyatzis, or (in the UK) the material produced by the Management Charter Initiative (MCI). A debate about the appropriateness – or, as many would see it, the inappropriateness – of a national list of competences may produce two not wholly intentional consequences. The first is to make organizations think specifically about what managers in those organizations need *to be able to do*, and the extent to which a nationally agreed list is appropriate. The second is to focus attention on the actual *content* of the competences, which has sometimes appeared to be a rather strange conglomerate of skills, attitudes and end results.

Although there has been this shift in at least some organizations towards what managers need to be able to do, the shift has in many not gone far enough, if it has even started. It is slightly surprising to see surviving into the 1990s one cause more understandable in the 1960s and 1970s – an over-emphasis on developing managers for the future instead of working on issues of *current requirements*. While organizations have certainly helped to sustain this emphasis, the argument applies with even greater strength to many training and educational institutions offering taught experiences outside the organization. The identification of the nature of effectiveness in management has scarcely influenced the design of their programmes – as distinct from making a contribution to parts of the syllabus. The traditional business schools, all of whom now offer in-house programmes, have not on the whole shifted themselves substantially towards issues of effectiveness. They have stayed in the areas which they understand – those of knowledge, particularly *conceptual or theoretical knowledge*. With few exceptions, their in-company programmes have largely mirrored such 'open' programmes where there has been an inevitability about the generalized views of management processes on offer. Although there has been some shift to the design of specific material for particular companies, it has been relatively cosmetic; again, one looks in vain in many programmes for sessions designed to help managers to define and improve their own *effectiveness criteria* rather than sessions designed to convey only generalized management knowledge.

If we look, as we should, on the traditional business schools as the intellectual leaders in defining effective managerial behaviour, we see them largely still locked in the confusion between efficiency and effectiveness described by Peter Drucker in 1974: 'Efficiency is concerned with doing things right. Effectiveness is doing the right things.'

DEVELOPMENT PROCESSES EMPHASIZING EFFECTIVENESS

Just as too much management development has been based on an inappropriate view of what managers need to be able to do in their specific organizations (an intellectual failure), so there has also been a complementary failure of a different kind. Management development processes have too often been detached from the reality of the *perception and understanding of managers themselves*. With rare exceptions, managers are not concerned about the knowledge possessed by a boss, colleagues or subordinates; their characteristic judgement on a manager's effectiveness is whether or not he or she can get things done. The fact that they are not aware of, and tend to be impatient about, the knowledge and skills required to enable a manager to get things done is not of course in itself an argument for not providing these things. It is a practical and psychological argument from two sides of the same coin – for starting from the reality of *where managers are*, rather than imposing on them our views about what they need.

Since effectiveness is defined clearly by managers in terms of the results actually secured, and not by the knowledge someone possesses, it would seem 7 sensible to concentrate in our processes on helping managers to learn from *actions undertaken*, rather than providing them with conceptual statements of what managers ought to do, or with analytical experiences of what other managers have done (or might have done). Instead of giving emphasis to the provision of knowledge and asking managers to interpret and use that knowledge in subsequent action, it would be both more appropriate and more likely to be successful if we gave attention to issues of *action*, and only secondary attention to issues of the required *knowledge*: knowledge and the capacity to analyse and produce solutions to problems are necessary but insufficient contributors to effective action. Primary attention to managerial skills may similarly be misplaced although not inappropriate: the first stage of attention should be on a *desired managerial result* rather than the skills required for managerial activities.

In the UK, of course, the original definition of the benefits to be derived from working through real past experiences was provided by Reg Revans (1980) and then by John Morris (see Chapter 9). My own research (1988, 1993a) follows their ground-breaking statements by putting forward views about the kind of development experiences it is possible to identify, and to use effectively.

It may be inevitable that good ideas are sometimes misunderstood and later watered down. The original work of Revans and Morris has frequently been misinterpreted simply as being about the use of a defined project by an individual, or the creation of a group of managers discussing their own projects; so, increasingly, management training and education courses have included projects as part of the syllabus, and in such cases projects have been yet another interesting variant within a set menu. Virtuous t hough this may be in programmes otherwise suffering from a surfeit of conceptual and analytical exercises, it is not an adequate representation of what is meant by using 'real-life experience'. Similarly, the view that managers ought to work on some kind of direct problem-solving, presented as a simulation of effectiveness issues in management, is a misunderstanding of what is desirable and possible. Whatever the arguments for introducing bridge-building with Lego bricks, or outdoor experiences requiring managers to bridge chasms and climb cliffs, they are stronger as arguments directed to providing variety in learning activity than they are to using real work issues for development.

Courses which give primary attention to managerial skills such as interviewing, negotiation or interpersonal relationships, or to skills involved in dealing with information technology, can be significant contributors to the improvement of managerial performance. This will, again, be more likely to be true if such courses are built on a proper analysis by the organization – and preferably by the managers themselves – of what they have to do, rather than on someone else's judgement that all managers need to be good at some given list of skills.

Four cases are now given, illustrating the kind of shift of emphasis in which I have been involved, and where I find other organizations working with what I

believe to be an appropriate idea of what can be achieved.

Case 1

The final stages of a two-week programme were geared to the participants reviewing the corporate strategy of the group for which they worked. The intention of the sessions, which included a presentation to the chief executive, was that participants should be more familiar with the reasons for the corporate strategy, instead of just criticizing it from their own level in the business. In later programmes we made a significant change, since it seemed to us less relevant that participants should know the corporate strategy than that they should be encouraged to *take action on strategic issues affecting their own business*. They were instead asked to make proposals on a significant business problem currently affecting most of them: one example was the nature of, and possible reactions to, competition from Japanese manufacturers. While they could not do anything about corporate strategy – except perhaps understand it better – they could do something in their own companies about the Japanese 'threat'.

Case 2

A company which had revised its sales objectives and organization structure had some concern that the managers involved might not have the skills necessary to achieve the changed objectives. As a result of analysis with them it became clear that although probably a number of them were lacking in some skills, the larger problem was that, while apparently committed to the revised objectives, they had not fully set up the action necessary to *implement* them. The prime effectiveness was not therefore the skills of sales management, but the identification of specific actions to implement the broad objectives agreed.

Case 3

A company which had changed the composition and structure of its marketing function found that a number of those managers involved would be unable to produce what was required because they were not fully equipped with marketing skills. In the course of discussion with them the emphasis was shifted from the *acquisition* to the *implementation* of skills. An in-house marketing programme was devised which, in addition to giving managers the necessary tools, took them through to the identification of specific marketing projects which needed to be undertaken. The programme was designed to meet general marketing skill requirements in the organization, the specific requirements of the projects which had to be undertaken, and the completion of real work to meet the needs of the business.

Case 4

MBA programmes normally provide participants with a better understanding of the various functional areas of management such as marketing, finance and production. The expectation is that managers who have acquired this knowledge may be able to manage these functions better, or may through a better understanding have an improved relationship with other departments. IMC's MBA programme starts at the other end of the process, by requiring our associates to analyse the nature of *relationships between their own function and others in the business*, and to make proposals for improvement. While we believe that it may be important for most managers to 'understand finance better', we see it as at least as important that they should be helped to take specific actions relevant to their own needs in dealing with other functions.

Some of the central principles of action learning have been misunderstood and misapplied (Mumford 1991). Another problem has been that the simplistic generalization that 'all managers should learn through doing a project' has too often been expressed entirely in terms of *doing* the project, and very little in terms of *learning from it*: learning processes concerned with effectiveness must always deal with the reality of the manager's job, and always involve her or him in action on it. A manager will, however, not learn enough simply by taking action, and it is clear from most of the literature on action learning that this is not sufficiently understood, and certainly is given too low a priority. The emphasis has been on projects and action to the exclusion of any serious discussion of the learning process while people are *undertaking the project*.

One other opportunity for development processes related to concern for effectiveness is now beginning to emerge. Managers have always expressed themselves in the cliché that: 'I have learned from experience'; it is often clear in fact that their learning has been partial, inefficient and ineffective – though that may not always be clear to them. One of the reasons is that learning from experience at work is very rarely designed, and even more rarely discussed; while formal management development processes will, for example, highlight the relevance of a particular job move from one function to another, from one country to another, or from one product to another, very little will have been done to make sure that effective learning occurs *within those experiences*.

We encounter now the essential paradox of management development, which is that managers claim to learn from experience; they talk about the jobs they have done, the projects they have completed, the bosses they have worked for and even about the courses they have attended (see Mumford, 1988). Yet management development – because, as I argued at the beginning of this chapter, it has seen itself as being concerned with formal processes – has paid very little attention to this. Management development has been defined purely in terms of formal off-the-job training and education, and formal processes for moving people around. Not only have these schemes offered a prescription which does not meet the managers' realities; as already described, the processes themselves have given no help to managers in reinterpreting, and making better use of, their on-the-job development opportunities.

Clearly if we actually want to focus our development on effectiveness, rather than purely on discrete knowledge or skills, the on-the-job experiences present the prime vehicle. What we need is both a conceptual understanding that management development must embrace those accidental informal opportunities, previously ignored by most management development advisers, and practical processes for integrating real work experiences and formal schemes of development. A great deal of that integration will be accomplished by managers and their bosses with no intervention from the management development educator or trainer, except perhaps through some introductory sessions on a course or the use of some reading material or workbook.

Our understanding of the opportunities here, first illustrated on a large scale by Revans and Morris, is now being enhanced by more recent work. In the USA the work of McCall and his colleagues (1988) describes and analyses the kind of experiences to which managers are exposed. My own work with my colleague Peter Honey (1989) builds on my original 1988 research work in spelling out how managers can actually engage successfully in learning terms with the opportunities open to them. The use of learning experiences at work is by far the greatest area for attention for productivity in management development; it meets the criteria suggested by centring on what managers actually have to do, and on issues of their personal effectiveness; it removes the problems of simulation and of transfer of learning. Increased recognition of such opportunities – whether at the design level by management developers, or by individual managers for themselves – will nevertheless not necessarily lead to effective learning. It is one of the most potent criticisms of formal management development schemes that in proposing to provide additional development opportunities – whether through courses or job assignments – we have largely assumed that *learning will necessarily follow*.

The argument of this section has been that formal management development processes can (and should) be focused on and operated through effectiveness issues, but that management development must also embrace the ways in which managers *learn to be effective* – learning by experience, largely outside normal schemes. The model I have developed to describe this view of management development is given in Figure 1.2.

One of the determining factors about the success of improved development on the job – Type 2 in my model – will be the effectiveness of managers in developing not only themselves but their subordinates and indeed their colleagues. In formal management development schemes the role of a coach or mentor has increasingly been identified. Important though such formal approaches can be, we really need a much more extensive understanding and use of less structured opportunities for one manager to help another (Mumford 1993b).

EFFECTIVE LEARNING PROCESSES

If we manage to work successfully on the issues of managerial effectiveness in the ways described, we create the potential for a virtuous learning circle (see Figure 1.3). It is clear that for many managers involvement in formal   *11*

Type 1   'Informal managerial' – accidental processes

Characteristics   – occur within managerial activities
                                   – explicit intention is task performance
                                   – no clear development objectives
                                   – unstructured in development terms
                                   – not planned in advance
                                   – owned by managers

Development
consequences   – **learning is real, direct, unconscious, insufficient**

Type 2   'Integrated managerial' – opportunistic processes

Characteristics   – occur within managerial activities
                                   – explicit intention both task performance and development
                                   – clear development objectives
                                   – structured for development by boss and subordinate
                                   – planned beforehand or reviewed subsequently as learning experiences
                                   – owned by managers

Development
consequences   – **learning is real, direct, conscious, more substantial**

Type 3   'Formal management development' – planned processes

Characteristics   – often away from normal managerial activities
                                   – explicit intention is development
                                   – clear development objectives
                                   – structured for development by developers
                                   – planned beforehand and reviewed subsequently as learning experiences
                                   – owned more by developers than managers

Development
consequences   – **learning may be real** (through a job) or **detached** (through a course)
                                   – is more likely to be **conscious, relatively infrequent**

Figure 1.2   Types of management development

management development processes off-the-job has created a vicious learning sequence (see Figure 1.4). Modern motivational theory tells us that behaviour which is not rewarded is not willingly engaged upon again. Some managers have had training or educational experiences they regard as useful or

12

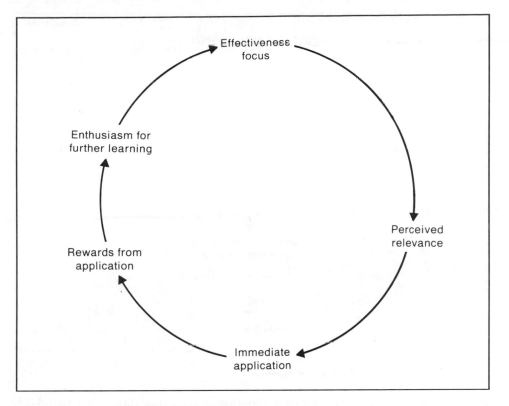

Figure 1.3   The virtuous learning circle

interesting or stimulating, and they are willing to return to similar experiences subsequently; others are relatively unwilling to attend in the first place and/or experience nothing like stimulation or utility during the course. All too often this can be traced back to the failure of courses to deal with the issues of what managers really do, and to deal with them in the ways most related to their normal managerial work processes. If trainers and educators have grappled successfully with the issues of *evaluation*, then corrective steps could have been taken to improve results; either the programme could have dealt with effectiveness issues in the ways I have recommended, or if they did not they would at least have dealt with broader issues of knowledge or skill in a more effective way. The absence of evaluation is particularly ironic in that, for those programmes which do emphasize the acquisition of knowledge or skill, evaluation is not only necessary but achievable (see Easterby-Smith, 1994); emphasis given to effectiveness issues makes the evaluation more difficult to separate for evaluation purposes. It is also probably less necessary; if you design a process actually to engage people in action you *reduce* the requirement to *test the extent to which they have applied that which they have learned:* I use the verb 'reduce', not remove.

The whole shift of emphasis to action-based learning helps us to remove one of the traditional problems of management education and training. It is a   *13*

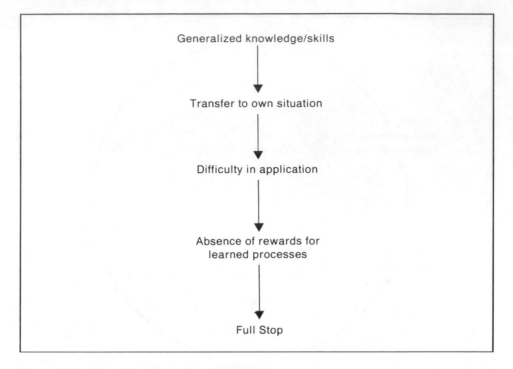

Figure 1.4   The vicious learning sequence

logical oddity that having created a situation of unreality (i.e. a structured off-the-job learning experience), and then having done in many cases very little about directing attention to those issues of real personal concern to managers, tutors and trainers have then complained and written learned articles about the problems of transfer of learning. If we create unreality and do not deal with issues of effectiveness, we ought not to be surprised that managers have problems in transferring what they are supposed to have learned back into their real job situation. Nor should we be surprised that the boss and colleagues to whom they return from the off-the-job experience gives no welcome to the kind of learning which the managers bring with them.

Concentration on those issues which are relevant to the manager and his colleagues in the real-life situation certainly reduces the transfer problem, both because of the perceived reality of what the manager is engaged in, and because there need literally be no 'transfer' in the sense that he can be involved in projects and real-time problems *drawn from his own work* which do not then have to be 'translated'. Where learning activities are not primarily and directly based on the manager's own work, we should tackle the transfer problem on our programmes instead of leaving it to the manager to resolve on his or her own on return to work; this means less time on teaching, and more time on how the manager will *implement* what he or she has learned.

Emphasis on effectiveness and reality will nonetheless not, as some writers seem to assume, in itself completely overcome the need for careful choice of

14

effective learning processes. Management development has been far too subject to 'flavour of the month' approaches, each of them claiming to be uniquely appropriate to developing managers. Over the years we have been told that T-groups, grid training, coaching, self-development, action learning and now outdoor training were, successively, the answer to our management development problems. In my view, the adoption of any single technique as the predominant answer to our management development problems is lazy and incompetent; nor is the answer a further proliferation of management development processes. In his most helpful book, Huczynski (1983) identifies around 300 management development techniques. While in no way wishing to inhibit future creativity, it is my view that productivity in management development will derive from the appropriate methods already relatively well-known and tried, rather than the identification of new processes. I take this view because the application of management development methods is at the moment so clearly both inefficient and ineffective; we have failed to fit our processes to the *needs of the learner*. Just as we have not satisfactorily dealt with the reality of how a manager *manages*, so we have not dealt with the reality of how a manager *learns*. Just as we have swept aside the common perception of managers that they learn through on-the-job processes (a matter of common experience apparently too simple for researchers to cope with), so we have ignored the reality that different managers actually *learn differently from the same process*. It is an extraordinary fact that educators, trainers and developers know very well that if Brown and Jones both have the same need to improve an aspect of their managerial performance, and both are taken through the same learning experience, Brown will learn and Jones will not. It seems that most tutors, having stumbled across this truth painfully when an individual reacts badly to a learning process, then pick themselves up and hurry on as if nothing had happened. In designing courses the best that may occur subsequently is that the designers offer a catholic menu of activities, hoping everybody will get something out of the course. Thus the supposedly well-designed course will include role-plays, films, case studies, lectures, an afternoon in the resource centre: if you are bored by one, there is always tomorrow.

It is an extraordinary commentary on management education in both the UK and the USA that only in the years since 1980 has there been attention at any level of significance to differences in the ways in which people learn. The field was for a long time dominated by fundamentally sterile debates about the virtues of case studies, of business games, or of experiential exercises. I emphasize again the absence of action on the part of the traditional business schools because of their perceived dominance in the rest of the management development world. I cannot think of any significant university-level contribution in this field apart from the original innovative work by Kolb, and the work done at Lancaster by the Department of Management Learning, who have made a considerable contribution in the literature on issues of the general design of different kinds of learning event, and the significance of the interaction between the tutor and the learner. Although much of their written work is understandably directed at the tutor, I believe they would share with me the view that one of the problems is that the tutor has been given too great a prominence in the learning process: their efforts, quite rightly, are geared to helping the tutor be more effective by assessing the learning situation in which he or she is involved.

No doubt because I started from a different kind of environment my own concern has been as much with the learner as the tutor. Peter Honey and I have developed Kolb's original concept of the learning cycle, and have advised the designers of learning experiences how they need to pay attention to *all stages* of the cycle, designing total programmes, sessions within programmes, or particular kinds of on-the-job learning experience. We also took Kolb's original concepts of individual learning preferences, developed our own method of determining these, and then provided direct guidance to the learner on how to make use of this information (Honey and Mumford, 1986, 1992).

Honey and I have also argued that knowledge of the *learning preferences* of managers actually arriving on a learning experience can be used to provide a more appropriate experience. We think it is irresponsible simply to throw a ragbag of activities at a group on the assumption that their learning styles will be different. Our general proposition is, of course, that the experience should actually be designed as a *learning*, not as a *teaching*, experience. This undoubtedly increases the difficulties for the designers and operators of learning events, and perhaps it is the prospect of such difficulties which has deterred training and education institutions from actually thinking seriously about the learning process. Nor would understanding by designers and providers of development experiences, while helpful, go sufficiently far. It is surely another prospective leap forward in management development that we should share with managers our improved understanding of learning and cause them to recognize and improve their own learning processes: that is to say, that we should incorporate our improved understanding not merely in the design of a more effective event, but that we should treat learning as an *overt part of the programme*. Instead of being an implied and unstudied part of most management development activities, learning should be placed in the forefront as an explicit activity; nor should it be confined to an interesting session at the beginning of a programme, with perhaps some review of personal development growth at the end of it. We must provide time and resources to help managers consider their learning processes *during the programme itself*.

I have carefully used the word 'programme' rather than 'course', because I see this as being applicable just as much in the situation in which an adviser is counselling someone's development on the job as it would be where a tutor is running an off-the-job experience. The reason for this extended attention to the learning process is not merely a matter of logic – of the extraordinary fact that many programmes which claim to help managers to learn never actually address that issue – but also that it is essential as one of the ways in which we will manage to draw together on-the-job and off-the-job development experiences. If in our off-the-job experiences we give sufficient time and

16

attention to engaging a manager in understanding his own learning, we can also help him to see how to apply this knowledge so that he *continues to learn* from similar or equivalent learning experiences when he is back on the job. Just as dealing with issues of effectiveness will help reduce substantially the problems of transfer of learning, so by giving substantial attention to the learning process itself we can reduce the notorious problem of managers seeing experiences as a series of one-off events, with no connection with each other in learning terms.

The phrase 'continuous learning' is now becoming popular; it will be no more than a promotional phrase if we do not provide the *learning processes* necessary to secure it. It seems clear that some of the people writing about continuous learning are really talking only about a series of training events, and not in fact about continuous learning at all; for learning to be *continuous*, rather than simply a series of events, we need to equip people to learn effectively *outside and around those events*: we need to do so for the obvious reason that for most managers most learning will occur – or not occur – *on the job*. Continuous learning and 'learning how to learn' will become empty clichés unless real effort is put into enabling individuals to understand what is involved, and to develop the necessary skills. In addition to our work on learning styles, Honey and myself have increasingly concerned ourselves with further practical exercises to facilitate an individual's understanding of his or her own learning (Honey and Mumford, 1989, 1990).

In the same way that definitions of managerial effectiveness are most sensibly couched in specific organization terms, effective learning processes are defined most appropriately by the *learner*, not by the tutor. In my experience, it is salutary for advisers and trainers to be exposed to an analysis of their own preferred approach to learning (see Chapter 7) and then to see how far what they offer – and how they offer it – is dominated by their *own preferences*, not by the individuals they are supposedly trying to help.

SUCCESSFUL MANAGEMENT DEVELOPMENT

I have used three different aspects of 'effectiveness' in this chapter. If we understood these issues better, and carried out our work on the development of managers more appropriately in relation to them, we would be much more likely to produce effective management development. Most specifically, we would increase the chance that we would be offering processes which managers themselves recognized as being effective, and were therefore prepared to engage in for themselves and offer to others. I think we need to recognize that the continued unpopularity of management development (the formal process) is due at least as much to our failures as designers and implementers of formal processes as it is to unwillingness of managers to spend time and devote energy to formal management development.

Of course, there is more to successful management development than the three main themes I have mentioned here. Margerison (1991) offers a substantial review of causes of success and failure in management *17* development; I agree with many of his items, but have expressed my own views as well (Mumford, 1988). It seems to me that too many management development schemes are dominated by issues about the 'system' and too little influenced by the needs, requirements and potential for growth of individuals. We will not have effective management development as long as we encourage systems which are in fact geared to processing people seen as a *concept*, rather than as *individuals* who can be assisted to develop. I shudder when I hear a personnel director or management development adviser say 'All our managers have been through …': it has become all too obvious that some management development schemes measure results by the number of people who have 'been through', rather than by *achieved results in development*.

I have already argued that we need a more substantial contribution from the organizations who ought to be leading management development. Definition of what effective managers do, and the identification of learning strategies and techniques – two out of my three areas of effectiveness – ought to receive much more attention. On the first, the marvellous work of Stewart (1976), Mintzberg (1980) and Kotter (1982) surely cannot be the last word. On the second we need a substantial research effort from the business schools; perhaps the subject is too difficult for them to tackle, because it raises too many questions about the purposes of management education. I have argued for a focus on effectiveness, and the practice of most business schools certainly does not take them in that direction. (If they had a coherent philosophy, perhaps that, too, would inhibit them from pursuing the areas I have indicated.)

Although I have particularly strong views about the associated issues of learning and effectiveness, I am not alone in my criticisms. Over the last twenty years we have seen the views of Livingston (1971), who told us that formal management education 'tends to distort managerial growth because it overdevelops an individual's analytical ability, but leaves his ability to take action and to get things done under-developed'; this kind of criticism was repeated by Peters and Waterman (1982) and Behrman and Levin (1984). There has been no equivalent research and analysis of the output of UK business schools. This is not to say that comment has been lacking – from business schools vocal about their excellent contribution; from individuals such as Gordon Wills critical of that same contribution; and from the potential customers who have voted with their feet to be absent. An optimistic view would be that the debate largely engendered by the Management Charter Initiative may encourage a concentration on issues of effectiveness. A pessimistic view would be that the traditional business schools will unconsciously follow the advice offered by Peters and Waterman, and that they will therefore stick to their knitting – offering programmes geared to a view of management education as essentially concerned with the identification and application of theory and concepts, with all too little emphasis on *application*.

REFERENCES

Behrman, J. N. and Levin, R. L. (1984) 'Are Business Schools Doing Their Job?', *Harvard Business Review* (January).

Boyatzis, R. (1982) *The Competent Manager* (New York: John Wiley).

Drucker, P. (1974) *Management Tasks, Responsibilities, Practices* (New York: Harper & Row).

Easterby-Smith, M. (1994) *Evaluation of Management Education, Training and Development,* 2nd edn (Aldershot: Gower).

Honey, P. and Mumford, A. (1986) *Using Your Learning Styles* (London: Honey).

Honey, P. and Mumford, A. (1989) *The Manual of Learning Opportunities* (London: Honey).

Honey, P. and Mumford, A. (1990) *The Opportunist Learner* (London: Honey).

Honey, P. and Mumford, A. (1992) *The Manual of Learning Styles,* 3rd edn (London: Honey).

Huczynski, A. (1983) *Encylopaedia of Management Development Methods* (Aldershot: Gower).

Kolb, D. (1984) *Experiential Learning* (Englewood Cliffs, N.J.: Prentice-Hall).

Kotter, J. P. (1982) *The General Manager* (New York: Free Press).

Livingston, J. S. (1971) 'The Myth of the Well-Educated Manager', *Harvard Business Review* (January).

Margerison, C. J. (1991) *Making Management Development Work* (Maidenhead: McGraw-Hill).

McCall, M., Lombardo, M. and Morrison, A. (1988), *The Lessons of Experience* (Lexington, Mass.: Lexington Books).

Mintzberg, H. (1980) *The Nature of Managerial Work* (Englewood Cliffs, N.J.: Prentice-Hall).

Mumford, A. (1988) *Developing Top Managers* (Aldershot: Gower).

Mumford, A. (1991) 'Learning in Action' *Personnel Management* (July).

Mumford, A. (1993a) *Management Development: Strategies for Action*, 2nd edn (London: IPM).

Mumford, A. (1993b) *How Managers Can Develop Managers* (Aldershot: Gower).

Peters, T. J. and Waterman, R. H. (1982) *In Search of Excellence* (New York: Harper & Row).

Revans, R. (1980) *Action Learning* (London: Blond & Briggs).

Stewart, R. (1976) *Contrasts in Management* (London: McGraw-Hill).

Wills, A. (1988) *Creating Wealth Through Management Development* (Bradford: MCB University Press).

Part II
PLANNING FOR MANAGEMENT DEVELOPMENT

2 Planning management development

Tony Vineall

The literature of management development planning has grown a great deal in recent years and with a more practical and less academically statistical slant. What this chapter aims to do is to answer the question which anyone who is believed to have some practical experience in the subject gets asked several times a year: 'How do we begin?'

The question usually comes from a senior executive who has been given the task of 'doing something about management development', usually in a medium- or large-sized group which operates in more than one country and in more than one product or service area. The group will often have been through several phases of management development. There will have often been a period in the past of excessive and over-structured activity, from which little remains other than a lot of forms collecting dust. Most commonly there is an active recruitment programme and some (not very long-term) succession planning for the very top jobs; and not much in between. The group wants to do something systematic to get a grip on its longer-term management resource situation.

What follows in this chapter charts a path to do just that: it will involve quite a lot of work, especially in the early stages, and serious commitment coming down from the top; but experience shows that the balance of what it can contribute over its demands in terms of inputs is such that it can rapidly become accepted as a valuable institution and be seen as just as indispensable as the basic financial accounting procedures or annual operating plans.

THE BASIC DISCIPLINES

Like all planning, much depends on the *quality of the basic data*. Certain preliminary activities have, therefore, to be carried out to provide the data on which all management development planning is based. Examples of such

23

activities are as follows.

A systematic grading of jobs based on their content

Job classification based on *content* is usually first introduced primarily for determining salary scales. It is, however, equally important to management development, providing a ready common language to describe and group jobs, according to content. Where management development is to be planned on an international group basis, the grading system should ideally be one which applies throughout the group. Where this does not exist, a series of *broad seniority bands* may have to be introduced for management development purposes, and local grades converted to them. One way or another there must be a clear and common perception of the *relative levels of jobs* before planning can begin – and job titles rarely suffice for this purpose.

A system of performance appraisal

Performance appraisal has also usually been devised initially for other purposes – to provide a basis for differentiating rewards; or for counselling the individual (or, less happily, to build up a case for remedial action or termination). Appraisal systems should, however, also serve to ensure that there is a *regular recording of achievement on the job* which forms, especially over time, an indispensable foundation for management development. Management development is not just about performance, but if predictions about the future are not firmly rooted in what the manager has *actually delivered,* the whole exercise will fall into disrepute.

Potential assessment

Performance appraisal is, however, only a beginning. More specifically relevant to management development planning is the assessment of *potential* – the judgement of how far the manager may be promotable in the future. Such judgement has to be related to performance, but goes further, and is, of its nature, more speculative and more judgemental than performance appraisal. The relationship between performance and potential is not a simple one – the best performers are not necessarily those of high potential. The process of potential assessment has accordingly to be more complex: whereas performance appraisal focuses on what the manager achieved, potential assessment is equally interested in *how he achieved* it, and it must involve more people, such as the boss's boss or the head of the appraisee's function, and also the individual himself.

Most organizations include a brief assessment of potential as something of a footnote to the annual appraisal exercise, and this is useful – although the form in which it is communicated to the individual needs care. It is also, however, desirable to organize more extensive potential assessment exercises at key stages of development. A few companies set up assessment centres, or use external ones; more commonly companies make some in-house arrangement to set aside time on specific occasions to think through, in a structured way, with the help of all those who are in a position to contribute, the likely future pattern of an individual's progress.

A system of development lists

The results of such potential assessment then need firming up in a form which can guide action and provide a useful input to planning. This is best done with a framework of *development lists*. Jobs are divided into three or four main levels, each therefore with a salary breakpoint about 50 per cent above the level below, and each of these main levels thus incorporating probably three or four normal salary grades. A development list will then be drawn up of those individuals in any one main level who are judged to have the potential to reach the next higher level within five years. If the main levels were termed 'junior management', 'middle management', 'senior management' and 'top executive', the first list would be those likely to be promotable from junior management to middle management within five years; the second list those promotable within five years from middle management to senior management, and so on.

Such a system of development lists contributes to management development planning in several ways. First, it focuses and sharpens judgement about potential by asking specific questions – judgement of potential can otherwise be sloppy, with too many people being vaguely 'promotable within a few years' without commitment to how many, or even how soon. Secondly, they provide the raw material for basic planning comparisons of promotable resources and known and likely future needs. Thirdly, they highlight training and development needs; challenging and testing opportunities, which are often in short supply, can then be directed to those on the lists. Finally, the system provides a useful language in which different parts of a large complex organization can communicate about the sort of people they want for a certain job.

People change and develop, and sometimes disappoint, and it is vital that names are *deleted* from lists as well as added to them. It may therefore be desirable not to tell individuals when they are put on such lists, lest the need to tell them that their names are being removed becomes a deterrent to actually deleting them.

These activities have been described as 'basic disciplines': they are to management development what the basic accounting records are to financial management. They do not themselves constitute or guarantee good management planning, but without them what follows will probably be in vain. It is now possible to consider the regular, usually annual, management development planning cycle.

MANAGEMENT RESOURCE PLANNING MEETINGS AT COMPANY OR UNIT LEVEL

Appraisals of performance have been completed, judgements of potential have been made. What happens next?

What happens next is the most central feature of a system of management development planning – *a review at unit level* (typically the operating company) which provides the focus for the appraisals and potential assessments and sets priorities and plans which will guide the individual appointments, attachments, training courses, etc. which will move the organization, and those who manage it, forward in the coming year. This is the crucial point at which, in respect of that particular unit, the organization 'gets its act together' in respect of management development – it is amazing how frequently the need for a well-prepared meeting of this kind is not appreciated.

The first thing to establish is who should attend, and that will depend on the structure of authority and responsibility in the particular business. For a subsidiary company the review is essentially between the chief executive and his boss – probably the director to whom he reports at group level. Indeed, together with the annual operating budget, this review is a key control for these two. Each will have his personnel executive with him, and where there is some other arm of the business closely involved with management development it should be represented also. The criterion is that anyone whose authority is needed to effect a major personnel change should be there.

This unit/company review should address the key areas of management development and ensure that they have a full picture of the management resources of the unit in the context of likely future needs. Accordingly, they will consider six areas:

1. *Major business plans* and any likely *organizational and establishment changes*. This link with operational planning is fundamental and should be clear and overt. For this reason, management development reviews can usefully be timed to follow long-term planning meetings. This will enable management development planning to accommodate the likelihood of a move into a new product area or an important technological change in the industry or plans to acquire subsidiaries in another country – or, indeed, a strategic withdrawal from a certain market segment.
2. An *individual review at the senior levels in the unit* – the level will be defined according to the individual unit, but as a guideline will, in an operating company, clearly cover the board members and the level immediately below them. This review should be based for each individual on a simple sheet recording:

    (a)   the basic *personal details* (age, service, qualifications, grade, pay, etc.)
    (b)   a brief summary of the individual's *performance appraisal*
    (c)   a statement of the individual's *potential*.

As the system becomes more sophisticated a statement of how the individual feels about *his or her own career* is a useful addition.

Those conducting the review must first establish that they really understand and agree with what is being said about the manager: then they should determine what to plan for the next stage of his or her development.

This may take the form of a recommendation that managers should be considered for certain kinds of job move – to widen their experience; to fill gaps in knowledge; to test them in a more demanding post; to extend their base by operating in another product area or country. Or it could recommend a training course. In other cases it may conclude that the manager is ideally placed for the time being and that the most important priority is that he or she should *not* be moved but should remain long enough both to contribute in, and benefit from, the job he or she is doing. Specific moves can be agreed in this way but that is not the main aim – what is basic is to establish agreement on the *priority for the coming year.*

3.   A review, on the same lines, of those who have been included on the development lists because of their potential. It will also normally be at this review that individuals will be *added* to these lists. In the case of such people it is particularly important to identify *gaps in their experience*, and to plan moves which will enable them to develop and further prove their abilities.

4.   Identification of possible *successors for vacancies* which are likely to arise at senior levels – because of retirements; or because the incumbents are likely to move; or because of organizational changes; or, where numbers are large enough, where past experience suggests that there may well be some losses to posts outside the organization. Such lists of possible successors are, of course, tentative, but like so much in this field, they begin to point the way to possible problem areas. The same few successors may keep appearing against several vacancies or, in some areas, all the candidates may look less than ideal. The reviewers will then want to reconsider the agreed plans for some of the successors in order to speed up or re-plan this development.

Succession will not always – particularly at the most senior levels – be provided within the individual company, and this succession planning at unit level is only one part of a wider exercise: the personnel executives involved must ensure that the particular succession planning is related to the wider group situation.

5.   At this stage it should be possible to take an *overall view of the company's situation.* No one can produce a checklist of precisely what should be discussed: in one unit it will be the lack of any managers of development potential in the engineering function; in another it may be the unfortunate coming together at a time of top-level retirements and promotions, and how to arrange them successfully; elsewhere it may be the fact that none of the financial managers seems to stay in the job for *27*

more than eighteen months. The review paperwork will have provided the basic data to show up these issues, but there is a skill in spotting them. If this skill – essentially, though not exclusively, a contribution of the personnel specialist – is lacking, no amount of forms and checklists will compensate: a system of management development planning needs a lot of *managing*.

6. The meeting should be summarized quickly in clear *action notes*. The temptation will be to record everything that was said; succinctness with an emphasis on action will not only make it more likely that the notes are not immediately filed, but may actually result in *people moving*.

REVIEW OF RESOURCES AT HIGHER LEVELS

Even at the level of the individual company or unit the review will inevitably (and rightly) consider issues of balance of resources and needs; but planning will not always be viewed within the group context and imbalances in particular units are, to an extent, to be expected. It is therefore important that a further review is conducted at a higher level – probably for *all group resources in a particular country*. Thereafter, a similar exercise needs to be carried out for the *total group*. These reviews may well address themselves to the individual details of the highest levels of management and to succession at that level. They will certainly give priority attention to a more 'aggregated' approach to management development planning: to reviewing the promotable management resources in the light of likely needs as determined by the age structure of the existing management, business plans to change the management establishment in the future, and best estimates of patterns of leaving. The kind of basic information appropriate to this exercise is set out in Figure 2.1. This review should certainly be prepared in total for all functions and a similar exercise carried out for specific functions.

In Figure 2.1 can be found the signposts to most of the management development *problems* which will crop up over the next few years. From an informed review of the data will come provisional conclusions, such as that:

1. There is a hump in the age distribution of senior executives and that those with potential to replace them (List III) are too few and, apparently, rather young.
2. The age distribution at the top (or at some other level) is such that, in combination with planned establishment reductions, there is going to be a shortage of promotion opportunities over the next five years, followed by a further five years of intense demand for replacements. How will the succession candidates be stimulated meanwhile? Or will they leave? Maybe someone should talk to them about it!

Once such problems have been identified, discussion must move to *specifics and individuals*. The review will have done the essential task of management development planning and drawn attention to a problem which, if nothing is

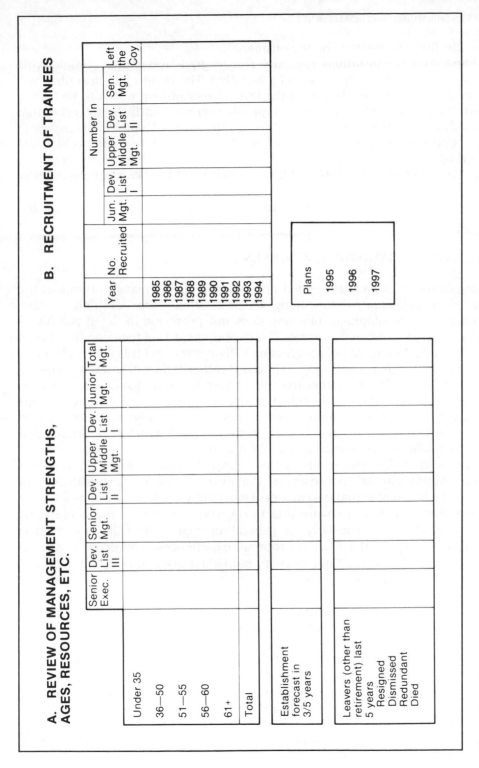

A. REVIEW OF MANAGEMENT STRENGTHS, AGES, RESOURCES, ETC.

	Senior Exec.	Dev. List III	Senior Mgt.	Dev. List II	Upper Middle Mgt.	Dev. List I	Junior Mgt.	Total Mgt.
Under 35								
36—50								
51—55								
56—60								
61+								
Total								

Establishment forecast in 3/5 years								

Leavers (other than retirement) last 5 years								
Resigned								
Dismissed								
Redundant								
Died								

B. RECRUITMENT OF TRAINEES

		Number In					
Year	No. Recruited	Jun. Mgt.	Dev. List I	Upper Middle Mgt.	Dev. List II	Sen. Mgt.	Left the Coy
1985							
1986							
1987							
1988							
1989							
1990							
1991							
1992							
1993							
1994							

Plans
1995
1996
1997

Figure 2.1   Human resources review

done, is likely to creep up on the business.

Most large organizations regularly recruit graduates either straight from university or within a few years of graduating. The review just described will form the basis for deciding what the level of recruitment needs to be for the next few years. Such trainees are typically recruited with the intention that they should progress fairly rapidly through the ranks of junior management in their first five–ten years in the business. Accordingly, it is useful to have the information in Section B in Figure 2.1, which highlights the success in retaining and developing the recruits and gives a picture of how careers are actually *experienced by those who join.*

These overall reviews at higher levels will form the basis of plans for the coming period.

PLANNING OF INDIVIDUAL CAREERS

Some further comment is needed on what 'planning' means in terms of the *careers of individuals* – something which is often misunderstood. Clearly, management development planning does not prescribe in detail the future advance of an individual's career. The development lists focus on how far an individual looks capable of progressing in five years, and it is also reasonable to forecast the *kind of job* – e.g. a specialist rather than a generalist, someone who will be in a line job rather than an adviser. It is right for the individual to know this information, although it needs to be communicated with clear indications of its limitations – in particular, that any such forecast is dependent on *continued performance in the job* (and, equally importantly, on the *availability of appropriate jobs* in the future).

The organization also needs to think through typical career paths in the main functional areas – not to ensure that everyone's career slavishly follows the model but to plan that the careers of most individuals will meet most of the requirements. This will ensure that those who progress to reach the most senior positions, particularly in general management, will have passed through a range of the most appropriate experiences. The detail of such a model has to be worked out in every individual organization, but a typical checklist could well be:

1. To cover the *full range of responsibilities in an individual's basic function.* It could thus be appropriate to plan that engineers have experience not only on development and design but also in the management of ongoing engineering departments, including maintenance, etc. Similarly, it might be decided that accountants should have experience of both financial management and management accounting; that personnel managers have experience of both industrial relations and pay issues.
2. To have operated in *more than one environment*, preferably at a reasonably early stage in a career. This means working either in a different market or in a different country.
3. To have actually been 'in charge' with responsibility for 'hands-on'

management of a *distinct part of the business*. Few people will have experience as general managers in an early part of their career, but it is important to ensure that careers do not continue permanently in headquarter organizations and that those of potential operate away from the company's base, perhaps running the accounts department or the engineering function at a distant site. Like riding a bicycle, this is something which has to be learnt in practice, and preferably when young.

It will never be possible to ensure that all careers meet all these criteria, but a regular analysis and the availability of the model as an objective can significantly raise the number of careers which meet most of them. Without such a model the tendency could easily be to use people's experience in further jobs which develop and further test only the same capacities. There is a huge difference between *ten years' experience* and *the same years' experience ten times over*.

CONCLUSIONS

These are the elements in a management development planning system. It is a 'system' in the sense that it is a series of regular tasks which highlights the shape of the present situation and points to potential problem areas. But how useful it is will depend on the *use made of it* – it will give no automatic answers. More than most planning systems, it will be a continuously rolling exercise, always an updated forecast, always open-ended, usually a bit untidy.

Three points are worth making in conclusion. The first is to restate the importance of the *middle levels* which are the most elusive in the process of getting a grip on the development of managers. It is very difficult – but vital – to plan and influence careers between the 'bottom-up' activities of recruitment and early training and the 'top-down' plans for top-level succession. One very experienced consultant who advised medium-sized companies in this field once put it more caustically when he said he usually found that management development consisted of 'an interest in young men and a sort of mafia surrounding the chairman'. It is usually because they are concerned to get more order – or less disorder – into that middle ground that groups want to institute management development planning, and it is by progress in that difficult area that it will in the end be judged.

The second point underlines a theme running through this chapter: that the regular systems are valuable to point to a *specific trend or problem*. Accordingly, there will be frequent occasions when it is right to follow this up by setting up *ad hoc* exercises: a senior working group to study the high turnover of engineers, or to look at the gap between well-trained accountants and their ability to move on to financial director jobs between which there are many discontinuities in the skill requirements, for example. Such exercises, as well as coming up with a good answer, can put the right political clout behind development programmes. The need to set up such *ad hoc* exercises is not a

31

weakness of the regular system: the fact that the need for them is perceived is, in fact, the system's strength. It is, however, also important that such one-off exercises do not get incorporated into the regular procedures, involving continuing work long after it has ceased to be necessary.

The final point is the most important of all. It has been stressed that the planning systems must be seen as a support for – and useful only insofar as they support and contribute to – good decisions about *actual people and their careers*. This is a two-way relationship. The systems must usefully guide the individual appointments: in addition, the appointments must be seen to forward the overall objectives of the plan. There is also an even more important interaction and mutually supportive relationship with the *organizational culture* – those shared attitudes and values in respect of people and their development which exist in the organization. The systems will be frustrated if the culture does not incorporate a belief that it is right – for the business – to regard longer-term career development as important, and on occasions to make short-term operational level sacrifices to that end. This will come about only if the systems make it reasonable to assume that such sacrifices are not in vain – and, above all, that the systems bring benefits in terms of the availability of well-developed people as well as demands for the release of others. It is such a culture which marks the company which has really integrated its management development planning into the running of the business.

REFERENCES

The Institute of Personnel Management publish pamphlets on many of the individual activities in the field. For a further and deeper treatment, reference could usefully be made to:

Bennison, M. and Casson, J. (1984) *The Manpower Planning Handbook* (London: Institute of Manpower Studies/McGraw-Hill).

Hirsh, W. (1990) *Succession Planning* (London: Institute of Manpower Studies).

Walker, James W. (1980) *Human Resource Planning* (London: McGraw-Hill).

3 Diagnosing needs

Andrew Stewart

Managers often try to solve assessment or development problems by adopting new techniques; if those new techniques are seen not to be successful, the techniques themselves are blamed as being ineffective. The fault more probably lies with an inadequate or non-existent *diagnosis of the needs which the technique was trying to meet*: if the problem is not properly defined, a solution is likely to be elusive.

This chapter is primarily concerned with the training and development needs of individuals and groups, but there is another set of needs which should be established before specific training and development needs are addressed: these needs have to do with the *commercial or functional effectiveness of the organization*, and may be seen to exist at three levels:

1. At the *strategic* level, the question is whether there are shortfalls in the performance of the organization – now or in the future – which can properly be traced to ineffective performance on the part of some managers of employees. In addition, new developments in the market or customer base may create a demand for different ways of doing things, which implies no criticism of current performance, but which will lead to difficulties if no change in approach occurs.
2. At the *manpower planning* level, the question is whether the stocks and flows of people through and around the organization are appropriate – both to current needs and to future trends. More importantly, perhaps, is the quality of individual concealed in the statistics such that the operation will be enhanced rather than held back for lack of talent?
3. At the *individual* level, it is advisable to check whether there are people who are under-performing compared to expectation, and if so, *why*. They may have reached their level of incompetence; or they may simply be in the wrong job, or they may be perfectly capable of performing better with some developmental help.

These three levels of question are primarily concerned with the way in which the business of the organization is being conducted, whether this be in the commercial style of private enterprise or in the service-orientated style of the health service, local or national government. If it can be shown that the performance of individuals or groups is impeding the attainment of the organization's declared objectives, then it may be worthwhile to probe training and development needs in some depth to establish *what kinds of intervention* are going to yield the best pay-off. This chapter is primarily concerned to present a range of techniques for probing those needs.

TYPES OF TECHNIQUE

Training needs analysis techniques can be classified in two distinct ways. There is a distinction between *group* techniques and *individual* techniques; and there is another distinction between *deficiency-* and *ideal*-based techniques:

- Group techniques are particularly useful at a *macro level*, for strategic planning and for deciding training priorities; individual techniques are designed to make accessible the training needs of *single persons.*
- Deficiency-based techniques are aimed at discovering shortfalls in *current performance* in order to design remedial action; ideal-based techniques are designed to achieve statements of what, in the best of all possible worlds, people *should be doing*, and then set out to help people to get closer to that ideal.

The trainer needs to know about both the ideal and reality, but the order in which this is achieved may be determined by the diagnostic techniques used. Most of the techniques presented in this chapter can be used in either group or individual mode; only some of them can be used in ideal mode, but most of them can help to uncover deficiencies.

CRITICAL INCIDENT

In this technique, the interviewer selects a group of managers who are representative of the target population, and asks them to talk about the most difficult problem they have had to deal with in the last period of time. This period can vary from around one week to not more than six months; memory for detail will fade seriously after this time. Six weeks is often chosen as a period of time which will be meaningful to most people, and the starting question might be: 'Can you tell me about the incident in the last six weeks which has caused you the most difficulty?' Follow-up questions might include:

- When?   One-off problem or regular?
- Why?   Your problem or someone else's?
- Who with?   What caused it?

- At what cost?   Will it happen again?
- How was it solved?   Any long-term effects?

After a number of interviews have been conducted, it then becomes necessary to *classify the information*. Some categories which have emerged from the data include:

- Alone/other people involved
- Technical/financial/managerial
- Type of product/service involved
- If other people involved, insiders/customers/suppliers/others
- If other people involved, senior/peer/junior/other
- Producing new ideas/servicing old ideas
- New problem/old problem.

Although it is more difficult, it provides a more accurate reflection of the data if the *interview content is allowed to dictate the categories into which it is sorted*. In some other systems the interviewer comes with a prepared list of categories into which the data will be fitted; this seems to suggest that the content is already known, in which case it might be hard to justify the research.

Critical incident technique is fairly rough and ready, but will give fast information about priorities. For example, a service engineering organization was putting about 80 per cent of its training effort into technical product training and 20 per cent into interpersonal skills. A critical incident survey showed that less than 15 per cent of the problems were generated by the equipment, and that all the rest required customer handling skills. A rapid shift of priorities could then be seen to be justified, together with con-gratulations to the technical trainers who had clearly been doing a good job.

Critical incident interviews do carry an implied commitment to those interviewed that something is about to be done about their problems; if no tangible results appear within a relatively short time those interviewed may well feel let down. Some form of *feedback and action* should therefore be made apparent at the earliest opportunity.

SELF-REPORT QUESTIONNAIRES

In self-report questionnaires managers are asked fairly straightforwardly *what training they think they need*. The manner of putting the question varies from providing a list of courses to tick to providing a list of skills to tick; sometimes the managers are simply given a blank sheet of paper. The problems with this approach are that the managers may not know their own training needs, may not know enough about the training courses on offer, and may regard the questionnaire as just another piece of paper to be filled in and leave it in their in-tray, or fill it in negligently.

Self-report questionnaires are more useful on the technical and financial side than on interpersonal relationships. A good questionnaire begins by   *35* providing some background information and asks the respondents to refer to their year's objectives or to think of their most recent critical incident. Then it asks respondents to tick relevant courses or to tick the skills and knowledge they feel they lack. Some typical answers include:

- Management training
- Management of people
- Encouraging creativity
- Joint problem-solving
- Problem definition
- Management by objectives
- Experimental design.

Statistics
Survey methodology
Finance
Negotiating skills
Interviewing
Technical updating
Influencing company policy.

These answers are not condensed, except in the area of technical updating. They are a good example of the lack of detail which most self-report questionnaires yield. The technique is very frequently used, but cannot seriously be recommended.

STRUCTURED INTERVIEWS

In a structured interview the trainer visits a number of managers with a standard list of prepared questions which it is hoped will throw light on their training needs. Clearly the questions will vary from company to company and from situation to situation, but once the list is prepared it should remain *constant across all interviews*, otherwise any differences that appear between interviewees may be due to the questions they have been asked rather than to any real differences.

One typical set of questions is as follows:

1. What sort of things in your job give you most *satisfaction*?
2. What *changes* would be needed to make your job more *effective*? *Who* could make these changes?
3. What sorts of *activities* take up a lot of your time? Does this please you?
4. How far are you *responsible* for planning the way you use your time?
5. What proportion of your activities do you have *no choice about*?
6. Which aspects of your work *interest* you the most? Which the least?
7. Where is the work you do *initiated*?
8. Do you often come *under pressure* for quick results? *Where* does the pressure come from? *How* do you react?
9. How are your *standards of performance set*? By *whom*?
10. How do you get *feedback* on the results of your work?
11. How, and by whom, does the work you are doing get *stopped*?
12. How much *public presentation* of your work and your department do you have to do?
13. Do you find yourself working very much in *committees*?
14. How much do you have to do with the *data processing* department?

15. Do you have much to do with *unions or staff associations*?
16. Do you find the job *different* from what you were expecting?
17. Has any job you have been involved with *failed to reach completion* because of lack of technical knowledge or skill on someone else's part?
18. Have you any skills you feel are being *inadequately used*?
19. Where do you see your career going over the next *year*? The next *five years*?
20. What *training* have you *had*? Do you remember any training as particularly useful, or useless? Why?
21. What *training* do you think you *need*, either that you know is already available or that you would like to see introduced?
22. What kind of person would you advise the organization to recruit to *replace you* if you were to move on? What technical knowledge should they bring with them? What training and experience would you want them to be given in the first three months? What advice would you give them? What sort of mistakes do you think they would make at first?

Some questions will be more fruitful than others. Questions 9 and 10, for example, did not work with some technical/professional managers since they had not considered that setting standards of performance and organizing feedback systems was a useful activity: for them, the technical job set its own, unique, non-negotiable standards of performance. In the case of a company legal department it was held to be unethical and an invasion of privacy to even attempt such a thing, since it implied that their legal qualifications were in some way unequal one with another and did not represent the ultimate statement of legal competence! Questions 18 and 22 usually unleash a great deal of information, regardless of occupation.

The results should ideally be *analysed independently by two or more people*. In this way, any classification which emerges has the added reliability of having been arrived at by two or more separate individuals, and is less likely to be influenced unduly by one strong set of values. Generalization should wait until all the data have been sifted.

Structured interviews are usually better than self-report questionnaires for anything other than the most straightforward needs diagnosis, but they do take time. Only some of the questions will pay off, and it may be difficult to achieve standardized administration between two interviewers, or from the same interviewer on different days. The critical incident technique may yield more information faster, but carries a greater implied commitment to action.

DIARY METHOD

In this method, those involved are asked to keep diaries which *record their activities under a variety of headings*; this record is then analysed to deduce the demands being made on the individual, and the skills needed to do the job. This form of analysis moves away from the identification of deficiencies towards the description of *actual* performance, and the deduction of *ideal*   37 performance; this feature can help to obtain people's commitment to the work involved in making the record.

Diaries can be general (attempting to cover a whole range of potential needs) or highly specific (when one or two needs are to be examined in depth). For example, a supervisor in a garment factory was asked to keep a diary to assist in the introduction of new procedures under the 1974 Health and Safety at Work Act. She was asked to place a tick in the appropriate space each time she had to deal with one of the following:

- *Workshop tidiness*

  - materials obstructing free passage
  - made-up goods obstructing free passage
  - dangerous goods stacked at unsafe heights
  - personal belongings lying around.

- *Machine maintenance*

  - machines being serviced with power on
  - untrained people attempting to service machines
  - unsafe parts not being properly disposed of
  - machines left uncleaned
  - operatives transferring machines without permission
  - machines not being switched off during breaks.

- *Personal*

  - long hair in danger of being caught
  - smoking in prohibited areas
  - liquid refreshment being passed around at work stations
  - shoes making foot controls difficult to operate
  - pregnant operatives lifting heaving weights.

The supervisor ticked each item and used a code to show whether she had taken action herself, told someone else to take action, or taken no action at all. She was not asked to state how long each incident had lasted, or who else was involved.

Much fuller diaries have been sought in order to obtain a broad picture of the activities carried out by managers. In the example below, managers were asked to record the length of time spent in each activity, who else was involved, and the degree to which the activity was planned.

- *Activity*: Talking on the phone; with one other face-to-face; with more than one other face-to-face; and was the contact scheduled? Touring (inspecting the workplace); mail-handling, other paperwork; lecturing; travelling; operational work
- *Contact*: Alone, with boss; with secretary; with subordinates; with colleagues (i.e. peers reporting to the same boss); with peers (i.e. people

of similar level not reporting to the same boss); other senior; other junior; external (specify); new contacts

- *Interruptions*: In own office; other (specify)
- *Nature of activity*: Crisis (drop everything to sort out); choice (need not have done that day); deadline (done for a definite time goal); new work (different from anything done before); recurrent task; urgent work; unexpected work.

In addition, mail in and mail out was analysed, and the whole was supported by a detailed questionnaire. Results were classified into *choices, constraints, demands,* and *skills required.*

In designing a diary the following sequence has proved useful:

1. Conduct a *pilot investigation* to determine the greatest areas of interest, and whether they are general or specific to one or two skill areas.
2. Since the diary is intended to demonstrate the demands being made on the individual, some definition of the *specific demands to be investigated* should be made. Examples might include duration of activity, contact with others, amount of discretion in choosing the activities, need for information about the results of the activities.
3. Each of the desired categories is broken into codes – one for type of activity, one for contacts, and so on. If the length of time spent in each activity is important, then an appropriate breakdown should be offered. It is important to make the job of completing the diary as easy as possible by using ticks or some other simple code rather than seeking substantive written information.
4. A *questionnaire containing the diary* is then assembled, together with a statement of its purpose and instructions on how to fill it in. This is first piloted on one or two friendly individuals, and then sent to a small but representative sample of those from whom the final responses are sought. At this stage, irrelevant questions can be removed and those that have been found difficult to answer can be modified. The method of analysis should be tried out at this stage as well.
5. The full set of questionnaires is sent out, the returns analysed, and a report prepared on the demands made on respondents, broken down into sub-groups if this is useful. Full discussion of these demands is then followed by *decisions about the needs revealed,* and the early stages of *planning to meet them.*

Diary method can offer a complete and well-aimed account of the key areas of individuals' work and the support they need to do it. It can bring to light the dull, day-to-day training needs that few bother to look for, and it can provide an informative contrast between what really happens and the job description. It does, however, take time to set up and run, and some statistical skill to analyse. Respondents may resent the time taken to complete it, particularly if there is no space to record the time taken filling it in. There is also a slight *39* danger of asking questions because they look nice rather than because they will yield useful information about how the job is being done. Despite the labour, the diary method can be one of the richer sources of information about training and development needs in the organization.

PERFORMANCE QUESTIONNAIRE

This technique is useful particularly at the interface between *individual training needs analysis and organization development*. Having identified the level of individual whose training or development needs are to be investigated, a questionnaire is designed which contains a series of *bipolar statements* – describing, for example, managerial behaviour – with a five-point scale between the poles. Some items from a group of senior managers in an international bank included:

- Prefers to work in the field   Prefers to work in the office
- Is better at relationship skills   Is better as a technician
- Reacts   Anticipates
- Prefers action   Prefers evaluation
- Prefers the client to set priorities   Prefers the bank to set priorities
- Would rather explain a situation   Would rather improve a situation
- Knows when to cut losses   Does not know when to cut losses
- More concerned with short term (less than two years ahead).   More concerned with long-term (two years or more ahead).

The questionnaire is distributed to managers of the position under consideration, and if possible to current occupants of the position and those of their colleagues who have a close working relationship with them. Each is asked to think of the most effective holder of the given job they know, or have working directly for them, and to describe him or her on the questionnaire anonymously. Both *good and bad points* should be allowed to emerge. When the completed questionnaires have been returned a second set is sent out. These are exactly the same as the first set, but the instructions now ask the respondents to think of the least effective holder of the given job they know; anonymity is understandably even more important on this occasion. A simple statistical analysis of the comparisons between the two sets of returns will reveal which items discriminate between *perceived effective* and *perceived ineffective* performers. Other analyses will yield a list of items solely associated with effective behaviour, and a list of items solely associated with ineffective behaviour. (The analysis involves no more than counting the number of times each response option is used for each question.) There will be no particular pattern which emerges from some questions, and they may be discarded. In other cases there may be a clear pattern. For example, take the item:

40   ●   Reacts   Anticipates

Suppose that fifty people have responded to both the first (effective) and the second (ineffective) administration of the questionnaire. The results might look as follows:

- (1st administration)   Reacts 0 0 5 15 30 Anticipates
- (2nd administration)   Reacts 20 25 0 5 0 Anticipates

The results are now weighted to reflect the extremity of view expressed. Thus the frequencies in the outside two columns are multipled by 3; the frequencies in the next two columns are multiplied by 2; the centre column remains unaltered. The results now look as follows:

- (1st administration)   Reacts 0 0 5 30 90 Anticipates
- (2nd administration)   Reacts 60 50 0 10 0 Anticipates

The difference between the results of the first (effective) administration and the second (ineffective) administration are clear. The maximum frequency for the first set appears at the extreme right-hand side; for the second set at the extreme left-hand side. There is a clear picture of effectiveness in that virtually all votes went for anticipation; there is a clear picture of ineffectiveness in that the great majority of votes went for reaction. An unclear result is obtained when the votes are spread fairly evenly across all five options (a more detailed account of this procedure will be found in Stewart and Stewart, 1981b). The analysis of results thus yields the material from which a picture can be constructed, of both the effective and the ineffective holder of the position. In this way, both information about *behaviour for development*, and *behaviour to be avoided or trained out*, can be obtained

The items which make up the performance questionnaire can be brain-stormed or produced by selective interviewing, but the best method seems to be to conduct a short series of *repertory grid interviews*, which will yield results already in bipolar format. This method is discussed later in this chapter. The performance questionnaire has the advantages that the information has been generated directly by those who are likely to be involved in any action for change that may follow, and concerns *real people and real events*. It therefore provides a good basis for asking whether the characteristics revealed should be perpetuated or changed. It also tends to generate information of a kind which is directly observable and amenable to change, rather than personality statements which make for difficulty in observation and may not be possible or proper to try to change. The main drawbacks are that it requires that there be at least thirty (and preferably fifty) respondents for the statistics to be reliable, and it is therefore unlikely to be of use to very small organizations or at the top layer of any organization, unless great care is taken not to try to generalize the results beyond the immediate group surveyed. Further, if the questionnaire is not couched in terms which are in the *language and culture of the people responding*, and if they are not asked to respond about real people,   *41* the result will be a poor response rate and resort to 'ideal' types. This in turn leads to *unrealistic or inappropriate statements of needs*.

CONTENT ANALYSIS

This technique presents the analyst with an unusual opportunity to conduct a diagnosis of training or development needs which does not impinge directly on those being investigated. This *non-reactive research* depends on obtaining access to written records of various kinds, and going through them systematically to extract training needs. It is possible to look for skills being exhibited, for deficiencies being shown, for demands being made, or for all three. It can be done on a group basis, or for an individual; since historical data are being used, no one in the field is being disturbed, nor will the information be faked for the occasion.

Sources of information for content analysis can include performance appraisal records, internal memoranda, letters to outside people (customers, suppliers, competitors), complaints, training literature, sales proposals – indeed, almost any written material can prove a valuable source of information. For example, despite the existence of an in-house written communication course, it was clear that the reports being produced by one particular research organization were failing to meet their twin objectives of communicating the research and maintaining a high profile in the market place. It was agreed to undertake a content analysis of a range of reports recently produced. It was also, unusually, possible to gain access to previous drafts of the final reports, so that not only could the finished version be seen, but the contributions of the various reviewers along the way could also be analysed and training needs extracted. The following were found, with a note of the frequency of occurrence after each:

- *Strategic errors*
  - Facts not distinguished from opinion   7
  - Benefits not clearly stated   5
  - Context missing (and needed)   4
  - Purpose of report unclear   4
  - Political implications of work missed   4
  - Lack of awareness of readers' special needs   4
  - Statements made that could easily be taken out of context
    and misused   3
  - Too much claimed in the title   1

- *Grammar and syntax*
  - 'Data', 'criteria', and 'media' used with a singular verb   21
  - Subject not agreeing with verb   17
  - Spelling mistakes   15
  - Inappropriate use of brackets   14
  - Misplaced apostrophe in possessive cases   14

- Misplaced qualifying clause   7
- Confusion between 'its' and 'it's'   5
- Use of jargon abbreviations without explanation   4
- Use of quotation marks to show emphasis   2

● *Presentation errors*

- Unreadable handwriting   5
- Tables too dense   5
- Terms not defined clearly   4
- Results given without mentioning sample size   3
- Paper, to be read verbatim, clearly too long for allocated time   2
- Inconsistent typestyles used on final document   2

● *Editing and management errors*

- Paper too late for publication deadline   5
- Editor offers clarification; author responds with 'I know what I meant'   5
- Editor puts check mark instead of specifying what is not clear   4
- Editor, having asked for report, forgets why it was wanted   3

Two courses were set up as a result of this analysis. One replaced the existing report-writing course, which clearly either made assumptions about basic competencies which were not justified in practice, or failed to meet its objective to teach them. The second course was specifically aimed at editing skills. This was partly because they were clearly needed, and partly because senior managers were flattered to be invited on to an editing course, whereas they would be insulted by the implication that they needed help with writing skills. It is also worth mentioning that correspondence files were reviewed, revealing the fact that over 50 per cent of replies to external letters began with some variation on 'I am sorry for the delay in replying to your letter ...'. The improvement in style produced a dramatic change in the management of *customer relations*.

It may require some imagination to trace the places where information truly relevant to the diagnosis of training and development needs may be found, but because it is non-reactive, can be checked, uses historic and usually unfaked data, and can be fitted into odd time corners, content analysis is an attractive technique. New trainers can also be inducted into their jobs by offering them some content analysis in order to help them find their way round the organization and some of its problems. However, care needs to be taken about breaching confidentiality, so that personal records should be used with considerable discretion, if at all. The day-to-day paperwork of the organization will generate enough information for most needs.

BEHAVIOUR ANALYSIS

Behaviour analysis is a special case of content analysis in which *people's actions and statements* are categorized in a *running analysis performed by*   *43 themselves or by the trainer.* The behaviour of each individual, either alone or in a group, is monitored under a series of simple headings, and a check mark made every time one of the list behaviours occurs. The exact headings will vary with the area of need under investigation, but for a course in general interactive skills the following might be appropriate: proposing, supporting, building, disagreeing, criticizing, seeking information, giving information. The trainer looks for the *overall contribution level* of each person (too high? too low?), and the *relative importance* of the various kinds of behaviour. Building behaviour is usually important in developing a cohesive team, so people low on this behaviour may need help to increase it. People with a high level of proposing and giving information may need help in learning to listen.

Using different categories of behaviour, some ratios can yield useful information. The ratio of *caught* proposals to *escaped* proposals (those that get some attention even if only rejection, and those that get none) can be useful when helping someone to get their ideas accepted; the ratio of *bringing in* to *shutting out* behaviour can be useful for developing teamwork skills – it is frequently observed, incidentally, that those who profess most vehemently the virtues of participative management are those who most seriously exhibit shutting out behaviour. The ratio of *defending–attacking* behaviour to admitting difficulty can demonstrate a person's way of coping with challenge. For help with committees and other groups operating to an acknowledged formal structure, the ratio of *backtracking* to *jumping the gun* behaviour can be useful in helping control and to distinguish between (a) going over old ground or (b) leaping ahead to matters that are not yet ready to be dealt with. Feedback of the ratios, together with charting of changes in the ratios as the training progresses, can provide both an elegant diagnosis and a direct measure of change in the one package.

A full account of the use of behaviour analysis in training will be found in Rackham and Morgan (1977). To make the most effective use of behaviour analysis, simple category systems should be used with very few assumptions about what right and wrong behaviour look like; value judgements occurring too early will impede flexibility of styles and accuracy of self-analysis. *More than one person should be observing*, and the results should be frequently checked against one another. Feedback should be given early and often, as soon as the observations can be shown to be reliable. It should then be possible to depart in a controlled manner from the original training programme to address new needs as they emerge.

TESTS AND QUIZZES

One simple way of assessing training needs is to ask people questions and discover how many right answers they give. In technical areas, this is a useful and neglected approach to analysing training and development needs.

For example, as part of the diagnosis of training needs of personnel managers, questions could be asked along the following lines:

1. How many warnings must an unsatisfactory performance be given before dismissal?
2. How long must a woman have worked for an employer before she is entitled to maternity leave?
3. Give two examples of conditions of employment that might be construed as indirect discrimination against women.
4. Joe has been on the hourly paid staff for five years and four months. How much notice is he entitled to, should we wish to dismiss him?
5. Consider the following list of our suppliers. Tick those that operate a closed shop agreement. Name the main unions recognized by each of them.
6. On average, how long must a newly recruited salesman stay with the company before the cost of recruiting and training him or her is recovered?
7. An executive aged 55 dies while in our employment. His salary was £40 000 plus £5 000 profit sharing last year. What is the payment due to his widow?

It is not difficult to see how this kind of exercise can serve as a diagnosis of training needs, especially if it is self-scored and used from time to time as a progress check, perhaps involving a parallel-form version at the end of whatever remedial work takes place.

In order for this approach to work, the quiz constructor requires a clear idea of the *ground the training needs analysis must cover* and of the *objectives* of any course to which it is linked; the more open the question, the more difficult it will be to score. Interactive skills are less amenable to this approach, since questions which pose a hypothetical situation and then ask 'What would you do?' tend to receive answers of the kind that the respondent thinks are required rather than a genuine response; to make matters more complicated, the respondent may not know that he or she is doing this. Where factual information is concerned, therefore, the quiz can perform a valuable role; where interactive skills or matters of opinion are involved it is less effective and may actually be misleading.

PSYCHOLOGICAL TESTS

There is a mythology about psychological tests which it may be useful to dispel. A test is no more than a *conversation, frozen into a standard form*, so that as near as possible the identical 'conversation' is held with everyone who enters the situation. In this way, any differences which are detected between individuals are likely to be genuine differences and not caused by differences in treatment. That is all. The rest is merely technology to try to ensure that the tests work.

Tests are designed to provide answers to three levels of question: the more interesting the answer, the more difficult it is to provide.

● At the lowest level, tests provide answers to the question 'Has this person actually done or learnt what he/she claims to have done or learnt?' These are the *achievement tests*.

45

- At the next level, tests provide an answer to the question 'Could this person do the things we want him/her to if we gave him/her the task and trained him?' He has not done it yet, and has no relevant track record. These are *ability and aptitude tests.*
- Finally, there are tests which try to answer the question 'If we gave him this to do, would he choose to do it?' These are *personality and attitude tests.* They yield the most interesting answers, and are the most difficult to construct, administer and interpret.

Achievement tests will indicate at once whether there is a training need. Ability and aptitude tests will give an indication of whether the person has the brains or inclination to learn what has to be learnt. Personality and attitude tests (or, more properly, questionnaires, since there are no hard and fast right answers) may help to decide what likelihood there is that any training, development or appointment to a position may be successful.

Achievement tests are simple to score in that the person either does or does not produce a performance (typing speed, colour vision acuity, etc.) of the kind claimed. Ability tests are fairly straightforward in that a person achieves a score which can be compared with that achieved by other people, and conclusions can be drawn about the probability of his/her ability to do the job; perhaps for reasons of self-flattery, the level of ability judged necessary to perform many jobs is over-estimated. Personality questionnaires represent a quite different order of difficulty in interpreting. A questionnaire will permit some form of classification of an individual into a particular personality type. This enables the interpreter to say that some occupations will be more congenial than others, or that there may be a preference to tackle situations in one way rather than in another. But there are no absolutely right or wrong answers; there are simply new pieces of *technical information* upon which an individual or a manager has to make some judgement.

Tests and questionnaires are very high-profile techniques and are easy to challenge. It is both technically proper and tactically wise to ensure that the instruments used are properly validated for the kind of people upon whom it is intended that they are to be used. Such tests should have fairly bulky manuals containing a wide range of statistical information about both reliability and validity over a number of different groups of people; instruments which cannot offer this information, and whose proponents are making no systematic effort to produce such information, should be avoided. The best indicator of all is how easy it is to *obtain access* to the instrument; if it is freely available for a fee or licence, then it may not meet the necessary standard.

Reputable suppliers will insist that potential users of their tests are qualified to do so. This may necessitate undertaking a training course run by the supplier. By far the best approach is to ensure that test users are Chartered Occupational Psychologists, or at least possess the British Psychological Society's Certificate of Competence in Occupational Testing (Level A). This will give them immediate access to most tests of ability, or allow them to take only abbreviated training from the supplier in the specific instrument they require. Level B certification is to be introduced shortly to cover personality tests in the same way. Details of certification are available from The British Psychological Society, St Andrews House, 48 Princess Road East, Leicester LE1 7DR.

REPERTORY GRID

Most kinds of interview carry with them the danger that the results will be *contaminated in some way by the views of the interviewer*. The repertory grid approach is designed to go some way towards preventing this. A grid interview begins with the selection of the topics for discussion, called *elements*. These are concepts, items, people or behaviours representative of the area of interest. Examples of element lists might include:

1. Accidents, to discover the training needs of a safety officer.
2. Brand names of competing products or services, to discover the training needs of a marketing manager, or indeed some of the marketing needs of the organization.
3. Names of managers occupying the level for which replacements are ultimately to be sought lower down the organization.
4. Job activities undertaken by those managers.

Eight or nine elements is usually enough, although it is possible to use the technique with as few as three elements.

The interviewer checks that the interviewee is reasonably familiar with the elements on the list. Then the elements are taken, three at a time, and the interviewee is asked: 'Can you tell me some ways in which any two of these elements seem like each other to you, but different from the third?' If managers' names have been used, the interviewee might say that two of them are usually to be found in the field while the third is normally in his office. Another two might be thought to be approachable while the third was difficult to get to know. Yet another two might be described as fast workers while the third is thorough. Each of these bipolar distinctions is called a *construct*. It is the constructs which yield the information that is sought in a needs diagnosis.

By contrast repetition of the process, long lists of constructs can be obtained. The interviewee is then asked to go back over his or her list and to indicate which end of each construct is the preferred choice for effectiveness as a manager, or as an attractive feature of a product or service, or as having importance for a safety officer to deal with. At the end of such discussions with a number of interviewees, the interviewer will have accumulated lists of constructs with value judgements indicated by most of them. It is then possible to group the results in such a way as to produce a picture of the kind generated by other techniques. It is also possible to translate the bipolar constructs quite directly into bipolar items for a performance questionnaire. Note that the interviewer contributes no *content* at all, but merely *guides the process* along set lines.

This technique can be used to accumulate data from a range of people, or it can be used to interview a very few exhaustively. Only construct elicitation

47

has been described; to go on to a full grid requires some more steps in the logic, and may not always be a cost-effective approach for diagnostic purposes. Construct elicitation will often suffice. A fuller discussion of repertory grid and its uses in business will be found in Stewart and Stewart (1981a).

CONCLUSION

A number of techniques for diagnosing training and development needs have been presented in this chapter. They have in common that they are intended to provide a statement of what *people could do better*, expressed in *measurable terms*. The depth to which it is thought worthwhile to probe, the type of need to be investigated, and the breadth of coverage intended all influence the choice of diagnostic technique. The better the diagnosis, the easier it is to design the subsequent evaluation of the training or development, since the measures will already have been suggested. It has been indicated that desired *behaviours and performance* should be considered first, and translated into *training needs* afterwards; care should be taken not to present needs that are beyond reasonable efforts to accomplish; prospective trainees should participate in the diagnosis, and not have the results suddenly thrust upon them.

Finally, attention may well be given to something strangely seldom addressed when training needs are being considered – the preferred *learning style* of the individual about to be trained or developed. Honey and Mumford (1986) have developed a simple instrument to enable an individual to detect his or her preferred learning style: *activist, reflector, theorist* or *pragmatist*. Most people have elements of all four in their approach, but one or two are likely to predominate, and it is possible for training or development to be designed to take account of the learner's preferred style of acquiring information or skills: it seems unwise to spend a great deal of time and effort in diagnosing training or development needs if no effort is put into making the subsequent experience 'user friendly'.

REFERENCES

Guion, R. M. (1981) *Personnel Testing* (London: McGraw-Hill).

Honey, P. and Mumford, A. (1992) *The Manual of Learning Styles*, 3rd edn (London: Honey).

Miller, K. M. (1975) *Psychological Tests in Personnel Assessment* (Aldershot: Gower).

Rackham, N. and Morgan, T. (1977) *Behaviour Analysis in Training* (London: McGraw-Hill).

Stewart, R. (1982) *Choices for the Manager* (London: McGraw-Hill).

Stewart, V. and Stewart, A. (1981a) *Business Applications of Repertory Grid* (London: McGraw-Hill).

Stewart, V. and Stewart, A. (1981b) *Tomorrow's Managers Today* (London: IPM).

4 Performance appraisal

Andrew Stewart

A great deal has been written about performance appraisal; a great deal more has been said. It is odd that, despite all this attention, so few organizations say that they are satisfied with their particular way of conducting appraisals of employee performance. It is all the more strange since the task is, in principle, very straightforward. Two people, one the manager and one the managed, sit down together perhaps once during the year, in order to find answers to the following four questions:

1. What did we *set out to achieve* during the year?
2. Have we *achieved* it?
3. What are we going to do *next*?
4. How will we know *if we have done it*?

Anything more elaborate than the above could be said to be complicating a simple matter more than it merits, to the confusion of all concerned. This chapter presents some of the approaches that have been adopted in trying to obtain satisfactory answers to these four questions.

First, some of the more usual varieties of appraisal system will be described, together with a discussion of the performance criteria associated with them. Some comments will be offered about system design, and this will be followed by an account of some of the ways in which organizations try to train their managers to use their systems. Ways in which systems can be monitored and controlled will be presented, and then two further issues will be explored which often cause difficulty: *assessing potential*, and *problem performers*. Some future trends will also be discussed. Finally, there will be a simple checklist to help managers to ensure that all the necessary steps towards a successful performance appraisal interview have been carried out.

VARIETIES OF SYSTEM

People do not learn unless they are given *feedback on the results of their action(s)*. For learning to take place, feedback must be both *regular* and *frequent*, should register both *successes* and *failures*, and should follow soon after the relevant action(s). In the daily rush of getting things done, much of this can be forgotten or not put into effect. Performance appraisal schemes give people the chance to learn how they are doing, to correct their mistakes and to acquire new skills. Since manager and the managed are together reviewing past performance and planning to meet the needs of the future, it should follow that some of the necessary conditions for the *successful management of change* are also being met. A performance appraisal scheme can also offer the opportunity to consider and agree longer-range targets for achievement, thus making positive growth more likely for the organization, and avoiding the trap of doing nothing more than daily 'firefighting'. Finally, since employees are expensive, it makes sense to try to encourage their best efforts. A performance appraisal interview can be one of the most motivating events in an employee's year; badly handled, it can be a disaster.

There are usually four parties to an appraisal: the appraisee, the appraiser, the central planning and personnel departments, and external bodies such as training councils, trade unions and bodies set up in the interests of equal opportunity legislation. The interests of the first two parties should dominate; if the main focus is either planning or defence, then the chief objective of the exercise may be lost.

Appraisal systems may be used for three main purposes: *remedial, maintenance* and *development*. A system should have a mix of all three; systems become out of balance if any one purpose predominates. If the *remedial* purpose is foremost, then the appraisal interview may become a disciplinary interview, and the form a charge sheet. If *maintenance* is the main objective, then the process can become a short, skimped, perfunctory ritual. If there is too much emphasis on *development*, then the focus falls on the next job rather than the one presently in hand, and the interview may be construed as a promise of future progress.

Above all, the appraisal interview is a time for *listening*. The appraisee probably has a good idea of how his performance appears to him, and this is unlikely to be badly at variance with his manager's view: indeed, there is some evidence that an appraisee is likely to be harder on himself than his manager intends to be.

Many variations in appraisal systems have been tried in order to support the basic purpose of *looking backwards in order to look forward*. The chief ones appear to be:

1. *Eligibility*: all staff, or managers and salaried staff only.
2. *Appraiser*: immediate line manager, technical specialist, personnel specialist, 'grandfather' or 'grandmother' (manager's manager).
3. *Employee access*: employee sees all the form, some of the form, or none

of the form.

4. *Self-appraisal or preparation for counselling form*: used, or not used.
5. *Past performance only*: or past and present performance measured.
6. *Measurement against*: performance targets or objectives, rating scales of performance, rating scales of personality, or no measurement criteria specified.
7. *Rating scales*: present or absent, together with variation in the number of divisions on the scale.
8. *Opportunity to set targets for future performance*: or not.
9. *Discussion of training and development needs*: for present job, for next job, or for longer term.
10. *Potential rated*: on a one-dimensional scale, a multi-dimensional scale, or no formal rating of potential.
11. *Discussion of salary*: forbidden, mandatory, or optional.
12. *Appraisal interviews*: frequency and regularity.
13. *Disputes*: resolved by appeal to manager's manager, or personnel, or no procedure.
14. *Appraisal forms*: *who may see*: and for what purpose.
15. *Use of forms*: *for central planning* purposes.
16. *Use of forms*: *for day-to-day management* and *coaching* purposes.

Each of these variations is held to be helpful by different practitioners, depending on the circumstances in which they are working. It is not possible to offer a single best method, merely a selection from which a choice may be made. The area which seems to cause the most anxiety, however, is the link with salary. If salary is seen as compensation for work done, then perhaps the link with performance is more tenuous. If salary is used as an incentive – to reward outstanding work and to encourage rising standards – then some form of link seems inevitable. If salary review and performance appraisal occur at the same time, there may be a tendency to drift the rating unjustifiably upwards in order to be able to offer a satisfactory increase. One way to prevent this is to have both performance and salary rated on the same scale and in the same way, but to have the events occur *six months apart*; in this way, all concerned understand the system, but managers have the freedom to vary the salary rating if the employee's performance has either improved or worsened since the performance review.

PERFORMANCE CRITERIA

In order to be satisfactory, both to those directly involved and to the law, the criteria for a performance appraisal system should be *genuinely related to success or failure in the job*, and should be as far as possible amenable to objective (not subjective) judgement. In addition, it is helpful if they are easy for the manager to administer, appear fair and relevant to the employee, and strike a fair balance between sensitivity to the needs of the present job and applicability to the company as a whole.

Most appraisal systems offer some guidance to appraising managers on the way they should measure performance. There are two major kinds of measure: *personality* measures and *performance* measures.

Personality measures

These have largely fallen into disuse. They are difficult to apply reliably, depend too much on the quality of personal relationships rather than employee performance, and if the employee is judged deficient on a personality measure there may be little incentive or ability to change. Their use is now generally discouraged.

Performance measures

These have replaced personality measures in most cases. They have two main forms. There are *rating scales*, which are generally printed on the form and held to apply to all employees. There are *objectives*, which are an individual performance measure, agreed between manager and employee. Rating scales allow the measurement of change in one employee over time; they also allow comparisons between employees. They are therefore necessary if the appraisal records are to be used for any kind of central manpower audit, leading to the planning of salaries, careers or succession. They have the disadvantage that not all scales may be equally applicable to all employees, and that managers may not share similar standards in the use of the scales. Objectives give greater freedom to both manager and employee in deciding how performance will be measured. They may also have a greater motivational effect by demanding that standards be discussed and understood by both manager and employee, whereas rating scales can be imposed without the opportunity for understanding. The disadvantage of objectives is that no common yardstick may exist between different appraisers and appraisees. It may be possible, and desirable, to have both rating scales and objectives in one system.

Personality measures might include such items as drive, loyalty or integrity. Performance measures might include accuracy, clarity, analytical ability. Objectives might include 'sell x widgets by y date to z customers'. Clearly these measures are offered in increasing order of precision; some systems have aimed at maximum precision at the expense of measuring what is important but not easily quantifiable. Under these circumstances, a *qualitative* measure, the meaning of which is clear to both parties to the interview, is probably preferable to a *quantitative* measure which assesses with great accuracy something which is not important.

The derivation of performance criteria demands research. A specification for the universally effective employee does not seem likely to be a realistic target. Each organization should evolve its own performance measures, and should monitor them continuously to ensure their relevance. The needs of organizations, and of individuals, *change*: if the performance criteria do not change as well, preferably a little ahead of the need, then the appraisal system will serve no useful purpose, and may even do damage by insisting on performance measures which no longer relate to the work in hand. A variety of methods for establishing performance criteria will be found in Chapter 3 on diagnosing needs, and accounts of the increasingly used competence-based approach is given in Chapters 6 and 18.

SYSTEM DESIGN

Each of the four main parties to an appraisal has different but overlapping purposes, all of which have implications for system design. The four are as follows:

1. The *appraisee* will wish to make a contribution to the appraisal process, which implies a face-to-face interview. If acceptance of the appraiser's *evaluation* is to be indicated, or at least evidence that the appraisee has seen the comments is required, then the appraisee may need to sign the form at the end of the interview. If there is to be an opportunity for *long-term guidance*, then the system will need to provide for planning or objective setting for the future, together with discussion of ambitions, training needs, and abilities not yet evidenced in the work currently being done. If appraisal is to be used for *self-development*, then goals will need to be agreed during the interview, some variety of preparation for counselling form might be helpful, written objectives should be retained by both manager and appraisee, and there should be further mini-appraisals during the year.

2. The *appraiser* will want the employee to work to agreed goals, which implies the setting and recording of objectives and personal goals. These goals may need coordinating with those of other employees, which will require control over the timing of appraisals from the top of the organization downwards, with the minimum time lag possible between appraisals at top and bottom, and fairly close coordination and control of appraisals from the centre. Coaching the employee will require the setting of specific performance targets, as much as possible suggested by the employee, including both targets and measures, and both parties will need to keep records and use them for frequent and regular reviews. To encourage the appraiser to listen to the employee, a preparation for counselling form should be strongly encouraged, and the appraiser may wish to record the employee's comments separately, possibly for later integration. In order to make the early detection of problems more likely, general, open-ended questions should be used concerning aspirations, unused skills, constraints on performance and other self-rating techniques. The preparation for counselling form can be a vital aid here, as can the need for the grandparent to sign-off the appraisal form before the interview takes place. In this way it is also possible to achieve some   *53*

measure of equity between employees. The management information system can also be used to detect broken trends or unusual patterns if rating scales are being used. If the training of subordinates is to be controlled, then there needs to be a recordof both training needs and the extent to which they are being met. If money is being used as compensation, then a salary increase may be communicated at the appraisal interview, since pay and performance are not directly linked. If money is being used as an incentive then, as suggested above, the salary reviews should be a separate but related exercise.

3. *Central planning and control* may have a wide range of purposes, but some of the most common are mentioned here. A manpower skills audit will require that there are some common performance criteria across all employees, and that there be central collation of measures on these criteria. For manpower planning purposes the form may need to record not only the employee's performance as measured on required characteristics, but also information about age, job history, mobility and family circumstances. Succession planning also requires that some form of assessment of employee potential takes place, as objectively as possible, and that information about employee aspirations, judged suitability, and current performance is coordinated. Salary planning may require that the manager gives an overall performance rating across all characteristics, and central collation will be necessary, either with or without intervention, to produce conformity to agreed norms. A record of training needs will be required if overall decisions about training priorities are to be taken on an informed basis. Equity between employees can be monitored by defining and communicating the scope of the scheme to all concerned, by grandparent signing-off appraisal ratings, by central monitoring of both quality and promptness of appraisals, and by a formal system for handling unsatisfactory performers. Problem and grievance detection and handling becomes easier if the employee signs-off the completed form, if the employee is invited to comment on the form, if grandparent or central personnel have the power to intervene in critical situations, and if there is a formally defined and agreed procedure for improving the performance of those judged to be unsatisfactory, followed by a declared system for asking them to leave the organization. Finally, downward transmission of organization objectives can be achieved by centrally coordinated cascading of appraisals, so that no manager is put into the position of having to agree objectives with a subordinate in the absence of his own agreed objectives.

4. *Outside parties* can also have interests which impinge on the appraisal system. Local, industry or national codes of good practice can usually be adhered to by ensuring that the performance criteria are relevant to the job, that no group of employees is given special treatment, and that appropriate guidance is offered on the use of appraisals with poor performers. Pay restraint has often been a feature of the political

climate; in this case, the system needs to ensure that both immediate parties to the appraisal understand clearly any restrictions on the manager's discretion, and increased use needs to be made of the remaining motivational characteristics of appraisal. Finally, privacy or right of access legislation may require that forms be designed so that the employee can see the whole form, adequate safeguards are in place against misleading interpretation – such as employee sign-off and comment space, a formal grievance procedure is in place, and there is a clear policy about who has access to appraisal data and for what purposes, together with location and duration of storage of records. This is now a particularly sensitive area where any part of the records are stored in a computer.

Rather than approaching this set of problems in terms of the various purposes of the parties involved, it is very common to spend much time and effort designing the paperwork: given the strong arguments sometimes put forward for a blank piece of paper being the ideal appraisal form, some of this enthusiasm may be misplaced. Assuming, however, that the purposes have been thoroughly investigated, certain specifics then need clarification. If *individual objectives* are to form the core of the process, then a common form is simply a blank piece of paper divided down the middle, with objectives on the left-hand side and standards of performance on the right. It is important to offer some guidance so that managers do not try to set too many objectives, try to set objectives to cover the whole job, or set as objectives only those things that can be measured quantitatively.

If narrative summaries are to be used, then the form will contain a list of *key words* – such as accuracy, speed, cash control, or timing – and the manager will be asked to write a two-line summary of the employee's performance on each of these characteristics. This method has the advantage that it does apply *common yardsticks* across large groups of people, but does not demand undue precision. Differences may occur in the way in which individual managers interpret and judge these characteristics, however.

Rating scales require that the appraisee is rated on each characteristic, using a scale with a number of divisions. While useful, rating scales carry some issues which need resolution. There is no point in offering more than five divisions on the scale. Scales with seven, nine, or even thirteen points have been seen, and managers tend to use them as if they were slightly vague five-point scales. There is often dispute about whether there should be an odd or even number of points on the scale. It is possible to avoid this discussion entirely in the following way. Label the points on the scale, avoiding the use of the word 'average', so that the first four are concerned with above-the-line performance and only the fifth records below-the-line work. For example:

- Exceeds in all respects
- Exceeds in most respects
- Exceeds in some respects

- Meets basic requirements
- Fails to meet basic requirements.

In this way, ratings are being made against the *requirements of the job* and not against colleagues, and the scale can be described either as a five-point scale, or as a four-point scale with an extra box for the unsatisfactory performer. It can also be helpful to offer a separate 'not applicable' box. Any overall rating should follow the separate rating scales, preferably at a distance. It may also be useful to consider a separate column to record *immediate past performance*. This emphasizes the fact that the appraisal is supposed to be a review of the entire previous year, and allows any recent changes in performance to be noted without unduly affecting the rest of the year's evaluation.

Perhaps the most important consideration in system design is to ensure that the system *responds to the developing needs of all those using it*, and to avoid the situation in which an entrenched system dictates inappropriate behaviour by those upon whom it is inflicted.

TRAINING

Appraisal training falls into three parts. They need to be kept distinct and to be carried out in the sequence shown, otherwise confusion and ineffective implementation are almost certain to occur. The first stage involves obtaining managers' *commitment*. The second stage trains them in the *formal systems and procedures*. The third stage trains them in the *necessary interview and interpersonal skills*.

Commitment is best obtained by holding a series of meetings at which all those who will be affected by the system have an opportunity to hear what is being proposed, and to discuss it. It may be helpful to lobby one or two key managers in advance; there should be a clear statement about the purposes of the appraisal system and there should be a readiness to negotiate about system design, but it is better to avoid being side-tracked into form design. This should follow as simply as possible from the agreement of purposes. It may also help to de-emphasize the judgemental role of the appraiser and to stress the benefits that employees will gain from being appraised – in other words, help them discover what they will be able to do as a result of appraisal which would otherwise have been difficult or unlikely. If no such benefits are apparent, the value of the system as proposed must be questioned.

Training in the systems and procedures should occur only *after* commitment has been obtained, otherwise much time will be consumed trying to answer the question 'why' when the training is designed to answer the question 'what'. This stage of the training should include the history of the appraisal system and the organizational problems it is supposed to solve, what actually happens in the interview, how the form is filled in, when, and by whom, who receives the form, what happens to the information, and whose responsibility it is to see that actions recommended on the form are actually carried out. Special emphasis should be given to ensuring that managers understand the *grievance and poor performer procedures*. Practice in handling and completing forms should be offered, together with the opportunity to criticize and spot mistakes in forms already completed. This stage of the training responds well to some form of programmed instruction, either in text form or on a computer.

Training in *skills* depends on successful completion of the previous two stages, otherwise disruption is highly likely. Three training techniques may be worth considering.

1. *Role play* is used automatically by many trainers. It can have many drawbacks, including the passivity of most of the audience and the fact that participants can always opt out by stating, correctly, that it is not real life; poorly-chosen role plays can compound these difficulties. Role play can be useful, however, particularly where *attitude change* is important. Trainees can be asked to play the part of someone whose attitude they need to understand, such as someone passed over for promotion. They can also be useful in unfreezing people by trying on a completely new appraisal personality.

2. *Real-life counselling* involves one participant counselling another about a genuine work or personal problem, while the remaining participants observe. This certainly lacks the artificiality of role plays, but can get a little sharp. For this reason, perhaps, it is generally a better vehicle for learning counselling skills than the normal role play.

3. *Live appraisal of real* tasks involves the following sequence:

   ● A participant performs an *appraisable activity* while the remainder of the small group observe
   ● All prepare to *appraise the volunteer*, who prepares to be appraised
   ● One person then *appraises* while the rest observe
   ● All prepare to *appraise the appraisal*, while the appraiser prepares to be appraised
   ● One person then *appraises the appraisal*, while the rest observe.

   This module can be repeated as often as necessary, and concludes with a general review. The exact nature of the kick-off task is relatively unimportant, so long as there is enough to appraise. Subsequent appraisals quickly become surprisingly real, and the whole approach can be highly successful at making apparent issues of objectives, standards and measurement. *Rich feedback* is essential, and should be as accurate as possible, backed perhaps by video-recording the entire episode. *Objective matters* should predominate, such as the balance of talking at various points of the interview, the amount of time devoted to extremes of performance versus the amount of time used to talk about the regular performance, the use of open and closed questions, and the amount of positive versus negative feedback offered.

An interesting variant is to offer training in *being appraised*. This has worked particularly well where managers have been reluctant to appraise or to be   57 trained. The prospect of their subordinates being better equipped than they are has sometimes led to both appraiser and appraisee being better equipped to fulfil their roles.

The most common issues arising in the skills training stage include:

1. Knowing one's own *biases*.
2. Being prepared to discuss both *good and poor performance* in a straightforward manner.
3. Using *open, closed* or *reflective questions*.
4. Handling *conflict*.
5. *Listening* and *summarizing* skills.

The most common pitfalls encountered in appraisal, which therefore require to be looked at in training, include:

1. The *halo effect*.
2. Creating *extremes of rating*.
3. *Talking* too much.
4. Failing to support opinions with *evidence*.
5. *Inadequate briefing* of the appraisee.
6. *Pre-judging* performance.
7. Not allowing *adequate time* for the interview.
8. Choosing the right *environment*.
9. Basing assessment on *feelings* rather than facts.
10. Over-stating *weaknesses* or *strengths*.
11. Failing to take account of *special circumstances*.
12. Basing judgements on *too short a time span*.
13. Making *false assumptions*.

Understandably, looking at that list, skills training can be a fairly intense experience which has benefits far beyond the immediate task of the appraisal interview.

MONITORING AND CONTROL

All appraisal systems need constant *monitoring*, and from time to time they need *alteration* of some kind. In the early implementation of a system the designer should look out for two main kinds of misunderstanding.

1. Misunderstanding of *terms* may occur, particularly such common ones as 'objective', 'job description', 'person specification', 'training needs', 'development needs', 'counselling', 'personality', 'performance' and 'behaviour'. These may well be familiar to trainers and management developers, but many line managers have no real idea of what is meant by them, or may have developed some eccentric definitions.
2. Misunderstanding the *system* will be shown by forms going to the wrong

place or being filled in late, inadequate coverage of certain employees or groups, peculiar use of rating scales, or partial completion of the forms.

Later on, as part of a more general research programme, some other types of monitoring may seem possible and appropriate. Appraisal action may be checked by following up the actions recommended on the appraisal forms to see if anything has *actually happened* as a result; the types of *objectives* set can also be reviewed as part of this process. Appraisal predictions, particularly of potential, can be checked to see if they are actually proved to be *correct in practice*. Employee attitudes can be checked, either with a purpose-designed survey or as part of a larger *attitude survey*. Examples of some items that have proved significant indicators of effective interviews in the past include:

- I had a clear idea of his/her career path
- He/she and I had the same idea about the direction of his/her career
- My manager agreed with my rating
- My rating came as no surprise to him/her
- She/he accepted my rating of her/him
- My manager agreed with my rating of her/him
- She/he fitted in with the rest of the work group
- We wanted the same outcome from the interview
- I could visualize him/her as my manager some day.

Whether the interview was conducted in the office or outside, and whether the manager had selected the employee for the job initially or not, were not significantly related to the effectiveness of the interview.

As any survey of employee options will *increase their expectations*, there should be a policy about feedback of results, a method of feeding back locally useful results fast, and a commitment by top management to action should the results indicate a need for change.

IDENTIFYING POTENTIAL

Performance appraisal, as we have seen, is designed to *look backwards in order to look forwards*. The best predictions of potential, using performance appraisal as the basis, are made when the next job is not greatly different from the previous one. The greater the proportion of new demands, the less likely that track record alone will suffice. Performance appraisal seems to be essential but insufficient as a predictor of future performance.

Objections to the use of performance appraisal records for the prediction of potential include the following. Single-scale measures of potential, such as most systems still use, are too simple to permit a full statement of what the employee may be able to do. Although supported with words, it is the number that goes into the manpower planning system. In addition, a statement of the kind 'ready for next move in x months/years', if seen by the employee, can be construed as a promise. Managers' confidence in their ability to make ratings of potential is usually very low, and they are very rarely trained in using the potential assessment part of the form. They thus receive the least support at precisely the point where they feel they most need it. Managers find it difficult to assess potential for positions much above their own or in parts of the organization with which they are not familiar. Promotion solely on the basis of past performance almost inevitably leads to promotion to the person's level of incompetence. Discontinuities in the system will occur, where past performance is a particularly poor indicator of success in the next job – for example, the first move from a non-management to a management position.

Poor performers who are in the wrong job are difficult for the system to detect. For them, appraising potential on the basis of past performance is doubly unfair. Finally, in the absence of experience, the appraisee has no basis for judging whether the post under consideration would appeal to them. The more people know about the job for which they are being considered, the more likely it is that they will succeed in it.

If the performance appraisal system is to play a useful part in the prediction of potential, then it should ensure that appraisal is on the basis of *performance*, not personality; and the performance criteria should be related to success in the job for which potential is being assessed. Appraising managers should be trained to use this part of the form and to extract appropriate information during the interview and at other times. Promises of specific jobs should neither be made nor implied. Preparation for counselling forms should be used. Ratings of potential should be checked as a matter of course, rather than as part of the grievance procedure. There should not be sudden and major discontinuities in the requirements for jobs in adjacent grades. Finally, there should be a buyer's market for important staff.

Unsupported by other techniques, performance appraisal can be seriously misleading as a predictor of potential; but the information which it yields is a vital component of any decision reached by whatever other methods may be used.

There are many alternatives and adjuncts available to performance appraisal as a means of identifying potential. These include assessment centres, psychological tests, assignments, secondments, peer- and self-assessment and action learning programmes. Ideally, ratings of potential should involve the use of more than one criterion or trait, more than one assessor, and more than one technique. In this way, a more reliable judgement may be reached.

By far the most effective method of identifying and developing potential is the assessment centre, provided that it has been designed with your organization's needs in mind, not bought off the shelf. Adopted by the armed forces during the Second World War, used extensively by the Civil Service, and developed widely in varying forms in industry since the late 1950s, assessment centres have an excellent research base and track record. They consist of putting a group of participants through a series of work simulations (in-tray, leaderless group discussion, problem analysis, problem-solving, presentation, report writing, etc.) coupled with some psychological testing. Their performance during the exercises is observed by trained line managers against previously established criteria, recorded in a standardized manner, and then critically reviewed, before feedback is given to each participant, and development plans drawn up in conjunction with their line manager. Progress through those plans is then monitored. The cost of such programmes is not slight, but fades into insignificance when compared with the cost of a wrong promotion. Assessment centres can significantly reduce the risk of expensive mistakes.

PROBLEM PERFORMERS

People perform unsatisfactorily for a wide variety of reasons. The first task is to discover which particular combination of reasons applies in the specific case. The problem may lie in a number of factors:

- *Intelligence* – too little, too much, specific defects of judgement or memory
- *Emotional stability* – over-excitable, anxious, depressed, jealous, sexual problems, neurosis, psychosis, alcoholism, drug addiction
- *Motivation to work* – low motivation, low work standards, lack of organization, frustration, conflict
- *Family situation* – domestic crises, separation from family, social isolation from peer group, money worries
- *Physical characteristics* – illness, handicap, strength, age, endurance, build
- *Work groups* – fragmented, over-cohesive, inappropriate leadership, wrong mix of personalities
- *The organization* – inappropriate standards, poor communication, too little investment and management support, span of control too large, responsibility without authority
- *External influences* – employment legislation, consumer pressure, safety legislation, changing social values, economic forces, changes in location.

The appraisal system can be used as part of the process for dismissing people who do not perform satisfactorily. Alternatively – and preferably – it can be used to *manage those people so that their performance improves*. This can be achieved in a number of ways.

- *Counselling* – self-appraisal, preparation for counselling, some form of job climate questionnaire, vocational guidance, mid-career guidance, medical help, financial counselling
- *Training and development* – as a reward and encouragement, not punishment, set up with precise, measurable objectives, careful monitoring and close follow-up
- *Changing the job* – physical layout, timing, induction, responsibility *61*

without authority, no feedback on performance, late or distorted feedback on performance, too may figurehead duties, little or no control over the job content, insufficient warning of changes, shared management of subordinates

- *Termination* – which does not have to be rushed or graceless, can take proper account of financial arrangements, time off to look for a new job, vocational guidance, interview training and exit interview.

Note particularly that there is an option to change jobs *within the organization*. Several appraisal schemes specifically exclude this possibility; the options there are either to improve performance in present post to an acceptable standard, or to dismiss. This runs the serious risk of sending away someone who could do a perfectly satisfactory job if he or she were in the right place. While the logic of not wanting managers to shuffle poor performers around the system instead of addressing uncomfortable issues cannot be denied, it seems potentially wasteful to make a rigid rule that prohibits trying an employee in a different role.

There are particular groups who perform badly simply because they are unhappy or bewildered in some way. These people may include new graduates who are experiencing a mismatch of abilities and assigned task with inadequate induction. Old employees may be feeling that they have reached their ceiling or be experiencing difficulty with the slower learning patterns that can come with older age groups. People without clear career paths will appreciate information and options; people with a sad history in the organization need help to discover whether the problem is real and not merely a reputation which is following them around without justification. The performance appraisal system should be able to generate information, objectives and controls to assist with most of these situations, making the unhappy necessity to dismiss for poor performance rarer, but more sure-footed when it does occur.

FUTURE TRENDS

The only certain thing about today's business environment is that it is changing rapidly and somewhat unpredictably. It follows that no performance appraisal system should expect to be the same in five years' time as it is now. There is therefore a need for continuous monitoring and control of the *relevance of the system to the organization's shifting requirements*. Some of the primary influences on change as it affects performance appraisal include increasing public scrutiny of performance criteria, coupled with open record systems. It does, after all, seem perverse to deny access to information about someone when that someone is the person who might benefit most from knowing it – quite aside from the ethical issue about whether there is any right to deny access to information about an individual to that individual. *Self-appraisal* is a growing component of many systems, and is a logical outgrowth of the open record. The increase of on-the-job training and self-development, wherein people take responsibility for their *own learning*, increases the inevitability of self-appraisal, and matrix management makes the older, hierarchical approach to performance appraisal almost unworkable. Pressure towards professional and technical career paths to parallel the more traditional managerial career progression also puts pressure on performance appraisal systems. Managers have to be better informed about the technology they are managing, or have to hand over some of the responsibility for appraising performance to those who do not manage but do perform a technical or professional function. Special efforts need to be made to be made to counsel those who are experiencing mid-career change, possibly coupled with a personal life crisis. The phenomenon of middle managers who feel that their worth is in question, reinforced maybe by redundancy, is more common. Many more people are now questioning whether they are pursuing the right path, and would welcome informed advice about alternatives. There are pressures to bureaucratize. While it is true that some of these pressures can legitimately be traced to the door of government at various levels, more come directly from within the organization. The first reaction to difficult trading conditions is often to tighten controls and to administer more effectively what is already there, rather than go all out to discover new ways to do things, or new things to do. Under these circumstances, negative feedback and talk of where people are failing becomes the norm, and the appraisal system become the vehicle for *stifling initiative and motivation* rather than a stimulus to new directions and originality. There is a feeling that smaller business units may be helpful; some organizations have become too large to manage, and breaking up the monolith into more viable pieces needs to be accompanied by local control and adaptation of the appraisal scheme. It may be necessary for the large unit to put things on to a computer, but a manual system may be perfectly adequate for the smaller organization; the move to smaller units offers an encouraging chance to simplify over-elaborate systems. Finally, there is a greater inclination to treat people as valuable investments, not merely as units in a card index or computer file; the return to an organization on investment in good recruitment, selection, induction, appraisal and assessment of potential practices is now more rarely questioned. Performance appraisal systems are being seen as less concerned with discipline, control and record-keeping, and more orientated towards development, self-development and growth. This seems to me to be an invaluable trend.

PERFORMANCE REVIEW SEQUENCE

The following is offered as a rough guide to the sequence of events which a manager may wish to initiate in order to be fairly sure that nothing of importance in the performance appraisal process has been overlooked.

1. Agree a time and date for the review *well in advance*.
2. Arrange for the location to be *private* and *free from interruptions*.
3. Set aside *at least an hour and a half*, and possibly two and a half hours.   *63*

4. Bring *all relevant results and information* concerning the appraisee's performance in his/her area of responsibility.
5. Ask the appraisee to review his/her performance in the work situation *point by point.*
6. Ask the appraisee about any problems which might affect performance.
7. Ask the appraisee about the *implications of any problems or events*, and their effect on the individual, the team and the work.
8. Ask the appraisee what needs to be done by either of them to help *improve performance.*
9. The appraisee should ask about anything which he/she feels is *affecting his/her performance.*
10. Agree the *key result areas.*
11. The *appraisee* should *set/agree standards of performance* for the next review period.
12. The *manager* should *set/agree standards of performance* for the next review period.
13. Agree future action.
14. Close with a firm date for the *next interim review.*

REFERENCES

Boyatzis, R. E. (1982) *The Competent Manager* (New York: John Wiley).

Fletcher, C. (1993) *Appraisal – routes to improved performance* (London: IPM).

Fletcher, C. and Williams, R. (1985) *Performance Appraisal and Career Management* (London: Hutchinson).

Handy, C. A. (1985) *Understanding Organisations*, 3rd edn (London: Penguin).

Stewart, V. and Stewart A. (1977) *Practical Performance Appraisal* (Aldershot: Gower).

Stewart, V. and Stewart, A. (1981) *Tomorrow's Managers Today – the identification and development of management potential* (London: IPM).

Stewart, V. and Stewart, A. (1982) *Managing the Poor Performer* (Aldershot: Gower).

Woodruffe, C. (1990) *Assessment Centres – identifying and developing competence* (London: IPM).

5 Managing career choices

Charles Margerison

The importance of a career today is accepted, just as acquiring a trade was recognized in the days when craftsmanship was the basis for securing lifetime employment in a prestigious role. The concept of a 'career' now goes well beyond the original legal, medical, educational and religious professional positions which were the major professional roles prior to the emergence of modern industrial and commercial organizations. Today, when there are a vast number of people in universities and colleges acquiring qualifications in everything from accounting to zoology, there is a tremendous pressure for the development of a wider base for *career mobility*. The chief focus for this pressure is the work situation, and in particular the medium and large industrial and commercial organizations, together with public service bodies.

People who have acquired qualifications and skills in a particular area want to go on and use these and acquire roles in an organization. However, there are simultaneously the organizational problems of coordination and management. This brings to the fore different aspects of career work than the original technical specialization in which a person qualifies. In developing a career many people have therefore to look at the extent to which they pursue particular roles which concentrate more on administration and management rather than their original specialization.

The concept of the *managerial career*, in contrast to the craft and technical career, has become established only over the last thirty to thirty-five years. The predominance of the managerial role in terms of the status and rewards associated with it has, however, overshadowed the other equally important career roles in industrial and commercial organizations. This chapter concentrates on career roles related to organizational levels and performance criteria. Van Maanen and Schein (1975) argued that we should indeed examine 'the person within the total life space and throughout his lifetime'; it is important to identify the different *career roles* people can play in the modern organization and the transitions that need to be made for success at the different levels.

A number of approaches have been taken in the literature to the study of careers and career development. Several theories exist which explain careers in terms of *life cycle stages* (Miller and Form, 1951; Erikson, 1963; Levinson, 1978; Schein, 1978). Schein (1978) 'identified' three distinct models: biosocial life cycles, family–procreation cycles and work–career cycles. Within this last group the focus of attention becomes the stages through which managers move as they pursue an organizational career (Super *et al.*, 1957; Hall and Nougaim, 1968; Schein, 1971). In a different approach Holland (1973) distinguished six major orientations to work. Margerison (1980) showed that British chief executives ranked themselves in priority order as enterprising, social, conventional, investigative, artistic and realistic, in that order on Holland's scale. In looking at managerial career prospects, however, we need to examine the *key role factors* that should be used to assess *career progress* at both the technical and managerial levels.

As the traditions of long service, loyalty and the gradual evolution to a senior executive position in Western industrial organizations have declined, an increasing emphasis has been placed on *performance review and appraisal*. The essential aim of performance appraisal has been to assess people on their merit, and to ensure that promotions and pay reviews are related to a review of performance against agreed criteria. Alongside this has emerged the assessment centre method (Bray and Grant, 1966; Byham, 1970) for identifying in particular those with executive potential. These trends reflect the increasing competitiveness of organizational life.

In contrast to these developments are a number of organizationally-orientated problems which have a direct bearing on the development of careers. Van Maanen (1977) identified areas of concern such as the changing values relating to work life and leisure, alienation from work, reduced organizational effectiveness and lack of understanding of adult identity and development.

Too often, the study of careers concentrates exclusively on the managerial or executive role. However, for an organization to function adequately it needs to have policies and practices reflecting people's different roles and different expectations. This chapter therefore provides a model for comparing career roles at different levels and functions.

MANAGERIAL CAREERS AND ORGANIZATIONAL ROLES

There are many individual roles in organizations, which enable people to develop their career paths. Careers, according to Hall (1976), are 'the individually perceived sequence of behaviours over the span of the person's life'. However, these experiences and activities take place through recognized professional bodies and in employing organizations based on particular roles. The significance of roles at the general level of the organization has been well documented (Katz and Kahn, 1978). In the career context Louis (1980) has

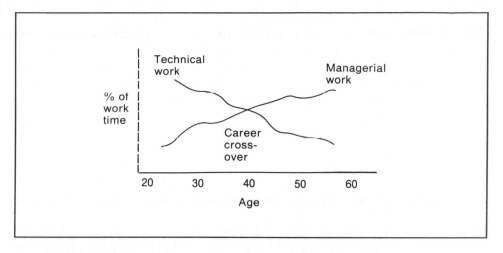

Figure 5.1   Career choice model

developed a typology of *career transitions*, comprising two main categories – *inter*-role and *intra*-role transitions.

Concern has been raised at the extent to which modern organizations force people to *leave their technical specialization role* in order to get promotion within the organization and the reasons for this (Jennings, 1971; Beckhard, 1977; Van Maanen, 1977; Vardi, 1980; Veigh, 1983). While financial rewards and higher status may result, they are often achieved at the expense not only of a person's original career interest, but also of *individual and organizational performance* (Peter and Hull, 1969; Jacques, 1976).

A key aspect of this process is the relationship of technical to managerial work. While each person has a personal career line, there is an overall trend which can be seen in Figure 5.1.

When a person starts in the workforce it is usually in jobs at levels that are primarily *technical*. Gradually, the person who is successful is asked to take on more responsibility; this usually involves supervising the work of other people and therefore involvement in the process of *management* is initiated. More time is spent at the next level in allocating and delegating work, reviewing that work, sitting on committees, ordering resources, budgeting and the various other tasks associated with management. There is for many people, therefore, a definite *role transition* from a technical to a managerial job in terms of the time spent, although clearly the technical background knowledge and experience is usually essential to do the managerial task. Nevertheless, as the role of senior managers has been examined in depth only since the mid-1970s (Mintzberg, 1975; Lau and Pavett, 1980; Kotter, 1982), the task of explaining the *personal processes* of such role transitions is not fully developed.

Driver (1979) postulated that individuals have one of four basic approaches to their organizational careers and personal development: transitory, steady state, linear or spiral, and has drawn on Schein's 'career anchor' scheme of career motivation (Schein, 1978) to develop further an *active/passive sub-type*   *67* within each main career concept type.

What seems to be missing from previous research are the critical factors that govern a person's *career prospects*. Is it possible to reduce the complexity associated with career assessment to two central factors: *competence* and *achieved capacity to manage*? If we extend this to identify the factors underlying promotion through various roles to a senior managerial position, then we should relate achievement specifically to the capacity-to-manage factor (Jacques, 1976; Stamp, 1981), and competence to a person's experience and expertise.

The capacity to manage others involves not only the desire but the ability to *exercise influence in a managerial role*. There are many people who would desire to reach a senior organizational level and have lots of people reporting to them. However, many do not have the interpersonal skills and ability to tolerate ambiguity while at the same time giving directions for action and achieving results through people. It would appear that the capacity to manage others is a very difficult concept to measure. However, most people know what it means. There are few people who voluntarily indicate when they have reached what they believe to be their preferred level; there is always the temptation to take on more than we can do, if only because the incentives – such as the rewards, the status and the fringe benefits that tend to go with managerial roles – are attractive. However, as Jacques (1976) indicated, there are individual differences in capacity and this relates to management as much as it does to any other aspect of life.

Likewise the achievement factor can be applied to the managerial role capacity just as much as it can be applied to a sporting role such as a golfer or tennis player. Figure 5.2 outlines the factor of managerial capacity contrasted with the competence (experience–expertise) factor. This produces four specific roles which have been named the *specialist*, the *adviser*, the *supervisor* and the *executive*.

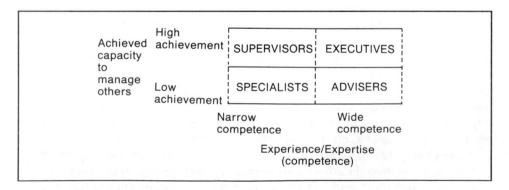

Figure 5.2   Types of role within organizations

The specialist

The specialist is a vital part of any organization. Specialists usually have very *narrow experience in a particular area*, such as a research chemist working on one product, or an engineer on one machine. In so far as they have penetrated their particular discipline or function to a considerable degree, they do it within narrow boundaries. Very often they have *low inclination to manage others*; their key interest is in pursuing that which they know best. They often like to do their work in their own way and with the minimum of interference. Very often they will not wish to have the responsibilities of administration or of managing others.

Such people are very important in research and development, in planning jobs, and in other technical work requiring concentrated endeavour assessing specific issues in depth. While such work must be done and must be done well, it is unlikely that people with such an orientation are likely to make successful managers: they have neither the interest in doing so, nor the experience. While they may be highly achievement-orientated in their own discipline, their achievement level in terms of management is low. Where specialists show an interest in managing others, their experience and work allocation will need to change in order that they gain opportunities as an adviser, a supervisor and an executive.

The adviser

The adviser usually also has a *low concern for managing others*. However, in contrast to the specialist who acts within a narrow field, the adviser operates on a very wide basis of experience and knowledge. The very nature of his or her job involves him/her in working with a variety of clients in different parts of the business. The accounting or finance person will usually, for example, have a wide understanding of the systems applying to production and sales and be able to make a substantial contribution to the personnel department in terms of wage costs. Through his/her own discipline he/she therefore picks up a very wide understanding of the overall business. This stands in contrast, for example, to the specialist chemist whose area of expertise does not facilitate the *crossing of organizational boundaries*.

The adviser, therefore, may have wide experience but little interest in managing subordinates. While his or her achievement-orientation in terms of managing is usually low he/she may have high personal needs for achievement within his/her discipline or function. If a person who is in an adviser role shows interest in the managerial role then it is important he or she gains a leadership position in a supervisory role, and if successful then in an executive role to test his or her abilities and achievement.

The supervisor

The supervisor is a generic term to cover those people who have a *high*   69 *capacity to manage others*, but only within *narrow functions and disciplines*. They enjoy taking on integrating and administering tasks, but do so within specific and limited areas of knowledge and experience. These are usually confined to their traditional area of technical training; they have not usually gone beyond that knowledge and training to acquire the language and skills of their functions. An example could be the foreman in charge of the engineering maintenance area. However, it could also apply to an accountant who reaches a high level in the organization but still has experience of managing people only in the financial area. Where a person shows an interest and ability in managing it is important to assess their performance by widening their range of experience and developing their competence; this can come only through real experience on different jobs.

The executive

The executive is the person who understands the three roles that we have mentioned and brings about an *overall approach* to what has become known as *general management*. The executive will have a high capacity for gaining achievement through managing others. He or she will have acquired wide experience and expertise through various job changes and self-development activities. His/her competence is therefore widely based so he/she can assess organizational issues on a broad front.

Executives develop a wide picture of the organization through gaining personal experience in managing different functions and tasks. They initially have team leadership experience in a specific area, but then move to manage a *cross-functional team* of people from different backgrounds. From there they often move into a role whereby they manage a part of the organization where they have *profit and loss responsibility*. Beyond this, they can, in large organizations, move to corporate roles involving the strategic management of many profit and loss units or divisions.

The executive role therefore demands widespread competence and understanding of the legal, financial, marketing, operational and personal aspects of organizations, combined with a high achieved capacity for managing others.

IDENTIFYING PEOPLE'S CONTRIBUTION PROSPECTS

In addition to the four main career roles identified it is also important to identify how well a person *works in a given role*. It is rare for a person to take on a role and immediately perform to a high level; normally there is a *learning period* during which adjustments are made. In choosing a person for a role we are always taking a risk that they will not learn and adapt quickly enough to perform the duties as required.

How do we assess whether a person can make the transition from one role to another? Organizations use a variety of means – interviews, psychological tests, temporary postings, special project assignments and other means.

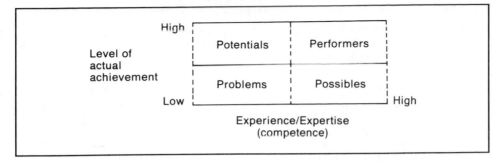

Figure 5.3   Model of perceived career prospects

However, one of the key tests is how well a person is performing in his or her *present role*. This may or may not have any bearing, however, on a person's output (for example) if moving from a specialist role to an executive role, or from a supervisory role to an advisory role.

Given the significance of the factors of achievement and competence that have already been identified, it is useful to outline a simple model for assessing a person's career situation within any role. Figure 5.3 shows a model designed to indicate the *perceived outcome of several role influences* on an individual, regardless of the level in the organization at which he or she is located. It is based on two criteria: the *level of achievement* that a person exhibits in a particular role and the *experience–expertise* (competence) that a person possesses. It is these two factors that are central to effective individual action. The model therefore produces four ways of viewing a person at a particular point in his or her career – namely, as a performer, potential, possible or problem. Let us examine each of these terms.

Performer

Those people who have a *high need for achievement*, and produce results based on a *wide background* of experience and expertise within particular roles.

Potential

Those people who have shown a *high need and level of achievement* but so far *do not have the range of experience or expertise* to do a wide range of work in their professional area.

Possible

Those people, by contrast, who have been exposed to a *wide range of experience* and have *expertise* but have yet to show *commensurate levels of achievement* in a particular role.

71

Problem

Those people who within particular roles have shown *little achievement* and have a *low level of expertise–experience*.

In any organizational position or level at which a person finds themself, the sum total of the role influences to which he or she is subjected may thus take on any one of the four dimensions.

MERGING CAREER PROSPECTS AND ROLES

Although the roles described provide a general framework for the analysis of organization positions and the skills associated with those positions, they indicate only half of the total picture. People can have a high desire to manage others and wide experience, but they may not have the *interpersonal skills* or *political awareness* to carry out their managerial role as an executive. It is thus essential that the concepts developed from Figure 5.3 be integrated with the roles developed in Figure 5.2.

A person can be a performer in an executive position but may be a problem in terms of his or her contribution to another role such as a specialist. This may be because the person has not occupied the role of specialist for twenty years, during which time the type of work in the area in which they originally qualified has radically altered. This could place the executive performer in the position of a problem specialist if they had to revert to that role. Likewise someone on a specialist role can be a performer in that role but may be a potential in one of the other roles, such as an adviser, through lack of experience–expertise in that role. In assessing peoples' careers we thus need to examine their *strengths in relation to particular roles*. As shown in Figure 5.4, for every role we need to assess a person's work.

This approach differs from that of Driver (1979) in that it applies regardless

Role	Role assessment			
	Problem	Possible	Potential	Performer
Specialist				
Adviser				
Supervisor				
Executive				

72   **Figure 5.4   Model for assessing role performance**

of the type of organization concerned or the level at which the individual operates within that organization. A trainee chemist in a bureaucratic organization may thus be a performer in that role but have difficulty in being a performer in a supervisory or executive role. A general manager in a multinational public company may be perceived as a problem in that role despite the fact that in his or her career he/she has successfully been a performer at the specialist, adviser and supervisor roles.

Figure 5.4 therefore provides a basis for making assessments within particular roles and a guide for manpower planning. People who wish to progress in their careers are normally expected to show performance in *specialist roles* before becoming advisers. Likewise there is usually an expectation that an executive will show prior performance as a supervisor and perhaps as a specialist and an adviser before an executive appointment. However, it is possible that people who can excel in an executive role may not be performers as specialists or advisers. It is therefore important to discriminate when making career promotions. Equally there are dangers in appointing supervisors and executives from people who succeeded as specialists or advisers. The oft-quoted example of the best salesman being promoted and becoming a poor manager can be replicated many times with chemists, engineers, computer specialists, teachers, accountants and others.

This is why it is important to identify the capacity to manage amongst those people who are to be promoted into supervisory and executive positions. The work of Ghiselli (1971) is instructive here, as is the work of Jacques (1976) and Stamp (1981) on managerial capacity. Essentially, those people who will become performers at supervisory and executive levels must have the desire and determination to influence others, as well as the competence of experience and expertise.

Margerison (1980) asked chief executives what were the primary influences that had helped them develop as a manager; they cited the following seven items in order of importance:

1. The ability to work with a wide variety of people.
2. Early overall responsibility for important tasks.
3. A need to achieve results.
4. Leadership experience early in career.
5. Wide experience in many functions prior to age 35.
6. An ability to do deals and negotiate.
7. Willingness to take risks.

The chief executives therefore recognized too that the capacity to manage depended heavily on the ability to work and influence others combined with wide experience and expertise plus high achievement. However, the important point emerging from this research is that the executives stressed the importance of *early leadership* and *wide responsibility at any early age*, building on their personal need for achievement.

73

Many specialists and advisers have high achievement but either do not wish to or are unable to influence people appropriately in the managerial role. It is increasingly recognized that career paths must be charted for such people so that they obtain the status, prestige and rewards that go with senior positions of a non-executive or supervisory level nature. A number of important organizations have now established such specialist–advisory career paths. This is akin to what happens already in hospitals where a specialist surgeon does not need to become chief administrator to gain similar rewards or status, or in a university where a professor can be a specialist or adviser and a senior member of the organization. There is a danger that in business organizations we will lose people who perform as specialists and advisers because they feel that career progress will cease if they do not become executives.

CAREER SELF-ASSESSMENT

Increasingly people want to chart and manage their own career rather than wait upon the call of the organizational hierarchy. In my work with Dr Dick McCann we have been able to provide managers and staff with ways in which they can gather data to assess their own career choices (Margerison and McCann, 1993). Firstly we identified through interviews major types of work which we were able to represent as a wheel (see Figure 5.5).

When we asked people what kind of jobs they had had during their career they could trace their movement around various parts of the wheel. We also discovered that each person had a preference for some types of work more

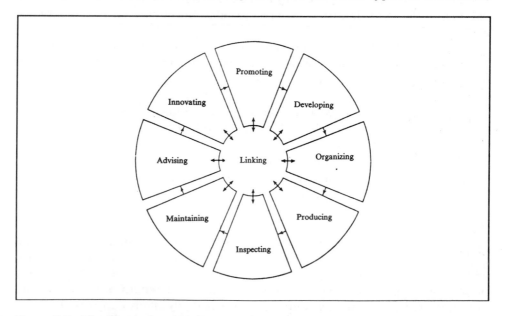

74   Figure 5.5   The Margerison–McCann types of work model

than others. We therefore developed two measures to help people gain feedback and make personal choices. These are:

1. The Types of Work Index – this measures the individuals' perception of their job on the key work functions of the Team Wheel.
2. The Personal Team Management Index – this measures a person's work preferences.

By matching the scores from these two instruments we are able to provide each person with a satisfaction score. This together with the personal reports provided enables each person to make assessment of what action they need to take.

It is through such models and feedback that individuals can make choices in their careers.

CAREER PATHS AND POSITIONS

Some implications

Clearly, a person's interpersonal/political skills and their leadership style have a lot to do with their overall success as a manager. However, far more attention needs to be paid to the person's *individual desire to manage* and *capacity to achieve* in that role as a basic measure of potential. Few organizations when selecting new managers from outside put sufficient emphasis on these issues. Alongside this there needs equally to be the recognition of experience being related to *outputs*, rather than just a series of involvements with different kinds of work.

It is possible to deduce from current research a number of strategically important issues which organizations need to address if they are to obtain the people who are best equipped to contribute to the organization in the future. It is also important to have a policy which enables the lessons of such research to be put into practice. This would certainly include many of the following points:

1. People should be *tested through experience in various roles* and enabled to gravitate to that which is their strongest role.
2. The *reward structure* of the organization should provide status as well as financial comparability to those who excel in specialist and advisory roles as well as supervisory and executive roles.
3. The organization should enable people to *assess themselves* as specialists, advisers, supervisors and executives through direct experience, through projects, task forces and other limited-term activities.
4. The organization should be sufficiently *decentralized* to enable people identified as executives at a young age to have a profit and loss responsibility to test their capacity to manage.

5. Opportunities should be provided for people who have been identified as supervisors and executives prior to the age of 30 to have an early chance to take on leadership positions where they will have the various *inter-personal issues* to manage.
6. The organization *structure* should facilitate the movement of people to meaningful jobs in different parts of the business where competence at wide level can be tested through experience.
7. The organization should establish a *career development structure* that is taken as a serious part of managing at all levels, so that appraisal and counselling form an integral part of management practice.
8. The organization should recognize people's *strengths* and enable them to work in roles where they can perform best without having to change for salary or status reasons.
9. A consequence will be that *specialist and advisory roles* are given equally high status as supervisory and executive roles.
10. The assessment of people for supervisory and executive positions should assess their capacity to *manage others*, rather than just technical performance in a previous role.

REFERENCES

Beckhard, R. (1977) 'Managerial Careers in Transition: Dilemmas and Directions', in Van Maanen, J. (ed.), *Organizational Careers: Some New Perspectives* (London: John Wiley).

Bray, D. W. and Grant, D. L. (1966) 'The Assessment Centre in the Measurement of Potential for Business Management', *Psychological Monographs*.

Byham, W. C. (1970) 'Assessment Centres for Spotting Future Managers', *Harvard Business Review*, 48 (July–August).

Driver, N. C. (1979) 'Career Concepts' in Katz, R. (ed.), *New Dimensions in Human Resource Management* (Englewood Cliffs, N.J.: Prentice-Hall).

Erikson, E. H. (1963) *Childhood and Society*, 2nd edn (New York: W. W. Norton).

Ghiselli, E. (1971) *Explorations in Managerial Talent* (Santa Monica, Cal.: Goodyear).

Hall, D. T. (1976) *Careers in Organizations* (Santa Monica, Cal.: Goodyear).

Hall, D. T. and Nougaim, K. (1968) 'An Examination of Maslow's Need Hierarchy in an Organizational Setting', *Organizational Behaviour and Human Performance*, 3, pp. 12–35.

Holland, J. L. (1973) *Making Vocational Choices: A Theory of Careers* (Englewood Cliffs, N. J.: Prentice-Hall).

76 Jacques, E. (1976) *A General Theory of Bureaucracy* (London: Heinemann).

Jennings, E. E. (1971) *The Mobile Manager* (New York: McGraw-Hill).

Katz, D. and Kahn, R. L. (1978) *The Social Psychology of Organizations* (New York: McGraw-Hill).

Kotter, J. P. (1982) *The General Manager* (New York: Free Press).

Lau, A. W. and Pavett, C. M. (1980) 'The Nature of Managerial Work: A Comparison of Public and Private Sector Managers', *Group and Organizational Studies*, 5, pp. 453–66.

Levinson, D. J. (1978) *The Seasons of a Man's Life* (New York: Knopf).

Louis, M. (1980) 'Surprise and Sense Making: What Newcomers Experience in Entering Unfamiliar Organizational Settings', *Administrative Science Quarterly*, 25(2).

Margerison, C. J. (1980) 'How Chief Executives Succeed', *Journal of European Training*, 4(5).

Margerison, C. J. and McCann, J. (1993) *Team Management* (London: Pfeffeir Mercury).

Miller, D. C. and Form, W. H. (1951) *Industrial Sociology* (New York: Harper & Row).

Mintzberg, H. (1975) 'The Manager's Job: Folklore and Fact', *Harvard Business Review*, 53(4), pp. 49–61.

Peter, L. J. and Hull, R. (1969) *The Peter Principle* (London: Souvenir Press).

Schein, E. H. (1971) 'The Individual, the Organization and the Career: A Conceptual Scheme', *Journal of Applied Behavioural Science*, 7, pp. 401–26.

Schein, E. H. (1978) *Career Dynamics: Matching Individual and Organizational Needs* (Reading, Mass.: Addison-Wesley).

Stamp, G. (1981) 'Levels and Types of Managerial Capability', *Journal of Management Studies*, 18 (3).

Super, D., Crites, J., Hummel, R., Moser, H., Overstreet, P. and Warnath, C. (1957) *Vocational Development: A Framework for Research* (New York: Teachers College Press).

Van Maanen, J. (1977) 'Summary: Towards a Theory of the Career', in Van Maanen, J. (ed.) (1977) *Organizational Careers: Some New Perspectives* (New York: John Wiley).

Van Maanen, J. and Schein, E. H. (1975) 'Improving the Quality of Work Life: Career Development', in Hackman, J. R., and Suttle, L. (eds), *Improving Life at Work: Behavioural Science Perspectives* (Washington, D.C.: Department of Labor Monograph Series, 2).

Vardi, Y. (1980) 'Organizational Career Mobility: An Integrative Model', *Academy of Management Review*, 5(3), pp. 341–55.

Veigh, J. F. (1983) 'Mobility Influences During Managerial Career Stages', *Academy of Management Journal*, 26(1), pp. 64–85.

6 Defining managerial skills and competences

Wendy Hirsh and Marie Strebler

MANAGERIAL SKILL LANGUAGE: A PRACTICAL PROBLEM

The drive to increase the quality of management, and hence of managers, has been an increasing preoccupation of recent times. Nowhere has this been more evident than in the UK where concern about management quality has been linked to both national and organizational performance (Handy, 1987; Constable and McCormick, 1987).

However, as soon as we start to examine how the quality of our managers can be improved, we hit a fundamental question. We need to be able to recognize a 'good' manager when we see one. To do this we need to be able to define what a 'good' manager is or has which makes him or her 'good' at their job.

Employers cannot avoid this need for some language in which to discuss management and managers. Without some idea of what they expect in a manager, they have no criteria against which to judge the performance of current managers, or to assess managerial potential. Without a reasonably well understood 'language' for defining 'good' managers, people inside a company cannot even hold sensible discussions about who to recruit, who to promote and what sort of management training to provide.

Individuals interested in pursuing managerial careers need similar information. They will ask: 'What skills do I need to be developing for my employer to see me as a successful manager?' And, 'If I move to another employer, will the same skills be important there?' Indeed, the trend towards self-development is very dependent on employees understanding what their current or future employers will value in them, and therefore what kind of development to seek.

As this chapter will show, expressions of many different kinds are used to describe what it takes to make a good manager. We will call these expressions managerial skill languages.

We examine the growing popularity of competences as one way of expressing managerial skills. We will look at expressions of managerial skills which are often seen in lists used by employers and the choices employers have for deriving their skills frameworks. The national definitions of managerial skills arising from the Management Charter Initiative will be discussed. The chapter ends with some practical problems which remain for those who seek to use competence frameworks and elements of emerging practice in employing organizations.

WAYS OF EXPRESSING MANAGERIAL SKILLS

Researchers and writers on management have had a significant influence on how we think about management and the terms in which we talk about it. We might reasonably expect that studies of management *activities* would help us define what good managers do. In fact, this branch of research (e.g. Mintzberg, 1973; Stewart, 1985) has served us with some useful warnings rather than with easy answers. Managers are engaged in a vast range of activities, many of which – like thinking – are difficult to observe. Some tasks are less common than previously believed (e.g. systematic planning) and some very time-consuming (e.g. short meetings with other people). Managerial activities are very fragmented, with wide variations from job to job. Job holders may also have considerable choice in how they choose to define and carry out their tasks. We should therefore have little hope that a standard list of managerial activities could be written which would apply equally to all management jobs.

These complex and varied patterns of managerial activities led to the notion of different *managerial roles*. These may vary from one job to another, and also individuals may prefer certain roles. Mintzberg defined roles, including, for example, leader, entrepreneur, resource handler, negotiator and so on. These terms have been influential in forming the way we talk about managerial skills. The work of Belbin (1981) suggests that organizations could do well to think about appointing teams of managers with complementary strengths in different roles, as an alternative to looking for 'superpeople' who can excel at everything.

Some have tried to produce simpler models by picking on *one set of activities* seen as central to managerial work. Viewing management as 'decision-making' or as 'leadership' are examples of this approach. Without further research they beg the question of whether these simplifications are valid and, if so, what underlying skills or attributes make people good at these particular functions.

A fairly natural next step for those engaged in management development is to try and convert such lists of activities or roles into lists of *skills* or *attributes* required by managers. As we shall see later, both the mapping of activities onto skills and the subsequent assessment of skills and personal attributes are fraught with difficulties. However, this has not prevented the dominance of lists of *skills* in definitions of what makes a good manager (e.g. if managers spend most of their time dealing with other people, then common sense would appear to indicate that 'interpersonal skills' – whatever they may be – are surely important in the job).

Lists of skills often become too long and detailed to cover all the aspects of management which people perceive as important. Such lists also fail to express some more deep-seated aspects of the person which other managers seem to want to look for – 'someone quick on the uptake', 'someone who will fit in', 'someone with new ideas'. For these reasons, underlying *personal attributes* are sought as proxies for skills or the ability to acquire skills. These fall into roughly three groups: *intellectual* attributes, *personality* and *attitudes*. There is indeed mounting evidence that intellectual ability correlates with managerial performance, and cognitive abilities can be assessed through tests. Some employers may feel that certain personality types suit the organization or particular management jobs, although there is disagreement on whether personality is a reliable factor in predicting management performance. It seems reasonable for organizations to want managers who have a positive attitude towards work and are highly motivated to succeed. Criteria concerned with attitudes are, however, quite difficult to define and also to assess. All these three aspects of the manager's 'self' – intellect, personality and attitudes – remain attractive to employers because they provide a shorthand picture of the 'kind of person' they want. Moreover, as management jobs become subject to rapid change in content, one can argue that personal attributes become more appropriate to use than detailed lists of activities, skills or competences, which will quickly become out of date (Barham *et al.* 1988).

By contrast with skills and personal attributes, the world of management education deals in yet another kind of commodity – *knowledge*. Effective managers may need to know about certain aspects of business and the business environment. In many management jobs this knowledge also needs to encompass functional or specialist knowledge. Organizations which look for *experience* to assess their managers are often using experience as a proxy for the knowledge which someone will have gained in certain situations. As such, experience is a better predictor of performance if we also know whether someone performed well or badly during that job experience. Expressions of output or *performance* can be used to assess managers directly, although they rather beg the question of what makes for good performance.

COMPETENCES

The latest in this long line of attempts to define what makes a good manager is the notion of *competence*. This developed into a veritable industry in the late 1980s and continues into the 1990s; it has also spawned a wide variety of definitions and even spellings.

Boyatzis (1982) returned to the notion of looking at performance in the job and examined the ways in which high-performing managers were different. His resulting definition of a competence or competency leans towards personal attributes, being:

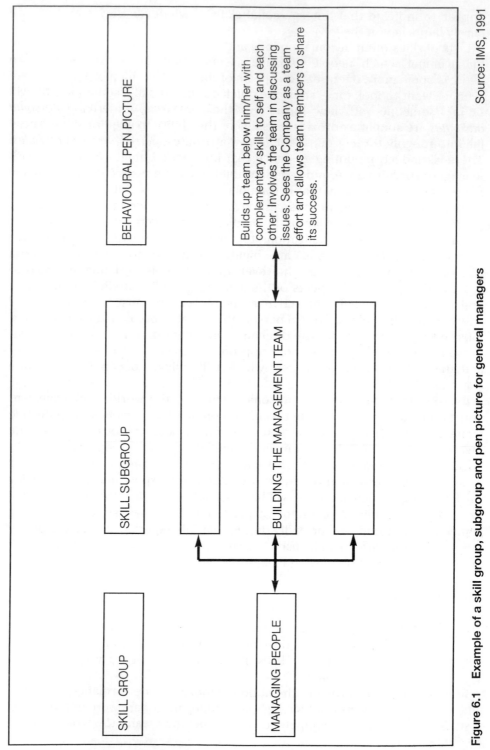

Figure 6.1   Example of a skill group, subgroup and pen picture for general managers

SKILL GROUP

SKILL SUBGROUP

BEHAVIOURAL PEN PICTURE

MANAGING PEOPLE

BUILDING THE MANAGEMENT TEAM

Builds up team below him/her with complementary skills to self and each other. Involves the team in discussing issues. Sees the Company as a team effort and allows team members to share its success.

Source: IMS, 1991

an underlying characteristic of an individual which is causally related to effective or superior performance in a job.

However, the development of the idea of competence also owes much to the shift in education and training towards the attainment of performance standards in job-related tasks. The use of assessment centres has also made it natural to look for aspects of job-related performance which could be observed in exercises or sought in tests. So the term 'competence' has come to mean any skill or attribute which relates to the ability to do the job better or 'the ability to put skills and knowledge into action' (Day, 1988).

Although different practitioners and researchers quibble over definitions, the notion of competence seems to have three recurring features:

- A competence is seen in the context of a particular job or job role and the organization in which that job exists
- Competences are positively associated with superior performance
- Competences can be described in terms of specific behaviours which can be observed in the job.

Competences are usually expressed by combining a set of headings and subheadings with so-called behavioural descriptions of what a manager would look like in the job exercising each of these competences.

For example, Figure 6.1 shows a typical cluster heading (managing people) and one of its competence subheadings (building the management team). This is defined in terms of some behaviours which indicate superior performance in this competence. They could be investigated in a practical way, for example by looking for evidence as to whether a particular manager does or does not involve his or her team in discussion of issues. It is this explicit definition of competences in a job context which has made them so attractive to human resource specialists and managers.

To summarize then, many approaches have been tried to the problem of defining what 'good' management consists of. Competences are merely the latest in this long line, which has included:

- What the job involves: activities, tasks, roles
- What the manager can do: skills, competences
- What the manager achieves: output, performance
- What the manager is: intellect, personality, attitudes
- What the manager knows: knowledge, experience.

SKILLS AND COMPETENCES IN COMMON USE

Many large organizations have been using skill frameworks for a number of years, certainly pre-dating the rise of the competence approach. It is quite instructive to see what aspects of management these organizations have highlighted as most important. The Institute of Manpower Studies conducted a survey of how over 40 leading UK organizations expressed managerial skills just as the competence boom was in its infancy (Hirsh and Bevan, 1988).

Although these organizations expressed the characteristics of good managers in very varied language, a few particular expressions were extremely common. The clear winners were *'communication', 'leadership', 'judgement', 'initiative', 'organizing'* and *'motivation'* (as shown in the 'Exact Words' column in Figure 6.2).

In addition to these prevalent expressions, there were some characteristics which were commonly sought but not expressed in exactly the same words from one organization to another (as shown in the 'Clusters of Meaning' column in Figure 6.2).

Intellectual attributes and *conceptual skills* formed a dominant cluster, as did aspects of *managing people*. This dominant cluster includes 'leadership', but also 'motivating others', 'developing subordinates', 'delegating' and the 'organization and control of staff'.

Organizations seemed to be able to handle only a *small number of criteria* against which to assess their managers. On average ten or so main skill items were used, some preferring to use five or so main headings with three or four subheadings under each.

Although the precise nature of the skill frameworks was endlessly varied some common themes emerged. Dealing with people was often seen as separate from dealing with projects or resources. Dealing with oneself, in terms of motivation, stress management and so on was also a popular part of an overall framework. The need for managers to deal with change was apparent in the frequent mention of adaptability, the capacity to deal with stress, and personal energy.

As skill descriptions have to be quite short and simple, it is hardly surprising that by picking one or two popular aspects of these different dimensions of management, the resulting lists tend to show a *close family resemblance* between major employers. However, commonly occurring terms had very different meanings in different organizations and processes. For example, 'leadership' tended to be seen as a personal characteristic in graduate selection, but more as a skill when used in appraisal of existing managers. Its definition across a range of organizations included delegation, motivation, control, training others and inspiration of values, goals or confidence. Clearly the word 'leadership' alone is not sufficient to ensure the same mental picture of what is being looked for.

Organizations followed up through interviews in the IES study stressed that they had to put more detailed descriptions to these broad terms to make them useful. These detailed descriptions were heading towards the notion of behavioural descriptions of competence already described.

An examination of more recently published skills and competence frameworks shows that many of the items shown in Figure 6.2 are still prevalent. Both changes in methods of deriving such lists and changing perceptions of management are, however, bringing about subtle shifts in language. For example, 'drive' has become fashionable in the early 1990s, and

Exact Words	Clusters of Meaning
oral communication	managing people
leadership	communication
judgement	intellectual/conceptual
initiative	job performance
organizing	organizing
communication (general)	motivation
motivation	specific skills
analytical skills	self-confidence
professional/technical skills	personal circumstances
planning	judgement
innovation	influence
appearance	professional/technical
interpersonal skills	innovation
experience	stability
numeracy	personality
maturity	career outlook

Figure 6.2   Common items of skill language   Source: IMS, 1988

there is a very strong emphasis on the personal competences of flexibility, adaptability and self-confidence. This is hardly surprising given the degree of business uncertainty experienced as a result of recession and restructuring.

DERIVING SKILLS AND COMPETENCES

Organizations wishing to generate their own framework of skills or competences for use in the selection, assessment and development of managers have a number of ways of approaching their task. They also need to have in mind the types of *use* the framework is intended for. Some common uses are shown in Figure 6.3. Use will affect the particular groups of managers covered by the framework. For example, a framework to be used in senior level succession planning will obviously need to target different job groups from one used for supervisory training. Use may also condition the level of detail required (e.g. training applications usually require more detailed descriptions than could ever be used for planning or held on a computerized information system).

The three main methods of approaching the task of defining skills and competences can be characterized as:

- Brainstorming
- Internal research
- Adopting or adapting an existing framework.

Brainstorming

Brainstorming has been widely used and involves groups of personnel   *85*

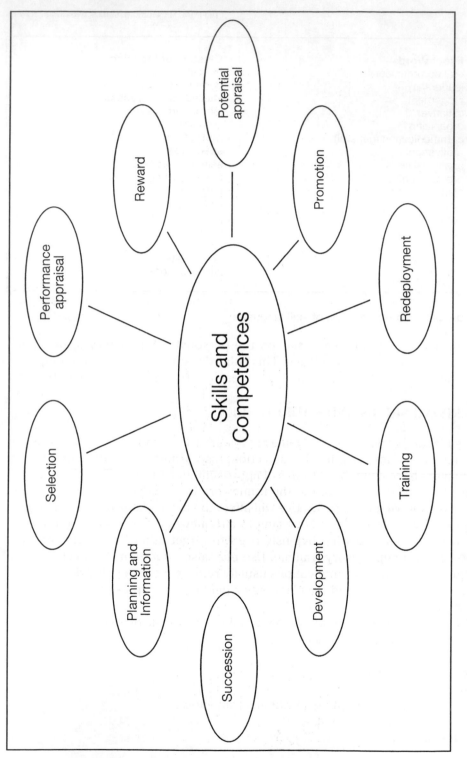

Skills and Competences

- Potential appraisal
- Reward
- Performance appraisal
- Selection
- Planning and Information
- Succession
- Development
- Training
- Redeployment
- Promotion

Figure 6.3   Uses of skills and competence frameworks

specialists and sometimes of line or senior managers. They generate and react to lists of expressions, and come up with an agreed list to use for a specific purpose. This method is clearly not very scientific but was still used by nearly half the IMS sample (Hirst and Bevan, 1988). It has the advantage of involving some people who observe a good many managers and tends to capture the prevailing culture of the organization, which may be an advantage or a disadvantage depending on the circumstances. Brainstorming tends to generate a language rich in expressions of personal attributes and heavily influenced by current fashions in thinking about managerial skills. Many of the items shown in Figure 6.2 came out of brainstormed lists and show a strong tendency to abstract nouns – 'leadership', 'judgement' and so on.

As brainstorming does not generate the behavioural descriptions needed to clarify competences it leaves the organization vulnerable to making very subjective judgements about people on the basis of abstract nouns alone. It also carries the risk of those doing the brainstorming being out of touch or out of date in their perceptions of managerial jobs.

Internal research

Internal research is becoming more common and was used in over 40 per cent of the IMS sample, often combined with the use of external consultants. Several types of research can be undertaken using interviews and questionnaires. Surveys of managers can ask about commonly used skills, and interviews can examine how managers deal with incidents critical to job performance. Research can look at all managers or focus on the attributes of managers seen as particularly successful. Interviews with job holders and those who work with them elicit the key skills, behaviours and personal attributes which seem to mark out high performers. Some organizations give high performers and other managers psychometric or other tests to try and find correlates of high performance. Internal research tends to lead to a skill language which is couched more in terms of observable behaviours at work, and less in terms of rather abstract personal qualities. The methods of such internal research are described in Chapter 3.

Internal research has two useful by-products. First, it usually generates the more detailed behavioural descriptions referred to above, as well as the global expressions of these skills. It therefore produces material which makes the skill language easier to use in practice. Secondly, it tends to highlight variations in skill requirements between functions, roles or levels in management which brainstorming may ignore. Internal research, although increasing in popularity, requires an organization to accept the need to conduct and use research in personnel areas. This may be more natural in organizations with a research or scientific culture in their main business. We also need to be aware that such research into skills and competences is still essentially subjective, although capturing the perceptions of people close to the job.

As an example of internal research we can look at the skills framework   *87* produced for general managers (GMs) in a leading company in the construction industry. The intended use of the skills framework in this case was very clear. It was to be used initially to identify potential general managers and to take selection decisions at that level.

There were also some particular requirements which made internal research an obvious choice. Senior management wanted some objectivity in this selection process but did not want a list of skills which seemed long and full of personnel jargon. They wanted something clear and simple and expressed in language people in management in the company could understand.

Background information was collected on the company, its manpower systems and career paths of existing GMs. Skill interviews using multiple methods (discussion, repertory grid and critical incidents) were held with a sample of directors, GMs and middle managers in several locations. The research was also used to examine the extent to which GMs in different business divisions had similar or different skill needs.

The resulting skill framework had four main clusters and 16 particular competences. Interestingly the word 'competence' was seen as jargon in itself and studiously avoided throughout the project.

As shown in Figure 6.4, each competence (or skill subgroup) was accompanied by a simple form of behavioural description. This took the form of a short paragraph (four or five short sentences) characterizing a 'pen picture' of a good performer against this competence. Pen pictures of poor performers were also found to be very helpful.

Once the headings, subheadings and pen pictures had been agreed by senior management, a simple rating scale was attached to each skill which enabled the managers to use the framework as a checklist to spot potential GMs. For its succession planning, the company now carries out a yearly audit of potential. This is done by checking each of the managers identified against the pen pictures to categorize their potential and identify their progress and development needs. The company is now able to draw up succession plans well in advance of a vacancy occurring. Senior managers have also found an added benefit from the competence list as they have spontaneously used it as a tool to structure their interviews when making appointments. The framework has also made managers think about their staff in a more rounded way. In other words, they now consider all the skills required to be an effective GM, not just an individual's dominant strength. Pen pictures have helped to promote consistency by providing a common standard for judging potential at this level throughout the company.

Of course, internal research methods can be tailored to the different kinds of outputs required in the expected areas of use. Organizations with existing skill frameworks, perhaps derived in the past by 'brainstorming', can use internal research to check out the validity of these models and amend them if necessary.

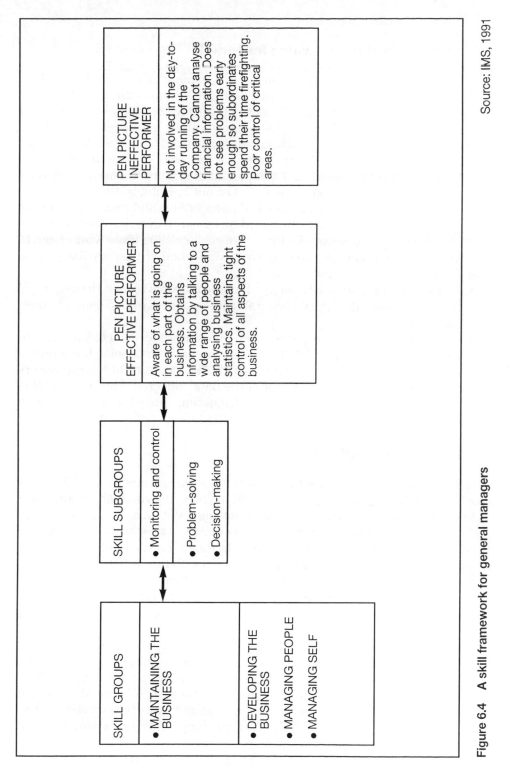

Figure 6.4   A skill framework for general managers

Source: IMS, 1991

Adopting or adapting an existing framework

Another option in establishing a competence framework is to find one which has been derived elsewhere and adopt it, with or without adaptation. One such framework is that derived in the UK as the basis for the Management Charter Initiative (MCI), which will be discussed below. Others have been based on the American work of Boyatzis (1982) and McClelland reported in Spencer, McClelland and Spencer (1992). Such general frameworks have the advantage that they are based on significant samples of managers in various organizations. Their disadvantages are that they are not specific to the organization concerned (although they can be tailored to an extent) and their language can seem rather abstract. They may be based on research done in other countries and a long time ago. So those wishing to use such existing frameworks need to consider when and how they were derived, and whether they are likely to be applicable to their own organization.

A number of large, often international, companies have used these general frameworks modified through considerable internal research to generate their own skill frameworks.

It is a delicate matter, especially when using external consultants, to discover the extent to which data from internal research is being fitted onto a standard framework and the extent to which the structure of the framework itself will be adjusted to take account of the data collected. This is something practitioners should discover when discussing possible projects with consultants.

PAST OR FUTURE SKILLS?

Whichever approach is taken to establishing a skills framework, skill needs derived from today's jobs may not turn out to correlate with high performance in future because management jobs are changing over time. This issue is most difficult where the time delays are long between the assessment of managerial potential and performance in the job. Graduate recruitment is the most obvious example of a process which has to deal with this situation. A common approach to this problem is to use more general attributes which are believed to correlate with performance in most management jobs. It therefore makes certain sense to look for graduates who are 'bright' (i.e. have strongly developed cognitive skills) and highly motivated. Expressions of flexibility, adaptability and willingness to change are quite commonly used and again attempt to deal with future uncertainty. Some organizations examine their corporate strategies and environment to look for more specific ways in which future managers will have to be different. Internal research can also ask job holders specifically about aspects of their jobs and skills they already see as changing. Using this approach to give current competence frameworks at least a flavour of the future can be valuable.

Global studies of future management skills have also been conducted, although these still rely on changes which can be seen on the way. Barham *et al* (1988) found that the image of the manager of the future may be a 'more holistic' one 'that integrates both skill requirements and the manager's attitudes, personality and values, or his or her "being"'. This study concluded that many of the more personal attributes and orientation will be as, if not more, important in the turbulent future of management than specific skills and knowledge. This argues for not undervaluing some of the generic personal competences.

A NATIONAL APPROACH TO MANAGERIAL SKILLS

Arising from the concern about the quality of UK managers, the Management Charter Initiative has evolved as a means of focusing attention on improving management development. One particular aspect of this initiative has been the derivation by the Training Agency and then the Employment Department of a generalized framework for management skills. This rather large and technical exercise took three years to complete and was essentially approached through the rather conventional method of job analysis. It is therefore not surprising that the resulting framework is structured around management tasks and activities rather than around skills and personal attributes. The resulting occupational standards for managers underpin and link with the National Vocational Qualification (NVQ) and Scottish Vocational Qualification (SVQ) frameworks for vocational management qualifications.

Management standards are in place for the following:

- Supervisory Management (MIS) corresponding to NVQ level 3
- First Line Management (MI) corresponding to NVQ level 4
- Middle Management (MII) corresponding to NVQ level 5

One of the difficulties with the MCI competence framework is that the structure of the edifice is quite complex. The task-based method of analysis led to definitions of management *roles* which are broken down into associated *units of competence* (rather like skill clusters) and *elements of competence* (like skill or competence subheadings). The *performance criteria* (the behavioural descriptions) form the basis for assessment (MCI, 1991). Although not all that different from the usual heading, subheading and behaviour structure used by many companies, the jargon takes some getting used to. Figure 6.5 shows an example of the MCI structure.

The MCI movement has attracted considerable support from organizations wishing to improve the quality of management development, with about 1,500 organizations subscribing to the MCI code of practice (MCI, 1993). However, the MCI framework for management competences has been much more contentious, with arguments both for and against such an approach (Thomson, 1991; Hirsh, 1989).

One argument is that many employers have either already developed their own competence frameworks or espoused one of the other generic models (Everard, 1992). For small employers the framework may be too complex and   *91*

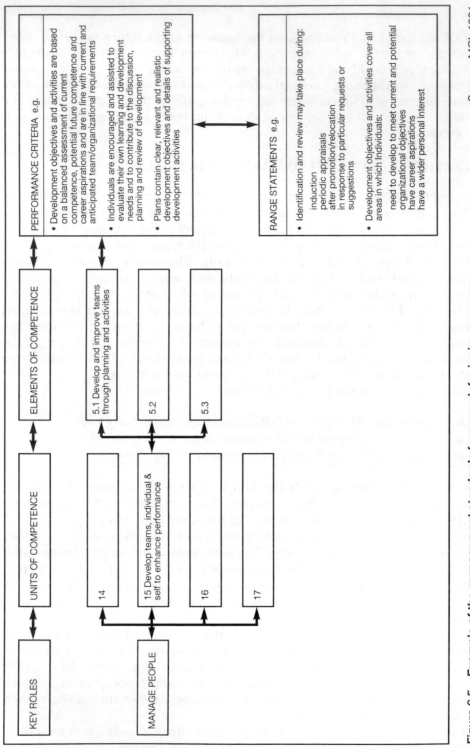

Figure 6.5 Example of the management standards framework for junior managers

Source: MCI, 1991

The text content within the figure reads:

PERFORMANCE CRITERIA e.g.

• Development objectives and activities are based on a balanced assessment of current competence, potential future competence and career aspirations and are in line with current and anticipated team/organizational requirements

• Individuals are encouraged and assisted to evaluate their own learning and development needs and to contribute to the discussion, planning and review of development

• Plans contain clear, relevant and realistic development objectives and details of supporting development activities

RANGE STATEMENTS e.g.

• Identification and review may take place during:
  induction
  periodic appraisals
  after promotion/relocation
  in response to particular requests or
  suggestions

• Development objectives and activities cover all areas in which Individuals:
  need to develop to meet current and potential organizational objectives
  have career aspirations
  have a wider personal interest

ELEMENTS OF COMPETENCE

5.1 Develop and improve teams through planning and activities

5.2

5.3

UNITS OF COMPETENCE

14

15 Develop teams, individual & self to enhance performance

16

17

KEY ROLES

MANAGE PEOPLE

the language too rigid. It is also unclear if and how personal competences are incorporated into such a task-based structure. There are doubts about the feasibility of an acceptable structure for senior management (Finn, 1993). These arguments are not purely academic and all represent real barriers to employers embracing the MCI framework for their own use.

It is too early to judge how many companies will use the MCI framework for their own internal use. They are likely, however, to have contact with it through college-based courses for managers. About 10 per cent of a sample of 535 organizations claimed to be using the MCI standards in training and development (MCI, 1992). It remains to be seen whether it will gradually gain wider currency for processes not directly related to formal qualifications.

The process of assessing managers against the national framework has also been hotly debated. If we are not to lose the possible encouragement to improve management development, assessment must not become the main thrust of the Charter Initiative. Our national bodies should remember, as companies have done, to keep definitions of management skills simple, clear, workable, and thereby acceptable.

ISSUES FOR PRACTITIONERS

Once practitioners have found their way through the problem of deriving a framework for managerial skills, there are a number of practical problems which arise.

Multiple skill frameworks and harmonization

A combination of decentralization, different uses for competences, and different groups of managers (by level, business area, function, etc.) can lead to a proliferation of different skill frameworks. This can be disastrous. Employees and managers move from having no language at all for managerial skills to a host of competing ones.

Using one identical skill framework will usually not be valid. Managers would be astounded if they were asked to assess supervisors against exactly the same criteria as board members. A middle ground in this dilemma is something we call *harmonizing* skill language. It consists of making the language appear similar and consistent where possible. When the same attribute really is relevant in different situations, then why not use the same word for it? That way the organization gets used to using that word with a consistent meaning. When skill needs vary, there are often families of skills, tasks, competences or behaviours which vary by job group but retain a family resemblance, and only require the language to be modified to express the changing nature of managerial skills. These families of skills are more apparent to managers if they are listed always in the same order and clustered in the same way.

For example, a competence concerned with 'interacting with others' at junior management level may be modified into 'interacting with staff in other 93

departments' by middle management, and turns into a 'representational role' for senior management. The logic of these changes can be made apparent to users, without compromising the real differences which exist. In fact, such variations by level can become a kind of prospectus for skill development. Harmonization can also be attempted by process (e.g. recruitment, appraisal of potential or performance, training, etc.) and across the organization (i.e. in different business areas or units).

Extending and updating skills frameworks

Most effort in the area of competences until recently has gone into looking at the managerial skills of staff in management posts, perhaps at a variety of levels.

Organizations are now looking to do a number of even more challenging things:

- To extend their frameworks to technical as well as managerial skills. This may require defining both function-specific and job-specific technical skills.
- Extending competences to cover the whole workforce. This presents challenges in research method to make the process manageable in terms of time and cost.
- Updating researched frameworks as jobs change. The initial effort to research competences can be costly. Must it be like a Forth Bridge which needs to be started again almost as soon as it is finished? Quicker, cheaper ways of validating and updating skills frameworks will be required.

Assessment and selection

The central purpose of competences is to make various forms of assessment less subjective. However, there are two basic problems with trying to use competence frameworks as a totally mechanistic approach to assessment.

Firstly we are assuming that assessors can rate competences as distinct from rating the overall performance of the individual in a set of tasks or activities. However, research indicates that assessors even in the most structured assessment environment – the assessment centre – appear to assess performance at a task rather than performance of a particular attribute (Sackett and Dreher, 1982; Robertson, Gratton and Sharpley, 1987). So even assessors briefed to look for several attributes in each exercise or task in an assessment centre actually score the candidates on their overall performance at that particular exercise or task.

The breaking down of activities into skills or personal attributes also leads to problems in adding them up again to reach an overall rating – do you want two measures of 'judgement' for every one of 'communication'? There is at present no simple way of defining such a 'recipe' for management with weights for different attributes.

It is perfectly sensible to use competence frameworks as powerful communicators of skill priorities. It is also sensible to use behavioural ratings on those competences to indicate areas of individual strength or weakness. It does not appear valid to treat such assessments, added up or weighted in any fashion, as accurate single measures of overall managerial performance.

There are, therefore, huge dangers in putting competence profiles on computers and using these scores to 'match' individuals against the supposed skill profile of a particular post. Current methods for profiling posts and assessing individuals are both too primitive to rely on. The notion of 'matching' also does not allow for developmental placements, or the creation of balanced teams.

Trends in practice

Researchers are divided over the validity and application of competence frameworks. Some see them as a dangerous over-simplification of the rich variety of managers and managerial jobs. At the other extreme some have a vision of worldwide databases of competences for every kind of management job and the capacity to 'dial a manager' to fit each post.

Employing organizations seem mercifully willing to use the concept of skills and competences in a pragmatic way. They see the benefits in terms of providing a language to describe managers in their own organizations, where none existed before (Glaze, 1989). Such frameworks can be expressed, through behaviours, in terms which managers seem able to understand. They also provide a vehicle for senior management to send messages to employees about what behaviours will be valued, especially in times of change. These messages can help to bind together diverse personnel processes ranging from recruitment to appraisal to promotion and development. They may help to make judgements about individuals less subjective and less open to discrimination.

Among the growing number of employers experimenting with frameworks for defining managerial skills and competences, some elements of emerging practice appear:

- Relatively *short* and *simple* lists of skills and competences are used
- There is recognition of the need to articulate *specialist or functional skills* as well as management skills
- There is acceptance that skill language may need to be a *pragmatic amalgam* of tasks or activities, knowledge, personal attributes and skills or competences
- Skill descriptions are made explicit and couched, wherever possible, in terms of *specific behaviour which can be observed*, rather than in more abstract terms
- Increased attention is given to *rigorous derivation* of skill descriptions *and validation*

- Some elements of skill lists need to be spiced with a *flavour of the future*, not just present and past. Frameworks need to be regularly reviewed to ensure they reflect changing skill requirements
- Skill languages are *harmonized* in terms of content and format as much as possible across groups of managers (functions, levels, etc.) and personnel processes (recruitment, assessment, management training programmes, etc.)
- *Consistent understanding* of skill terminology is helped by such harmonization and also by behavioural descriptions and simple lists. It can be further assisted by thorough appraisal and selection training, and experience of group assessment or group discussion (e.g. in assessment centres, succession planning committees, etc).

These practical approaches do not answer the very complex questions about what management really is, what kind of skill language is most rigorous, and whether good management can really be assessed. However, they do add up to ways in which the organization can set clearer signposts about which management skills will be particularly valued and what they might look like in practice.

REFERENCES

Barham, K., Fraser, J. and Heath, L. (1988) *Management for the Future* (London: Ashridge Management College and Foundation for Management Education).

Belbin, R. M. (1981) *Management Teams: Why they Succeed or Fail* (London: Heinemann).

Boyatzis, R. (1982) *The Competent Manager: A Model for Effective Performance* (New York: John Wiley).

Constable, J. and McCormick, R. (1987) *The Making of British Managers* (London: British Institute of Managers).

Day, M. (1988) 'Managerial competence and the Charter Initiative', *Personnel Management* (August).

Everard, B. (1992) 'Standards and NVQs: a time to reflect', *Transition* (July), pp. 12–14.

Finn, W. (1993) 'Is the top talent measurable?', *The Times*, 1 April.

Glaze, T. (1989) 'Cadbury's Dictionary of Competence', *Personnel Management*, 21 (7): pp. 44–8.

Handy, C. (1987) *The Making of Managers* (London: National Economic Development Organization).

Hirsh, W. (1989) *Defining Managerial Skills* (University of Sussex: Institute of

Manpower Studies, IMS Report No. 185.

Hirsh, W. and Bevan, S. (1988) *What Makes a Manager?* (University of Sussex: Institute of Manpower Studies), IMS Report No. 144.

MCI (1991) 'Occupational Standards for Managers, Management I and Assessment Guidance', London.

MCI (1992) 'Management Development in the UK', Market Research Report, 16–25 March.

MCI (1993) 'Corporate Membership' Leaflet.

Mintzberg, H. (1980) *The Nature of Managerial Work* (Englewood Cliffs, NJ.: Prentice-Hall).

Robertson, I. T., Gratton, L. and Sharpley, D. (1987) 'The psychometric properties and design of managerial assessment centres: Dimensions into exercises won't go', *Journal of Occupational Psychology*, 60, pp. 187–96.

Sackett, P. R. and Dreher, G. R. (1982) 'Constructs and assessment center dimensions: some troubling empirical findings', *Journal of Applied Psychology*, 67, pp. 401–10.

Spencer, I. M., McClelland, D. C. and Spencer, S. M. (1992) *Competency Assessment Methods: History and State of the Art* (Boston: Hay/McBer Research Press).

Stewart, R. (1985) *The Reality of Management*, 2nd edn (London: Pan Books).

Thomson, A. (1991) '10 good things about MCI and 10 bad things', British Academy of Management *Newsletter*, 8 September, pp. 8–9.

Part III
THE PROCESS OF MANAGEMENT DEVELOPMENT

7 Styles of learning

Peter Honey

In 1962, Chris Argyris predicted, amongst other things, a move:

- *From* management development programmes that teach managers how they *ought to think and behave*
- *To* MD programmes with the objective of helping managers to *learn from experience.*

Argyris argued that this was necessary because 'no one can develop anyone else except himself. The door to development is locked from the inside'. He went on to say 'Emphasizing the *processes* of how to learn, how to diagnose administrative situations, how to learn from experience – these are timeless wisdoms'. His conclusion was that we needed less emphasis on developing *learned* managers and more on developing *learning* managers.

When I first read Argyris' words I agreed with them wholeheartedly, but I did not fully understand how to put them into practice. What exactly were the processes of learning from experience? How could management be designed to give managers practice in these 'timeless wisdoms'? Was it just a question of exposing managers to different experiences and hoping they would learn from their successes and mistakes? Or did the *mechanics of learning* need to be understood and designed into management development as a deliberate strategy?

I confess I did not know the answers to any of these questions. Then I came across Kolb and Fry's Learning Style Inventory together with their description of the stages involved in the business of learning from experience. This was the spur for many years of work in conjunction with Alan Mumford resulting in *The Manual of Learning Styles* (Honey and Mumford, 1992), together with its sister booklet *Using Your Learning Styles* (Honey and Mumford, 1986). In these publications we describe the full range of uses of learning styles information in the design of programmes, boss–subordinate relationships and selection of structured learning activities.

In this chapter I intend to concentrate on the use of learning styles by individuals for themselves. I shall:

1. Examine the *process of learning from experience* and the short cuts that managers characteristically take to truncate the process.
2. Describe four different learning style preferences and show how they affect the *sort of activities managers learn from*.
3. Show how it is possible to develop an under-developed learning style, and thus become an *all-round learner from experience*.

THE PROCESS OF LEARNING FROM EXPERIENCE

Alan Mumford and I have developed (Figure 7.1) a simplified version of Kolb's (1984) model.

It is rare to find managers who consciously discipline themselves to do all four stages as shown in Figure 7.1. Depending on their learning style *preferences* (this will be discussed later) managers are likely to take a number of liberties with this process. Some of the better-known ones are as follows:

1. *Indulging at stage 1* (i.e. rushing around, having lots of experiences and keeping frantically busy but never bothering to review, conclude or plan). Such managers equate having lots of experiences with learning and conveniently assume that if they have experienced something they have automatically learned from it.

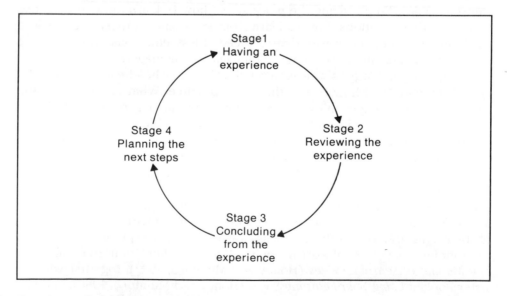

Figure 7.1 Learning from experience

2. *Limiting stage 1*, by repeating familiar experiences over and over again and never going out on a limb and trying something new or different.
3. *Avoiding stage 1*, by being a 'voyeur' and learning from other people's experiences rather than their own. This reduces the risks of making mistakes or making fools of themselves.
4. *Avoiding stage 2*, by having a stock of conclusions and forcing experiences to fit the conclusions rather than the other way round. This is closely akin to the well-known process of jumping to conclusions; the attraction is that it avoids the uncertainty of reviewing an experience and the hard work of reaching conclusions.
5. *Limiting stages 2 and 3*, by collecting ready-made ploys and techniques of the 'how to do it' variety. This avoids the hard work of discovering and creating practical ways of doing things via reviewing and concluding experiences.

Of course, all these short cuts are entirely understandable and all have their attractions, but they, and others like them, all tend to erode the amount that can be learned from experience.

DIFFERENT LEARNING STYLE PREFERENCES

Kolb's Learning Style Inventory suggested that people develop preferences for different learning styles in just the same way that they develop any other sort of style – management, leadership, negotiating, etc. Naturally I did the inventory to discover my own learning style and started to include it on training courses I ran as a way of predicting who would respond in what sort of way and so anticipating learning difficulties. Unfortunately, whilst I bought the theory, I found some problems with the inventory itself (the predictions were not as accurate as I wished and the face validity was poor). Accordingly, together with Alan Mumford, I started to develop a questionnaire that would do a better job.

After three years of intensive experimentation the result was an eighty-item questionnaire that takes ten minutes or so to complete and identifies whether someone is predominantly:

- *Activist* – What's new? I'm game for anything
- *Reflector* – I'd like time to think about this
- *Theorist* – How does this relate to that?
- *Pragmatist* – How can I apply this in practice?

The learning styles tie in with the four stages of learning from experience as follows:

- A preference for the *Activist* style equips you for *stage 1*
- A preference for the *Reflector* style equips you for *stage 2*
- A preference for the *Theorist* style equips you for *stage 3*

- A preference for the *Pragmatist* style equips you for *stage 4.*

All-round learners, or 'integrated learners' as they are sometimes referred to, are clearly best equipped to manage all four stages. However, most people develop learning style preferences that assist with some of these stages, and hinder others.

These style preferences very significantly affect the sort of activities that people learn best from.

Activists

Activists learn best from experiences where:

1. There are *new experiences/problems/opportunities* from which to learn.
2. They can engross themselves in *short 'here and now' activities* such as business games, competitive tasks, role-playing exercises.
3. They have a lot of the *limelight/high visibility.*
4. They are *thrown in at the deep end* with a task they think is difficult.

Reflectors

Reflectors, on the other hand, learn best from activities where:

1. They are encouraged to *watch/think/chew over activities.*
2. They are allowed to *think before acting*, to assimilate before commenting.
3. They have the opportunity to *review what has happened*, what they have learned.
4. They can reach a decision *in their own time* without pressure and tight deadlines.

Theorists

Theorists learn best from activities where:

1. They have time to explore methodically the *associations and inter-relationships* between ideas, events and situations.
2. They are in *structured situations* with clear purposes.
3. They have the chance to question and probe the *basic methodology, assumptions or logic* behind something.
4. They are *intellectually stretched.*

Pragmatists

Pragmatists learn best from activities where:

1. There is an obvious link between the subject matter and a *problem or opportunity on the job*.
2. They are shown techniques for doing things with obvious practical advantages *currently applicable to their own job*.
3. They have the chance to try out and practise techniques with *coaching/feedback from a credible expert*.
4. They can concentrate on *practical issues*.

The dovetailing between learning styles and learning activities has led us to postulate some key questions that people can use to assess the appropriateness of different learning opportunities.

Key questions for Activists

- Shall I learn *something new* – i.e. that I did not know/could not do before?
- Will there be a wide variety of *different activities*? (I do not want to sit and listen for more than an hour at a stretch!)
- Will it be OK to *have a go/let my hair down/make mistakes/have fun*?
- Shall I encounter some *tough problems and challenges*?
- Will there be other *like-minded people* to mix with?

Key questions for Reflectors

- Shall I be given adequate time to *consider, assimilate and prepare*?
- Will there be opportunities/facilities to *assemble relevant information*?
- Will there be opportunities to listen to *other people's points of view* – preferably a wide cross-section of people with a variety of views?
- Shall I be under pressure to be *slapdash or to extemporize*?

Key questions for Theorists

- Will there be lots of opportunities to *question*?
- Do the objectives and programme of events indicate a *clear structure* and *purpose*?
- Shall I encounter *complex ideas and concepts* that are likely to stretch me?
- Are the *approaches* to be used and concepts to be explored 'respectable' – i.e. *sound and valid*?
- Shall I be with people of *similar calibre* to myself?

Key questions for Pragmatists

- Will there be ample opportunities to *practise and experiment*?
- Will there be lots of *practical tips and techniques*?
- Shall we be addressing *real problems* and will it result in *action plans* to tackle some of my current problems?
- Shall we be exposed to *experts* who *know how to/can do it* themselves? *105*

BECOMING AN ALL-ROUND LEARNER FROM EXPERIENCE

A knowledge of learning styles can either be used to help dovetail learning activities to suit learning styles or be used as a starting point for *self-development*. The latter option is the one I want to explore now.

The advantages of having a broader range of learning skills are that you become a more effective learner from life's events and, if you are a trainer as I am, you are more likely to be able to help a greater range of trainees by being a more effective trainer. I want to illustrate how I personally have made use of a knowledge of my own learning style preferences to become a more effective trainer, as a means of trying to encourage readers to develop their own learning skills and thus become better at helping other people to learn.

THE TRAINER'S LEARNING PREFERENCE

I have been a trainer since 1965, but it was only in the late 1970s that the implications of my own learning styles really dawned on me. My own preferences are for the Activist and Pragmatist styles. This means that my strengths and weaknesses tend to be as follows:

- As an Activist, my strengths are that I am:

  - flexible and relatively open-minded
  - happy to have a go
  - happy to be exposed to new situations
  - optimistic about anything new and therefore unlikely to resist change.

- As a Pragmatist, my strengths are that I am:

  - keen to test things out in practice
  - practical and realistic
  - businesslike and down-to-earth
  - keen on specific techniques.

That's the good news! On the other hand, my preference for the Activist and Pragmatist styles means that I have some important weaknesses:

- As an Activist, my weaknesses are that I am:

  - likely to take the immediately obvious action without considering alternatives
  - likely to take unnecessary risks
  - likely to do too much myself and hog the limelight
  - likely to get bored with implementation and consolidation.

- As a Pragmatist, my weaknesses are that I am:

  - likely to reject anything without an obvious application

- not very interested in theory or basic principles
- likely to seize on the first expedient solution to a problem
- impatient with disorganized people who 'waffle'.

Clearly these strengths and weaknesses affect my performance as a trainer. For example, I am likely to design training courses that are packed with lots of activities and to sell people short on theory and basic principles. I am likely to warm to trainees who display Activist tendencies and to have difficulties with trainees who hold back and are more cautious and less assertive. Also, paradoxically, the more I try to jolly along trainees who have Reflector–Theorist preferences the more likely they are to take fright and withdraw still further.

THE CHOICE OF SELF-DEVELOPMENT

Once I knew my own learning style preferences (the Learning Styles Questionnaire together with its score key come as a package with *The Manual of Learning Styles*) and realized their implications for me as a trainer, I had two choices. Either I could specialize and train only fellow Activists and Pragmatists or I could set out to develop my under-developed Reflector and Theorist styles so that I was better equipped to help a broader range of trainees.

The idea of specializing has some practical difficulties and having seriously toyed with the idea, I dropped it in favour of self-development. The practical difficulties are not by any means insurmountable – indeed, on an in-company basis where there may be a team of trainers with various styles there is much to be said for more thoroughly matching trainer and trainee styles. It would require a system where trainees' learning styles were identified *before* they attended a training programme so that they could be catered for either by allocating them to courses designed to suit their styles or to trainers with compatible styles.

I decided to set about consciously strengthening my Reflector and Theorist styles so that, through an extended repertoire, I would be in a better position to adopt styles suitable for all types of trainees. More specifically, I set myself the goal of strengthening my Reflector style by becoming:

- More thoughtful, thorough and methodical
- Better at listening to others and assimilating information
- More careful not to jump to conclusions.

In order to strengthen my Theorist style, I set about becoming:

- More rational, objective and disciplined
- Better at logical (vertical) thinking
- Better at asking probing questions.

SELF-DEVELOPMENT PROGRAMME

Here are some of the things I did in order to strengthen my Reflector and Theorist styles.

1. Each month I sat in the public gallery at the Town Hall observing our local councillors during their meetings (for an Activist this is ideal, because you are not allowed to speak – only to observe). I kept a careful record of what was said and later did an analysis of the arguments used, and the processes that led up to a decision.

2. A general election was called soon after I had embarked on my self-development plan: I bought myself copies of the manifestos for the three main parties and did a painstaking analysis of the policies each was advocating. Having done this, I designed a self-scoring questionnaire to help people decide which policies they agreed–did not agree with.

3. I put myself on a Rational Emotive Therapy (RET) course. RET is a rigorous form of therapy that brings out and challenges your irrational beliefs, and as such is an excellent vehicle for developing the theorist style in particular.

4. I read articles in the 'quality' newspapers and did a thorough analysis of the arguments they were using, and tried to identify and write down the fundamental assumptions they were based on. I compiled a list of probing questions that I wished to put to the authors.

5. I forced myself to compile lists for and against a particular piece of action. I tried this on domestic decisions, not just work ones, and it nearly drove my wife mad! Never mind, it helped me to think of alternative courses of action rather than revelling in instant (Activist) on-the-spot decisions.

6. I deliberately increased my serious reading. To give myself an incentive I volunteered to write reviews of books. This is an excellent way of forcing yourself to read the book in question carefully enough and analyse its good and bad points.

7. I took a list of criteria to be used as the basis for designing an assessment programme for middle managers and broke each down into a number of specific behavioural indicators. Previously, the criteria had been global and vague (leadership, flexibility, decision-making, etc.). I spent a concentrated day pinpointing six key behaviours for each criterion.

8. Finally, and perhaps most helpful of all, three times a week I made an entry in my learning log. The procedure I devised is as follows:

    (a) start by thinking back over an experience and selecting a part of it (a 15-minute period or so) that was *significant* or *important* for you

    (b) write a detailed account of what happened during that period; do not at this stage put any effort into deciding what you learned – just concentrate on describing what actually *happened*

(c)   then, list the conclusions you have reached as a result of the experience; these are, in effect, your *learning points*: do not limit the number, and do not worry about the practicality or quality of the points

(d)   finally, decide what learning points you want to implement in the future and work out an action plan which covers what you are going to do and when you are going to do it; spell out your action plan as precisely as possible so that you are clear *what you have to do*, and that it is *realistic*.

I have been so impressed with the value of keeping a log like this that I have introduced it as a twice-a-day feature on most of the training programmes I run. Activists need some cajoling: Reflectors, Theorists and Pragmatists take to it more easily.

STRENGTHENING THE ACTIVIST AND PRAGMATIST STYLES

Of course, none of my personal examples will help those who want to develop their Activist and/or Pragmatist styles. Here then, taken from *The Manual of Learning Styles*, are some 'thought starters' for people in that position.

Self-development activities to develop the Activist style

1.   At least once a week do something new, i.e. something that you have never done before. Visit a part of your organization that you have neglected, go jogging at lunch time, wear something outrageous to work one day, read an unfamiliar newspaper with views that are diametrically opposed to yours, change the layout of furniture in your office, etc.

2.   Practise initiating conversations (especially 'small talk') with strangers. Select people at random from your internal telephone directory and go and talk to them. At large gatherings, conferences or parties, force yourself to initiate and sustain conversations with everyone present. In your spare time go door-to-door canvassing for a cause of your choice.

3.   Deliberately fragment your day by chopping and changing activities each half-hour. Make the switch as diverse as possible. For example, if you have had half an hour of cerebral activity, switch to doing something utterly routine and mechanical. If you have been sitting down, stand up. If you have been talking, keep quiet, and so on.

4.   Force yourself into the limelight. Volunteer whenever possible to chair meetings or give presentations. When you attend a meeting set yourself the challenge of making a substantial contribution within ten minutes of the start. Get on a soapbox and make a speech at your local Speakers' Corner.

5.   Practise thinking aloud and on your feet. Set yourself a problem and bounce ideas off a colleague (see if between you you can generate fifty ideas in ten minutes). Get some colleagues–friends to join in a game   *109*

where you give each other topics and have to give an impromptu speech lasting at least five minutes.

Self-development activities to develop the Pragmatist style

1. Collect *techniques* (i.e. practical ways of doing things). The techniques can be about anything potentially useful to you. They might be analytical techniques such as critical path analysis or cost benefit analysis. They might be interpersonal techniques such as transactional analysis, or assertiveness or presentation techniques. They might be time-saving techniques or statistical techniques, or techniques to improve your memory, or techniques to cope with stress and reduce your blood pressure!

2. In meetings and discussions of any kind (progress meetings, problem-solving meetings, planning meetings, appraisal discussions, nego-tiations, sales calls, etc.), concentrate on producing *action plans*. Make it a rule never to emerge from a meeting or discussion without a list of actions either for yourself or for others, or both. The action plans should be specific and include a deadline (e.g. 'I will produce a two-page paper listing alternative bonus schemes by 1 September').

3. Make opportunities to *experiment* with some of your new-found techniques. Try them out in practice. If your experiment involves other people, tell them openly that you are conducting an experiment and explain the technique which is about to be tested. (This reduces embarrassment if, in the event, the technique is a flop!) Choose the time and place for your experiments; avoid situations where a lot is at stake and where the risks of failure are unacceptably high. Experiment in routine settings with people whose aid or support you can enlist.

4. Study techniques that *other people use* and then model yourself on them. Pick up techniques from your boss, your boss's boss, your colleagues, your subordinates, visting salesmen, interviewers on television, politicians, actors and actresses, your next-door neighbour. When you discover something they do well – emulate them.

5. Subject yourself to scrutiny from 'experts' so that they can watch your technique and coach you in how to *improve* it. Invite someone who is skilled in running meetings to sit in and watch you chairing; get an accomplished presenter to give you feedback on your presentation techniques. This idea is to solicit help from people who have a proven track record – it is the equivalent of having a coaching session with a golfing professional.

6. Tackle a 'do-it-yourself' project – it does not matter if you are not good with your hands. Pragmatists are practical and, if only for practice purposes, DIY activities help to develop a practical outlook. Renovate a piece of furniture, build a garden shed or even an extension to your house. At work, calculate your own statistics once in a while instead of relying on the printout, be your own organization and methods man, go

and visit the shopfloor in search of practical problems to solve. Learn to type, learn a foreign language.

CONCLUSION

If management development is designed to provide managers with learning opportunities, then the process of learning from experience is an essential ingredient, perhaps the *most essential*. In my view, any respectable management development programme should offer explicit help with *learning how to learn*, by doing some or all of the following things:

1. Help managers to know the stages in the process of learning from experience and how their learning style preferences help (and hinder) them with parts of this process.
2. Help managers to work out how to develop an under-developed learning style so that they can aim to become better 'all-round' learners.
3. Provide managers with a safe haven where they can practise developing an under-developed style and help learning from experience to be a deliberate, conscious process.
4. Help managers to identify *learning opportunities* in their current jobs, and plan how to *utilize* them.

REFERENCES

Argyris, C. (1962) *Interpersonal Competence and Organizational Effectiveness* (Homewood, IL.: Irwin-Dorsey).

Honey, P. and Mumford, A. (1986) *Using Your Learning Styles*, 2nd edn (London: Honey).

Honey, P. and Mumford, A. (1992) *The Manual of Learning Styles,* 3rd edn (London: Honey).

Kolb, D. (1984) *Experiential Learning* (Englewood Cliffs, N.J.: Prentice-Hall).

8 Self-Managed Learning

Ian Cunningham

I and my colleagues coined the term Self-Managed Learning (SML) in order to distinguish this approach from close relatives. I was particularly interested in bringing together the advantages of various learning methods whilst avoiding some of their disadvantages. I shall in this chapter give a practical example of a Self-Managed Learning (*SML*) course, before commenting on some of the methods and theories I drew on.

SML has been used in a wide variety of settings over the last 15 years. It has mainly been used with managers, but programmes in, for example, Cable and Wireless have shown the value of the approach for secretaries, technical staff and others.

I have always been keen to include assessment of people's learning in SML programmes, and in some cases this has led to qualifications being gained by course participants. In Shell, for example, we negotiated with BTEC for managers to gain the Certificate in Management Studies as a result of carrying out a Self-Managed Learning programme.

In other organizations, assessment of learning has had a purely internal focus. In British Airways successful 'graduates' from an SML programme for younger managers were given accelerated promotions. In the BBC, a one-year programme for newly recruited personnel staff provided the basis for them gaining managerial posts. In contrast to these examples of SML being used for more junior staff, Allied Lyons (see Hurley and Cunningham, 1993), the NHS and the London Borough of Lewisham have used the approach for senior managers.

A CONCRETE EXAMPLE

I need to provide some information as to what SML means in practice. In contrast to the organizational examples mentioned above, here I shall focus on the part-time postgraduate Diploma in Management (by SML). (See Cunningham, 1981 for details of this course's development at the former North East London Polytechnic, now the University of East London.). I will describe incidents an observer would actually see or hear, and follow each of these with an explanation of why they would observe such episodes; I hope that this will provide a better insight into the course than a purely abstract discussion.

Observed

New members arrive on a Friday evening in October for the opening of the diploma at a residential weekend. They join with existing (second-year) course members and do some fairly standard 'getting to know each other' exercises, along with sessions to find out more about the course. So far, this looks very similar to many other management courses. However, as the weekend goes on, differences become apparent. The residential weekend has been organized by a planning group consisting of second-year course members plus two staff. This group steers the weekend, but staff, whilst actively involved in particular sessions, are not controlling what goes on. On Saturday a session is devoted to helping first-year course members form into 'sets'; the sets are groups of five or six course members along with a staff member and a second-year course member (who together act as co-set advisers). The session is disorganized and sometimes chaotic as people try to find a sensible basis with which to group themselves. Eventually they do, and the sets settle down to their first meeting of many they will have over the next two years.

On Saturday, all first- and second-year course members and staff gather together for a *community meeting*. This meeting discusses and decides upon course issues. It is chaired by a course member, and whilst staff join in on discussions they have only a minority voice in the proceedings. The community meeting decides who shall be on the planning group for the next residential weekend. It also decides which workshops and other events shall take place before the next residential weekend, which is in the next term.

Explanation

1. SML is not necessarily an individual activity. Managing one's own learning includes *involving oneself in the learning of others.*
2. SML events are sometimes quite tightly structured. The difference between SML and other modes is *where the structure* comes from. In most college or university run courses, tutors lay down the structure: in SML the structure comes from collective agreement involving course members and staff.

   This issue of structuring is important. Just because course members control their own learning it does not make the course unstructured. 'Structure' and 'direction' (or control) are two relatively separate *113* variables, and courses can be more or less structured and more or less directed by staff; this can be shown as in Figure 8.1.

A course can, for instance, be highly directed with little structure. This fits certain T-group or interpersonal skills programmes where staff dictate a low structure format. Most so-called 'taught courses' have high direction and high structure: staff impose both content and timetabling (structuring). Certain self-development groups come into the low structure/low direction category: the trainer adopts a low profile on content and structure. The SML mode is unusual in providing a great deal of structure within a framework which has little staff direction over course content. In Figure 8.1 I am suggesting that a total lack of structure is not possible: an unstructured course is a logical nonsense since to have a course is to provide a structure of some kind, even if it is only to arrange a time when people meet together.

3. The community meeting is a key event as it demonstrates the notion of a self-managing community operating to make collective decisions about the course. All course members are able to be directly involved in decisions about what goes on, though the community meeting delegates specific tasks to groups (such as the residential planning group).

4. Sets are important in providing *support groups* besides meeting other needs. Each set is assisted in its operations by the presence of the co-set advisers. Second-year course members who want to develop their skills in this area have found it valuable to apprentice themselves to a staff member in order to work with a first-year set. The set also gets the benefit of the presence of someone who has been through the first year.

Figure 8.1   The issue of structuring

Observed

After the first residential weekend, John, a manager in a construction company, is at home in the evening working on what he should put into his programme of study. He knows he has to write a learning contract which he has to present to his set for approval. Some aspects of this contract seem much easier to write than others; he has had no problem in covering his past experience, and he has had a reasonable shot at describing his strengths and weaknesses (helped by diagnostic material provided by the college). However, working out learning goals is proving less easy; he knows he wants to advance within his own company, but specifying a balance of objectives is not simple. He decides to take a rough draft of what he has written to his next set meeting in order to get the feedback and comments of others.

Explanation

Paul Tillich called the fatal pedagogical error, 'To throw answers like stones at the heads of those who have not yet asked the questions' (in Brown, 1971). Managing involves asking questions and formulating problems *before* looking for answers and solutions. So for managers to manage their own learning they need first to formulate the questions: the problems.

I define a 'problem' as existing when we cannot go from where we are to where we would like to be simply by action. If I want to know something about company procedures, and these are written in a company manual, I can simply go and look it up; that is no problem. However, if I currently feel unassertive and lacking in confidence (and I want to be assertive and self-confident) I may well have a problem. It is probably not at all clear how I can move from my current to my desired state. In the diploma course, managers are advised that they may find it helpful to address themselves to five questions:

1. **Where have I been?** – What are my past experiences?
2. **Where am I now?** – What strengths and weaknesses do I have? What is the current situation that I am in?
3. **Where do I want to get to?** – What goals/targets/objectives do I want to set for myself?
4. **How will I get there?** – What programme of study should I design to achieve my goals?
5. **How will I know if I've arrived?** – What criteria can I apply to assess my learning?

Most people find these questions helpful in assisting them to formulate and choose their problems. I say 'choose' because any problem is a choice. If one decides to accept the situation and does not wish to change, then there are no problems. It is only when a person *chooses* to change that problems become identifiable. This situation can be shown diagrammatically as in Figure 8.2. This indicates the link with the five questions outlined above.

In Figure 8.2 the person has the problem of going from **A** to **B**. The position is chosen on the basis of the person's values and beliefs: it is not an externally defined objective reality. My stance then is to reject what I often hear from trainers and lecturers. 'That manager says he wants to learn **X**, but that is not the real problem. What he really needs is **Y**.' The arrogance of such statements is in part based on a notion that 'real problems' exist out there in the world, detached from people; I regard this as an unacceptable standpoint. I may *115*

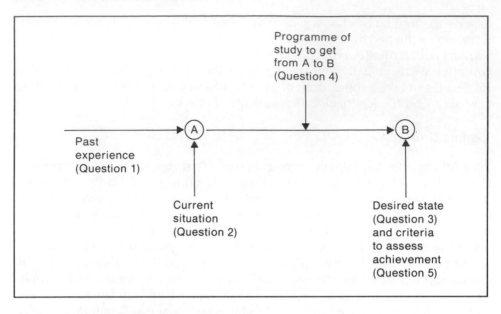

Figure 8.2   The problem of going from A to B

disagree with the goals a manager has set, but that is just my view against his or hers. I believe that I have the right to challenge and question a learner, and in the process they may change their formulation of the problem. However, in SML courses the staff do not have the right to impose goals on learners, no matter how subtly they may wish to do it.

I have argued here for the principle of learners setting their own goals; however, there are also practical reasons why this is important. The research evidence on managerial learning is quite conclusive in supporting the notion that learning is enhanced if managers consciously *set their own goals*. Kolb and Boyatzis (1984) quote a number of studies which demonstrate remarkable improvements in learning and performance when managers were given the chance to set their own goals, and such changes tend to be independent of how difficult the goals are that people set for themselves.

Observed

John has returned from the set meeting where his draft learning contract has been discussed. His proposals have been analysed in detail, and many of his ideas have been exposed, under questioning, as being ill-thought out. He had been a bit annoyed at the time, as he felt he had put a lot of effort into his draft contract. However, now that he can re-read his proposals he realizes that they were not as solid as he had thought. Just saying that he wanted to 'learn about management finance' and to 'improve interpersonal skills' clearly was not specific enough. He decided to talk to his boss, because part of the reason he had put in 'improve interpersonal skills' was on the basis of feedback at his last appraisal interview. He now realized that he needed to be clearer about what his boss actually meant by this.

Explanation

1. Sets are often at their most supportive when they confront individuals about what they *are or are not doing*. Woolly non-judgemental feedback ('I like what you've done') is as inappropriate as destructive judgemental assessment ('You'll never make a good manager'). Supportive confronting involves supporting the person as a person and valuing their worth as a human being, whilst commenting, positively and negatively, on what they do. This can be expressed simply as: support *being* (that is, the person); confront *doing* (that is, what they do).
2. Part of helping people to manage their own learning is assisting them to specify the precise problems which they wish to tackle. In order to get *good answers*, one needs first *good questions*.
3. It is valuable if managers can build into their learning contracts evidence they gain from colleagues, bosses, subordinates and others at work. However, our experience is that much of this evidence is too vague. We have encouraged managers to go and *seek out good feedback*, so that they can have a better basis on which to decide what to learn. Sometimes set members (staff or course members) have gone to a person's place of work to assist in this information gathering, especially if the boss or work colleagues get built into the contract as sources of learning.

Observed

Jane has had her contract agreed by her set at the end of the first term, and she now finds she has to start to put her plans into operation. She decides that her desire to learn about basic elements of marketing can best be met by attending a module on this topic, which is already provided on the Diploma in Management Studies. The module is one evening a week for one term. She has been given study leave for one day a week by her employers, so she comes into the college to use the library in the morning, prior to going to her set meeting in the afternoon. She feels she has a problem in running meetings, and looks for books in the library on this topic. However, she comes across an entry in the catalogue of a video tape on the subject. She signs out the tape and views it in one of the soundproof booths provided in the library.

Later in the term she decides to pluck up courage and tackle her antipathy towards statistics. She arranges a meeting with a tutor, and he shows her how to use material on the PCs on open access in the computer room. She realizes how valuable it has been for her to have discussed her concerns about statistics in the set, as her colleagues were not only able to reassure her, but also helped her to clarify the kind of questions she needed to put to the tutor. She finds that the tutor occasionally gets over-enthusiastic about pushing her *117* into the broader aspects of the subject, but because she is clear about what she wants she is able to steer him back to her own needs.

Explanation

1. A person managing his or her own learning can choose a *variety of ways to learn* what he or she wants to learn.
2. *Back-up learning resources* are important, though many are ill-designed for easy access. Libraries are often organized to suit librarians, and it can be a problem getting the flexibility and responsiveness needed for SML work. The use of learning resources in SML programmes is unlike their use in so-called open and distance learning; much of the latter is not very 'open' at all, being predefined packages which give little or no choice to managers – they are like Tillich's stones being thrown at the heads of managers who have not formulated the questions (and are not going to be allowed to). It is a Henry Ford approach to learning ('You can have any course you like, so long as it's this one').
3. Tutors may also not be ideally responsive. However, part of the skill of managing one's own learning is to *manage experts*; the experts do have things to offer, and it is short-sighted of managers to ignore this. Managers are, though, rightly suspicious of experts who wish to push their own field of interest too much. To quote Greenberg's First Law of Experts: 'You don't ask a barber if you need a haircut' (Peers and Bennett, 1981). However, if you decide for yourself that you need a haircut, a barber can be useful.

Observed

Jim, a senior manager in local government, meets his tutor from college. They sit down in Jim's office and go through a time diary Jim has kept for the last two weeks. As they analyse his activities, Jim realizes how much time he has been devoting to unproductive work. He appreciates now why his staff have complained about the amount of time he is out of the office or otherwise not available to them. He discusses with his tutor ways in which he could reorganize his time to fit more closely with his priorities.

After they have been through the time diary, they discuss how Jim processes paper (since this is another problem he has decided to tackle). Jim calls in his secretary, so that with the tutor the three of them can consider how to change the filing system.

Explanation

1. SML can involve learning both high-level abstract theory and 'nitty-gritty' practical skills.
2. Learning can take place at work, in college (or anywhere).
3. Course members choose one staff member (not the set adviser) to act as

a 'specialist tutor' to assist them with specific learning which needs expert help; ideally, the specialist tutor works with the learner over the two years, although in practice people often switch tutors as their interests or requirements change. This special relationship does not preclude the course member from using other tutors on an occasional basis.

Observed

It is a sunny July Saturday afternoon and this is the third residential weekend of the year. Course members can be observed around the building and outside it. Eight people are struggling with a computer-based business game: some are from the public sector, and they are finding the commercial aspects of the game difficult to handle. Ten people are in a seminar on industrial relations negotiations run by one of the tutors. Tom, Jenny and Tim are busy in the computer room, each working on his or her own specific work problems. Tim has been testing out some proposals his employers are about to implement, and he finds a serious flaw in their calculations. He subsequently reports this to his organization, and they save a seven-figure sum by redoing their sums along the lines that Tim suggests.

Arthur sits under a tree in the grounds reading a book on operations research, and every so often he glances at a group of nine people on the lawn who are painting and drawing. They are in a session on integrating left-brain and right-brain working. Later on, he observes them all lying down listening to a guided fantasy, and he wonders whether he should not have joined that group rather than choosing to work on his own.

Meanwhile, in a darkened room in the main building, a group of seven is watching a video of Tom Peters, oblivious of the sunshine outside. Along the corridor Tony, Mike and Sue are using video equipment to practise their counselling skills. Janet, who is on the course, but is also a management tutor in a college, is assisting them, as she runs counselling training courses in her own college.

Down by the lake, well away from the main building, Simon and Carol sit on a bench. Simon is crying: his father died a few days ago; he does not feel able to attend the planned activities, and Carol, who is in his set, has agreed to sit with him for the afternoon. Simon is confused because his dominant feeling is one of anger, not sadness, at his father's death. Carol knows that Simon's relationship with his father has been fraught, as it has come up in the set discussions, and she tries to help Simon make sense of his feelings. Eventually, they wander slowly back from the lake.

It is now late afternoon and a discussion group is about to start on the lawn, led by one of the tutors. Tim and Jenny leave their computers to join it, along with Simon and Carol. Mike and Sue emerge from their video session to take part, and Arthur decides to take a break from his book to join them.

Inside the building, a session on theorizing is being held, and people do various exercises to assist them in being more effective at developing theory from their experiences. In one exercise, course members form into small sub-groups. One person (the problem owner) talks about a problem whilst the others write on cards the concepts used by the person as he or she talks. Together they arrange the cards in a 'concept map' in order to help the problem owner to *model the problem*. The problem owner is then assisted in elucidating the hypotheses with which he or she is working, so that concepts, models and hypotheses can be linked together as theory.

Explanation

1. Residential weekends provide a range of options to cover what course members request. Sometimes people spend time outside formally organized sessions: this is part of *managing one's own learning*.
2. The activities exemplify the *holistic orientation* of the programme; most people are pleasantly surprised at how valuable it is to attend to their learning needs as whole persons: they find they change intellectually, emotionally, physically, socially and sometimes spiritually. All of this is relevant to management.
3. Course members *learn from each other*. The course provides a network which allows people to meet others with matching interests and concerns: it also facilitates mutual support in times of personal difficulty.

   This networking often continues after the formal ending of the course. There are facilities for ex-course members to meet and contact each other. (One set which went through the programme in 1980–82 has continued to meet of its own volition up to the present day.)
4. The style of the residential course is in keeping with a both/and orientation: people work hard and they have fun; they are active and passive; they engage in rational and non-rational activity; they plan rigorously and they respond to serendipitous whims.
5. I like to feel that the SML approach is genuinely scientific in the sense that Bateson (1973) has supported; that is, that one counterposes theory and existing knowledge with experience, and tests each against the other. I agree with Sirag (1979) that 'the future of physics rests in the hands of those who have an equal toleration for mathematical rigour and free-wheeling fantasy'. A similar statement could be made about management.

Observed

The two-year course is coming to its end for Mike's set, and they are dealing with assessment, in order to decide on who gets the diploma and who does not. Mike has already presented various essays and reports to the set, and these have been discussed. He is now at the set meeting at which they are looking at the totality of his work. He first shows a video tape where he is counselling someone, and after that he gives his reasons why he thinks this has satisfied the criteria in his contract on this subject. Other course members and the staff member (set adviser) question him on this, and eventually they agree he has met the required standard. Mike then distributes copies of assessments carried out by his boss and his subordinates on aspects of his performance at work. In discussion it seems that there is doubt on some aspects of these, particularly as to whether Mike has met all his previously contracted criteria. The set agrees that they cannot make a decision on this information, and the task of going to Mike's company to talk to his boss and his subordinates is delegated to two set members. After this discussion, Mike's specialist tutor joins the set, and he reports on Mike's work in the areas of finance and economics. The set quiz him on his report, and eventually agree with Mike and the tutor that the required criteria have been met. The set then consider Mike's other (written) work which they have already seen. They agree that if the two set members seeing Mike's boss and subordinates get the required information, they can proceed at the next set meeting to decide on a pass.

Explanation

It is central to SML that the learner manages the assessment process in conjunction with *relevant others*. In the context of this diploma course 'relevant others' means at the very least other set members and the specialist tutor. In Mike's case above, the person's boss and subordinates were also involved. At no time are judgements imposed externally on the learner: the assessment process matches the initial contracting process in being a *collaborative negotiation*. I have discussed elsewhere other aspects of assessment (see Cunningham, 1983).

WHERE DOES SML COME FROM?

The roots of SML lie in: a particular view of learning; and a range of methods and approaches to learning.
  Some of the latter are outlined below.

LEARNING APPROACHES

Independent study

From work in the North East London Polytechnic, I wanted to use the idea that individuals can *plan and carry out their own learning programmes* (see Cunningham, 1981).

Action learning

The value of individual managers *assisting each other* in their learning (through the use of sets) was clearly demonstrated in various action learning   *121* programmes in which I was involved (e.g. GEC's Developing Senior Managers Programme; see also Casey and Pearce, 1977).

Autonomy labs

The work of Harrison (1974) in creating courses where managers were free to do what they liked (almost) impressed me. Restricting the trainer role to providing *rich resources and to assisting others in their learning* (through counselling and coaching) seemed a healthy stance.

Humanistic education

Rogers (1969) has been an influence on many management developers in the UK, and his passionate advocacy of a *person-centred* approach provided important philosophical underpinnings for SML.

Holistic education

It seems self-evident to me that managers are not disembodied brains (see also Mant, 1977): they exist in physical bodies, they feel (even if they pretend they do not), they value and believe in particular ideals (even though it is not always apparent). Schutz (1979) is one of many writers who have promoted a *holistic perspective* on learning. His holistic studies MA at Antioch University in San Francisco was one of a number of American programmes I was able to experience at first hand when working in the USA in the late 1970s.

Self-development

Self-development methods and ideas flourished in the late 1970s. The idea of managers managing their own development through starting with their *own needs* has proved very effective. However, 'self-development' has tended to become a catch-all term to include almost anything that is not traditional learning. Some of the proponents of self-development also started to see the need to consider the *context* within which the person was learning (usually their organization). Hence the idea of developing 'learning organizations' came more to the fore.

Work-based management development

These are the methods one can use to assist managerial learning *without managers leaving their place of work*. Coaching, the use of work assignments, job rotation, and apprenticeship are examples of such unglamorous (but often high valuable) methods. My experience of consulting in various organizations indicated that these approaches could be the most cost-effective learning modes for much managerial learning (see Mumford, 1993 for further discussion of this topic).

OTHER INFLUENCES ON SELF-MANAGED LEARNING

As well as influences from learning approaches, SML has benefited from:

1. Developments in *psychotherapy*, which have provided ideas on how people change (for example, neuro-linguistic programming – see Bandler and Grinder, 1979).
2. Research on the *nature of management* (for example, Stewart, 1982), which indicates that managing is not a neat subject discipline that can be taught in compartmentalized, standardized chunks.
3. Research on *brain functioning*, which shows up the different contributions that the left and right hemispheres of the brain contribute to our ways of thinking (see Mintzberg, 1984).
4. Ideas from philosophy about the *nature of knowledge and of reality* (Bateson, 1973 and Watzlawick, 1978 were specific influences); the notion that 'reality' cannot sensibly be conceptualized as a concrete entity outside of ourselves is a central tenet of SML. Managers create their own reality, and teachers and trainers have to respond to that.
5. *Eastern philosophy*, particularly Taoism, has provided a subtle and powerful antidote to narrow Westernized modes of thought; this is especially so in relation to the idea that one can work in a *both/and* rather than an *either/or* mode: I shall comment specifically on this in the next section.

BOTH/AND OR EITHER/OR?

In organizing SML to get the benefits of the different strands outlined above, I was guided by the notion that we could work in a both/and rather than an either/or mode: we did not need to choose between apparent opposites, since many things that are supposed to be opposites are not. Let me pick out one writer (amongst many) who has categorized management education programmes on an either/or basis, and indicate how his reasoning is unhelpful.

Handy (1975) identified what he claimed were the polar opposites in management education – instrumentalism and existentialism, and argued that management teachers had to choose between these two schools. He described the *instrumental* school as believing that education was *subject-oriented*; that one teaches things to people; that the success of a course is judged on the basis of the person's contribution to society or to an organization; that reasoning and learning are deductive (practice follows theory); that entry to courses is on the basis of organizational sponsorship only. The *existential* position he described as concentrating on the individual (and his or her freedom), not on the group. The view of reasoning and learning held by this school, he said, was *inductivist* (theory emerges from experience). He stated that teachers in this camp disliked assessment and talked instead of allowing feedback. They also preferred to take people onto a course on the basis of *123* personal choice rather than organizational sponsorship.

Handy also argued that it was not possible to 'ride two horses at once', and that all management teachers had to choose one or the other position. The evidence I have gathered from my own research (Cunningham, 1984) indicates that effective management teachers or trainers do not conform to Handy's assumptions. The people in my research talked very much in terms of working with *both poles at the same time*. Everyone was, for instance, in some way interested in the development of the person and in the person's contribution to society, their organization or their area of work. The notion that a management teacher *has* to choose to help *either* the person *or* society (and cannot do both) is nonsensical. For one thing, the notion that 'organizations' and 'society' are objects which can exist separately from persons is difficult to sustain; secondly (and conversely), it presupposes that managers can manage *outside a social context*.

To refer back to the case of the course I described earlier:

1. We recruited individuals as self-sponsored *and* as organizationally sponsored.
2. We took assessment seriously, and pass or fail decisions were faced not as a necessary nuisance but as an important judgemental process to be set *alongside* the less judgemental feedback mode.
3. We valued people who were independent *and* interdependent. The course could work only if people *both* considered themselves and worked on their own problems *and* considered others and worked with them on their problems.
4. The course demanded that a person be involved in a *learning community*, as well as pursuing *individual* and *small group* work.
5. Course members used subject-based knowledge *and* they used their personally-created knowledge. Theory and practice were continually counterposed in ways which transcended simplistic deductive-inductive modes.

I have indicated here the notion of a holistic integration of poles, but I recognize that there are 'management teachers' who operate according to one or other of Handy's opposites. I have come across messy, self-centred existentialist programmes which have degenerated into chaotic disasters. The history of much of the 1960s–1970s radical and humanistic education movement showed that many programmes collapsed because of this unbalanced mode of operation (see Swidler, 1979; Rogers, 1983; Leonard, 1979; Deal, 1975).

Equally degenerate instrumental programmes have tended to survive because of a combination of authoritarian control mechanisms, the exclusiveness and secretiveness of staff, and the investment by course members in pretending that their course is satisfactory (otherwise it would undermine their qualification, and if they have learned the hidden curriculum of instrumentalism they would not want to put their careers at risk).

What I have expressed above is my own interpretation, based on my experience of a number of institutions. However, in my research, people time and again expressed their rejection of narrow instrumentalism; they criticized the lack of involvement of such programmes with the lives of course members; the wastefulness of fixed curricula; and the lack of effectiveness of standardized taught courses.

CONCLUSION

SML approaches have been tried and tested in a wide variety of contexts over many years and with thousands of managers. Evaluation studies have shown the depth and breadth of learning for individuals from this approach. More importantly, people who have been through SML programmes comment on the way they learned to learn for themselves for the rest of their lives. They say, in evaluation studies carried out in a variety of organizations, how much they value becoming self-managing learners. Ultimately it is the *process* of SML which appears to provide the richest and most profound pay-off for learners and for their organizations.

REFERENCES

Bandler, R. and Grinder, J. (1979) *Frogs into Princes* (Moab, Utah: Real People Press).

Bateson, G. (1973) *Steps to an Ecology of Mind* (London: Paladin).

Brown, G. L. (1971) *Human Teaching for Human Learning* (New York: Viking).

Casey, D. and Pearce, D. (1977) *More than Management Development: Action Learning at G.E.C.* (Aldershot: Gower).

Cunningham, I. (1981) 'Self-Managed Learning and Independent Study', in Boydell, T. and Pedler, M. (eds) *Management Self-Development: Concepts and Practices* (Aldershot: Gower).

Cunningham, I. (1983) 'Assessment and Experiential Learning', in Boot, R. and Reynolds, M. (eds) *Learning and Experience in Formal Education*, Manchester Monograph (University of Manchester).

Cunningham, I. (1984) *Teaching Styles in Learner-Centred Management Development Programmes*, PhD thesis (University of Lancaster).

Deal, T. E. (1975) 'An Organizational Explanation of the Failure of Alternative Secondary Schools', *Educational Researcher*, 4 (4), pp. 10–16.

Handy, C. B. (1975) 'The Contrasting Philosophies of Management Education', *Management Education and Development*, 6 (2) (August), pp. 56–62.

Harrison, R. (1974) 'Developing Autonomy, Initiative and Risk-Taking Through Laboratory Design', in Adams, J. D. (ed.) *New Technologies in O.D.* (La Jolla, Calif.: University Associates).

Heron, J. (1977) *Dimensions of Facilitator Style* (London: British Postgraduate Medical Federation).

Hurley, B. and Cunningham, I. (1993) 'Imbibing a New Way of Learning', *Personnel Management* (March), pp. 42–5.

Kolb, D. A. and Boyatzis, R. E. (1984) 'Goal Setting and Self Directed Behaviour Change', in Kolb, D. A., Rubin, I. M. and McIntyre, J. M. (eds) *Organizational Psychology: Readings on Human Behavior in Organizations* (Englewood Cliffs, NJ: Prentice-Hall).

Leonard, G. (1979) 'Frontiers in Education: Past and Present', *AHP Newsletter* (May), pp. 5–6.

Mant, A. (1977) *The Rise and Fall of the British Manager* (London: McGraw-Hill).

Mintzberg, H. (1984) 'Planning on the left side and managing on the right', in Kolb, D. A., Rubin, I. M. and McIntyre, J. M. (eds) *Organizational Psychology: Readings on Human Behavior in Organizations* (Englewood Cliffs, NJ: Prentice-Hall).

Mumford, A. (1993) *Management Development: Strategies for Action*, 2nd edn (London: IPM).

Peers, J. and Bennett, G. (1981) *1001 Logical Laws* (London: Hamlyn).

Rogers, C. R. (1969) *Freedom to Learn* (Columbus, Ohio: Charles E. Merrill).

Rogers, C. R. (1983) *Freedom to Learn for the Eighties* (Columbus, Ohio: Charles E. Merrill).

Schutz, W. (1979) *Profound Simplicity* (London: Turnstone).

Sirag, S. P. (1979) 'Physics Education', *A.H.P. Newsletter* (May), pp. 17–18.

Stewart, R. (1982) *Choices for the Manager* (London: McGraw-Hill).

Swidler, A. (1979) *Organization without Authority* (Cambridge, Mass.: Harvard University Press).

Watzlawick, P. (1978) *The Language of Change* (London: Basic Books).

9 Development work and the learning spiral

John Morris

BRINGING WORK AND LEARNING TOGETHER

What did you learn at school? How did you learn it? Could you teach what you have learned to others? These are formidable questions. Your answers might be: 'I learned a set of subjects which I've mostly forgotten'; 'I learned by being taught and from studying'; 'I don't think I could teach all that, but then I'm not a teacher'; followed by 'Anyway, it was all a long time ago'.

But suppose the same questions were applied to the *work you are now doing*: What have you learned from doing your job? How did you learn it? Could you teach what you have learned to others? Are these questions any less formidable?

The experience of learning from doing your work is more recent, so you could probably go into far more detail in your answers; but you may still find that you are inclined to answer the last question with 'It's not my job to teach.' And yet, in the constantly changing and demanding world of management, it would be enormously valuable if experienced managers were able to pass on to others what they have learned. Maybe that help would not take the form of 'teaching' in the traditional sense: it could include other skills – such as 'adviser', 'mentor', 'tutor' or 'coach' – that refer to the ability to enable others to improve their knowledge, their skill, or whatever else it is that they want to improve.

Many of us would like to do this, but find ourselves in difficulty: *work seems to drive out an awareness of learning*. While we were at school, or taking part in a training course, we knew that we were supposed to be learning. But at work the learning seems to happen without our knowing it. And yet we know that in many ways this is the very best kind of learning – that is why we often claim that 'learning from experience' or 'learning by doing' are the keystones of all real learning.

The problem seems to be this. How can one clearly distinguish 'work' from 'learning', and yet find ways of bringing them together skilfully and deliberately in a *self-managed flow of learning from experience*? In helping managers to tackle this problem, various models of learning styles have been immensely useful. Probably the best known approach is still that of David Kolb (Kolb *et al.*, 1979). This takes the form of four phases, each phase neatly contrasting with another in an elegant cross-formation. If you want to see your preferred style of learning, you complete a simple questionnaire and see yourself clearly represented on the model. You can then compare yourself with other people, of different ages, sexes, occupations and so on.

The four phases are given rather jaw-breaking names, but these can be quickly understood. 'Abstract conceptualization' is the process of *thinking about one's experience*; 'active experimentation' is the *application* of the *results of one's thinking*; 'concrete experience' is the emotional impact of being *actually in a new situation*; and 'reflective observation' is the process of *conscious reflection* on what has been *perceived* and *experienced*. The four phases also include contrasting aspects of the learning process: involvement and detachment, action and reflection.

Good models are for focusing our attention on something that interests us, not for covering everything in their domain. It is a tribute to Kolb's model that it has fostered variants – some would say improvements. It has also attracted sharp criticism: in my view another tribute. I came to the model rather late, from a background in social and developmental psychology. My appetite had been sated with the rich fare of psychological research into learning processes (in fact, it had given me acute indigestion). Human learning turns out, as you can imagine, to be a fantastically complex affair, made even more complex because our *study of learning* is itself a *process of learning* – or, rather, a complicated hierarchical network of processes. When rich food fails to satisfy, something simple and salty is refreshing, and may prove far more nourishing. For me, the Kolb model met this need. His later work in developing the model shows how soundly based it is.

But I also found the Honey and Mumford model (1992) very attractive, especially in working with busy managers in short events. The words describing the phases were simpler than Kolb's, though they were turned into *types of managerial behaviour* rather than phases of learning. 'Activist', 'Theorist', 'Pragmatist', 'Reflector': everyone can readily recognize these, and I found the questionnaire meatier than Kolb's. Add to all this a users' club in which members pool their scores and experiences of working with the approach, and we have a learning model which takes its own lessons seriously.

A further model of learning, in the form of personal development, was developed by Bert Juch (1983). Juch locates his learning model in a rich context of other studies, drawn from many fields. For good measure, he embeds his research investigation in a personal history, showing how he came to develop the model and what his experiences have been with it.

I have found these models illuminating and useful, but have also found it
128 helpful to use another, which is close to them in its structure, but is more

'organizational' in its focus. Organizations are systems for getting work done, by dividing it up (usually very efficiently) and then putting it together again (notably less efficiently). The learning model that I have been using links directly to an *organization for doing work*.

Just a word or two on why I call the model a 'spiral' (Figure 9.1). I join with Juch here, it is really a preference for an open metaphor, rather than a closed one, like 'cycle' or 'style'. Juch talks of 'whirling cycles within a lifelong spiral': I find it useful to think of turnings in a spiral rather than sharp discontinuous levels of learning. But I cannot deny, from frequently repeated experience, that some of the turns can be very abrupt!

From Figure 9.1 it can be seen that at the bottom is the earthy activity of '*doing*' (that most flexible of terms), grounded in a *situation*. Above it are the classic managerial activities of *planning*, *monitoring*, and *reviewing*, and above that *forming* a purpose. If I had to find an extended phrase to include these phases of learning, it would be something like this: learning from trying to express a *purpose* in action within a situation; *planning* being the shaping of an appropriate action, *monitoring* being the control of action as it occurs, and *reviewing* being the comparison of the action with the purpose. The model has the virtue of being easily transposed from the individual to the group level, and to the organizational level. Since I am interested in linking individual, group and organizational levels of learning, it has been useful to have a model that seems to move so readily from individual to organization.

Another useful aspect of the model is that it enables one to see very clearly an unfortunate side-effect of the conventional form of organization. I call it 'splitting the learning' (see Figure 9.2). This obviously happens because of the manifold advantages of the division of labour, as against the organizational advantage of singleness of overall purpose (survival, for example, or growth). But when we look at the implications of the division of work for the continuity

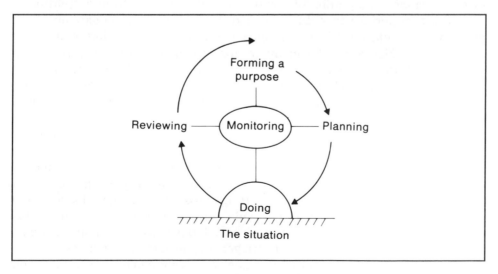

Figure 9.1 The learning spiral approach

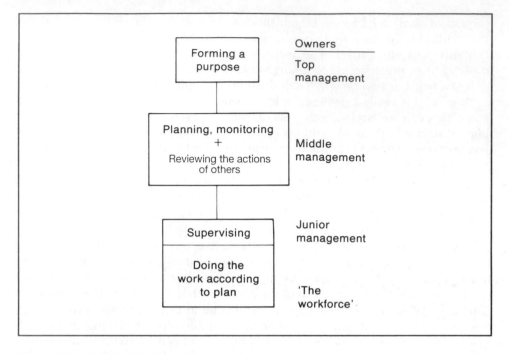

Figure 9.2   Splitting the learning

of learning, it is clear that the devices used within organizations for turning purposes into action may not be those that occur in individuals when strongly-felt purpose is expressed in action. By and large, conventional organizations replace *strong feeling*, which is the individual link between purpose and action, with *tight control*. This produces one of the most depressing effects of this kind of organization – a splitting of commitment that results from a splitting of purpose from performance. I have called this 'the motivation gap' and have conservatively placed it below the managerial level of planning, monitoring and review in Figure 9.3. But many groups of managers I have worked with suggest that the motivation gap is often above that level, so that one commonly finds a highly motivated board of directors signalling their purposes wildly but ineffectively to a distinctly unmoved group of executives (see Figure 9.3).

There seems to be a powerful and attractive way of getting purpose and performance close together again: it is the direct-action approach (see Figure 9.4). The purpose is embodied in a *leader*, rather than a mere owner, or director; the leader, full of the energy that flows from purpose, makes direct contact with those who take action, cutting across the managerial layers, and especially those with a concern for planning and review. One finds this commonly enough in small, entrepreneurial businesses, and in 'real-time management', celebrated for its hair-trigger response to emergencies.

Unfortunately, the bypassing of planning and review can have dire effects on many kinds of action. New products and services may take years to gestate,

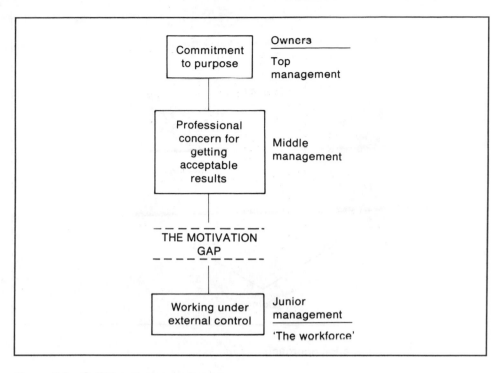

Figure 9.3   Splitting the commitment

and will never appear if direct action rules. Routine performances may need to be carefully assembled and rehearsed, but will be ignored or under-valued by direct action. Direct action is splendid when it works, and often disastrous when it does not: it is all or nothing, and it certainly has no time for fostering learning, for enabling it to become conscious and reflective. Such qualities are seen as pernicious, as the forerunners of 'paralysis by analysis'.

Is it possible, then, to find other ways of countering the fragmentation that is all too common in the conventional organization, with its disastrous effects on an energetic flow of learning? Can we combine work and the whole spiral of learning? Clearly, to do so effectively requires an unconventional organization, one in which *purpose can infuse performance without loss of planning and review*. One way in which this purpose can be achieved is in the deliberately small world of a development programme, in which learning comes from project work – not project 'exercises' or project 'recommendations' but real *development work*, in which actual needs are met and there are real changes for the better.

In a development programme, based on live projects, the energy that flows from purpose needs to be shaped into coherent activity through a process of continuous planning, monitoring and review. Instead of these 'managerial' activities being operated through a formal procedure of decision and control, the people who are engaged in the operational work of the project are able to relate their experience to the guiding purpose, which is very much *in*   *131*

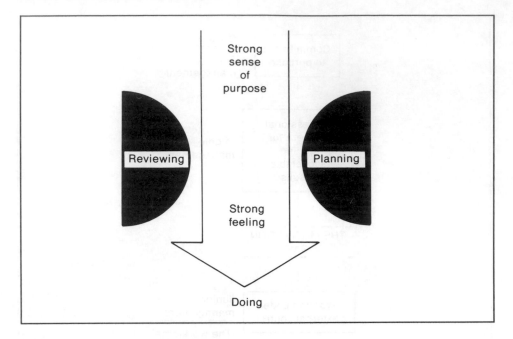

Figure 9.4   The direct-action approach

themselves. If we still wish to use the invidious term 'control' (invidious only when it comes to controlling people) we could say that a project is a *continuing experience of self-control* in the light of a *guiding and energizing purpose.* This stands in the sharpest possible contrast to the conventional organization, in which the work done by the 'workforce' is based on the distant and often inscrutable purposes of owners and investors, mediated by complex and often contradictory control procedures.

The development programmes I wish to comment on now have been part of the work of the Development Consortium, which is an innovative venture in management development, hived off from Manchester Business School in 1982 with the aid of the Foundation for Management Development. It is independent and self-funding, existing to foster initiatives in action learning and other forms of development work that seek to bring work and learning into the same set of activities. Unlike the usual management centre, it does not have a fixed staff, apart from the two managing partners and administrative support. It works wherever possible with practising managers as learning consultants and advisers. If other staff are needed, they are brought in for a specific programme. The basic unit of work is a *development programme,* usually consisting of several linked projects.

We often think of a 'consortium' as an *ad hoc* association of several substantial businesses coming together to manage an important project. The Development Consortium is a more informal association, bringing together

individuals and teams, rather than institutions, in development programmes of many kinds. These have focused on the needs and interests of directors, senior managers and project leaders in organizations faced with major organizational change. Clients have included a wide variety of enterprises in financial services, engineering, information technology, music, transport, industrial products and utilities; together with public sector organizations such as health services, educational institutions, development agencies, and local authorities.

What do all these diverse activities have in common? They all take the form of *development activities*, rather than educational programmes or training courses. They all struggle to identify complex issues of real concern to the managers taking part, and they are all closely associated with managerial work, rather than being uncoupled from it. There is one other thing that these activities have in common. They all follow through the *whole learning spiral*, often through several turns. They relate purposes to performance, planning to review. They question purposes in the light of experience, rather than force experience (or reports of it) to conform to fixed purposes. They recognize that an effective development activity must find its own strong purpose, since it is exposed to so many sources of disturbance that lack of purpose will swiftly lead to its dissolution.

But any further search for common factors in diverse activities would probably be mistaken. One great value of development activities is that particular issues can be addressed in all their uniqueness. What might prove useful, however, is to note some of the experiences that seem pertinent to getting the learning spiral to work. The experiences are not pointed enough to be called 'lessons', and they are not solidly enough based to be claimed as 'evidence'. But they may indicate questions for later consideration.

DEVELOPMENT CULTURE AND DOMINANT CULTURE

Development projects bring two cultures closely together; these are the *dominant* culture and the *development* culture. The dominant culture is the set of values and ways of doing things that predominate in the organization, the tone usually being set by the central group of top management (or, in owner-managed enterprises, the owner). In a successful organization, the dominant culture will usually have strong developmental aspects, but these have to fit into many other day-to-day requirements and pressures (see Chapter 17). The development project, on the other hand, has a licence to establish a development culture – and certainly a practical necessity to do so, if it is to be effective in achieving its task. Much of the literature dealing with developmental failures reveals situations in which the two cultures came into collision and, in the short run at least, the dominant culture won.

In the activities of the Development Consortium, the two cultures are brought together from the beginning, because a steering group is invariably part of the programme design. The steering group contains senior line managers from the organization or organizations taking part in the programme; they are members of the dominant culture, faced with the   *133* challenge of enabling the two cultures to work together to mutual advantage. The development culture knows all about mutuality: thrives on it, in fact. Not so the dominant culture. Most dominant cultures are greatly concerned with the maintenance of the *existing pattern of authority*, often exercised through a clearly-defined line of command. The task of balancing the two cultures provides a powerful learning experience for members of the steering group, and a continuing insight into the challenges each poses to the other.

COMING TO TERMS WITH TRIBES

Of course, there are far more than two cultures living within the organization; there are also the powerful *sub-cultures of the main business activities*: marketing, sales, production, distribution, finance, accounting, technical services, personnel. Many of these sub-cultures have been lovingly nurtured by professional education and training. Some of the professions provide traditions, career paths, rewards (and punishments) of great power and long standing; they cut across the dominant culture of the business, often providing opportunities for development, and sometimes unintentionally producing inertia, confusion and cynicism.

It does not seem too fanciful to see these sub-cultures as the sustaining elements in organizational tribes, and whenever I have discussed this notion with groups of managers, they have accepted it readily (particularly where other tribes are concerned). Indeed, in many an organization, the tribes and their mutual antipathy are taken for granted: a fact of life. Yet the experience of working with 'multi-tribal' project teams suggests that tribes are to some extent conventional metaphors, rather than all-powerful realities. Tribal loyalties may quickly be contained when a demanding and engrossing task is in hand.

Successful businesses seem to be able to bring the tribes together in a durable confederation, with the larger commitment of securing the success of the business as a whole. In a sense, the whole business becomes an effective blend of tribal loyalties and corporate commitment, like a small nation with a limited set of purposes.

HUNGER FOR UNDERSTANDING OF STRATEGY

Managers who are working on projects quickly find themselves looking beyond their usual boundaries. Partly this is because development projects are chosen to widen their perspectives, and are invariably successful in achieving this; but it seems also to be a matter of getting a sense of how the organization as a whole is moving, and perhaps a hope that this will provide a set of useful guidelines for one's daily work, and a reasonably clear context for the project work. There is also a sense in which 'strategy' becomes a synonym for 'the overall purpose of the business'. Development work encourages questioning, and questioning sooner or later becomes a questioning of purpose: 'What are we doing this for anyway?'; 'How does this fit in with the other activities going on?' As the questions becomes wider, one can see them as expressing a real hunger for an understanding of the overbranching purposes of the organization.

The sheer sense of urgency that project work engenders – or perhaps it is rather a sharpened sense of organizational opportunities – leads to confrontations which are focused on the feasibility of current organizational stances. In one of our programmes, managers in a project set accused top managers of leaving a 'strategic vacuum' within the business; when this was discussed, the top managers argued that the 'vacuum' was one of the many signs of the intractability of an old, highly ramified business with structural abysses a century old. The question for them was: 'How do we slowly form a strategy that can gain the commitment of all the varied interest groups sharing the business?' Within the heightened consciousness of the project set, fresh from disturbing extrapolations of future business threats, this 'slow but sure' approach seemed unacceptably complacent.

It is characteristic of development work that it encourages these issues to be raised, and perhaps coped with; and it reminds us that the hunger for an understanding of strategy is part of the deeper need to couple performance with a durable sense of purpose: performances, however efficient, are not self-sustaining, especially when one begins to question them. At this point, the issue of *leadership* arises.

LEADERSHIP

There seem to be many kinds of leader. One well-known political figure was reputed to have said: 'I don't understand all this fuss about leadership. You just tell people what to do and they do it!' Another kind of leader would see this as domination, acceptable only in emergencies, and even then building up a formidable weight of resentment and subversion.

My own experience in project teams brings out a familiar insight: leadership flows from *demonstrable commitment to purpose,* which releases energies that focus attention. For those who share the purpose, this kind of free-flowing energy is attractive: the person imbued with purpose becomes a readily identifiable focus, an embodiment of what needs to be done. Because a project team is a kind of small world, capable of following through the whole learning spiral (usually several turns of it) in a manageable timescale, the presence of leadership is usually easily recognizable. Because the purpose is so clear and readily available, all members of a project team commonly find occasion to act as leaders, according to skill, sensitivity and circumstance.

KEEPING IT SIMPLE

In a major programme in the public sector, a visiting speaker from an entrepreneurial business made a great impact with his succinct and salty list of Do's and Don'ts for successful management. One of the best received of these was 'Keep it simple, stupid!'.

We can understand why senior managers from an uncomfortably visible part of the embattled public sector should hunger and thirst after simplicity. All the more when the relevant Department of State complicates life for these managers by imposing its own notions of simplicity on their planning and operations. Yet it seems clear that success in most activities depends on holding the essentials of the business in mind (and at heart) as a set of vital priorities: 'as complex as you must, as simple as you can' emerges as a lesson from work in development projects, where it seems at times that almost everything is relevant to the project work, yet pressures of time and resource impose severe limits.

LEARNING FROM BEST CURRENT PRACTICE

Reg Revans (1983) identified a common weakness of senior managers which can seriously inhibit their capacity to learn. He noted that they eagerly accepted the influence of top managers who are undeniably successful, but they failed to appreciate that they might have something to learn from their colleagues, especially those who were lower down the organizational hierarchy. 'Best current practice' can be found in many places and at many levels, and it is vital for the manager not to be blinkered by the achievements of his seniors, or to become parochial in his or her choice of practices to emulate. By consciously adopting a broader perspective, the manager becomes able to learn from failures as well as from successes, and from a whole host of contacts, irrespective of formal status.

It is interesting from this point of view to look at the lessons drawn from two influential studies of best current business practice: the McKinsey study of American firms *In Search of Excellence* (Peters and Waterman, 1982), and the British study *The Winning Streak* (Goldsmith and Clutterbuck, 1984). Despite some interesting differences between the two, successful companies emerged as those with a *strong, distinctive culture*, represented by the top management. They were firmly based in products and services in which they had a widely recognized competence, and which the managers knew how to manage. And they all had a distinctive ability to do a number of simple things well. But many of the simple things pulled in different directions and had to be skilfully balanced.

From the descriptions given in both books, it is clear that successful companies have dominant cultures with a strong and continuing thrust towards development – particularly to do things *better than others*. They succeed in countering their own tendencies to fragmentation by a great variety of devices: early fostering of general managers; high visibility of top managers and their priorities; internal promotion; continuing attempts to work with their members on the basis of mutual advantage; strong emphasis on informal communication, semi-autonomous business units, and careers open to the available talent.

One might wonder what semi-autonomous business units are doing in a list of ways of countering fragmentation: it is the *fragmentation of learning and commitment* that is of concern here, and small business units, with a close association of purpose and performance within the working group, come very close to providing a natural flow of learning from business experience. Many of these ways of countering fragmentation are open only to top management, and not the whole of top management at that. In order to effect the kinds of changes in structures and systems that many of the successful companies display, one would need a substantial mandate for reorganization. But this is only because we are seeking a solution to fragmentation on an organizational scale. If we reduce the scale, it is possible to see possibilities for bringing the key phases of the learning spiral energetically together on *any* scale of human activity. For example, the release of energies and creativity in those who choose to leave formal employment in order to start their own business is striking, yet commonplace. And within the organization, the current emphasis on self-development programmes enables individuals to look carefully at their own jobs in order to find opportunities for 'negotiated change' in line with their under-used skills and interests. It is perhaps not surprising that many of these programmes focus on the same issues as sophisticated studies of corporate strategy: identifying one's strengths and weaknesses in relation to external opportunities and threats; mobilizing one's resources; setting priorities; and developing the capability of continuous learning from experience.

It seems to me, then, that all the ways of countering the deep-seated drive to organizational fragmentation link up with one key theme. The task is to turn as much work as possible into *development work*, without seriously unbalancing the organization and wasting resources. It is worth recalling at this point, that I have not been arguing for the 'direct-action' approach, though that has an intuitive appeal to most of us, with its sense of energy and commitment. The whole argument has been for opportunities for us to move purposefully through the *whole learning spiral*, with our own purposes providing the energies.

The learning spiral, seen as a whole, gives due place to planning and monitoring and review – all of them highly conscious, deliberate, responsible activities. The planning of development work must take into account its effect on other work; if this is not picked up in the planning phase of the learning spiral, it should be evident at the monitoring or review phases. Those development activities that incur avoidable costs or unbalance the system of which they are a part must be carefully checked against their initial purpose. Was the purpose over-ambitious, or naive? Since the purpose itself is part of a set of wider purposes, it can itself become the *focus of learning*. In fact, we all too often take our purposes for granted, and doggedly keep them uncritically fixed, while we continually fail to produce the performances that would adequately express them, or achieve them. If we are committed to continuing learning, we need to keep our purposes *under continuing review*. In this way, as we change and the world changes around us, we can relate them to more comprehensive and coherent purposes: a sure sign of maturity. I know that it can sound rather odd and confusing to talk about 'learning to learn'. But we can easily recognize that one of our purposes can be to *manage our own learning*: to become aware of how we are currently learning, and to find ways of improving it. If we do not manage ourselves, we will find no lack of other people willing and eager to manage us, to their own advantage, and often at our expense.

Not all development work has to be cast in the form of a project (though there is nothing to stop us seeing our own learning activities as personal projects: it sharpens the mind). Most enterprises, however enterprising, use the term 'project' rather sparingly, to describe major initiatives or 'one-offs'. And yet every really successful organization is full to bursting with development work, because people have become members of a culture which places great emphasis on doing things well, and then doing them better.

To return to the theme of my chapter: if we want to get the learning spiral to work, we must treat it consistently as a *development spiral* focusing on the endless opportunities for development work – from the smallest improvement in working practices or product quality to the most cosmic 'great society' that our collective imaginations and skills can devise. In development work, small or large, the divided activities of work and learning, purpose and performance, long separated by conventional forms of organization, come together in a continuing process of *changing for the better.*

REFERENCES

Goldsmith, W. and Clutterbuck, D. (1984) *The Winning Streak* (London: Weidenfeld & Nicolson).

Honey, P. and Mumford, A. (1992) *The Manual of Learning Styles*, 3rd edn (London: Honey).

Juch, A. H. (1983) *Personal Development* (Chichester: John Wiley).

Kolb, D. A. *et al.* (1979) *Organizational Psychology*, 3rd edn (Englewood Cliffs, N.J.: Prentice-Hall).

Peters, T. J. and Waterman, R. H. (1982) *In Search of Excellence* (New York: Harper & Row).

Revans, R. W. (1983) *The ABC of Action Learning*, 2nd edn (Bromley: Chartwell-Bratt).

10 Management Learning Contracts

George Boak

The aim of management training and development is to help individuals to improve their performance as managers. The kind of help each manager needs is particular to their individual abilities and circumstances, and it is important for them to be able to apply any ideas they acquire or skills they develop.

These simple facts can cause problems for management trainers. Trainers from the Northern Regional Management Centre (NRMC) have, since 1983, used Management Learning Contracts (MLCs) to help a wide variety of managers from different organizations. A development of Action Learning (Revans, 1980) and Learning Contracts (Knowles, 1975), MLCs represent a flexible, focused and effective approach to management development (Boak, 1990).

This chapter introduces the reader to MLCs by summarizing key points and principles about their use, and by presenting some examples of practice.

WHAT IS A MANAGEMENT LEARNING CONTRACT?

The definition of the MLC is that it is a formal agreement between a learner/manager and a trainer or learner's boss about what the manager will learn and how that learning will be demonstrated. The agreement also specifies an action plan and the resources that will be needed. The agreement is formal in that the terms are set down in writing and the document is signed.

The subject of the MLC is a matter of individual choice. Ideally it will be a skill the manager wishes to develop to improve his or her job performance. The degree of development – which is defined in the MLC – will depend in part on the time the manager can invest in learning, and the timescale of the contract.

At NRMC we have used MLCs with managers from a wide range of organizations, on programmes leading to qualifications and also on programmes purely for management development. Many diverse learning needs have been satisfied by the MLC approach. A brief survey of the main broad areas of learning would include: finance skills and techniques; information technology; interpersonal skills – including interviewing, counselling, training, chairing meetings, negotiating and persuading, making presentations, delegating; self-management skills – including time and stress management; and others – including how to apply particular organizational systems, how to comply with legislation, how to acquire a working knowledge of a foreign language, and so on.

Box 1   Contents

The MLCs used at NRMC have the following headings:

GOAL	the broad area of the contact, e.g. Time Management Interviewing
LEARNING OBJECTIVES	a more specific description of the knowledge the learner will acquire and the skills they will develop
ACTION PLAN	what the learner will do to achieve the above objectives
RESOURCES	a specification of the time, help, opportunities and other resources they will need to meet the objectives
ASSESSMENT MEASURES	what the learner will produce or demonstrate at the end of the MLC to show they have met the objectives.

For short contracts, all the information may be set out on one side of A4. For longer and more involved contracts, for example at MBA level, the proposal may cover ten pages or more.

The MLC has obvious advantages:

Flexibility: it can be used to address any learning area, to suit the needs and abilities of the learner.

Participation: the learner/manager can take the lead role in designing the MLC. This has a tremendous potential effect on motivation. Where appropriate, the line manager of the learner can also be closely involved in discussing and designing the contract, and this may be of great practical value.

Relevance: real job issues can be the focus of the MLC. The flexible and participative nature of MLCs tailor them to each individual situation.

Structure: the detailed and formal nature of the agreement can provide a firm structure to support each individual contract.

These benefits accrue when each of the parties to the contract plays their proper part: the learner/manager must be prepared to learn to identify areas for development and to see the contract through; the trainer must be prepared to listen and to help the learner/manager define their aims: to suggest effective approaches and sometimes to provide necessary resources; and the organization – represented by the learner's line manager – must be prepared to allow some time to be given to learning in the short term, in the expectation of improved performance in the longer term.

Where advice, time and other resources are made available, the value of the MLC can be enhanced.

BASIC PRINCIPLES

The MLC approach is founded on certain basic principles of learning and development, of which the Learning Cycle, the principle of Staged Improvement, and Learner Ownership are the most important.

The Learning Cycle

The Learning Cycle is a framework for explaining how people develop skills, and in particular the different types of activity they need to undertake in order to be effective learners. The four stages (Figure 10.1) of the Learning Cycle are Planning, Action, Reflection and Theory (Honey and Mumford, 1992). To develop any skill, a learner must undertake each of these activities, perhaps on several occasions.

Suppose I wish to learn how to construct a profit and loss account. I may start with *Theory*, by reading about how such accounts should be constructed. I then think of my own requirements, and begin *Planning* by selecting the relevant parts of the theory and setting myself some targets. I then attempt to set out an account for my company – the *Action* stage of the cycle. And then I should *Reflect* and evaluate how well I have done: which parts have I done correctly, where do I still need to learn? And then I may go through the cycle again. It may take many circuits before I am as proficient as I would like to be be.

This cycle of activities would apply whatever the skill I am trying to learn.

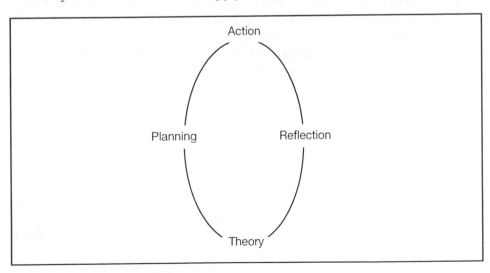

Figure 10.1   A learning cycle

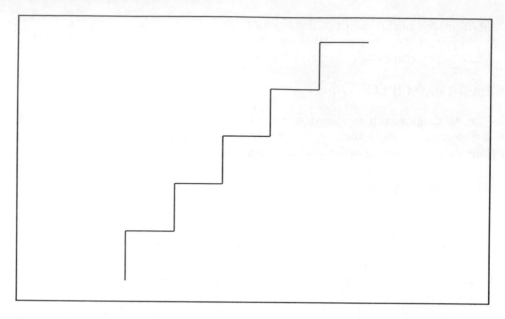

Figure 10.2   Learning stages

The MLC makes explicit use of the stages of the cycle, setting clear targets for development, identifying relevant theory to be consulted, planning for the manager to take action in the workplace, and providing a review and evaluation of learning.

Staged Improvement

An equally important principle is that learning takes place in stages (Figure 10.2). As a newcomer to management accounts, for example, I am unlikely to become an expert in a short period of time. But I can improve on my previous level of ability – I can understand more of the accounts, if not all of them. The MLC will recognize this by taking as its starting point the learner's initial level of ability, and seeking to agree a target for development that is realistic given the time and other resources available.

Learner Ownership

A third important principle concerning the use of MLCs is that the learner must own the contract. Ownership is most likely to bring the motivation necessary to achieve the MLC's objectives. Learners who have chosen their own contract objectives, who have made a strong contribution to the design of the action plan, and who have participated in agreeing the assessment measures, are likely to feel that they own the MLC. Learners who have been told what their contract should be about – whether by their boss or by the trainer – are likely to feel that the contract belongs to someone else. Only very

---

Box 2   Ownership

Line managers are often tempted to see the MLC as an opportunity to make the learner address an aspect of their behaviour which is seen by the line manager to be a problem. In the experience of NRMC these MLCs are only effective if the learner:

- *Accepts there is a problem:* in other words, agrees that some part of his/her job performance is not up to standard

- *Believes something can be done about it:* in other words, does not accept the present level of performance as inevitable or unchangeable

- *Is prepared to do something about it:* sees the area as a priority and is willing to concentrate on it.

If any of these conditions does not apply, learning – and change – are very unlikely to take place.

---

rarely does this imposed form of contract lead to positive results. (See page 148 for further discussion of this.)

PREPARATION

The effectiveness of the MLC approach depends to a large extent on what preparation takes place before the parties meet to negotiate the contract. This necessary preparation is of two kinds: Priming and Needs Analysis.

Priming

Participants new to the process need to be briefed, or primed. This role generally falls to the trainer. Priming may be broken down into three separate, but related, parts:

Explaining what an MLC is and why it is being used

An explanation will include being explicit about the advantages of MLCs, and explaining the basic principles of the Learning Cycle and Staged Improvement. These explanations contribute to the second part.

Building confidence in the MLC approach

It is essential to gain the trust of the learner/manager in the MLC as a reliable vehicle for development. Such confidence-building techniques include describing the range of situations where MLCs have been used successfully. The trainer should demonstrate competence and confidence in the process.

Making clear what the learner is expected to do

The trainer must make clear what specific actions the learner/manager is   *143* asked to undertake. For example, to select a learning area by a specific date; to meet with a trainer at an appointed time; to make a specified amount of time available to work on the MLC and so on. The clarity of these requirements helps create a supportive structure within which the individual manager can feel more comfortable in exercising the freedom of choice available in the MLC.

Box 3 Rules

Clear rules in some areas provide the necessary support for learners to exercise freedom of choice in others. As an illustration, the rules of MLCs on the Certificate in Management Studies programme at NRMC are:

1. The MLC must be about some aspect of management. This is very broad, but rules out the proposals by engineers to learn more about some aspect of engineering, and librarians to learn more about libraries.

2. It must be a Learning Contract. It involves learning and development.

3. It must be a live proposal. It is not a summary, after the event, of learning objectives already achieved. It is establishing a target one hopes to achieve.

4. The initiative in establishing the goal and the objectives of the MLC rests with the programme Participant.

5. The MLC is agreed by the Participant, Trainer and a representative of the Participant's employer – usually the line manager – and assessed by them.

6. At least one of the MLCs (out of three) must be about some aspect of interpersonal skills. This is a good rule, requiring some self-examination and preventing a simple chase of techniques or knowledge.

7. THE MLC should take about 40 hours to complete over a six- to eight-week

---

Needs Analysis

It is important that the learner/manager undertakes some serious reflection on what skills he or she wishes to develop. This informs their choice of MLC and may increase their commitment to it.

This individual needs analysis can be assisted by: structured feedback from colleagues; self-analysis questionnaires; models of good practice; or providing a framework for self-evaluation.

Whatever system of needs analysis is used should be guided by the criteria of accuracy, acceptability and economy.

Accuracy should go without saying. There is little point in a learner/manager investing time and effort in developing a skill they already possess in abundance, particularly if they have shortcomings in other areas.

It is important not to overlook acceptability in the pursuit of accuracy. If the learner/manager does not accept the diagnosis, they will not take the medicine – that is, they will not accept ownership of the MLC. Self-analysis questionnaires with sophisticated coding systems run the risk of producing prescriptions the learner will not swallow. Questionnaires completed by colleagues can all too easily be discounted.

The economics of the needs analysis system can be overlooked in a theoretical discussion of possible methods, but economic considerations will influence, if not actually dominate, what measures are used. The most thorough form of needs analysis – shadowing by a trained consultant, accompanied by interviews – is obviously very expensive. Assessment centres and sophisticated self-analysis exercises coded by professionals – forms of needs analysis that are likely to provoke serious reflection – are also expensive. Good results can be obtained, however, simply by providing a structure within which the learner/manager can discuss their profile of strengths and weaknesses with colleagues.

For example, learners may be required to use a particular self-analysis questionnaire and to discuss the results with their line manager. If the line manager is new to this process, then some form of briefing for them is very desirable.

Box 4   Second options

One large company includes in the first stage of its development programme for Junior managers a morning when the learner/manager uses the Woodcock and Francis (1975) Blockages Questionnaire and his/her line manager also fills in the Questionnaire as if for the learner.

They then spend time together discussing similarities and differences in the profiles they produce, and are encouraged to make some decisions about development priorities.

Managers have included the use of self-analysis questionnaires in their MLC activity on a number of occasions. The most frequent use has been of the Honey and Mumford (1992) Learning Styles. The Learner answers on a self-analysis basis: he/she asks others to answer as if for his/her preferences and typical approaches. The difference can reveal self-delusions or inadequate communication.

NEGOTIATION

Reaching an agreement on the format of a simple MLC may take less than an hour. For more complex MLCs, several stages of agreement may be necessary, and the dialogue may extend over several weeks.

In either case, the aim of the trainer in negotiating an MLC is to produce a contract that is realistic, that is precise and clear, and that is owned by the learner.

First and foremost, of course, it should be a learning contract. The potential for combining work activities with relevant learning is a potent attraction of the MLC approach, but the danger is that work pressures will prove stronger than development motives, and the result will be not an MLC, but a project.

Projects and MLCs

Because MLCs involve action in the workplace to improve performance they are often confused with projects.

Projects are essentially about changing (or more often analysing) the practices of the organization. They can be about evaluating existing practices, creating new systems, proposing new procedures. They can be about developing teams and training (or more often informing) individuals. They can be about (quite simply) achieving results in the short term. They usually involve using management skills – particularly analytical, presentational and persuasive skills. Unlike MLCs, they are rarely about developing skills. (And even on those rare occasions they are never *explicitly* about developing skills.)

Managers often propose project goals rather than learning objectives. It is easy to see why: the manager's most pressing need may be to deal with the immediate problem, to produce the short-term result. And projects have a value: it is a manager's job to achieve results. Projects are usually also easier to understand and to describe. Trainers who negotiate MLCs will be offered many project proposals along the way.

MLCs can have a more enduring value for the individual and the organization, however, by helping the individual to develop transferable skills that will produce results over and over again in the future.

We now return to the three main aims of an MLC.

Box 5   The pure project

For example, Mark presented the following proposal as his learning objectives:

1. To produce a manual of services provided by the Manpower Planning Section.

2. To improve understanding, by other departments, of the role of the Manpower Planning Section.

The focus in the first objective is an activity and producing an artefact; in the second case the focus is on the behaviour of others. The underlying knowledge and skills Mark was using (and possible developing) could be described as the ability to write, structure and present an appealing manual or the ability to relate what the Manpower Planning Section could provide to what the other departments might need.

Realistic

A realistic contract is one where the objectives and the assessments are set at the right level. It takes into account the learner's level of ability at the beginning of the MLC, the amount of time and other resources available, and then sets targets that the learner/manager may reasonably meet. Part of the trainer's role is often to establish these key factors with the learner.

Learners are often unrealistic about how much can be achieved, and they may volunteer unreachable targets. The trainer's role at this point is to remind them of the principle of Staged Improvement, and to suggest setting an intermediate target.

Even more often the learner/manager makes assumptions about the availability of resources, and the proposed contract depends upon something outside the control of either learner or the trainer, which neither of them have thoroughly investigated. For example, such dependencies may be:

- the manager in another department who is expected to give the learner some information which is crucial to the completion of the MLC
- the computer equipment, which is expected to be installed and available next week
- the series of meetings where the learner/manager will practise being assertive.

Naturally, most MLCs will depend on resources of various kinds – it may be the assistance of others, or suitable equipment, or books and training courses, or opportunities for practice. Most are based on assumptions about how much of the manager's own time will be invested in the contract. The availability of these resources should all be checked before the MLC is agreed – or as soon as possible after agreement. Where access to a resource appears doubtful, the parties should discuss contingency plans.

Of course, unexpected changes in circumstances can render null and void even a carefully researched MLC. Many difficulties can be anticipated, however, and it is the trainer's job to steer the MLC round them.

Precise and clear

The MLC should be expressed in writing, in a form of words that is clear to all the parties, and that accurately expresses what the learner intends to achieve.

With MLCs of the type used at NRMC, with a Goal Statement, Learning Objectives and Assessment Measures, there are levels of gradually increasing precision and clarity. The Goal Statement may be broad, the Learning Objectives should be less so, and the Assessment Measures should be very precise. The Action Plan and the Resources statements provide a cross-check on the MLC, and they should spell out what the individual will do as part of the contract.

It is particularly important for the action plan, the statement of resources and the assessment measures to be precise and clear. For example, if the learner/manager proposes to 'read books on time management', the trainer should clarify which books (and even which parts of those books). If the proposal is to 'interview other managers', the trainer should clarify how many other managers will be interviewed. Where the learner proposes to demonstrate their development in part by producing 'a report', the trainer should clarify what the report will contain. These clarifications should be   *147* written into the contract, as a guide and reminder to all the parties.

Even where the contract proposal does not contain such obviously grey areas, it is sound practice to go over what has been written, to question and explain, and make sure the same words mean the same thing to different people.

Box 6   Precision

It is important to establish specific targets as a means of motivating and measuring learners who are using MLCs.

One contract had as an activity:

● To record a series of time logs

which was to be carried forward into assessment as:

● Comparison of daily time logs.

Experience shows that it is essential to make a more precise statement at this point, and to specify the number of days the learner will log. Not only does this need to be precise, but also realistic: learners/managers who propose to keep detailed daily logs for every day of the next six weeks must gently be dissuaded from doing so in most cases. The task is unrealistic. On the third day they will give up.

The point and purpose of the comparison should also be defined: what was it designed to reveal?

The written word of the MLC, quite apart from its value in legislating for matters of assessment, can crystallize and target certain actions and results, and can act in natural and positive ways on the learner's motivation to succeed.

Ownership

It is a fundamental principle of the MLC approach that the learner should own the contract.

Ownership of the MLC gives rise to commitment to seeing it through, overcoming obstacles and achieving its targets.

Ownership means that the learning area has originated with the learner and that he or she has set out, or participated in setting out, the written contract.

Throughout the process of negotiating the MLC, the learner should initiate proposals, exercise choice between alternatives and accept or reject proposals from others. Ownership means that the learner is in control of the MLC.

It is not always easy to get the learner/manager to take control. Much of the Priming process we discussed above is in order to prepare the learner for this leading role in the MLC process. But even where the learner accepts this role, there is still the danger that control can pass to another person.

The learner's boss – if they are involved in the MLC – may take control away from the learner. This may be because the boss may feel more comfortable in a telling/directing role, or because he or she is convinced they know best what the learner needs to develop, or because they have a special pet project they want the learner to complete, or out of frustration with the learner's reluctance to take the initiative.

The trainer, too, may take control for a number of reasons: through inexperience, because the trainer feels more comfortable in a directive role, through frustration with the learner's apparent inability to make a decision, or through wanting to define the 'best' contract.

Obviously, there can be a conflict between agreeing an MLC that is realistic, precise and clear and is also owned by the learner. If the learner's proposal is unrealistic, vague and unclear, then the trainer should intervene. Part of the trainer's difficulty lies in finding a way of intervening without taking control away from the learner.

For the most part this means asking questions and posing alternatives, rather than directing the learner down a particular path.

THE FIRST PROPOSAL

The learner/manager should take the initiative in defining the MLC, and so the normal pattern of a negotiation should be that – after some briefing and some form of needs analysis – the learner presents the first proposal to the trainer.

Proposals are likely to range from the detailed and specific plan which has been developed as far as explicit assessment measures, to the vague suggestion that the learner/manager wants to learn 'something about interviewing'. Different degrees of commitment may also be very evident at this stage.

Proposals are also likely to fall into one of a number of pure types, and it is helpful for the trainer to recognize these types and to know generally how best to respond to the proposal.

Project proposals

We have already contrasted projects and MLCs, but even with careful briefing some managers will propose project goals rather than learning objectives.

The trainer's role is to point out the difference between a project and an MLC and to remind the learner/manager of their briefing on this point. Useful questions are: 'What are you going to learn?' and 'What will you be able to do better at the end of the contract?'

Where a development programme contains a number of MLCs it is best to be firm and to ensure that the first MLC is a true MLC and not a project.

The broad skills collection

This type of proposal is often based on the series of activities needed to complete a project. For example, the manager who has been given the task of leading a project group to analyse a departmental procedure and to produce a report for senior management may propose a list of broad skills as 'learning objectives', such as:

149

- Analytical skills
- Chairing meetings
- Persuasion skills
- Report-writing

All of these are very broad skill areas. Any one of them could be an MLC Goal. Learning objectives should be more precise and clear and spell out which analytical skills, which aspects of chairing meetings, and so on, will be developed.

Faced with this proposal, the trainer should point out that it is very broad and needs to be defined more specifically. Which of the proposed areas for development is the most important to the learner? Perhaps the MLC could be re-written to focus on that one area?

A common, and related, type is the simple Broad Skill proposal. Here the learner/manager offers a broad skill as a learning objective – for example, 'Interviewing', 'Time Management' or 'Delegation'.

The role of the trainer then becomes one of helping the learner express the aspects of that broad area they most want to develop. One way forward is to encourage learners to formulate their own models of effective practice – which are influenced, but not controlled, by reading or ideas provided by the trainer.

Box 7 Interviewing skills

In some cases, learning about the skill area and learning where one needs to develop can form a useful part of an MLC. For example, Gillian was a junior manager who expected to be involved in recruitment interviewing in the near future. Her learning objectives were:

1. A clear understanding of the procedures to be followed in recruiting a new member of staff to the organization.

2. An understanding of the skills necessary to be an effective interviewer.

3. Recognition of my own strengths and weaknesses in using these skills.

4. Development (through practice) against priority areas of weakness.

The MLC involved Gillian setting out the required skills in a clear grid and seeking feedback from others on her relative ability in each area. This can be an effective general approach to a Broad Skill proposal, which helps the manager to focus their efforts on areas of real need.

Knowledge proposals

Some learner/managers – particularly low Activists – may present proposals that are exclusively about gathering information or knowledge. This may be theoretical knowledge – for example, to understand the principles of chairing a meeting – or practical and specific information – for example, learning the procedure for making capital expenditure proposals within the manager's company.

Knowledge proposals make such limited use of the potential of MLCs for management development that the general approach at NRMC has been to encourage the learner/manager to expand them.

All skills have a knowledge component, and the trainer can suggest that the MLC incorporates other parts of the Learning Cycle. If the learner proposes to research ideas of good practice, can they audit themselves (reflection) against what they discover? Can they then put into practice (action) a plan for development (planning) in the appropriate areas? If they are researching a procedure, can they then go ahead and apply it? Or can they evaluate the skills they will need to apply it and identify areas for personal development?

Skills and techniques proposals

There is no hard and fast line between skills and techniques, although at their extremes they are very different. Typically, techniques require the learner to follow clear, prescribed rules – some of which may lead to counter-intuitive behaviour. Skills may include the selective deployment of techniques.

We have already discussed the problematic Broad Skills proposal. Some managers – particularly on their second or third MLCs – will produce thoughtful, realistic and acceptable proposals to develop skills they have identified and defined with a degree of care. The trainer's role in these cases may be little more than one of suggesting minor amendments and ensuring clarity.

One question that should always be raised with a skills or a techniques proposal is why the learner wishes to develop in this area. Often the answers are straightforward and acceptable. Sometimes, however, they lead to an entirely different MLC (see Box 8).

One other aspect for negotiation may be the specific/generic dimension of development.

A learner/manager may be concerned to improve his or her own ability to

---

Box 8   The wrong solution

Mike wanted to improve his performance in meetings. Recently he had been embarrassed on more than one occasion in meetings with clients. He presented his contract as one which focused on better preparation for these meetings, and an improvement in his abilities to make formal presentations to customers.

Fortunately, discussion with his line manager before the MLC began cast doubt on the benefit of these measures. It was indicated that some specific aspects of presentation skills could be improved upon, but that another dimension of the problem concerned self-confidence in discussing matters with customers and more senior managers. It was decided to focus the MLC on Mike's feelings, through a logging process, and on developing 'scripts' to handle situations he found difficult – which meant changing some of the sentence structures he commonly used.

Preparation and formal presentation skills did not appear in the MLC. They were actually low priority – or no priority – learning areas.

lead a particular team, or to motivate an individual member of staff. The trainer can sometimes help the development of a more generic, transferable skill by encouraging the manager to think more broadly – for example, by learning a general model of leadership, or motivation, and by considering what contingencies apply in their particular situation. This may be a more valuable MLC for the individual and the organization.

The problem-based proposal

The final recognizable type of proposal is where the learner/manager describes a situation they would like to handle better, and admits that they don't know what specific skills are needed to do this.

Formulating the MLC can prove hard work for the conscientious trainer and the learner, but the benefits can be well worth the effort.

Generally, the trainer should spend some time questioning the manager to try to arrive at an accurate assessment of the nature of the problem: beware of the temptation to jump to the first half-likely conclusion! A good use for the MLC is for the learner/manager to spend time analysing the problem and coming to a clear understanding about what skills need to be developed – or the actual MLC can be delayed until such an analysis has taken place.

THE BALANCED RESPONSE

So far we have seen that a number of the proposals for an MLC put forward by learners may be in some degree problematic, and that some interventions from the trainer in response to these problems may be necessary. By questioning, suggesting, summarizing and occasionally telling, the trainer must balance the objective of achieving a contract that is technically perfect in its clarity and realism with the objective of agreeing a contract that the learner owns.

CONTRACTUAL RELATIONS

We have given a leading role – or at least a strong supporting role – to the trainer in what we have discussed so far. Of course, there is no reason at all why a learner should not set out their own learning objectives and assessment measures, establish their own action plan and explore their own resources, and then take action on their own to develop their knowledge and skills. People do this every day.

As it has been defined in this chapter, however, the MLC approach involves at least one other person in addition to the learner/manager, to discuss and agree the contract. This is one of the strengths of the MLC concept, because it helps learners/managers to structure and refine their thinking about what they want to learn (and why). The other party may also be able to suggest approaches and resources the learner might use. The learner/manager may emerge from the discussion with a clearer and more realistic plan. There should also be a deadline date, at which point the contract will be assessed. Realistic deadlines generally improve learning.

So far, we have spoken of the second party to the contract as a 'trainer'. He or she might be a professional management trainer from the organization's training department, or from an outside organization. As such, he/she may bring to the contract: a certain degree of experience of helping managers to develop; experience and expertise in the business of negotiating contracts; and a degree of detachment – and perhaps perspective – to the learner's aims and problems.

Alternatively, this role might be taken by the learner's immediate manager or boss. There are several advantages in this. The boss is perhaps more likely than a trainer to have an accurate insight into the learner's strengths and weaknesses, through frequent contact at work. The boss may also have a better idea of the demands of the job and the opportunities for development within the job. The boss may be able to give the learner/manager access to particular learning opportunities at work, for example by delegating appropriate challenging tasks, and may also be a natural witness of the learner/manager's performance and therefore be in an ideal position to give feedback.

The drawbacks to the boss playing this role may be that he/she is unable to bring expert advice to the contract and may be unable to offer the perspective that an outside party could provide. There may also be areas where the learner/manager feels unable to disclose weaknesses to the boss and may be more inclined to do so with an outside trainer. These advantages and disadvantages can be weighed up in each case.

Thoughtful and caring bosses can make good use of MLCs to clarify coaching and development targets for their staff. In larger organizations, training staff and training materials may be used as resources to support an MLC agreed between the learner and the boss.

Where organizations have appraisal systems, managers are usually required to discuss areas for development with their staff. In this context, MLCs can help to establish clear and realistic action plans for individual learner/managers. The use of formal MLCs (covering the points set out in Box 1) has much to recommend it in this situation, because it asks for explicit learning objectives and performance outcomes. Without this there can be a danger that development needs are addressed in terms of activities alone (for example, attending courses, gaining experience in new tasks and so on) without thinking clearly about what the activities are designed to achieve.

Perhaps an ideal partnership is for the learner, the immediate manager and a trainer to negotiate the MLC together. The learner can then benefit from the strengths that each of the other two parties brings to the table, and can draw on them for ongoing support of different kinds throughout the contract.

ASSESSMENT

Specifying assessment measures and carrying out some form of assessment *153* are integral parts of the MLC concept.

Assessment enables progress to be evaluated and success to be recognized and rewarded. It enhances motivation and sharpens the focus of the contract. The assessment measures for each MLC are negotiated and agreed in much the same way as the other components of the MLC, although in this area the trainer often has scope and legitimate cause to be a little more directive.

There are three main reasons why this should be so:

1. The assessment measures set the specific target for the MLC. A contract that is broad, vague or unrealistic in its goal or learning objectives can still be saved by clear and realistic assessment statements.
2. Learners often have difficulty in proposing effective assessment measures, and so are more likely to look to the trainer for advice than in any other stage of agreeing the MLC.
3. The assessment measures should be the last part of the contract to be agreed. By the time this point in the negotiation is reached, the learner/manager should feel considerable ownership of the MLC, and the careful trainer can exert influence without hijacking the contract.

The actual methods of assessment will depend on the particular MLC and also the context in which it is undertaken. There are, of course, many difficulties and problems in assessing managerial skills. This is an area which has attracted much lively debate in recent times with the advent of National Vocational Qualifications in Management (see, for example, Eraut and Cole, 1993; Mitchell and Sturton, 1993; Mullin, 1993; Wills, 1993). The assessment of MLCs raises similar issues of the validity, authenticity and sufficiency of evidence. In this short chapter I will do no more than note that the main methods of assessment are: demonstration of the skill, written report, witness statements and feedback, products and outcomes, and interviews (Boak 1990).

REVIEW

The MLC can be a very effective vehicle for helping managers develop skills. As we have seen, MLCs are very flexible and can be made relevant to any learning need; they enable managers to play a major role in designing their own development programme, and yet they provide a firm supportive structure.

To be effective, however, MLCs rely on skilled application. They are not a procedural device that can be implemented without thought or care. Much depends on the way in which the learner is prepared for using MLCs and on the way in which each contract is agreed. With a little practice and a little thought, most trainers and line managers can learn how to use MLCs effectively, and make the most of the benefits that are potential in the approach.

REFERENCES

Boak, George (1990) *Developing Managerial Competences: the Management Learning Contract Approach* (London: Pitman).

Eraut, Michael and Cole, Gerald (1993) 'Assessment of competence in higher level occupations', *Competence and Assessment* Issue 21, Training Enterprise and Education Division, Moorfoot, Sheffield.

Honey, Peter and Mumford, Alan (1992) *The Manual of Learning Styles*, 3rd edn (London: Honey).

Knowles, Malcolm (1975) *Self-Directed Learning* (Chicago: Follett).

Mitchell, Lindsay and Sturton, Jackie (1993) 'Doing to or working with? The candidate's role in assessment', *Competence and Assessment* Issue 21, Training Enterprise and Education Division, Moorfoot, Sheffield.

Mullin, Roger (1993) 'The competence debate', *Training and Development* (UK), (May).

Revans, R. W. (1980) *Action Learning* (London: Blond and Briggs).

Wills, Stefan (1993) 'MCI and the competency movement', *Journal of European Industrial Training*, Vol 17, No 1.

Woodcock, M. and Francis, D. (1975) *50 Activities for Self-Development* (Aldershot: Gower).

1 1 Mentoring and coaching

David Clutterbuck and Bernard Wynne

Mentoring and coaching are both techniques used by managers and organizations to enable employees to grow to their full potential. In describing either technique it is important to understand that the use of the term 'enable employees to grow' is very much a key to what the techniques are and how they are used. Both are driven by the active participation of the trainee and cannot be effective if they are primarily manager-driven.

The notion of the passive learner receiving an input of knowledge from an instructor is one which was acceptable even in the recent past – indeed, this still forms the bulk of training in many organizations.

Mentoring and coaching, on the other hand, represent an increasing trend towards helping the individual take charge of his or her own learning: the primary driver of the acquisition of knowledge and skill becomes the employee; the coach or mentor is available to give guidance, insight and encouragement in the learning process. The nature of various types of learning relationships can be seen in Figure 11.1.

Educationalists sometimes comment that this model unjustifiably downgrades the role and skills of a teacher. We would argue, however, that good teachers – like good managers – are able to play all these roles as circumstances require.

Mentoring and coaching, then, can work as effective techniques for developing people only with their active participation. In addition, while both are effective techniques for improving job performance in the short term, they are most effective when they take account also of some of the long-term development needs of the individual.

MENTORING AND COACHING: WHAT IS THE DIFFERENCE?

Coaching is a management skill which can be practised by all managers in

EXPLICIT	TEACHER	PUPIL	TELL	DISTANT RELATIONSHIP
	TUTOR	STUDENT	SHOW	
	COACH	LEARNER	DISCUSS/SHOW	
	MENTOR	COLLEAGUE	STIMULATE	
IMPLICIT				CLOSE RELATIONSHIP

Figure 11.1 How people learn

developing the people in their team. It is, perhaps, best used when it is applied to the development of one explicit skill at a time. For example, coaching to develop an individual's skills in customer handling will be more effective when kept separate from coaching an individual in improving his or her skills in using technology.

The ability to act as an effective coach is one of the key skills in mentoring. Mentoring is a more structured, deeper, more involved relationship, typically outside the normal direct reporting relationship. It is a cluster of skills and roles which relate mainly to the passing on of intuitive skills and knowledge and focuses on either specific or general skills according to the mentee's needs.

WHEN TO MENTOR, WHEN TO COACH

Mentoring is most effective when it is part of a structured approach fully integrated into the organization's process for developing people.

This requires that both mentor and mentee have a clear understanding of their roles. For both parties, guidance and training in how to manage the relationship is usually beneficial. Experience in the USA suggests that over-structured programmes become bureaucratic and lose the spontaneity that characterizes successful relationships. On the other hand, insufficiently structured relationships tend to degenerate into unfocused, pleasant discussions with little developmental value. At a minimum, there should be agreed learning objectives and meetings at regular intervals to review progress and plan the next steps.

Coaching does not have to be part of a structured programme, but the manager – who is concerned to develop people and who has an agenda for their development – will naturally see it as an opportunity for development.

As a very general distinction, mentors tend to focus on the medium- to long-term development needs of individuals in the organization – on future jobs. Immediate line bosses tend to have a stronger emphasis on improving the capability of the employee in the current job – with the increased importance of coaching as a skill.

WHO CAN BE COACHED AND MENTORED?

In practice, coaching and mentoring can be applied to any group of people, or to any specific individuals. For example, the emphasis on mentoring only young graduate recruits in the early 1980s has now spread to encompass high flyers, directors, women managers, women returners, racial minorities and professional groups such as headteachers.

THE SKILLS REQUIRED

The skills required for both mentoring and coaching are to a large extent those of a good manager. If the modern manager is an enabler and developer of people, being effective as a coach requires the manager to enhance those basic skills and to be able to recognize automatically when each is appropriate.

Perhaps the most important skill in coaching is being aware of what it can deliver. We mentioned earlier that the effective manager has an agenda for the development of people. The creation of this agenda is perhaps the main skill required. Part of this agenda is to develop in the individual the desire for, and awareness of, the need for personal growth.

To understand these necessary skills we can look at what good coaches do and, in doing so, we note that they place the individual firmly in control. While the coach is always on hand to support, to guide and offer advice, the coach does not take responsibility for the learning, this must remain with the individual.

The skills required of a coach include:

- Active listening, giving full attention, and banishing any distractions while engaged in the coaching process.
- Reflective listening, 'reflecting' back to the individual what they are doing in order to help the learning. This helps to clear up misunderstanding early, engages people in analysing their own views and ideas in a critical way, and demonstrates the coach giving full attention.
- Drawing out, encouraging the individual to talk about their feelings, ideas and aspirations.
- Recognizing and revealing feelings, identifying the feelings of others and yourself and being able to talk about them. To disclose information about yourself encourages others to share their feelings with you. Making comment specific, giving clear reaction to specific behaviour with sensitivity, in a constructive way, and being non-defensive when receiving feedback about your role as a coach.
- Agreeing goals, making sure that each side of the partnership understands exactly what they have to do.
- Summarizing, concluding all exchanges with a summary to draw together and state for joint agreement action to be undertaken.

```
Listen
See issues from others' viewpoint
Give feedback
Clarify shared understanding
Plan who does what and when
Take action
```

Figure 11.2   The coaching code

All of this can be summarized and stated in the coaching code (Figure 11.2).

WHAT EFFECTIVE MENTORS DO

At its simplest, the mentor is there to help the mentee to learn. Not all the knowledge passed on comes from the mentor's experience – much of the learning takes place by guiding the mentee into learning situations. We can define four key mentoring roles: coach, counsellor, networker, and facilitator.

Coach

The coach helps the manager build understanding of the way formal and informal systems work; helping him/her to gain personal insights; and providing opportunities to learn.

Effective coaches emphasize seeking rather than telling or teaching. The aim is to stimulate the mentee to come to his/her own conclusions; to work through issues together rather than provide ready-made answers. This is particularly important at the level of senior management, where there often is no *right* answer.

The core skills of coaching as applied to mentoring include:

- Suspending judgement
- Putting yourself in the other person's shoes, to understand their problems and perspective
- Working with the mentee to identify weaknesses that need to be tackled
- Providing considered, constructive feedback
- Checking comprehension
- Breaking processes down into steps that can be followed through with the mentee.

Counsellor

Counselling is most commonly seen as dealing with problems. Although the mentoring relationship may discuss problems, its primary focus is opportunities, for both personal development and career progression. The effective counsellor helps the manager work through his/her own ambitions, *159* motives and emotions, as a part of the process of making choices. These choices may be about career direction, how to handle specific work situations, or even about issues unrelated to work.

The core skills of counselling include:

- Keeping one's own counsel (listening more than talking)
- Helping the individual understand his/her own motivations and feelings
- Helping the individual focus on the real problem
- Moving the discussion as rapidly as possible from discussion of the problem to searching for viable alternative solutions.

Networker

In most organizations the informal networks are as important as, and frequently more important than, the formal. The scope of a manager's networks is a major factor in his or her ability to influence events and decisions.

The effective mentor gives the mentee access to parts of all of his/her networks. This can only happen in a relationship of trust, however, for the mentor will normally be concerned to protect the integrity of his/her network – and will naturally be careful not to allow relationships with key individuals to be damaged by insensitive behaviour on the part of the mentee.

The key benefits of networks are:

- To acquire resources or influence
- To acquire information (e.g. to make informed decisions or to avoid problems)
- To save time, by getting things done through informal rather than formal routes.

The key roles for a mentor here include:

- Helping the mentee get to know relevant parts of your network
- Helping the mentee map and make better use of his/her existing networks
- Helping the mentee expand his/her own networks.

Facilitator

Facilitation is the process of helping to make things happen. The mentor uses his/her influence with other people – often part of his/her network – to open doors or to help the mentee achieve work goals.

Good facilitators in mentoring are able to:

- Recognize and explain clearly what needs to be done and why
- Assess barriers to achieving goals, and suggest ways round them
- Understand and explain to the mentee the politics behind operational problems or discussions, which get in the way of achieving goals
- Smooth the path for the mentee (e.g. by dropping positive hints in the right places when the mentee wants to present a good idea; by trading favours with key people; or by making important introductions).

The danger of facilitating is in going too far to help the mentee. Wherever possible, the mentor should encourage the mentee to sort out his or her own problems, with advice and guidance. If the mentor sorts out the problems it removes a learning opportunity for the mentee.

HOW MENTORS HELP MENTEES MANAGE THEIR OWN LEARNING

The four roles involve a wide variety of developmental behaviours. Among them:

- *Challenging*: questioning the mentee's assumptions; forcing the mentee to think them through
- *Using personal examples*: drawing parallels with their own experience, e.g. 'When I faced a similar situation, I ...'
- *Guiding*: suggesting where the mentee might look for new knowledge or insights; pointing him/her in the right direction
- *Suggesting*: 'Why don't you try this?'
- *Encouraging*: helping the mentee look back at previous achievements as a motivator for new achievements; generally building confidence
- *Stimulating*: sharing the mentee's enthusiasm and helping direct it where it will achieve greatest impact
- *Confidence-building*: drawing on current projects the mentor is tackling, to illustrate how he or she goes about them – in particular, the thinking process behind the judgements the mentee makes.

ORGANIZATIONAL AND PERSONAL BARRIERS TO MENTORING AND COACHING

The organizational barriers which get in the way of effective mentoring and coaching are those which prevent many progressive changes being introduced. These include: lack of vision; no desire to enable people to achieve their fullest potential; creation of a culture against the development of the level of trust and openness required; lack of resources to enable managers to be trained in mentoring and coaching skills.

The personal barriers include a lack of understanding of mentoring and coaching and the skills that enable it to happen. In some cases there may even *161* be a fear of allowing people to develop in case they eventually bypass the manager.

A pilot programme recently conducted in an international company asked managers participating to identify barriers to coaching. Their response follows. (The company acted on the results of the pilot programme which led to a coaching initiative.)

Barriers to coaching

In the coach

1. Shortage of time.
2. Lack of preparation.
3. Lack of appropriate skills.
4. Lack of interest/commitment.
5. Resistance to change.
6. Cynicism.
7. Lack of information about opportunities, company requirements, and so on.
8. Being subjective/prejudiced.
9. Lack of confidence.
10. System raises expectations for which he/she has no answers.

In the individual

1. Inadequate or inaccurate self-assessment or goal-setting.
2. Lack of confidence/trust/motivation.
3. Fear of exposing weakness, especially related to self-assessment.
4. Lack of information about the company.
5. Time.
6. Fear of reaction of line management.
7. Poor preparation.
8. Resistance to change.
9. Satisfaction in current job.
10. Lack of mobility.

In the climate

1. Lack of action: no visible delivery.
2. Poor communication.
3. Salary policy.
4. A job posting system that is not really open.
5. Coherence/flexibility of all company systems.
6. Management commitment/personalities.
7. Lack of training.
8. Negative networks (e.g. cliques).

9. Lack of feedback.
10. Lack of promotion opportunities/commercial reality.

Overcoming barriers to coaching

We overcome these barriers through the following actions:

Barriers in the coach

- Develop greater understanding and skills
- Demonstrate its importance to the individual, the coach
- Help with time-planning
- Reward good coaches
- Develop personal confidence.

In the individual

- Improve personal development planning process
- Review appraisal, feedback and career planning processes
- Reward performance improvement
- Encourage wider, more demanding job roles
- Demonstrate commitment to developing people.

In the climate

- Communicate the benefits widely
- Improve training for coaching
- Reward effective coaches
- Reward performance improvement
- Encourage a culture where development is seen as the norm
- Develop positive networks.

A fairly similar picture emerges of the barriers to effective mentoring.

Overcoming barriers to mentoring

It is important that both mentor and mentee understand the traits that make a successful relationship. Mentees who gain greatest benefit from their relationships with mentors tend to be people who:

- Demonstrate a great deal of commitment to the process, and particularly to self-learning
- Understand their own responsibilities to the mentor
- Recognize the limitations of the relationship as part of management
  learning.

163

Taking these in turn:

Commitment to the process

Finding the time to devote to the relationship may be as much of a problem for the senior management mentee as for the mentor – indeed, sometimes more so. It often takes a good deal of organizing simply to undertake the formal learning opportunities, and there are always pressures of work. Indeed, the manager in a new job usually needs to spend more time learning about and getting to grips with the job. Time management and delegation skills therefore become important foundations for a successful mentoring relationship. If you, as a mentor, feel your mentee is having problems acquiring such skills you should discuss the matter with him or her.

Demonstrating commitment is also important. In many fruitful mentoring relationships, the discussion at each meeting usually starts with a review of the mentee's successes since the previous meeting.

Key behaviours the mentee should demonstrate include:

- Open-mindedness: being willing to listen and consider
- Seeking opportunities to put new knowledge into practice
- Practising taking different viewpoints and perceptions
- Being honest, especially about strengths and weaknesses.

Responsibilities to the mentor

Although the mentor may be more experienced than the mentee, the essence of the mentoring relationship is *mutuality*. There must be mutual respect and, where possible, mutual learning. At the very least, the mentee should be aware of the need to avoid:

- Intruding too much on the mentor's time – establish early on what calls the mentee would like on your time and what you feel is reasonable
- Disrupting or misusing the mentor's networks
- Breaking the confidentiality of discussions within the relationship
- Asking the mentor to act as a sponsor, except in very special cases
- Using the discussions to explore personal issues – e.g. serious domestic problems – unless the mentor has indicated a willingness to counsel in these circumstances.

Most of these points are common sense and should not really be an issue at senior management level.

Limitations of the relationship

Some mentoring relationships flounder because the mentee expects too much. For example, it may be expected of the mentor to give all the answers to problems, rather than help the mentee work out his or her own answers. Or that the mentor will arrange the next career step, on a patronage basis. Again, at a senior management level, such problems should not normally occur. However, it is useful for both partners to examine periodically whether they are being sufficiently realistic and pragmatic in their expectations.

Maintaining the relationship

The length of time formal mentoring relationships last varies considerably. For young graduate recruits, who have to make a major transition in thinking patterns from the world of academia to the world of work, it is common to maintain the formal relationship for two years or more. Senior managers, however, typically need to absorb a significant amount of intuitive knowledge in a much shorter time. At their level, it is important to become effective in the job as rapidly as possible, not least because they and their colleagues are looking for results.

For these reasons, mentoring relationships at this level tend to involve a relatively short formal element – typically six months. The informal relationship that develops between all successful mentoring pairs therefore emerges much sooner.

The formal relationship usually goes through three stages:

Phase 1: a somewhat wary relationship, where both parties assess the other and attempt to establish mentoring goals. This phase tends to be marked among senior managers by a businesslike approach, where professionalism is of more significance than friendship. The focus at this stage is largely the task.

Phase 2: as enthusiasm for the project grows, some of the professional barriers come down and the two develop a much more collegial relationship. The mentor, too, begins to learn from the association, and the nature of the confidences exchanged becomes much less constrained. The focus now becomes the two individuals.

Phase 3: as the mentee gains from the insights exposed, he or she becomes increasingly confident and competent. The volume of learning decreases from a flood to a trickle. This is the point where the formal part of the relationship should end – to continue may either devalue the relationship or cause resentment among one party or other.

The informal relationship is essentially a maturing process. Friendship remains, as does mutual respect, but the predominant attitude of the mentee towards the mentor is gratitude. Over the following years, the two individuals may form close parts of each other's networks. They may continue, from time to time, to discuss work problems (less on a 'What shall I do?' basis than 'What do you think of the way I am tackling this issue?'). And they may well collaborate in mentoring other managers.

Even though the mentee may eventually overtake the mentor in seniority terms, the informal relationship will normally endure, with the mentor taking pleasure in the progress of someone he or she has helped.

In summary, it can be said that the most important element in overcoming *165* the barriers is to identify them and work at eradicating them.

WHAT'S IN IT FOR ME?

It is clear that mentoring and coaching will only happen if individual managers make it happen. Organizations may initiate schemes and processes to encourage managers to mentor and coach, but unless individual managers recognize the personal gains they will not undertake it. Any scheme is only as good as those responsible for its implementation make it. So what does a manager get out of taking these approaches? We have identified some specific benefits which managers can gain from mentoring and coaching.

Benefits of coaching

- Provides opportunity for training and development relevant to the immediate needs of the job holder
- Provides opportunity for open and honest feedback on performance and development
- Encourages managers to actively plan with individuals their development
- Helps create a learning climate
- Supplements the formal training process in a cost-effective way.

Benefits of mentoring

Effective mentoring programmes benefit everyone involved.
    Within the mentoring relationship, the mentee gains:

- An opportunity to explore his/her own strengths, weaknesses and ambitions in confidence with someone who has 'been there before'
- A source of challenge to his/her assumptions about the job and how it should be done
- Growth in self-confidence and self-awareness
- An informal audience, on whom to try out new ideas and approaches, before presenting them to working colleagues
- The chance to learn from someone else's mistakes
- Insights into the politics and real decision-making processes and structures in an organization – how to get things done
- Faster career progression
- Encouragement in self-development.

Within the mentoring relationship the mentor gains:

- Peer recognition – good people-developers are increasingly highly regarded in the 1990s organization

- Opportunities to learn – whether teachers really learn much from their pupils is doubtful, but most mentors do find the relationship a valuable learning experience
- Talent-spotting – many mentors find these relationships a useful way of acquiring knowledge of the capabilities of potential recruits to their (or other) parts of the organization
- Greater ability to understand and relate to their own direct reports at the mentee's level
- Motivation and job satisfaction – most effective mentors uniformly say that they gain significant self-improvement from the relationship.

There is often a strong mutual benefit, too. Many – perhaps most – successful mentoring relationships result in deep and enduring friendships.

Benefits for the organization

The organization benefits in several ways, too:

- Newly appointed managers become more effective more rapidly
- Communications, especially between different layers and different functions, is improved
- Implementation of equal opportunities policies, in terms of promotion of women or minorities into more senior management jobs, can be boosted by making mentoring available to people from these groups
- Both mentors and mentees become more aware of the need to develop their direct reports
- Being actively involved in developing others acts as an inspiration for more self-learning. It promotes an active involvement in the process of continuous professional and personal development.

SETTING UP A MENTORING PROGRAMME

Our experience suggests that the most successful approaches follow an approach something like the following:

1. *Gain a clear understanding within HR of what mentoring can and can't do.* There will frequently be a requirement to make the case for mentoring to top management or senior line managers, who are distrustful of new ideas from personnel. If appropriate, invite an external expert – a consultant or an HR practitioner from another organization which has previously introduced mentoring, to make a short presentation to the executives.
2. *Be very clear about the target audience.* Schemes that start too large and too general tend to lack credibility. Best results appear to come from piloting with a relatively small, well-defined group – for example, high flyers at specific grades or at a particular point in their careers, graduate

167

recruits, or female managers. Successes with the pilot group will pave the way for extending the approach to other groups.

3. *Prepare the participants to make the most of the relationship.* By participants, we mean not just the mentor and mentee, but the mentee's line manager as well. One of the most common problems with mentoring is that the mentee's line manager is unsupportive, and the main reason for this attitude is that he or she may feel left out and threatened. All three need to understand:

- How the relationship is to be managed
- What the expected outcomes are
- The need to avoid conflict between the mentee's development needs and the line manager's need to get today's work done
- The different development roles of line manager and mentor.

This is where training comes in. The line manager's awareness may be sufficiently handled through discussion with HR and through initial (and in some companies, subsequent regular) meetings with the mentor and mentee. But the mentoring pair need a deeper understanding of how the relationship can be made to work for mutual benefit. Training usually requires one day for mentees, one to one-and-a-half days for mentors (although at very senior level, half a day often has to suffice!).

In particular, the training should cover the establishment of learning objectives and how to work towards achieving them.

4. *Prepare the climate.* Mentoring can easily be seen as elitist, if it is introduced insensitively. We find that everyone in the company – particularly working colleagues of the mentees, who are not assigned mentors – needs to be aware that mentoring is just one development option among many. Encouraging employers to seek informal mentors can also help defuse any resentment.

5. *Provide opportunities for feedback.* Best practice suggests that in a formal programme both mentors and mentees should meet as groups regularly (at least once a year) to review progress and share experiences. These review meetings provide an opportunity to adjust the programme and to assess its impact, both in general and on the individual participants.

FURTHER READING

Clutterbuck, D. (1992), *Everyone Needs a Mentor*, 2nd edn (Wimbledon: Institute of Personnel Management).

Hamilton, R. (1993), *Mentoring*. (Managers Pocket Guides, Industrial Society).

Megginson, D. and Boydell, T. (1984) *A Manager's Guide to Coaching* (London: BACIE).

Moorby, E. (1991), 'Mentoring and Coaching', *Gower Handbook of Training and Development* (Ed: John Prior) (Aldershot: Gower).

Singer, Edwin. J. (1974) *Effective Management Coaching* (Wimbledon: Institute of Personnel Management).

12 Facilitating management learning with interactive video

Don Binsted and Susan Armitage

Early in 1984, at the Centre for the Study of Management Learning (CSML), at the University of Lancaster, a number of ideas for future research into the use of technology in management learning presented themselves. These stemmed from the following:

- The publication of the Binsted/Hodgson positional paper 'Open and distance learning in management education and training' (Binsted and Hodgson, 1984). This research was funded by the Manpower Services Commission and indicated the need for further research to be carried out in a number of areas.
- The realization that CSML had this far only done a great deal of research into various aspects of management learning, where there was direct contact between learners and teachers, trainers, tutors, developers, etc. This opened up the question of whether theory and practice developed in that situation was relevant when learning was facilitated at a distance via media and technology.
- The highly innovative approach, developed some years earlier, by Richard Boot and Philip Boxer into computer-facilitated reflective learning (Boot and Boxer, 1980). This work indicated huge potential for the use of computer-based learning and for designs which bore no relationship to programmed learning.
- The exciting potential of interactive video (IV) which was becoming apparent from the limited number of examples then available.

This led us to devise a two-pronged research strategy in open and distance learning, as follows:

1.   Field studies of learners' experiences of engaging in open and distance

learning (for a definition of open and distance learning, see Binsted and Hodgson, 1984). Two extensive studies were carried out funded by the Foundation for Management Education and the MSC. Reports are available (Hodgson, 1986; Mann, 1987).

2. Laboratory studies which involved making and testing highly innovative IV programmes. This was funded in three stages by consortia of large organizations over a period of five and a half years (March 1985 to October 1990), with a total budget of £245 000.

This chapter gives an overview of what we did and what we learned from the laboratory studies.

DESIGN PRINCIPLES

It took one year to set up the first consortium of 11 organizations, but in this time we gathered much information about those computer-based and IV programmes that were commercially available. We formed a view about what we wanted to do, and perhaps more importantly, what we did *not* want to do.

Our preliminary investigations of a variety of computer-based and IV programmes revealed that, at that time, the underlying design of these programmes was based on programmed learning. The underlying theory of design came from the conditioning school of thought which is based on ideas of linking stimuli with appropriate responses, reinforcement, etc. (Burgoyne, 1977). In practical terms this led to programmes which made frequent use of multi-choice questions with right/wrong answer judging, remedial loops, etc. Compared with random access text or the old programmed learning technology, computers offered an increased level of speed and sophistication.

As computer-based and IV-authoring languages and systems became available, they became more and more trainer-friendly, so that trainers with little or no computing experience could produce their own programmes. These authoring languages or systems had easy-to-use multi-choice question-and-answer-checking routines built into them. In some of the IV systems it was impossible to escape these. This led to the view that in some way the logic of the computer would only support conditioning-based designs. This of course was not true; it was the design of software and the extension of programmed learning principles which produced this effect. When we tried these designs out on managers we found they became very frustrated, and simple right/wrong answer-checking was quite inadequate.

There is no suggestion here that conditioning-based learning is inappropriate for certain types of learning, for example, where there are right answers or where operating routines must be memorized and acted upon in stressful situations. However, in our research we set out to produce programmes which were not based on conditioning theories of learning nor programmed learning designs, since this would not be appropriate for managers and was against the espoused view in CSML about the desirability of 'openness'.

171

In practical terms we set out to make and test (on real managers) programmes which would:

- be based on cognitive and experiential theories of learning (Burgoyne, 1977)
- allow learners to exercise judgements based on their past experience
- give learners choice about how they interact with the programme
- explore designs which involve learner/learner interaction in programmes designed for more than one learner
- make imaginative use of video
- let the clever stuff go on inside the learners' heads
- use principles already established in CSML
- allow for substantial open-ended input by the learners
- have application to 'back home' work situations
- design programmes which require no direct tutor intervention.

It is important to note that we were trying to avoid being led by technology. The technology developed as our study progressed, but this was never the driving force behind our development of the programmes. Our approach was to design programmes which were educationally sound and then look for IV systems which could handle our designs. We found it necessary to evaluate both hardware and software. Apart from authoring systems which locked one into conditioning-based learning, we found combined IV hardware and software systems which could be made to do a number of things we *did not* want to do, and could not do some vital things we *did* need to do.

In the end we found only one system which was entirely satisfactory for our designs, and this was the 'System T' tape-based system currently available from Dr Paul Topham. (Acknowledgement at end of chapter.)

WHAT SORT OF LEARNING IS POSSIBLE?

In management development a variety of different types of learning is required. One of the principal objectives of the research was to discover which types of learning could be facilitated with IV. Figure 12.1 shows diagramatically the basic types of learning and their relationship to each other.

The three most fundamental types are cognitive learning, skill development and affective learning (sometimes described rather loosely as knowing, doing and feeling). Skill development is often concerned with psychomotor skills which are not generally associated with management, although this is changing (for example, when developing keyboard skills for computer operation). We found from earlier research that each type of learning requires different facilitation by the tutor (Binsted and Snell, 1981). This suggested that different IV facilitation might be required for each type of learning, another aspect to be illuminated by the research.

There are three hybrid types of learning which are of particular interest in

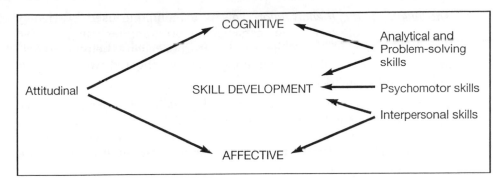

Figure 12.1 Learning domain map

management development:

1. *Analytical and problem-solving skills.* Learning in this area has an affinity both with cognitive learning and skill development, and learning needs to be facilitated both by cognitive and skill facilitators.
2. *Interpersonal skills.* Learning in this area has an affinity with skill development and affective learning. Learning needs to be facilitated by both skill and affective facilitators.
3. *Attitudinal learning.* This has an affinity with both cognitive and affective learning, since attitudes generally have a thought-through, rational component, as well as an emotional and, possibly, irrational component. Attitudinal learning needs both cognitive and affective facilitators to be present.

We consulted our co-sponsor group as to which types of learning they wanted us to investigate, and this dictated the programmes we made and tested. The programme titles developed are:

- Problem-solving and decision-making
- Interpersonal skills
- Attitude change
- Management of change
- Team-building
- Tutoring skills.

THE VIDEO COMPONENT

One of the first things we investigated was the question of where video elements are either desirable or vital. Clearly many learning situations do not need a video element, and straight computer-based learning is most appropriate. The video element is, however, very powerful when used in the right way. The various uses we made of a video element were as follows:

173

1. *The talking head, friendly tutor.* This is a technique used by Henley Management College in their management programmes using passive video. A commentator chats to the learner giving helpful advice, instructions, and 'jollying them along'. We investigated two particular talking head elements:

   a) Process-talk, where the talking head gives instructions and advice about what the learner should do next. Although this can be done with computer-generated text, the talking head introduces some level of relationship and appears less impersonal. It is important, however, to give the learner the option of seeing process-talk video again, because if distracted or not understanding, the learner may otherwise be at a loss as to what to do next. Back-up using text is another alternative.

   b) Content-talk explanations are another application for the use of talking head video. These are situations where the amount or complexity of content to be communicated is such that text would be long and tedious to read and would approach using the technology for electronic page-turning. A clear explanation by a talking head or voice-over graphics (talking blackboard) is then most effective. This technique is used extensively in the Open University programmes.

2. *Situational background.* Video can give the learner a rich picture of the situational background of work environments, especially when these are learners' own work environments. In a very short space of time a great deal of varied information and emotional data can be made available. This is particularly useful in case study-based learning as an alternative to reading text. This is particularly the case when interpersonal situations are involved, which is often an element in management situations.

3. *Models of behaviour.* These can be negative (models of inappropriate behaviour), or positive (models of appropriate behaviour) (Binsted, 1986). Negative models have their uses but are often overplayed, for example showing a human interaction where someone models a situation which is so inept that the learner is unable to take it seriously. Such modelling tends to be high on entertainment and low on facilitating learning. Positive models demonstrate effective behaviour which the learners can practise and appropriate for themselves. There is a difficulty in using the extremes of positive or negative models (i.e. totally right and totally wrong). Apart from the difficulty of being able to produce the former in a complex interpersonal interaction, the learner begins to get conditioned into copying the positive model. Again, may we say that this is acceptable in certain types of training, but is less acceptable with managers under development, and does not fit with the ideas of openness already commented upon. As an alternative to 'wrong/right' comparisons we developed 'not-so-good/better' models. The learners were asked to say what they thought was good or bad

about the 'not-so-good' model. There was no use of multi-choice questions to check answers; the learners were asked to form their own judgements. The better models were offered as improvements which could be bettered still further. This established much more productive learning than would 'wrong/right' models.

4. *Student interaction.* This use of video was the most innovative and powerful for facilitating learning. We won the National Award for Innovation in Education and Training Technology 1988 for this approach. We call this IV+. It requires that two or more learners work through the programme together, and at some point interact with each other. This interaction is automatically recorded by the VCR in the system via a camera. Thus live video of learner interactions can be integrated into the programme with pre-recorded video. One design we used for two learners was to start an interpersonal skills programme with a 'not-so-good/better' comparison of models. Having got the learners to explore what was good and what was not so good about each model, they were then invited to interact with each other on camera. They were thus able to play back and compare their behaviour with each others and the models. From the learners' point of view two very important changes in the learning process now occur:

a) The learners move from learning by demonstration to discovery learning. This is essential for skill development (Binsted, 1986).
b) They can also move from a hypothetical situation to a real work 'back home' situation, which brings in work cultures and systems, and focuses, for example, on issues such as 'what sort of behaviour would be appropriate back home?'.

THE OVERALL RESEARCH APPROACH

The progression in the research design was:

- Decide on the learning area to be researched (see Figure 12.1)
- Make the programme
- Test on real managers
- Revise
- Re-test
- Make final version.

We did this with the six programmes identified earlier and then experimented with embedding a set of the programmes in an organization. In parallel with this we did extensive experimentation with hardware and software systems.

AN ECONOMIC MEANS OF PRODUCTION

Right from the beginning we became aware that for commercially made   *175*

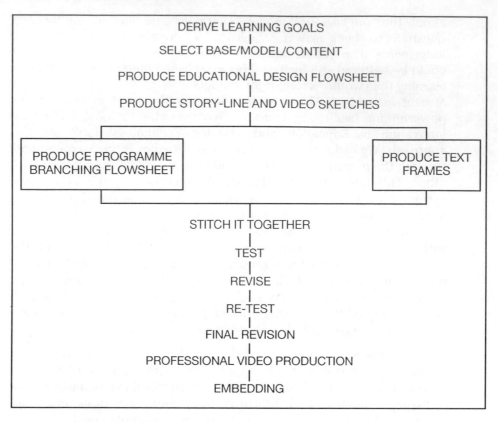

Figure 12.2   The CSML approach

programmes the cost can be high. One of our research goals was thus to explore ways of minimizing production costs. We wanted to do this for two reasons: to make the best use of our co-sponsors' money, and to pioneer ways of reducing cost for anybody trying to establish IV programmes in their organization. The overall approach is shown in Figure 12.2.

THE EDUCATIONAL DESIGN

This is *the* most important aspect of design. We used theories and principles stemming from the CSML work in management development over the years. This included such principles as whole cycle learning (Binsted, 1980). At this stage the programme has to be constructed from the two basic elements, video sequences (already discussed) and text frames. These latter are computer-generated text and graphics which are accessed by the learners. These all have to be linked together in various ways to facilitate learning. We constructed educational flowsheets for the learning design, an example of which is in Figure 12.3, which is part of an interpersonal skills programmes, using IV+ technology.

176

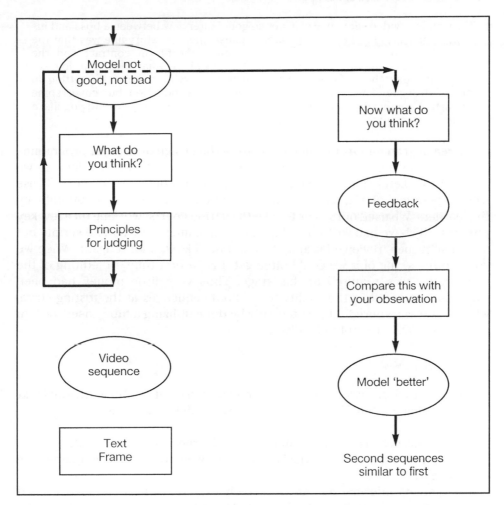

Figure 12.3   Example of educational flowsheet

At the educational design flowsheet stage of design the outline of the video sequences has to be decided and the outline of the text also needs firming up. The detail of each individual text screen follows at a later stage.

MAKING THE VIDEO SEQUENCES

Having specified the area of learning and the function of each video sequence, a story-line needs to be developed and some idea of the words to be used to enact the situation (Binsted, 1988). This will include the content of talking head explanations or process-talk already referred to. An example from the programme shown in Figure 12.3 is as follows:

We wanted a video sequence of a 'not-so-good' interview between a boss and his subordinate around the issue of career counselling. The story-line was that the subordinate, a computing graduate, was on a short-term contract and the purpose of the interview was to help her to think about what she might do next. We wanted only the first few minutes of such an interview to cover the setting up of the dialogue. The boss would dominate the introduction but cover some important points aimed at putting the subordinate at ease (e.g. 'would you like a coffee?'; 'I've had the 'phone transferred', etc.).

We reached an important conclusion from the design of our first programme – that *this was not the time to make a professional-standard video*. Instead we made video sketches which we shot ourselves with one fixed camera. These were of poor technical quality but the interactions were judged as authentic by the learners. We used ourselves to take the various parts, working off a few key phrases which we had written on flipcharts, off camera. We had no scripts but shot a sequence, reviewed it and, if we did not like it, shot it again. When we got into the swing of it we could often get it right first time. No editing of the video tapes was required at this stage. Thus very little money had been expended, and we had the facility to re-shoot sequences at the testing stage, when this was required. This could only be done utilizing a tape-based system (Armitage, 1992) (i.e. not videodisc).

TEXT SCREENS

Having made all the video sketches, we could then draft out the individual text screens, using 'System T'. These were of several different types:

- Process instructions, explaining to the learner what to do next.
- Learner choices (e.g. checking if they want to see a video sequence again).
- Content, information, ideas, principles, etc., where a talking head explanation is not required, or a talking head explanation needed to be summarized.

In general we did not make much use of graphics on text screens. When presenting diagrams we used video made with a rostrum camera with a voice-over. One advantage with the 'System T' is that the text screens generated are in 40-column text. Not only is this easy to read, but it severely limits the amount of text possible on one text screen. This we see as a positive advantage which discourages the similarity with a book, even if the pages are turned electronically.

Text screens are developed simultaneously with the production of a programme branching flowsheet (Topham, 1989a). An example is shown in Figure 12.4. This plans the various paths the learner can take through the programme. The more choice offered to the learner, the more complex is the branching. In the flowsheet, learners can focus on any one of six episodes of an interaction in any order. Having selected this, they can then review the

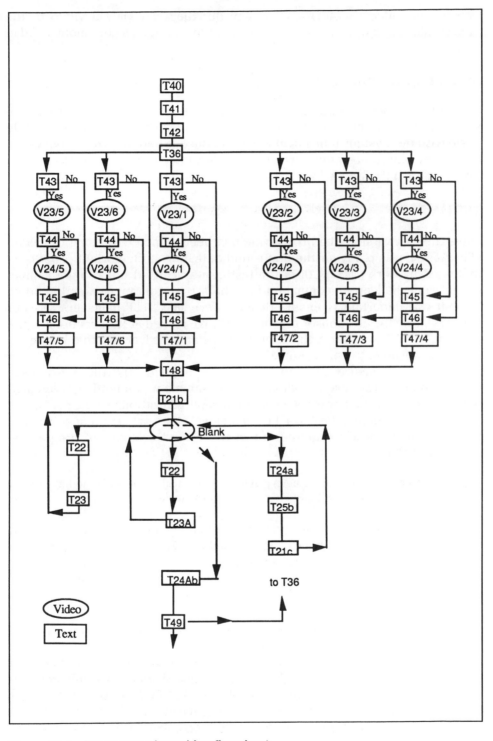

Figure 12.4   Programme branching flowsheet

episode on video (or not) and, if they do, they can view a video of the consequences (or not). The development of the text frames goes along hand in hand with the creation of the flowsheet (see Figure 12.2).

STITCHING IT TOGETHER

The video sequences and text frames now have to be linked together (the process called 'branching'). Even the most complex branching is very simple to do with the 'System T'. In effect this is the stage where the video sequences are edited, often merely topped and tailed. Unwanted sequences are left on the tape and are not branched in.

TESTING

Once the first version of a programme had been completed (using the video sketches), it was ready for the first round of testing, an important process as indicated by Bork (1987). All of the testing was carried out using a sample group from the learner population for whom the programme was intended. Thus it was important to ensure that we were sent 'real' managers (i.e. not trainers) from the co-sponsor organizations. We looked at the reactions of the learners as they went through the programme and the learning that had taken place as a result of the programme.

In order to ensure that the learners 'supplied' by the co-sponsor organizations were those for whom the programme was intended, a *research participant specification* was issued to all those organizations taking part in the research. For example, the extract given below is the participant specification for the type of learners required to test the Team Development programme (Topham, 1989b):

> A group of 4 people who have been given a specific task to do and who have the authority, power, responsibility etc. to see that the task gets done.

During the course of the five and a half years of the project, several different evaluation methodologies have been pursued (see Figure 12.5), and overall the testing methodology was developed as the project progressed.

Each methodology is described briefly in the following sections. Fuller descriptions of the methodologies can be found in Topham (1989c).

Semantic differential scales

This methodology was used to evaluate the first programme produced ('Problem-Solving and Decision-Making') (Beynon, 1986), using a simple rating scale (Osgood, 1952). The learners used the scale to rate 11 questions on 11 different 7-point scales. Their responses were then averaged and compared, to establish learner perceptions of the technology, the learning process, and their own problem-solving behaviour.

```
Semantic Differential Scales

Post-Event Interviewing

Structured Observation

Structured Observation + Pre/Post-Event Questionnaire
```

Figure 12.5   Evaluation methodologies

The main disadvantage of this methodology was the difficulty of relating the learner perceptions to specific design steps within the programme. That is, it established that greater learner awareness had occurred, but not the specific educational design steps that had facilitated this increased awareness. This was one of the critical purposes of carrying out the tests, and so other evaluation techniques were used on subsequent programmes.

Post-event interviewing

The use of post-event interviewing employed semi-structured interviews, allowing for maximum dialogue whilst ensuring that answers to some critical questions were obtained. Once all the interviews were completed, collating and making unbiased sense of the data in terms of the educational design steps tended to be rather subjective. However, the learners' workbooks, completed as a result of going through the programme, served to focus attention on the important design issues.

However, the data was still based upon the learners' perceptions, which were gleaned as a result of the evaluators' questions. These questions were based upon what the evaluator thought was, or could be, important and may have missed some 'unknown' that had affected the learning outcomes.

This led to a radical review of our testing process, resulting in a technique which we call 'structured observation'.

Structured observation

The term 'structured observation' reflects directly the two elements involved in this methodology. 'Structured' refers to the educational design flowsheet used during the development of our programmes (Topham, 1989a). The 'Observation' was achieved by the continuous video filming of the learners as they engaged with a programme.

After the learning event, the video tape of the learner(s) is played back and matched to the educational design steps on the flowsheet. The learners' workbooks are an additional source of information and provide backup or clarification about what is being seen. The advantage of this approach is that the evaluation is not relying on the learners' perceptions of what happened, but allows analysis of learner behaviour during the learning event.   *181*

Not only did this allow the major design steps to be checked for their effectiveness, but it also allowed us to identify and eliminate 'niggly' problems, such as unclear or ambiguous instructions, which learners did not always recall during the interview phase of the evaluation. It also allowed us to observe the different ways in which learners progressed through the programme, with managers from engineering occupations involved in very little discussion, whilst those from a banking environment discussed each point in detail (Topham, 1989c).

Structured observation + pre/post-event questionnaire

The last programme developed as a part of the research was aimed at trainers, and explores the subject of 'Tutoring Skills'. In using the structured observation methodology, we picked up that, although the programme itself achieved its educational design goals to a certain extent, something was preventing the learners engaging fully with the programme. This appeared to be something to do with the learners' preconceptions of what this programme would do for them, or in some cases the fact that they had been 'sent' to sample the programme, rather than perceiving any need for such training on their part.

In order to try and access these feelings and attitudes we decided to use two questionnaires: a pre-event questionnaire to try and determine why people had come to do the programme and their expectations of it; and a post-event questionnaire to try and determine how their attitudes had changed towards the programme and whether their expectations had been met.

Although, as for the semi-structured interviews, the questions were around what the evaluator considered important, some useful insights were gained into the external factors that influenced the learning process (Armitage, 1990a).

Revising

Following the first tests the programme will almost certainly need revision. In our research this varied from a fundamental re-design, involving re-shooting video sequences to a tidying-up of text screens. Our video-sketch technique made it very easy (and cheap) to re-shoot video.

MAKING THE FINAL VERSION

After the second test we revised the programme again and were then ready to make the final professional version of the video (see Figure 12.2). This is where significant sums of money can be expended, and problems can arise in briefing the video producer. We were most concerned to minimize costs at this point. We found our video sketches were an ideal way of briefing the video maker. We could say in effect 'make this to your high standards, because educationally we know this works'. In our first programme we used professional actors. In all the others we used ourselves. We learned four simple rules about making the professional video:

1. There was a level of technical acceptability. The video did not want to appear amateur.
2. Human interactions and situations needed to be authentic *as judged by the learner*. They needed to be 'real life'.
3. Dramatization of situations should be avoided.
4. Work with a sympathetic video maker who understands the educational use of video. We used Visual Link of Carlisle, one of our co-sponsors who produced excellent work for us.

EMBEDDING IV IN AN ORGANIZATION

It became clear from the outset that the question of embedding programmes in an organization was of equal importance to the need to make programmes that 'worked' educationally. Put simply, it is no use having excellent programmes which nobody uses. This was a view supported by research done into the design and delivery of Open Learning material (Mann, 1987), and the embedding methodology we used was based upon the findings of this research.

The final phase of the co-sponsor research, then, was to look at the process of embedding IV, and investigate what kind of infrastructure would be required to support the introduction and use of IV, within an organization. In this phase of the research the programmes and equipment were sited away from CSML and were left to 'stand alone', as they would, for example, should a company decide to put such equipment in an Open Learning Centre.

Thus we were looking at factors external to the programmes themselves. This made the structured observation methodology impractical. Given that the evaluators would also be absent from the 'test site', the most useful evaluation tool was that of a post-event questionnaire. The questionnaire probed why learners had come to do particular programmes, and what support they had, or felt was required, for a venture such as this. The results of this part of the research are discussed briefly as follows.

Our embedding design involved five stages. These were:

1. *Interactive video and the organization*. Identification of a 'key person' willing to take responsibility for IV within the organization. Plan the provision of adequate resources, both staff and equipment.
2. *Selection of appropriate programmes*. These need to be suitable both in terms of the intended learner population, and the level of learner support required.
3. *Publicity*. Production of appropriate publicity material and its targeted distribution.
4. *Implementation*. Ensuring that the key person and support staff understand the system and programmes in order to deal with minor technical problems or learner difficulties with material.

5. *Evaluation.* An appropriate evaluation process should be set up to monitor the use of the IV systems.

For the purposes of the research, evaluation of the whole process was carried out, not just after the implementation phase.

One of our co-sponsors agreed to host this part of the research, and also took the role of 'key person' within the organization. This role involves the co-ordination of all the five stages of the methodology. The equipment and programmes were made available for a two-week period, from 9.00 am to 5.00 pm, Monday to Friday. We were necessarily restricted in the programmes that we could offer, as the only ones we had available were those produced during the course of the research programme. This did cause some comment from learners about the appropriateness of material and would seem to support the need for careful choice of programmes as stated in Stage 2 of the embedding process.

Publicity material was produced and distributed to the target learner population, and the resulting demand for access to the programmes meant that two work stations had to be provided, rather than the original intention of providing one. These were housed in two separate rooms as some of the programmes involved two learners and live recording of their interactions. A booking system was in place at this stage in order that potential learners could call and reserve time on the work stations to complete programmes.

Shortly before the two-week period began, a training day was held to familiarize the staff with the equipment. The level of learner support required during use of the programme was extremely low as the programmes had been designed to run without the need for a tutor. However, responses to the post-programme questionnaire indicated that the learners felt this kind of training should be used as part of a wider training programme (Armitage, 1990b).

It was suggested that IV could be used, either to get all learners to the same level before a face-to-face learning event, or as a means of revision/reinforcement of the learning after an event.

The research findings would seem to suggest that the embedding process followed was successful within this organization.

CONCLUSIONS

Overall our conclusions were very simple:

1. The basis of theory and good practice we have developed in CSML are equally applicable for the design of IV programmes. In fact we would take the view that without such a basis, design is likely to be inferior.
2. It is feasible to facilitate learning in the areas of:
   Problem-solving skills
   Interpersonal skills
   Attitude change
   The management of change

Team-building
Tutoring skills.
(Significant learning was achieved, with a very wide variety of learner. In general they found the programmes enjoyable.)

3. Programmes written for two or more learners open up a number of learning possibilities stemming from learner interactions.
4. This coupled with the use of IV+ technology opens up a new set of learning processes not normally achievable with standard videodisc-based IV.
5. It is possible to introduce degrees of openness into IV programmes, and designs do not have to use conditioning.
6. The level of engagement in the programmes was in general very high. So much so, that we had to include text screens encouraging learners to take a break.
7. The embedding process used for the last part of the research worked well and demonstrated the ability of the programmes to 'stand alone' without tutor support.

A COST-EFFECTIVE APPROACH TO THE USE OF IV IN AN ORGANIZATION

If an organization is exploring whether to make extensive use of IV or IV+ for training, there are a lot of questions that need answering, and in general these answers are not readily available. We believe the safest way to proceed is to follow a similar pattern to our research approach, incorporated in a pilot programme. This will provide accurate answers to questions which relate to the specific organization, with minimum expenditure. The sequence of events would look like this:

1. Buy a tape-based system with IV+ capability which uses an easy-to-learn authoring system. Tape-based so that video sketches can be produced and modified easily and cheaply. Some authoring languages take in excess of three months to learn. 'System T' is the only one we have located which fulfils these conditions. (A final choice of hardware and software for the programme delivery will occur near the end of the whole process.)
2. Find some training needs which when met will have a good pay-off which can be measured. Choose a client in the organization who is keen to try something new and is keen to be actively involved.
3. Define the area of learning to be facilitated, and the learner population. Check out that this really needs the video element: if not, choose another area of learning.
4. Produce the educational design flowsheet and proceed to make the programme as already described. Test it on members of the learner population, revise, re-test, and revise again if required.
    (At this point a programme will be available which has been proven but is still based on rough video sketches. This is the point where *185*

professional video could be made, but this could wait until later. If the sketches cause negative comment at the testing stages it would be wise to make the professional video at this point. Assuming the sketches are adequate, the next stage continues with 5.)

5. Design and set up the embedding and monitor the results.
6. Make the professional video. This will not yield any new data but could be useful from two points of view. One is to test out the communication with the video maker, and explore the sort of relationship which could be established. The other is to have a finished article to show to people who need to be impressed and supportive.
7. Now it is known that IV is a workable way of facilitating learning in the organization, major expenditure in a project can be proposed based on sound data. Decisions can be made on hardware to be used, authoring system or language, and who will be the video maker. The overall decision then needs to be made as to whether to contract out any or all stages of the process. We would argue that a successful pilot programme is essential to proposing a major IV project involving substantial expenditure. Following this proposal ensures a basis of reliable data for minimal expenditure.

Another relevant factor is that it is feasible, in a five-day workshop, to develop the skills in a competent trainer to make and test a short innovative IV or IV+ programme.

ACKNOWLEDGEMENT

The authors wish to acknowledge the great contribution Dr Paul Topham made to this work. Further details of 'System T' can be obtained from him at this address:
4 Claughton Street
Kidderminster
Worcs. DY11 6PR

REFERENCES

Armitage, S. (1990a) 'Tutoring Skills', Co-sponsor Project Report (Lancaster: CSML).

Armitage, S. (1990b) 'Embedding IV in Organisations', Co-sponsor Project Report (Lancaster: CSML).

Armitage, S. (1992) 'Interactive Video: Using a Videotape-Based System for Management Learning', *Interactive Learning International*, 8 (1), pp. 37–44.

Beynon, A. (1986) 'Problem-Solving and Decision-Making', Co-sponsor Project Report (Lancaster: CSML).

Binsted, D. S. (1980) 'Design for Learning in Management Training and Development: A View', *Journal of European Industrial Training*, 4 (8).

Binsted, D. S. (1986) *Developments in Interpersonal Skills Training* (Aldershot: Gower).

Binsted, D. S. (1988) 'Creating Video Sequences for Interactive Video for Management Education and Training', *Journal of European Industrial Training*, 12 (6).

Binsted, D. S. and Hodgson, V. E. (1984) 'Open and Distance Learning in Management Education and Training: A Positional Paper' (Lancaster: MSC/CSML).

Binsted, D. S. and Snell, R. S. (1981) 'The Tutor Learner Interaction Part 1', *Personnel Review*, 10 (3), pp. 3–13.

Boot, R. and Boxer, P. (1980) 'Reflective Learning' in Beck, J. and Cox, C. (eds) *Advances in Management Education* (Chichester: Wiley).

Bork, A. (1987) 'Lessons From Computer-Based Learning', in Laurillard, Diana (ed.) *Interactive Media* (London: Ellis Horwood: Books in Computing Science).

Burgoyne, J. (1977) 'Management Learning Developments', *BACIE Journal*, 31(9), pp. 158–60.

Hodgson, V. (1986) 'The Relevance and Effectiveness of Distance Learning for Management Education', Report for the Foundation of Management Education (Lancaster: CSML).

Mann, S. (1987) 'The Effective Design and Delivery of Open and Distance Learning for Management Education', Project Report (Lancaster: MSC/CSML).

Osgood, C. E. (1952) 'The Nature and Measurement of Meaning', *Psychological Bulletin*, 49, pp. 197–237.

Topham, P. (1989a) 'Developing "Open" Interactive Video Coursework for Management Learning', *Interactive Learning International*, 5 (1), pp. 9–18.

Topham, P. (1989b) 'Team Building', Co-sponsor Project Report (Lancaster: CSML).

Topham, P. (1989c) 'Methodologies for Evaluating Interactive Video Courseware', *Interactive Learning International*, 5 (1), pp. 19–23.

NOTES

1. *Dr. Paul Topham*: Further details of 'System T' can be obtained from: Dr Paul Topham, 4 Claughton Street, Kidderminster, Worcs. DY11 6PR.
2. *Susan Armitage* is a lecturer in the Department of Management Learning at Lancaster University, and can be contacted regarding the work in this   *187*

chapter at: Department of Management Learning, The Management School, Lancaster University, Lancaster LA1 4YX. Tel: (0524) 594063, e-mail: mtaøø 4@uk.ac.lancs.cent1.

3. *Don Binsted* is at the time of writing a Senior Fellow in the Department of Management Learning at the University of Lancaster.

Part IV
MANAGEMENT DEVELOPMENT IN ACTION

13 An in-house senior managers' programme for organizational change

Bruce Nixon

We live in exciting times: changes are taking place which would have been inconceivable only a few years ago; rising expectations and the forces of necessity are compelling us to learn and find fresh solutions both globally and in the workplace (Naisbitt and Aburdene, 1985). Demographic changes are giving new urgency to the need to make better use of women, black people, young people, older people and the disabled. People expect to be treated with respect and are less willing to tolerate the old, relatively oppressive ways of managing that many of us have grown up with. More people expect their work to be *qualitatively connected to the rest of their lives*; they believe that work should be, and can be, fulfilling, exciting and fun and that there should be excellent opportunities for development and self-expression.

Organizations which meet these expectations are likely to be the ones which survive and prosper in the 1990s; they will attract and inspire the best people and learn how to release their energies and initiative in achieving corporate goals. Only in this way will organizations respond to the unpredictable changes and upheaval which lie ahead.

I believe that this situation requires a new style of leadership (Simmons, 1989) which is more *empowering and supportive*. Key elements of this are likely to be:

- Holding out an *inspiring vision*, based on values and beliefs, which appeals to people at every level
- Inviting others to *contribute their own exciting vision*
- Creating a *climate* in which everyone will offer their full energy, vision and talents
- Becoming a *leader of leaders*, not followers; releasing individual initiative
- Learning to *welcome change and upheaval*, and encouraging others to do so

- Making fresh, appropriate responses to *each new situation*
- Creating an *environment* where there is praise, encouragement, support and challenge, instead of criticism and blame
- Seeing the *whole situation* and deciding to see to it that everything goes well
- Giving up the pretence that the leader knows best and always knows what to do; instead, admitting that *we are all apprentices*, constantly learning how to do the job well
- Giving up blaming and complaining, and instead taking responsibility for *deciding and acting.*

I do believe this is not merely an enlightened way of managing: it is fast becoming an economic necessity.

This situation, if I have diagnosed it correctly, presents people in management training and development with an enormous opportunity. To rise to the occasion we need to see ourselves as *leaders of organizational change and development*; it will not be enough to continue traditional management training and development with its emphasis on teaching knowledge and skill. Instead, we shall need to create learning situations in which managers can work on the actual opportunities and problems they face in their own jobs. This requires an approach which puts managers in charge of their own learning by providing a flexible but rigorous structure and a supportive but challenging atmosphere.

The following case study describes an attempt to provide such an approach: to bring out and support the managers' desire for change and for new ways of managing people; to help them translate their vision into reality. The work described was started in 1986 and since then many more programmes like it have been run in Sun Alliance and still continue. The author is now working as an independent consultant and finding widespread interest both in a new leadership style and in new approaches to management development which focus on planning and implementing change and put managers in charge of their own learning. At first they find it strange, and it needs to be carefully presented to them. Once they start to experience it there is no looking back. They say it is exactly what they want.

CASE STUDY SYNOPSIS

Most programmes for senior managers are either run in business schools or management colleges, or largely employ external resources. What is unusual about this case study is that it describes a successful programme designed and run *in-company*. It is based on the philosophy that the trainers and the participating managers collectively have all the resources they need. It is a 'nuts-and-bolts' account which will interest other trainers who want to initiate something similar in their own organizations.

Two training managers (Richard Allen and Bruce Nixon) took the initiative to start a senior management development programme; they overcame the resistance to such an initiative; they pilot-tested the concept with six 'sympathetic' senior managers who later helped sell the new programme to twelve colleagues. We shall see the lessons they learnt from this pilot programme: how, in their experience, a programme for senior managers needs to differ from one for middle management. The programme is now helping to change the way that managers in the Sun Alliance Insurance Group manage.

The study describes how the participants were recruited, and what the selection criteria were; the organizational issues that had to be confronted as part of the long-term strategy for organization development in Sun Alliance are set out. The study also gives specific details of the objectives and structure of this twelve-month programme, and the issues and needs that emerged in the pre-course briefing meetings. It describes the design philosophy, and how the first workshop was designed; how we overcame our own fears in conducting the programme, what actually happened, and how that compared with our expectations. We also quote from the reactions of the delegates themselves.

BACKGROUND HISTORY

The need for management development for senior managers (i.e. those at the level below top management) had been widely recognized in the company; external programmes had been used for a time. However, this approach had largely ceased, mainly because it was difficult to establish what benefits managers (and hence the organization) gained. The feedback received typically showed difficulty in applying any learning back in the workplace. We had developed a range of in-company programmes for junior and middle managers; we were also doing a great deal of work with management teams. In all of this in-company work our approach was to help managers develop themselves by tackling the key business and organizational issues confronting them (Allen and Nixon, 1986). However, some key issues could be resolved only by senior and top managers; their role in strategic management and in creating an organizational climate in which people would give their best was crucial. Yet hitherto they had seldom been directly involved in management development programmes. Earlier proposals for the development of senior managers had not met with success (for reasons about which we will speculate later, reasons connected with some of the key issues facing the organization). Despite this, we knew from our contacts that there would be extensive support for a programme amongst senior managers themselves. So we decided to take the initiative. We invited six managers to a small-scale pilot programme; with their help and support we learnt a great deal about how to design and run a programme for senior managers (our previous experience had mainly been in work with junior and middle management). We incorporated what we learned from the pilot in the more ambitious programme.

After many years of working with managers at middle levels and talking with senior and top managers, we had considerable information about the *needs* and *key issues* of the organization. In their view, the key areas where   *193 improvement* was needed were:

- Strategic management
- The management of change
- The leadership and motivation of large numbers of people
- Gaining commitment to common purpose and agreed strategies
- Creating effective teamwork and trust
- Creating a climate in which people will give all they are capable of and which encourages them to develop themselves
- Articulating values and beliefs as a basis for strategy.

From talking with managers, it was apparent that some of the difficulties that *got in the way* of these improvements were:

- Competitiveness
- Inter-divisional rivalries
- A tendency to 'trash', blame and criticize rather than to take initiatives and to support one another
- Lack of trust or openness
- Unwillingness to acknowledge development needs in case this was seen as weakness
- A tendency to over-control
- Fear and feelings of personal inadequacy ('Who am I to change things?').

Managers in other organizations and industries will no doubt recognize most or all of these, as they are common difficulties. (It must be added that this is not how people behave most of the time; they are usually responses to very stressful or difficult situations.) Some of these were the very issues which had frustrated earlier attempts to initiate a programme. So we knew that we should be 'taking on' these issues in trying to start and successfully complete a new programme.

The Senior Management Development Programme would be a major further step in a long-term strategy to tackle these issues; if we chose the participants well, they would be respected people who would be widely influential, and many of them would move into top management over a period of time. If the first programme was successful, many more could take place and thus, over a long period, the programme could be extremely influential. We believed it would help considerably in bringing about beneficial changes in the way the group was managed. It was a very exciting opportunity.

SELECTING THE DELEGATES

We knew from the pilot programme that the selection of delegates would be critical. We wanted twelve participants representative of all the key trading and service divisions of the group; we knew from experience that there would be varying degrees of support from top management. Therefore we approached most participants direct and made it clear to them that it would be their responsibility to secure approval to attend; the delegates supported this approach as the most appropriate way of quickly and easily securing approval. We were open about our *specification for delegates*; they should be:

- Determined to achieve excellence
- Open: about themselves, their needs and difficulties, and to what others have to offer
- Keen to learn and develop
- Willing to share what they have to offer
- Willing to be supportive: both encouraging and prepared to tackle difficult issues
- Prepared to be rigorous in tackling important issues
- Already successful in a key senior role, and likely to progress further
- Committed to see the programme through regardless of changes in their job.

We approached people who we thought met this specification, people with whom we already had a friendly working relationship and most of whom knew about the work we had been doing with middle managers and supported our approach. In some cases, we asked them who they would find it exciting to work with on a programme like this, and we followed up these suggestions. One or two declined our invitations but we soon had twelve would-be participants. Our thinking was to work with people who were 'ready' and would carry back to their job and their colleagues what they had gained. We were not at this stage aiming to 'take on' people who were reluctant or resistant to change.

It may help at this point to define what we mean by 'senior managers': the managers were at the level below top management and typically in charge of substantial parts of major service functions or major business sectors (e.g. the chief accountant; the overseas division manager in charge of all services; the manager, computer services; the manager, linked life and unit trust business area; the commercial business manager; the deputy investment manager). Many have since been appointed to the boards of the newly formed companies within the group.

PITFALLS TO AVOID

We wanted to avoid the pitfalls of traditional management training. In our experience, these are:

1. Insufficient research before designing programmes to find out what individual managers *really need and want*.
2. No steps taken to *build relationships with the managers* before the programme.
3. Not enough emphasis placed on building the trust and the safety to talk   *195*

about *what really matters* and the *real difficulties* people have.

4. Emphasis upon knowledge and skill rather than helping managers bring about real changes in their *work*, and continuing changes in their *attitudes* and *behaviour*.

5. *Individual* and *organizational goals* not properly set, and not enough time devoted to planning, and planning the support for acting.

6. Insufficient attention to *individual needs*, and participation may be low because of a high participant–tutor ratio, rigid course design and lack of opportunity for managers to take responsibility for their own learning.

7. Content is regarded as *too theoretical*, and *not relevant*.

8. Contrived situations used as vehicles for learning rather than the living reality of the *participants' own work*.

9. Insufficient *organizational support* for participants, on return to the job, to apply what they have learned.

We were determined to avoid all of these pitfalls by talking to each participant about his or her own goals and needs, building relationships, developing trust, focusing on their work and the changes they wanted to make, creating a *long-term learning structure* that would support change, build in support and give responsibility for personal learning.

PROGRAMME DESIGN

Lessons learned from the pilot programme

What would be different about working with senior managers, as compared with middle managers (Nixon, 1985)? Some differences would be obvious: the focus would be broader and more long-term; on strategy rather than operations; and it might well be harder to develop an atmosphere in which people would be really open about their needs and difficulties – at least, that was our irrational fear. (Why is it that we see senior people as more inhibited and somehow less human?) Among the lessons we learnt from the 'pilot' programmes were that:

● Full representation of all the key *trading and service divisions* was extremely important to senior managers

● *Selection* was vital: one or two people with severe difficulties in trusting others or difficulties with our design philosophy could impede the progress of others

● More structure was expected by senior managers, but the right balance between *structure* and *flexibility* was crucial

● Talks and handouts had to be very polished and confidently delivered; hence more time for *preparation* was needed

● Unlike middle managers, the senior managers did not initially take to the idea of learning to counsel each other and preferred *private*

consultations with tutors
- Nevertheless, they would welcome the formation of *support groups* which would meet between the formal events of the programme
- It was important to keep the pace brisk, to be flexible and responsive and to be decisive (and right!) in making *changes* to the programme
- We should progress from strategy to managerial skills and issues, and finally offer the opportunity to deal with key personal issues, only when enough *trust and safety* had been established
- Senior managers often have expectations of a structured and largely didactic design; therefore the design should be thoroughly explained *before* each delegate decided to attend; for this reason we decided to hold a 'pre-day' fully to explain our approach
- They wanted practical help and guidance on *real back-at-work issues*, and very little theory
- Despite our fears, we were *fully capable of running the programme ourselves* and had a great deal to offer at all levels – knowledge, skills and attitudes
- The managers wanted, and expected, us to *stand up and express our views* – not to be cautious or 'hold back'.

Principles of design

The principles on which the programme design was based were as follows:

1. The subject matter of the programme would be the *strategies of the participants*, and whatever plans, actions, skills, attitudes and issues needed to be worked on to implement them.
2. There would be no *contrived exercises* (e.g. simulations, role-plays, case studies or games).
3. Learning would be largely by planning, acting, reviewing, and reflecting – and (most important) *learning* from each other.
4. On the basis that there would be twelve well-informed participants from a wide variety of disciplines, we decided *not to invite in any expert speakers in advance*; we would discuss the need with them during the first workshop and subsequent briefings. We also decided not to invite top management to participate as speakers, on the basis that these senior managers had good access to top management back in the job. In making this decision we did calculate the disadvantage of not having their active support; however, we judged that the results would speak louder than anything else.
5. Tutors would give short talks on key issues that might not otherwise be addressed, and provide suitable videos, papers, articles and books; some inputs would be on tools and techniques. We would also 'speak out' on major issues, say things that we thought needed to be said. Otherwise, our role would largely be to offer appropriate *structures and methods*, to lead sessions or small groups, and to coach and counsel.   *197*

6. Delegates would work in a variety of forums: in the plenary group; in support groups; in topic or interest groups; in pairs; in private consultations with tutors; or on their own. Three tutors would be provided. The *individual and distinct needs* of each participant could thus easily be provided for.

7. The programme should be a *twelve-month experience* on the basis, first, that such delegates are concerned with longer-term change and strategy and, secondly, that significant learning requires a sufficiently long period for planning, acting, reviewing, reflecting and trying again.

In many ways the approach was similar to that adopted with middle managers (Nixon, 1985). The most significant differences were:

- *Three workshops over a twelve-month period* as opposed to two over four–six months
- The emphasis on *long-term change and strategy*
- The relative caution that we expected about learning to *counsel each other* or deal with *key personal issues* other than in private consultations with tutors
- That a programme at this level could have a *profound influence* on the way in which managers in the group manage.

PROGRAMME STRUCTURE

The structure of the programme is shown in Figure 13.1. The purpose of the 'pre-day' was thoroughly to explain the underlying design and the principles, and to get real commitment to the programme before 'signing on'. We wanted delegates to be *sure* beforehand. We were considerably helped by two delegates from the 'pilot' programme who gave a frank account of their experiences and the benefits they had gained, as well as the difficulties they had encountered. We chose two people who were respected, well-known and would be frank about their experiences.

The individual briefing meetings were designed to enable the tutors to build relationships with the delegates; to help the delegates think clearly about their needs, and how they would use the programme; and, finally, to enable the tutors to collect information about the needs of delegates and their key issues so that they could design each workshop appropriately.

Each workshop would be of about three-and-a-half days' duration. Between each workshop delegates would implement their plans, and it was our hope and expectation that they would meet each other in small 'support groups' to give each other help and encouragement in implementing their strategies. This has happened. The objectives of the programme and an outline of each workshop are shown in Figures 13.2 and 13.3 respectively.

This was the programme which we presented to twelve potential participants in June 1986. Eleven ultimately emerged as firm participants and we started the briefings at the end of the summer.

Pre-day	June 1986
Individual briefings	August–September 1986
Design work	September 1986
Workshop 1	October 1986
Implementation	
Support groups meet	
Individual briefings	
Design work	
Workshop 2	February 1987
Implementation	
Support groups meet	
Individual briefings	
Design work	
Workshop 3	June 1987
Review of design	

Figure 13.1   Programme structure

To:
– Explore the changes taking place in the UK, and global environment (economic, technological, social . . .) relevant to Sun Alliance
– Build a vision of how Sun Alliance and your part of it needs to respond
– Decide how you and your team need to contribute
– Develop career strategies and plans which you will implement
– Identify the key issues you need to resolve, and changes you need to make in order to achieve your goals
– Further develop any crucial skills
– Build a cross-divisional support network for achieving excellence

Figure 13.2   Programme objectives

THE KEY ISSUES FOR THE PARTICIPANTS

From the briefing meetings the three tutors gained a clear picture of the key issues facing each delegate, his views on the best ways of using his time in the first workshop and the 'pay-off' that would result if the workshop fully met his requirements. With the flexible structure and the high tutor–delegate ratio it would be perfectly possible to meet these needs and expectations.

A number of common issues emerged:

- Creating a *shared vision of the future* to which all are committed
- Dealing with *change* in a *relaxed, flexible* and *optimistic* way
- Coping with *increasing pace and pressures*
- Getting things done without *bruising people* (others or oneself)
- Creating an *environment* in which people can achieve all they are capable of
- Building *trust, support* and *cooperation*

Workshop 1   Developing a strategy for excellence

- Scenarios: scanning the business environment
- Making Sun Alliance No. 1 – what that means
- Creating a vision for my sector
- Objectives, strategies, plans
- Key issues for me

Workshop 2   Leadership in Sun Alliance

- Review progress since previous workshop: successes, new developments, difficulties
- Key issues to emerge
- Leadership in Sun Alliance
- Developing really effective teams
- Managing change
- Other key issues or topics
- Update and further develop plans

Workshop 3   Consolidating success

- Further review of progress
- Further work on key issues or skills
- Developing people and creating the environment and support for people to achieve excellence
- Further plans
- Review of whole programme

Figure 13.3   The three workshops

- Using our own creativity and skills in a *positive* way.

Reassuringly, these issues were similar to those identified by the three trainers prior to initiating the programme. On the basis of these needs the first workshop was designed, as shown in Figures 13.4 and 13.5.

WHAT HAPPENED IN PRACTICE – THE FIRST WORKSHOP

In practice, the first workshop far exceeded our expectations. In a relatively short chapter such as this it would be inappropriate to describe the workshop in detail; we will instead comment on some of the factors which seem to have been crucial to its success:

1.   The introductions were absolutely crucial in creating a *climate of openness and trust*. So often introductions are a superficial ritual; we devoted some three hours to this session, and the questions each participant addressed were extremely carefully thought out:

- Your name
- Where you are from – brief history
- Three things it is important for us to know about you (that aren't obvious)

By the end of this workshop you will have:

1. **Built a clear vision** of the way ahead for Sun Alliance, for you and your part of the organization – fully consistent with you, your values and your beliefs.
2. **Explored** and shared ideas about **the major changes** taking place in the UK and the rest of the world
3. Developed **clear objectives, strategies and plans** you will implement
4. **Identified** the **key issues** you need to deal with now and the **changes** you need to make
5. Identified and started to develop any **skills and knowledge** you need to achieve your objectives
6. Built **a support group** for yourself

Figure 13.4   Objectives of workshop 1

Day 1   (Starting mid-afternoon)
S1   Welcome and introduction
S2   Introduction
S3   'In Search of Excellence' (video)
Day 2
S4   Creating vision and strategy
S5   Scanning the environment – major trends
S6   Implications: for you and your team; key issues to be resolved
S7   The key to it all: you
Day 3
S8   Identifying and planning key changes
S9   Work on key issues and changes
Day 4
S9   Further work on key issues and changes
S10   Commitments: plans to implement strategies and arrangements for support groups
S11   Review

Note:
*S = Session

Figure 13.5   Programme for workshop 1

● Current important issues for you as a manager – opportunities or difficulties
● Something you are proud of about yourself
● Aims for the programme and for this workshop.

Before the introductions took place participants paired up to work through what they would say. Their chosen partner stood beside them whilst they introduced themselves. The tutors started by introducing themselves in an attempt to set a standard of openness; this was commented on by the delegates as having been *crucial in setting the tone*.

2. The use of the video 'In Search of Excellence' was useful (at least to some), in that it raised a wide range of managerial issues and in a sense 'legitimized' being *visionary*.

3. All the major sessions were introduced by tutors who gave short inputs on the key issues involved; they said the things that were hard to say, and thus perhaps made it easier for others to say things that might otherwise have seemed too risky – e.g. encouraging them to talk about how it really is at their level, the difficulties they face as men, and how they *really feel*.

4. The session on 'Creating Vision and Strategy' was also crucial. We stressed that their strategy should be based on a vision that was rooted in *personal values and beliefs*; that this was how to create a strategy to which they and their team would be fully committed. We stressed that the vision should be *complete* – not just of their sector of the business but of the Group as a whole, and that it should include their personal life, otherwise it would not be integrated. We encouraged them to use pictures, symbols and music – not just words – to describe their vision. Some of the work on vision and strategy was done individually and some in syndicate; but perhaps the most crucial part was at the beginning when we encouraged each of them to choose a 'friend', who would listen and give encouragement whilst he talked about his vision. As in the introductions, the senior managers were being introduced to the power of being listened to (without noticing it). This was followed by a plenary session in which everyone shared their vision. The atmosphere was emotional and 'electric'.

5. Another key feature was the use of *feedback*. So much of the time organizational life is about criticism, 'trashing' and complaining (whether face-to-face or behind one's back), rather than taking positive initiatives. What would it be like in an environment where people were given appreciation and friendly advice instead? We decided to show people what it would be like. Session 7 (Day 2) was an opportunity for people, first, to celebrate their own successes, achievements and qualities, and, secondly, to receive from others both sincere appreciation and friendly advice. Most people found the first part extremely difficult and yet a *full appreciation of oneself* is so crucial to achieving excellence. The managers were learning to do amongst themselves the very things that would pay dividends in their own teams back on the job.

6. It was important to work *one-to-one* with the managers and to encourage free expression of thought and feeling. Several managers had very strong feelings about issues, both personal and work-based, and they could see clearly that these affected their performance. Working on these feelings enabled them to make clear decisions about what they needed to do.

7. The formation of '*support groups*' was crucial. Their formation was encouraged during the first workshop; the process began with the

choice of a 'friend' during the introductions. Each pair then chose another pair to form a support group which regularly met for the rest of the workshop. We encouraged these support groups to meet after the workshops – and they did.

8. Finally, the *support the three tutors gave each other* was vital. We were trying to confront some of the rigid patterns of the organization (Nixon, 1986); doing this requires confidence and courage: you can easily lose your confidence, even think you are the 'lunatic' who has 'got it all wrong'. Yet the situation *requires* you to do it, and managers want you to do it. If you open up the issue it makes a huge difference, as others then feel safe enough to follow and speak freely too. If you do not, nothing changes and the opportunity is lost; you have played safe when the task required you to take the risk. It is stressful and at times frightening; it requires the support of your colleagues to encourage you to keep doing it, to say to you 'Yes, you've got it right' or, even, 'Go further!' The feedback we received from the pilot programme confirmed this: this is what the managers expect you to do – to 'stand tall' and state clearly what you believe.

Why do we feel able to say that the first workshop 'far exceeded our expectations'? Surely it was too soon to evaluate the programme after one workshop? Indeed it was. But the comments of the delegates were astonishing, and their vision of how they wanted the organization to be was inspiring. Their diagnosis and their vision was almost exactly the same as our own. This was very exciting and encouraging to us. We quote part of a summary of the common features of their visions in Figure 13.6; their strategies were based on these visions of the future. In Figure 13.7, we quote some of the comments on the workshop.

WHAT HAD HAPPENED THREE MONTHS LATER?

At the end of January 1987, before designing the second workshop, we contacted the participants to find out how they had been getting on. All the managers had met, typically off-site at a hotel, at least once in their 'support groups', and reported that these meetings were highly productive. Apart from the support this provided in achieving their goals, there were other benefits: managers of service functions were building (much needed) closer relationships with their 'customers' (managers of trading units); trading unit managers were getting expert help; some of the barriers mentioned earlier were being broken down; certain key issues for the Group to tackle were emerging in these meetings which they wanted to work on in the second workshop; the managers were clearly excited about the whole development.

What were the individual managers doing differently? Most reported *significant changes in how they were managing*:

Human environment – belief in people

- Good leadership – top management in front
- Freedom and encouragement
- Dealing with conflict openly – not shirking it
- Tolerant and patient
- Good supportive place to work
- Working towards a common purpose
- Cooperation – energy directed outwards – not in competition or holding on to power
- Not bureaucratic
- Not perfection – allowing mistakes
- Valuing ourselves and each other

Posture towards change

- Quick to respond
- Innovative
- Correct definition of the business
- Hopeful and optimistic
- Good strategic planning

Figure 13.6   The vision of Sun Alliance

- A different way of life
- I've appreciated how much better I could be
- Nicely flexible – able to get out of it what was necessary
- Learnt to appreciate my strengths
- If only the office was like this we'd get a lot more done
- Tremendous supportive atmosphere from the first day
- One thing: I came battered and bruised. It has restored my self-confidence. Everyone has similar problems.

Figure 13.7   What participants appreciated

- 'I am pacing myself better; I have learnt to say "No" and to be "selfish" when I need to be; I am keeping better contact with people; I am feeling better about myself.'
- 'I have been very active with seniors and colleagues in developing the strategic corporate plan. I have made progress in getting the support of colleagues.'
- 'I am enjoying the job more. I am looking forward to changes with enthusiasm.'
- 'I have come back with a very positive attitude. I have always been fairly emotional. I've accepted it. I have tried to be more conscious of my impact on others.'
- 'John and I are more open with each other.'
- 'Things have gone very well. There is a better understanding amongst the team. Interpersonal relationships have developed in the right

direction. We have moved forward in the right direction. We are performing up to best expectations. There is a good chance we shall evolve the correct philosophy from here – not yet completed, but it is easy to envisage. The task for 1987 is to move on this process of evolution and implementation.'

- 'What am I doing differently? I am working at breaking down the barriers and misunderstandings. I am generating a team spirit … It is very much appreciated. I found it difficult.'

- 'I am very keen to motivate people properly and get the best out of them. I am breaking down the office "aura" and people do speak up more. I am developing a different way of working – different from what people are conditioned to. Progress so far is encouraging.'

- 'I have thought deeply about what I really should be involved in; what others should be involved in. I have sorted the structure and processes out. I have sorted my role out.'

THE SECOND WORKSHOP

The second workshop was conceived and designed to build on these successes, and also to help the participants continue their development and tackle any further blocks or obstacles. There was a real fear (both amongst the delegates and the tutor team) that the second workshop could not live up to the heights and standards achieved in Workshop 1; these fears proved unfounded judging by the end-of-workshop plans and comments of the participants. Most explicitly stated that Workshop 2 had been of even more use than Workshop 1.

So how did we build on the successes of Workshop 1? Again it is not possible or appropriate to describe the workshop in detail (the outline design is shown in Figure 13.3), but several factors were crucial to the continued success:

1. We again created a climate of openness and trust through detailed 're-introductions' covering both successes and difficulties since Workshop 1, and current thoughts on how to use Workshop 2. As in Workshop 1, these introductions took three hours to prepare and complete (longer again than we anticipated), and were enormously valued by everyone.

2. We introduced the concept of 'Influencing through a Network' and identifying key people with whom to build links; this proved very useful to many. So often managers devote an inordinate amount of energy to getting things done only through the very formal channels, and not using their 'friends' in the business. Most participants included better use of their network in their end-of-workshop plans.

3. For Day 3 we offered a range of sessions to enable participants to tackle their own priorities (as they had emerged during Days 1 and 2), and we included space for private thinking and planning. Having three tutors allowed the flexibility for the following structure to emerge:

Plenary session
To explain the proposal structure for the day and to enable people to choose options:
Options 1
Presentations; managing stress; team-building; personal thinking time.
Personal counselling sessions
One-to-one sessions or personal thinking time. The timetable provided for two 45-minute personal counselling sessions with a tutor or another participant – one before and one after lunch.
Options 2
Counselling skills; influencing; managing a secretary; personal thinking time.
Support groups
To compare the functioning of the support groups in the workshop with that, of 'back at work' teams.

4. The option groups provided a 'bonus' in mixing up the support groups; it gave everyone the additional opportunity further to develop their links with the whole group, and thus their *personal networks*. This was a specific request which emerged from Workshop 1.

5. We encouraged the participants to see the benefits of, and make full use of, all the resources and expertise available to them, and *overcome the fear of asking for help*. This was emerging as a key factor in the whole process – it is very often difficult for senior people (particularly men) to ask for help. It may show 'I have a weakness' or 'Something I am not fully in control of'. The logic then goes something like: 'To be a Senior Manager you shouldn't have to ask for help or even feel as if you need it – if you do have any weaknesses you hide them away so that no one can see or suspect'. As we in the UK are slowly discovering, this thinking is fundamentally backward: people are very perceptive; they can see when senior managers are having difficulties and are in need of help. It does not help anyone to try and disguise this, or pretend it is not so. We are slowly creating an environment through the programme where people are *taking charge of their own learning*; asking for help and gradually dealing with more fundamental issues (e.g. getting a better balance between work and home life; dealing with feelings such as resentments or anger, and other personal issues affecting work).

6. Again we provided a strong push to produce *concrete strategies* and *action plans* to be shared with the whole group. The commitment and excitement generated by doing this provided crucial support to the participants and increased the probability that they would successfully implement them.

THE THIRD WORKSHOP

Once more, we went out to talk to the participants to find out what they wanted in the third workshop. The enthusiasm of these extremely busy senior managers to return for Workshop 3 was overwhelming, and their encouragement to the tutors was to 'tell us all you know and don't edit your thinking' – quite a different situation from the caution shown at the start. From the comments we received, the main attraction and stimulation was to return to a safe, open environment with space and time to think with friends who would be straight but supportive.

The design that we developed differed from the original intention (as shown in Figure 13.3) and included: celebrating successes; taking responsibility for leadership in the Group; why leaders need to counsel, be counselled and teach others to counsel, and then, as in Workshop 2, a day for options (influencing, running meetings, dealing with difficult people, delegation, etc.). Again, the managers took charge of attending the sessions to suit themselves, which included having personal time to think. Many had periods of 1:1 time with each other.

EFFECT OF THE PROGRAMME ON THE BUSINESS

In truth, we do not know. We have not systematically asked, nor are we likely to. In the world of business, managers are impatient of research. They are pragmatic: if it helps, they want more of it; if it does not, they stop it. In this respect it is significant that by 1989 seven programmes had been held, and two more were planned for 1990. We now realize it is a very *long-term initiative* whose benefits will take years to have their full effect and to be evaluated. The best indications we had at the end of the second programme were the final comments of the participants.

- 'I now find myself once again firmly in touch with my personal philosophy and, more importantly, confident and excited by what we can all achieve within the Group. Words somehow seem inadequate – a breath of fresh air, a common-sense revolution, of great significance to us all for the future – all these things and much more.'
- 'As a result of this programme, the integration of the two companies [Sun Alliance and Phoenix] has been made easier and less painful. For this alone . . . the . . . Group owes a considerable debt.'
- '[The] management development function . . . is already changing the culture within the Group'.
- 'I've enjoyed these three sessions a tremendous amount and am very different as a result. I'm more confident and am carrying through the changes very much into my working life. It's continuing as well. Some courses you forget everything in six months, but with these sessions, they're remembered and it impacts all aspects of managing a team . . . This will change the attitudes of Group management and really make Sun Alliance No. 1.'
- 'This has been the best experience of my working life . . . I find it difficult to describe what I have got out of it but . . . I have been inspired, encouraged and supported. This has given me the confidence to make it

happen for me, my patch and my group. I am positive the benefit will be lasting and . . . when I recall [the] event . . . I will gain strength.'

Another interesting indication was that the participants asked us to arrange a fourth workshop twelve months after the third – something we never anticipated. As the reputation of the programme spread, demand for places on future programmes grew.

CONCLUSION

Reflecting on the experience, our principal conclusion is how much we underestimated ourselves. We used to see ourselves as 'professionals'. What a limiting and disabling view that is! If we see ourselves as *leaders*, and we are prepared to give a few years to the task, we are quite capable of helping to bring about enormous changes in the way managers in an organization lead. We can do this by creating conditions which will release the vision, optimism, creativity and energy of managers themselves. It involves us in taking risks and dealing with fear of failure; it involves working through one's friends to get things done, not ignoring the formal structure of an organization, but recognizing that change comes about through *mutual support*, *cooperation* and *friendship*.

NOTE

1. Bruce Nixon, now an independent consultant, acknowledges with gratitude the considerable help and encouragement he received from Richard Allen (then Home Division Training Manager) and Don Hole (who succeeded to that position) in conceiving, designing and implementing this programme. Richard is now an independent consultant, and Don now works with Equitable Life.

REFERENCES

Allen, R. and Nixon, B. (1986) 'Effective In-House Management Development: Challenging Tradition', *Industrial and Commercial Training* (July–August).

Naisbitt, J. and Aburdene, P. (1985) *Re-inventing the Corporation: Transforming Your Job and Your Company for the New Information Society* (London: Book Club Associates).

Nixon, B. (1985) 'Some Effective Ways of Working With Managers', *Industrial and Commercial Training* (July–August).

Nixon, B. (1986) 'Power and Patterns in People and Organizations', *Management Education and Development*, 17 (4) (Winter).

Simmons, M. (1989) 'Creating a New Men's Leadership', *Industrial and Commercial Training* (September–October).

14 Action learning – a questioning approach*

Jean Lawrence

> Learning and progress accrue only when there is *something* to learn from, and the something, the stuff of learning and progress, is any completed action (Peters and Waterman, 1982).

> There isn't a logical difference between how American and Japanese managers think about decision making but the weight of experience in decision making can be very different. The Japanese tap into their experience to inform their understanding. They regard their day-to-day corporate experience as a learning lab from which they may acquire wisdom (Pascale and Athos, 1981).

McKinsey and Co., with whom the four writers above were associated at one time, are not known for their enthusiasm for action learning. But their statements express truths, gleaned from their own experience, about the approach we are to explore.

Reg Revans has been working with managers in action learning since his days in the coal mines in the early 1960s. But there was a long gap in UK activities while he worked in other countries; no one here caught up with his thoughts until 1971, when a group of us began to work with him (as a 'set', in action learning terms) to promote this 'new approach to management education'. Revans had (in 1968) developed the Belgian programme as the first action-learning-based programme of management development (see Revans, 1971). Action learning is relevant to all the issues of the day – and many of the day after! – but in this chapter we will concentrate on its application to management development.

Out of our experience together we formed ALP (Action Learning Projects) International and, after about a year of 'talking about action' in our meetings

*I am grateful to my partner John Morris for the suggestion that I write in a questioning way about the questioning approach! – and for much else over the years!

209

and seminars, we were fortunate to be able to take action[1] developing a management development programme for GEC. This programme, the first in the UK, is fully described in *More Than Management Development* (Casey and Pearce, 1977), mainly by GEC managers. I remember that the 'crunch' in the process of contracting for the programme (some eight months later) came at the Reform Club – and at that time I, a woman, had to enter via the basement! I believe we *all* learned from that – a good many changes were made.

Since then, action learning has spread round the country and almost every management education institution claims to be doing it somewhere in the mix of their activities. Some other organizations have also developed ways of working with the ideas. It seems to be 'done' in a wide variety of ways, some of which are described in *Action Learning in Practice* (Pedler, 1991) by practitioners. I want in this chapter to use some of my own experience of management development programmes over the years to try to discuss some of the questions I am often asked. I remember that as I went through that original set experience in our group of ten, meeting once a month or so, I had as many sceptical questions as I now hear from others – and still new ones occur to me.

Questioning – *more and more discriminating questioning* – is at the heart of action learning. The reciprocal process in a set is not feasible in a book, but let us move now to some more or less discriminating questions and try out the approach as best we can.

'ISN'T ACTION LEARNING JUST "LEARNING BY DOING"?'

It is learning by doing – but not '*just*' learning by doing. We learn by doing from the cradle onwards: in action learning, we go further by making arrangements, often very simple arrangements, to *enhance the opportunities to learn from our experiences*, and to *speed up the process*. The arrangements create a structure within which people can explore their own experience and that of a few like-minded others, as they move cautiously further and further into new and challenging activities.

The small basic structure is a 'set' – a group of five or six people who work to test and question each other until each is much clearer about what he or she wants to do, and why. Each member knows that after they have taken their next step it will all be re-examined in order to learn from that particular event and to plan, with their involvement, the next possibilities. After the discussion the individual will, by themselves, choose the next step – and the work of the set will proceed in this way until the set disbands. The support given by the set provides quite a different picture from the 'learning by doing' concept, which is often used in relation to infant and junior learning. Here the child tries something, fails, tries something else and proceeds to success in this way, supported mainly by the teacher. In management, the work that is pursued in action learning is important, and failures can be tolerated only marginally. The support of the other members of the set minimizes the possibility of serious failure, and tests plans for 'trials' so thoroughly that even minor failure is unlikely. The support comes mainly from the set, not from the 'teacher'.

So in this 'set process' step-by-step analysis is undertaken, and each move is brought into consciousness by reviewing it and exploring its significance. Day-to-day events are exposed and understood in their own right, but also as part of the rather lengthy process of *getting change to happen.* In its turn, this interpretation and digestion of the small events week by week can be understood by each individual as part of the progress he or she and the others are making in their learning. Perhaps even more individually and deeply, the experiences can be consciously accepted as part of the *person's own growth.* Each can 'reorganize his own experience' as Revans has it or 'reframe his problems' as Braddick and Casey (1981) suggest. Individual behaviour can be observed in the group; gradually, as the set matures, insight can be gained into the way each member behaves in back-home situations, and into values and attitudes which have a vital influence on effective management.

When changes in behaviour occur and are noticed by a member of the set, others can provide support with their own recollection of his or her previous ways of behaving. There is then agreed evidence of *personal learning* – and encouragement to hold on to the change.

Learning is by no means confined to the sets. In the part of the organization in which the set member works, many managers may begin to take a new view of the task – and also, perhaps, of the way to tackle a problem of this kind. A client (later a managing director) in a senior management exchange programme wrote that he had benefited both from the work he had done with the visiting participant and from his contacts with his own staff member working in another company:

> This company has undoubtedly benefited enormously at all levels at which [the visiting participant] has had contact and where the concept of action learning is understood. I for one would welcome further involvement in what I believe to be the most practical and useful Management Training Programme that I have had the good fortune to be involved with.[2]

'ACTION LEARNING SEEMS TO HAVE A LANGUAGE OF ITS OWN'

'P & Q', 'problems and puzzles', 'clients', 'sets' and 'set advisers'. They come from Revan's writings. *P & Q* and *puzzles and problems* refer to a basic distinction of great importance in action learning. 'P' is programmed learning, available knowledge. 'Q' is questioning where there is no certain answer – question flows from question and more than one response can be accepted as sensible. One of our difficulties in tackling some of the intractable economic social and political problems that beset us may be in part that while our education system is more and more full of 'P', our lives are more and more full of huge issues susceptible only to the process of 'Q'.

Puzzles have a solution, however difficult it may be to find – we will all agree with it when it is presented. *Problems* – and *opportunities* – are the stuff of action learning. We can work on them in a variety of ways and come to many *211* different conclusions, all open to discussion and disagreement.

These concepts can be used when we face any dilemma – how much P &Q? – Is it a puzzle or a problem? In this chapter I shall be talking only about action learning in management development, but it is relevant to all kinds of problems – on the shopfloor, in hospital wards, in communities – and work in these areas in the UK and across the world has been described elsewhere (Revans, 1980; Pedler, 1991).

I should like to quote here an example of the relation between P & Q in management. If my problem is to find a way to create some activities to improve the public relations of the water industry, I can ask many experts about public relations techniques, analyse the cost, look at how it is done in other industries, nationalized and private, and in other organizations – gather as much 'P' as I can (and incidentally a good many new questions). But no book will help me to see how to persuade X (a senior manager) what should be done, nor reassure me that it is indeed X who should be persuaded first, nor whether to write a report, nor why I find it difficult to decide to call that particular meeting together – which, on the face of it, looks eminently sensible. Nor, indeed, will the book define the odds on my losing my hoped-for promotion if I do stir up the wrong kind of interest in high places on the issue. Problems of this kind involve uncertainty and the questioning process in the sets gradually ensures that a wide variety of directions are carefully explored, leaving, at each stage, the project champion (see below) to make his or her own decisions, justify them and then live with them.

Much has been written about *sets* (Revans, 1983).[3] I have said something about the process in responding to the previous question, and will say more in the comparison with consultancy later on. For me *action learning* has three essential characteristics – the participants work on *real work* (not exercises or cases); *they learn from each other by a questioning process* (not from teachers); and they carry through the work to *implementation* (not just to a report or analysis, recommendation and planning).

The logical outcome of these three requirements is a structure in which a few people work together on one or more real tasks until they have made a *visible contribution to progressing their problems*, and have themselves *inevitably changed* in the process. Their work has included their *recognition* of these changes, and their *derivation*. We call these structures 'sets'.

Project champion is the name I have given to a set member who is working on a particular task and is learning from it. 'Championing' is described in Peters and Waterman (1982). The task he or she is working on has many of the characteristics of other projects, but he or she has no particular expertise in that area of work, and, in addition, there is a continuous effort in the set to make the learning explicit.

Clients are the *problem owners*. They are the people who, at this moment, want an answer. Clients will pose the problem, and will be available to hear progress and to support the implementation as they agree a way forward with the project champions. They remain responsible for what finally occurs, but will be greatly influenced as the project champion develops his or her investigation, hypotheses and experiments, and then asks the clients' agreement on a plan of action.

Nominators or sponsors select the participants for the programme and usually play a part in selecting the problems to be worked on.

The *set adviser* is the person who helps a set to work well, and is interested in promoting the achievements (and in particular, the *learning*) of the members of the set. This role has been described in a number of articles by practitioners (Casey and Pearce, 1977; Harris's and Pedler's chapters in Pedler, 1991),[4] and the work of the set adviser is referred to later in this chapter. Set advisers can be, and often are, consultants or trainers, but other managers can fulfil the role, especially if they themselves have participated in an action learning programme.

The *programme* provides an 'envelope' in which all this can occur legitimately, and provides added learning opportunities through coordination of meetings and interaction of sets. The arrangements may also help participants to enter more quickly into learning and to take back with them into their 'normal' lives what has occurred, with minimum attrition; the 're-entry problem' in the form familiar to course organizers is virtually unknown. The form of the programme should reflect a clear understanding of the agreed objectives, and is discussed fully in a later section.

'IT ALL SOUNDS VERY OPEN-ENDED'

How do we know what we are becoming involved in? Isn't it a political hot potato? It is open-ended, but we can manage the process. We can agree carefully what we are trying to do, and for whom. We can be clear about our priorities – for example, are we focusing on developing managers for later promotion, or on changing the culture of the organization? Are we developing a level of management in their present jobs, or reorganizing a department in the face of a change in its environment? Often we are concerned with more than one objective. Several goals will be achieved in the programme – managers will develop and changes will occur in the organization – and work will be done on the specific agreed tasks. But it helps if those who are setting it up are clear at the outset about the *balance of aims*.

We can reduce the uncertainties still further. We can foresee some of the likely outcomes of the programme; in general, we can predict who will be affected and how we will try to meet the objectives we have set ourselves. Additional beneficial results, which we could not predict, may occur, as they did in the GEC programme.[5] Admittedly, we cannot foresee with any clarity the outcome of the tasks the participants take on – as we cannot when we tackle real problems in our own jobs; this difficulty is inherent in the kind of problems we have chosen to tackle. Authority for action, however, always remains with the client. The participant will always be no more than transient in his or her commitment to that work – unless arrangements are changed towards the end (and, in my experience, that would be very unusual). The participant's task is to learn how to get action to happen where he or she has   *213* no direct authority but strong commitment as a project champion. In 'own-job' projects he or she has direct authority derived from his/her 'normal' client, his/her boss. But the participant will probably designate part of his or her work, probably new work, as the focus for attention, and agree this with his/her boss and colleagues. He or she may risk trying out new ways of working in this designated area and will be scrutinizing, with the set, each step as he or she takes it.

Clarity of agreement about the nature of the task to be worked on, how it is to be evaluated, and what resources are available, are all necessary at the beginning – but even more important is the recognition that these matters are likely to be *renegotiated as the work progresses*. Unlike 'filleted projects', found in some training courses, real work will take a path that cannot be forecast with confidence; the definition of the task may change as more information is made available. The subsequent renegotiation often includes a change in the focus on a particular manager as the 'client' for the work being done – the 'owner' of the problem. As the problem is explained and symptoms are identified which lead to diagnosis of the 'real' problem (itself perhaps a temporary diagnosis), all may agree that the *ownership has in fact changed*, and a new 'client' is named.

Politically this can be a 'hot potato', if there is a lack of confidence that change will be accepted if it is promoted from below. It is necessary that top people – those whose decisions can encourage or forestall most important changes in the policies or shape of their organizations – believe that *things will change*, with their agreement, as a result of the programme. Often this does mean the exercise of political skills by those who, within the organization, are introducing action learning. The process of introduction, in itself, may provide considerable learning for the organization and, unavoidably, for those who introduce it. As in all developments, *timing* is important; often as the likely results are understood the chief executive will take the lead.

Even then, a lot of preliminary work may be needed to help senior managers to appreciate that what is being embarked upon is not just another training course where the manager's 'knowledge in the head' will grow. The manager returning from such a course may have very little effect on the work of the organization. Signing a cheque and putting forward a name, however carefully selected, is not enough to promote learning and change in the organization, and change is inevitable if learning has taken place.

So, yes, action learning does require top management commitment to organization learning – and therefore change – and if this seems like a 'hot potato', there should perhaps be a number of ways of cooling it! But it is *not* a charter for chaos. The meat of the programme is all that occurs after this top management commitment is obtained. Those involved can be trusted to work on it with no more hiccups and difficulties than are involved in any change process. Probably there will be less difficulty here because so much attention and analysis is focused on these particular changes, in order that maximum learning is achieved.

'WHERE DOES ACTION LEARNING MAKE ITS BEST CONTRIBUTION?'

Does its whole success rely on the choice of 'problem'? Its most valuable contribution is to increase general management skills at all levels: not to make an accountant technically more competent at manipulating data, for example, but to help him or her to influence others from his/her expert base. Action learning will tackle how he or she can get ideas across; see the value of one's role more clearly, lower the fences around one's department; indicate better ways to make one's data useful to one's peers, staff and boss, and help one to recognize that it is valid to work on unclear human organization problems using as much skill and care as one would usually spend on reaching technically correct answers.

This can be achieved for every manager at every level. One managing director said he had not realized he could give attention *of the same kind*, to personnel matters and the way people behave, as to his business problems of marketing, finance, etc., till he met action learning, in a lecture by Revans. As a result he got his entire management staff working in mixed groups on his business problems and monitoring their learning.

Action learning is not useful for increasing technical competence, nor for increasing knowledge about management. Talking *about* management, gaining new knowledge that the manager may need ('or thinks he may need'), can be done in a thousand ways more effectively than through action learning. It is useful only if the need is for more *effective managerial action*.

In business schools and colleges a great deal is done to improve knowledge, techniques and particularly analytical skills. I recall that after the Manchester Business School and London Business School had been running for five years, the Owen Report (BIM, 1971) said that, while they were very effective in teaching these skills, they did little to help their students work with people, or with the implementation of decisions. It was difficult to see, at the time, how they could, but that was the nudge I needed to pursue action learning with vigour. I got in touch with Revans.

At Manchester, I was building on experience already gained through a growing commitment to use projects (a huge variety within the species) in our programmes; joint development activities were a feature from 1971, and 'stretched' courses with projects woven into the programmes began in 1972. The first 'stretched' courses provided group project work for operational managers in manufacturing units other than their own. Twenty days' work was spread over four months. (The organization had originally asked for a three-week management course.) Action learning including a full phase of implementation has proved difficult to integrate into a business school or college, except in lengthy qualification programmes (e.g. MBA part-time programmes). Several institutions in the UK and Ireland offer these long programmes, based on action learning using real problems in organizations, centrally in their work.

If the special contribution is in the area of general management and we are to learn by taking action, then we need 'whole business' problems, or as near

215

to that as we can find. Since we are not involved in passing on or applying known answers, the *choice of problem*[6] is vital to success. Often a list of problems can be generated with ease; it seems that the better the organization the greater the number of *real problems* that are on their agenda. We need to select problems that will stretch the participants we have in mind; these problems will often be the ones which would normally be on the desks one level above. They must certainly be inter-departmental, not already studied and reported many times, and be of appropriate size for the length of programme. The most difficult criterion to handle concerns the obvious requirement – *reality*. If it is real, how can it fit into the pattern of a programme? If it is implementable – a feature of a real problem – how does that relate to urgency? If we want something done – to make a contribution to this problem – can we wait six months, starting next March or May, perhaps?

One way of working at these issues, and ensuring the connection between the reality of the work that is to be done and the central concerns of the organization, is to work through a steering group. Garratt's programme manager[7] may be an alternative; here is a designated member of the steering group, often called 'programme coordinator'. Line managers concerned with getting things to happen join with developers, and perhaps external consultants, to take responsibility for the form of the programme. They select the participants and the 'projects', and ensure that a 'client' is identified for each, sometimes a member of the steering group. The first part of the work ends with one-page descriptions of projects written by clients, and a list of participants ready to enter a programme whose broad design they have agreed.

The distribution of problems to individuals or groups can be done in a variety of ways. In many programmes, the clients present the problems publicly to all the participants and all the other clients, the tutors and training staff. Usually more problems are presented than are required so that real choices are available. In the Consortium programme, after the presentation, the sets go away by themselves to discuss the possible projects and come up with their individual choices. (They had already developed criteria for choice, which included not working in their own company and working in an area of management with which they were not familiar.)

If participants can choose the task they will work on and with whom they will work we can expect high motivation to work and learn. Some say, though, that this is not like real life. My experience is that quite often participants can choose their own projects and sometimes their sets. For group projects, they may be able to form their own group. More frequently, groups and sets are formed by the steering group. In GEC, each participant was allocated his project and his set by the central management development manager. In more recent programmes, much more choice has been made available to participants.

In a complex programme where there are many groups or sets, the process of choice can be fairly chaotic and should, in my view, be encouraged to be lengthy. The explanation of choices, the criteria on which they are based and the stresses that are generated are (or can be) an important part of the learning process. It is the first occasion in the programme where participants have to *live with the results of their choices.* That will re-occur on many occasions later, but perhaps at no point with such immediate and clear results for the participants themselves. Later in the programme, a review of the choices made can provide useful personal learning, not least about organizational pressures and culture.

As the set work begins, the role of the steering group changes to monitoring the progress of the programme, being visibly interested in the *results* of both the project tasks and the learning, but not judgemental about the way each project task is being achieved – that is the job of the client and the set, with the help of the set adviser. An important role of the steering group is to 'hold the ring' and to manage effects in the organization which may be inimical to the continuation of a series of programmes.

Examples of potentially damaging effects have included demanding too much time from top managers too soon, over-burdening a single department with reports and change proposals, or giving working papers to interested staff without due clearance. After the start the steering group will be supporting particularly the credibility of implementation, ensuring that their colleagues (above and below them as well as at their own level) do actually expect that change will result from the programme. This may later include informally helping clients to get items onto the agendas of influential meetings. A strong factor in enabling programmes to continue is that acceptable changes are made, especially those benefits top management *did not expect to occur.* This seems to be true even when other objectives (e.g. manager development) are important, often more important.

Steering groups for programmes change their roles after a few programmes. They may be thought to be a good forum for working on wide management development issues, putting organization strategy and development together; or they may take responsibility for other particular groups (e.g. graduate intake) and reconsider, with their new joint experience, appropriate methods of development for them; or they may say, 'This is fine for those top-level managers, what about those one level down?', and work step-by-step towards a full role in management development.

'HOW CAN WE ARRANGE EXCHANGE PROGRAMMES?'

We have heard of exchange programmes where senior people go to work in other organizations. How is all this arranged? Like porcupines making love – with difficulty! Many current top managers have experienced a period of secondment, an opportunity to work in another industry, country, organization or role, and all seem to look back on it as a highly developmental period. A manager moving to a new job has a short but exciting learning period and often in retrospect recognizes the struggle as having been highly developmental. The trick is to give more people these opportunities without disrupting current performance in the sending or receiving organizations: *217* gone are the days when someone good, useful or promotable could be 'spared' for an extended period; or when someone with few skills in the work could be accommodated and take the place of a hard-pressed good performer, in order to learn. Job swops, secondment and job rotation are even more difficult in the current climate and, although they may be feasible for junior managers, usually cannot be contemplated at relatively senior levels.

But there *are* real problems to be tackled, issues to be explored, in every organization at every level. The more managers are hard pressed by change and cost-cutting, the more there are opportunities for special effort to be applied to important one-off problems. If the work is real, it has to be done somehow. So projects or tasks can be tackled in a special way and managers can learn from that experience, bringing with them to the task the advantage of good managerial experience. In addition, *project exchanges* do not have the same difficulties as job swops – the effect of ignorance of the precise field of action is limited. Indeed the project champion often stimulates a new view of the problem precisely because of this ignorance. If it is thought that a consultant from outside, or the line managers in their normal roles, can get to a better solution and get the change made more easily and quickly, surely this should be carefully considered; then the only remaining issues are who learns from the process, and how are managers to be developed here?

Some time will be required from the current managers working as resources in the area of the project, but that will be essential, anyway, if the work is to get done at all. The kind of work required of them may well be different. For example, they may be involved in initial information giving, then authorizing, and arranging resources for implementation. In other circumstances they will perhaps be managing the data-gathering, doing the analysis, developing alternative strategies and scenarios, and planning and monitoring the implementation. The 'project champion' participant is likely to take on these activities; as the project progresses he or she will be authorized to do so and may well need more junior people to help – they would have been equally necessary in other circumstances.

There are, then, few difficulties in finding problems or in expecting results in terms of changes and managerial learning. The difficulties arise from the lack of inter-organization communication channels and the problems of getting like-minded companies and institutions to take decisions together, matching their participants and dovetailing their requirements in terms of time. There is a role here for an established organization to provide an 'exchange' of information on needs and opportunities at this high level, and to play a part in managing such a network of programmes. The Consortium Programme (sometimes referred to as the Rolling Programme) in 1975–8 met this need, providing a top-level exchange programme which involved nine UK organizations. It failed to continue after three years because it could not extend its base to involve enough organizations so that very high-level participants would be available regularly for each programme. At that time, none of the organizations involved would contemplate basing the programme in an institution, particularly a business school, believing (rightly in my view) that it would be emasculated by institution pressures. A steering group of the participating companies organized the programme in hotels and conference centres, and I provided a focus for communication at the Manchester Business School.

I was somewhat anxious about letting go the central administration, fearing dilution of the sharp-edged and seemingly risky activities we were involved in; I feared pressures to make it too tidy and simple so that the learning opportunities provided by the uncertainties of tackling real problems (not filleted ones) would be diminished. I had seen too many projects made progressively simpler to fit course, staff and institutional requirements. Staff enjoy preparing projects and learn enormously in the process – often, quite unintentionally, at the expense of the learning of those they mean to teach; managers too are often concerned about the acceptable risks within their own organizations; administrators like things to happen in a regular convenient pattern and prefer not to have to adapt too frequently to the demands of real life. Things have changed since then. As understanding of how to manage this kind of programme has increased, the anxieties have faded; the risk of promoting and administering a network of programmes of this kind from an institutional base should surely now be taken.

In the current climate, more and more institutions are recognizing that work is the best base for learning, and that managers learn best by managing difficult situations (taking on new jobs, starting new ventures, changing organizations are examples in many managers' experience). A catalytic organization promoting a partnership between those who wish to speed the change towards learning while working, and those who represent the variety of organizations in which managers work, would provide a way of helping the porcupines to be productive. We still need an aphrodisiac in British management learning – maybe just an encouraging arrangement would do!

'ARE THERE GROUP PROJECTS IN ACTION LEARNING?'

The Belgian programme (Revans, 1971) *was based on individual project work. More recently I have heard of group project work in this connection – is that really action learning?* Yes, for me it can be. These programmes *can* meet my basic criteria – real projects, learning from each other and implementation. But because the set work is different it is more difficult to hold the programme at a high level of learning, and thus the tutor-set adviser role is even more demanding. Implementation, though achievable, is often less focused; participants learn in their groups from the activity while in the programme, but often only a few (not the whole group) continue to be marginally involved after returning full-time to their jobs.

Set work in group project programmes differs considerably from set work in individual programmes. The group itself is not a set, though its members probably come from a wide variety of backgrounds – and should, in my view, always be working on 'new' work. The individuals in the group are working   *219* towards a single objective and exploring their part in progressing the work. This kind of group is in danger of becoming only a good and useful task force, so *learning* has to be a clear and important *objective*: unless they define their individual roles very clearly, the pressure the group can put on each individual, and he or she can put on himself or herself, is not of the same order as that in the individual or paired project set. When the group works well, the work and learning are brought together by a process of critical examination of what is being done and an exposure of the difficulties; members of the group question each other from their own experiences.

There is a qualitative difference, however, between this kind of questioning and the questioning of individuals who are *entirely responsible and at risk* in their own project. The individual needs the questioning of other members of the set who will not share the direct responsibility for what happens on that project, but reciprocally need his or her help for their work. To get the benefit of these *open confronting questions* born of an equal need for help, we experimented in group project work with putting two (or perhaps three) project groups together for a day to work in a set. In these sets, time was allocated so that one group would question the other about their project, and then reciprocate. The original groups had been formed of people who had no recent experience in the area of their group project. When this joint set meeting occurred, fairly expert people in the field of the project from the other group were able to question those who were struggling to find effective ways of progressing their unfamiliar work. Some of those asking these questions from their expert positions would also be involved in the implementation of the project work at a much later stage; this enhanced the benefits of the cross-group questioning. The sets were huge but the participants seemed to be able to cope with that by working as a team in their own groups, asking questions of the other group. We also created mixed groups towards the end of a group programme to share their experiences of the learning processes in each of the groups.

Inter-group meetings are akin to the meetings with other programmes (in Belgium and Sweden) arranged in the Belgian, GEC and Consortium programmes. The level of commitment in sets and in action learning programmes creates difficulty in sharing, especially early in the programmes. It takes a very mature group to attend as much to the outside world as to the inside. More work needs to be done to experiment with increasing the learning group to group, set to set, and programme to programme. Much of the learning in one set on one project (or, say, five projects) is at present lost to others. Perhaps more use of delegates or representatives may help?

'WHAT FORMS OF PROGRAMMES ARE APPROPRIATE?'

Is it true that top management programmes are always full-time exchanges? Are other forms appropriate only to other levels? No, there are other versions for top managers and many variants to meet different needs at different levels. It is true that a full-time exchange programme, probably running over six months, must involve a number of different organizations in making a high investment in the development of single members of their workforces, so it will be likely that participants will be limited to very senior influential managers. In the UK these programmes have involved managers likely to be appointed to company, division or group boards, and in many cases this has happened. So we can expect this form to be used only at top level. But the reverse is not true; very senior managers can be developed in programmes with a different design, particularly if the objectives are different (e.g. the priority objective is team-building in a board).

The form of a programme is very much dependent upon the purposes being addressed. There is an enormous range of choice. Action learning is well placed to meet three objectives: (a) management development; (b) organization change and development; and (c) task achievement. Tasks will be tackled and some progress will be made whatever choices are made about the form. The main influence will come from the priority given to one or other of the first two objectives, management development or organization development, though both will no doubt occur to some extent. Numbers involved and the level of investment in money, time and support facilities, may also play a part.

Decisions about the form will include whether other organizations should be involved, or the programme should be entirely domestic, and how limited within the domestic world; and whether work should be taken on individually, or whether there would be more benefit to be gained by working in a group. Managers may be challenged to work in an area of management of which they are ignorant, or on a familiar task, and there may be good reasons for them to work part-time.

Often a priority for organization change may influence form in the direction of own-organization, part-time and perhaps group work, while a strong need for manager development suggests perhaps individual work, several organizations, exchange and full-time. But many variants are possible to fit the needs of many different organizations. Sorting out these issues and gaining commitment to the form can be a fairly lengthy process. Some examples are given in Figure 14.1.

The GEC programme (1) was full-time but not an exchange programme, though there were some exchanges between companies in the group. It also included a number of other variants of both organization and task.[8] In GEC, managers were 'one below eye-level' because Sir Arnold Weinstock regarded his 100 or so managing directors as 'eye-level' – they had face-to-face contact with him. So it was a senior programme involving high-level projects worth six months' full-time work.

The Consortium programme (2)[9] was also full-time but involved 'exchange' projects; its aim was to develop top-level managers. It required a considerable investment in time and money, and participating companies regarded it as an alternative to, say, Harvard.

The Social Services programme (3) was devised to develop managers at a particular level, but also to increase mutual understanding of the work of the various departments and functions. The large manufacturing company (4) wanted to raise the competence of its managers in project management in one department and to share some understanding, knowledge and skill from one specialist area in the department to another. Similarly, an eight-month part-time programme in the water industry (5) was intended to develop 24 individual managers in each programme, as well as to increase the common appreciation, across the regions, of what went on in the water industry. This programme included two taught modules – they were in fact the starting point for the programme and the project work was built round and through them.

In the large retail organization (6) some gaps at the top were foreseen and development of selected individuals was regarded as urgent. The complexity of the organization, its long history and current reorganization indicated an internal programme. The need to develop a few very senior managers suggested individual projects. In the small transport company (7) the whole management team needed development both as individual managers and as a group. The new managing director, a family member and an MBA, felt over-trained compared to his managers, and wanted them to gain some understanding of the whole system of the small company and to develop towards board roles.

The Management Action Group (8)[10] was director and managing director level, each manager working in his own company and meeting for a day every five or six weeks. After an introductory week, the programme, in this case, consisted only of the set, and a series of set meetings. The set has met consistently for more than 12 years. One new member has been recruited to replace one who had to leave, and the set has survived a number of job changes and promotions. The members continue to come because they find the thought-provoking day away fruitful. As one said, they found at each meeting, 'nuggets in the gravel' of great value.

The result of the analysis is the same for the action planning in the African planning programme (9) which involved twenty or more managers from different African countries each time. But as explained in the penultimate section in this chapter there can be no implementation within the African programme.

The final example, for interest in the comparisons, is quality circles. As can be seen from Figure 14.1, the form differs strikingly from the other programmes. This may be appropriate. As I see it, quality circles are a very low-risk form of action learning related to everyday work, and the priorities in the objectives are likely to be different.

Whatever the form of the programme, it goes through a similar process from introductory work and identification of the projects to investigation and analysis, testing the arguments and ideas. At around the mid-point there is usually a pause and a very stringent evaluation of the proposals before moving further into action. The second half is concerned with experimenting and implementation, review and disengagement, and later reviews of the learning and achievements.

In the single long-running set at director level (8), each member went

Example	Organization		Task		Time
	One or several	Own or exchange	Group or individual	Own or other	
(1) GEC	One group, several companies and customers	Both	Individual or pairs	Both	P/T F/T
(2) Consortium (or Rolling) Prog.	Several	Exchange	Individual	Other	F/T
(3) Social Services	One	Own	Group	Other	P/T
(4) Large Mnfg Co.	One Dept.	Own	Group	Other	P/T
(5) Water Industry	One (10 regions)	Own	Group	Other	P/T
(6) Large Retail Org.	One	Own	Individual	Other	P/T
(7) Small Family Trpt Co.	One	Own	Individual	Other	P/T
(8) Manag. Action Group	Several	Own	Individual	Own	P/T
(9) Africa (Planning only)	Several	Own	Individual	Own	P/T
Quality Circle	One	Own	Group	Own	P/T

Figure 14.1   Choosing the form of management development programmes in action learning

through this cycle many times as he defined for himself new tasks and projects, within the overall project of managing his organization. A new task usually overlaps with the last one, which is by then perhaps in the early stages of implementation.

'DO YOU NEED OUTSIDE STAFF IN THE GROUPS/SETS?'

Why can we not do it ourselves? I am not sure you always do need outsiders, except at the beginning; but even those whose training and professional interest is in how people work together, and how groups work (or fail to work), find it quite difficult to be one of a working group which is making its way of working explicit and open to examination and interpretation. I have found this to be true for myself when working with social workers, psychologists, development managers and trainers. An outsider (who, essentially, is not involved in all the processes leading up to each participant facing this new experience which is to be real and evaluated) can work without the level of anxiety, discomfort, and defensiveness present in the others. He or she can help members of the set towards the *open, communicative, risk-taking, thoughtful, caring, imaginative, reflective behaviour* which is needed. Then there is a chance that the realities of working relationships, the members' area of ignorance and the many constraints on action, can be exposed and accepted, and the difficulties overcome. Not that the outsider is free from anxiety. But this kind of anxiety – about starting a familiar process with new people – is well recognized and can be managed, so it is not likely to impede the work. It is important that someone has as his or her priority the way the set is developing as a *challenging supportive working unit*, while others have quite different priorities in these early stages. They may be more concerned with finding a way of *surviving in the set,* understanding what is expected of them, dealing with doubts about the value of the experience just beginning, wondering why they were nominated for it, and sorting out why the outsider is not teaching or leading in the conventional sense, says very little, and does not 'keep order' in the set.

The outsider, the set adviser, is not the same as other members of the set, but need not be from outside the organization. A supervisor or colleague may feel confident to fulfil the role though he or she will have additional difficulties in dealing with the set's expectation based on their own past experience; an internal trainer or manager from another department or function or company in the group will have fewer difficulties on that score. This arrangement has often proved successful especially after the first programme. Preliminary work on understanding the role (both intellectually and emotionally) is of course necessary. Nothing can replace the experience of being a set member, as a starting point. Working in a set alongside someone experienced in helping sets to start and to work well is one way to gain further experience; another is to work with a set alone but alongside a more experienced person working in another set. Then a discussion of each meeting can take the form of a review of the role and how it was taken up in each set. It is usual, in my experience, gradually to transfer the work to internal staff in the later programmes even if external experienced staff are used at first.

Once work has started, the set adviser will re-examine with the set his or her usefulness on a number of occasions (though not at every meeting!) and may withdraw as the programme progresses. The difficulties of implementation are frequently underrated and the set may well need the help of a set adviser for at least part of this process. There is often a role in helping to legitimize micro-politics at this stage. Often the set adviser has more varied (but recognizably secondhand) experience of organizations, their structures, culture, power systems, than members of the set and may be able to help by providing frameworks for analysis. This may be less appropriate in mixed sets where there must already be considerable experience of organizations. Even today, there is less written about implementation than analysis, and the function of helping the set members to generalize their experiences may be especially valuable.

It is possible, particularly at this later stage, that the balance between attention to task completion and making learning explicit can move too far away from learning in the absence of a set adviser. This phenomenon varies from set to set, and pressure from the client system is usually part of the reason for over-concentration on the task at the expense of monitoring the learning. The task can *drive out learning*, as it so often does in ordinary managerial life.

'IS ACTION LEARNING SUITABLE ONLY FOR THOSE ABOUT TO BE PROMOTED?'

We are involved in developing managers to be more competent in their own jobs – there's little chance of promotion at the moment. Would Action Learning help? Yes. Action learning is an enormously flexible approach in terms of the needs it can meet, as long as the need is not met just by familiarity with techniques or a 'prolonged learning' approach.

The design of the programme and the choices made about the form it will take (see Figure 14.1) will be highly influenced by the need to *develop people in their own jobs.* This does not necessarily mean an individual project/own-job/own-organization/part-time programme. There may be a strong case for 'team-building' where group projects or exchanges within a department are indicated. This was the situation in a Social Services programme: there was a strong need to understand others' jobs and roles. Group projects where there was no recent specialist experience in the group featured in the programme; a side-effect was a much increased understanding of the *difficulties and constraints in top jobs* previously seen as remote – names had been known but not persons; and responsibilities, far from the sharp end, were little understood. The top people were enormously impressed by the unusual initiatives taken by those further down the system and appreciated their own previous neglect of these resources within the organization. Nothing changed in terms of promotion, but there was an identifiable change in the way those in   *225* the *organization worked together.*

'ISN'T ACTION LEARNING JUST "CONSULTANCY"?'

No. In consultancy, the consultant's learning is incidental to the task in hand, and the client should be alert to ensure that it never takes priority over task completion and client organization learning. In many assignments organizational learning is likely to be in the form of acquiring digested expertise from the consultant (very near to 'P'). The consultant appears as an expert in the field in which he or she is to work, and has often been asked to help because his or her 'P' in that situation is higher than that of the internal managers. Good consultants work hard to reduce the organization's dependence on them (and spend less energy than most of their colleagues on preparing the ground for the next – and continuing – jobs), but their own learning is not part of the design. At the worst, the experience can be likened to an excellent oft-repeated lecture, and at the best, as in 'teaching', the edge of the subject is explored mutually and the excitement of learning is shared, but unevenly. The client's learning, both in quantity and rate, is highly influenced by the consultant, as it is by the teacher.

In action learning, the *excitement of learning is built in from the beginning,* both in the set and in the client organization. There, perhaps only after the very early stages, the deep exploratory questions a good manager asks generate the excitement of shared insights and learning. The stuff of the set is this questioning, and the excitement is now inevitable as the challenge of the exploration is pursued. The participant who, in the parallel situation, is the consultant, has to struggle with perennially questioning colleagues who will explore every argument or idea he or she puts forward knowing he or she has no expertise with which to blind them. They do not assume that the participant is right or likely to be right; they know they are uncertain in their own work and need this examination process to give them confidence, but have high trust that with the help of the set he or she *will* get it right. When the participant returns to his or her client organization he or she is again subject to questions and exploration, for they too are sceptical and cannot completely rely on his or her expertise. Once again back in the set, the participant will be supported in whatever difficulties he or she has with the client system – 'It's the same for all of us in our different ways, we are all struggling' – and given the confidence, with ideas thoroughly re-examined, to go back and continue. 'Comrades in adversity' indeed, as Revans put it (1982). As the participants survive this process they no longer fear dealing with peers who have expertise which they do not have, but value their contribution. And the participants no longer doubt their ability to influence work where they have no formal authority.

'HOW DOES ACTION LEARNING END?'

Can the participant implement it completely? In earlier project work aimed at the development of learning within courses, the implementation phase hardly existed. The project would typically end with a report and recommendation to the client – often a teacher, standing in! The process of getting an organization not only to accept the recommendations but actually to *make the changes* challenges the project champion and the other members of the set. The project champion has done the work in developing the ideas, but has a limited time in which to see the implementation begin and to make sure it is progressing well when he or she leaves. The project champion has to foresee the real difficulties he or she will encounter and cope with determination with those he/she does not foresee. The recognition of political pressure and the need to work with the power system is often a revelation to people who have worked only within a function. They may have seen the structure in which they work encouraging sniping across the boundaries, without any obvious opportunity to use the real relations between groups within the organization to achieve important progress. Now they can find new ways of influencing change.

It seems that it is hard for participants as they approach the end of a programme to see how to disengage from their project work. The idea that implementation has occurred is difficult to accept when they know that a final report has not been written (they have already decided that will not help), that the final memos have not been sent, that the person they think should be appointed is not actually in place. *It seems helpful to suggest* that implementation has occurred when the participant leaves the organization in which he or she has been working on his or her project, or leaves the project work itself, in such a state that the work is more likely *to progress than to cease*. The reverse is frequently true in organizational life – change processes can easily be killed off. If the project champion is no longer there to hold the boundary and the change relies on him or her, organization forces can collude to stop it; the organism rejects the foreign implant and rapidly reverts to normal. However, if the project champion in an action learning programme has done his or her job well, he/she will have arranged that enough powerful people in the system are involved in the work on the project with him or her, so that his/her disappearance is hardly noticed and the energy remains with the powerful group, and they or one of their number becomes the project champion. The powerful group ensures that the work is unlikely to be able to be scrapped by organization forces of rejection, lethargy or resistance to change: the organism itself is mutating and the 'external' influence becomes irrelevant.

The programme does not end there. Usually the sets review this work a week or two before they are due to return to their normal jobs or to leave the programme. This review provides an opportunity to look back at the experience and to work at the process of disengagement from the project work. They can also face up to re-engagement in a normal managerial role full-time and wonder what will change, and for how long. Often career planning features in this discussion. Differences as they experience them, between the person who entered the programme and the one who now leaves, are   *227* identified and evaluated.

Later reviews (perhaps one month, and then six months, after they return) also give programmed opportunities to see the direction of changes in the light of their experiences, and to support those for whom the direction is not always seen as entirely positive.

'HOW CAN ACTION LEARNING FIT INTO TRAINING PROGRAMMES AND COURSES?'

On the face of it, it can't! It is not possible at one and the same time to say, 'Within this programme of x weeks, we are teaching you management, you are receivers, we are givers, we will arrange for you to go through some clearly defined exercises. Each of them can be evaluated in terms of performance of the giver and the ability of the receiver to respond in a predicted way by performing well-defined tasks'. And also to say, 'We are here to help you to interpret your intentions and your actions within a programme bounded only by time, place and agreement on a task – an objective for work over an extended period, maybe six months.'

Nevertheless, as Revans has so often said, 'P' is also necessary. It is possible (though difficult) to combine 'project experience', 'work experience', 'projects', etc. with a taught course. The combination of such disparate activities carries the danger that the programmed activity drives out the unsure, unplannable leaps into reality. The integration of the project work into the programme, so that it does not stand alone as an 'add on' or 'something other' is difficult *and* essential. It will always be second best to promoting an action learning programme on a base of previously understood and well integrated 'P' (e.g. if a new graduate intake are taught *about* management, perhaps two or three years later an action learning programme can build on this early knowledge and experience). The programme can then be based wholly on the performance of real work and carried right through to implementation and review.

Where the attempt is made to combine action learning with taught modules, much of the real work has to be done in the design stage. This is true of all programmes involving experiential work; it is difficult to achieve integration within the staff group so that staff in taught sessions and those in experiential work (where they are not the same people) all feel a responsibility for the success of the total programme. Time will be allocated so that they will have worked together sufficiently to appreciate the way the whole programme will develop and where the 'joints' may at first creak. Also they will have noted how in management games or perhaps structured behavioural exercises, the excitement of highly programmed and carefully arranged sessions (arranged not least in order to provide excitement) can compete (and usually win) in gaining the temporary allegiance of learners.

Less programmed work, with its intrinsic excitement but apparent lack of shape and defined ends, cannot survive alongside the short-term demands of clear deadlines in a business game. Given space and careful introduction, and clever timing of sessions within a programme, commitment to real project work is easily gained and grows with increasing understanding of the realities in which the learners are involved. Then the energy and excitement knows no bounds. In many institutions this is the way that real project and eventual action learning work may be introduced. It usually means dismantling a programme so that it is spread over a period of perhaps six months (or in degree programmes, an academic year), with the whole group meeting for an introductory period, other residential phases, and a review period just before the 'end' of the programme. In this way work done in organizations can begin at the beginning of the programme, be supported by all the 'course' work and 'end' as the results of the work are embedded in the organization when the programme ends. That it grows and does not wither as courses are repeated requires high skills (political as well as professional) on the part of the 'introducers'. It can so easily become a routine problem: 'the part of the course that is seen as difficult'; 'it's a bit of a nuisance to set up'; 'perhaps we can simplify it this time'; and thus you can lose most of the learning.

Staffing such a programme seems to present minor practical difficulties. Often, here, groups will work on a single project. The groups can be left to tackle the work without help; but often the intention is to facilitate their work and raise their level of awareness of the learning opportunities presented. 'Tutors', used to tutoring exercises, business games and teaching in formal sessions, perhaps on the same programme, find it difficult to justify being 'out' for a day with a group where the group is doing the work and does not need direction. The tutor is being asked to be a set adviser and the last thing he or she will have the opportunity to do will be to tutor; perhaps he or she will say very little in the day, but what is said at that one moment may have great value. Often in practice, tutors find other priorities take them away and groups are 'visited' less frequently than might seem useful. One group recently reported 'our thanks also to our "tutor" – they call it distance learning, I believe!'

'ARE THERE HEAVY REQUIREMENTS FOR SKILLED RESOURCES?'

This is a difficult question. Taught courses are perhaps being regarded as the norm, and measurement of the resources used in them is frequently controversial. Senior courses might perhaps be nine or ten weeks long; planning them is not very demanding on resources once a pattern has been set, though very high on resources the first time through. Running such a course might require a director (perhaps half-time), a 'teacher' each day on average, and quite demanding administration backup.

For an action learning programme of similar calibre there is more work each time at the planning stage, though first time round it would certainly not require more resources than the taught course. When the programme runs, administrative backup is markedly less, but of a high order – remarkably adaptive, for instance. Participants' meetings are short and infrequent, and residence is hardly a feature. Participants are not usually away from home and do not need 'looking after'. Few materials are circulated or prepared, and most   *229* of those which are needed are provided by the participating organizations. Academic or trainer resources are required on a much higher staff–student ratio, say 1–6 rather than $1^{1}/_{2}$–30, but for far fewer days. The requirement will vary considerably with the design, but perhaps it will be fifteen to twenty – instead of sixty – days; and normally there is no need for a separate extra course director. The 'programme manager' may well be a manager in the organi-zations concerned, a member of the steering group, and has usually worked on the development of the programme. Some specialist help may or may not be required for (say) five days overall. In many programmes, particularly after the first time, set advisers are drawn from a wider field than just academics or trainers.

So from the academic–administrative side for a group of thirty there may be little difference in resources in man-days. A taught programme can increase its intake above this figure with very little more staff time, and perhaps little loss of value – though many would question this. In action learning more people means more sets of five or six people, and each set needs a member of staff (academic or manager) for some days – perhaps fifteen to twenty. Increased numbers may also provide enhanced learning opportunities, because more groups can learn by sharing their work on the projects, and be stimulated by the set work in other sets. Administration may be slightly strained by the increased comings and goings. An individual project programme of this size needs more setting up and more administration while thirty projects are running.

The main difficulty in embarking on such programmes, for the academics, trainers and administrative people (apart from any role change), is that the *patterns of work* are so different from those required for the normal course offered by an institution. Booking whole days and three-day meetings, often off the premises, for a number of staff (possibly coinciding), may interrupt the academics' other plans and not fit with terms or avoid rush periods on other courses, etc. So the demands may seem greater than they are, and are often said to be so. Course or programme prices must be realistic so that those involved feel equally rewarded – institutionally or personally – not for the number of words said but for their *personal involvement in the work*.

Client organization staff are much more involved in an action learning programme. The participant will typically be working on his or her job part-time and on the project part-time (perhaps one day per week) for about six months. Colleagues in his or her department, division, or company may be involved with the participant's work. Someone senior, probably a chief executive, will have become involved at the beginning of the programme discussions to ensure that change action is expected and accommodated.

Development managers become *partners* (with line managers and perhaps outside help) in the 'design' of the programme, and take the *risks* involved. But they and their staff working in the programme in any way will be unable to deny that they have learned themselves, and most feel that, first time round at least, it is an important developmental experience, so the resources in the organization are enhanced and strengthened. Many clients and colleagues associated with the programme have made similar statements. But it must be recognized that the project of (joint) development of the programme does use resources and tests the reality of the commitment to management development and this form of organization change.

'HOW DO LEARNERS RATE ACTION LEARNING?'

Most of the popular training approaches are low on risk and high on consumer satisfaction. How does action learning rate? It is much more difficult to get an immediate standing ovation! We have all heard the lecture which consists of little more than a series of anecdotes, many of them humorous and received enthusiastically – some of the jokes are memorable. In action learning we are asking good competent managers to face difficult problems which may be well outside their normal competence, perhaps in another organization, with the spotlight on them, and often they will believe that their future careers will be much affected by their performance. We offer them nothing more than each other and expect an act of faith.

By the end of the programme, we can hope for enthusiasm. Participants will be aware of what they have learned, and may have seen changes in behaviour in themselves and others. They may have achieved a task and seen a change (probably four or five changes) of some importance begin to take shape, and know they had considerable influence – for they will have followed closely the work of all the others in the set. They will have taken high risks on entering the programme, and have felt themselves at risk many times as the work progressed, and they will have survived in good order. A very few leave the programmes part-way through, and a few emerge unmoved and unscathed, as reported by one participant in the GEC programme.[11] There must be similar experiences on taught programmes, though physical withdrawal (as opposed to mental or emotional withdrawal) occurs equally seldom, and leaving unscathed is not always highly visible.

The risk for trainers and developers is higher in starting out in action learning. Most trainers enter a programme not having worked with a set, and they convince their management on the basis of theory (Revans) and 'it seems to have worked there' – and often they seek the help of an experienced ally. Fortunately, most people (though not all) are aware of what they are taking on and prepare the ground carefully, getting help as they need it, and sometimes very early in the process. The steps to be taken have been carefully outlined in an 'action manual'.[12] The idea seems so simple: put a few people together, get them to take on a task or tasks, and let them get on with it. But most institutions have too many rules and procedures, too many sensitivities about authority and too much vagueness about their own purposes and their expectations of others, to find that comfortable. So it is complex – to give a degree of authority, to let loose an open mind on a problem not in his or her own backyard, and to work to get his/her mind more open, his/her behaviour more innovative, does involve risk. The rewards can be huge, an encouragement to moves in these directions in the culture of the organization, *231* as well as achievement of changes in each single problem area; and more competent managers using more imagination and strategic thinking, more easily able to get things done once decisions are taken, and more able to make good actionable decisions. Consumer satisfaction is not usually a problem at all. Most programmes are repeated (e.g. seven of the nine in Figure 14.1) where there is still a need. The difficulty, in 'market' terms, is in maintaining the integrity of the product so that learning remains equally as important as task.

'ARE ACTION PLANNING AND ACTION LEARNING DIFFERENT?'

Why is the action planning done at the end of our courses not action learning? The last time I heard this question I was talking to a colleague who works in action learning about the work I had been doing in Africa. At the centre there, technically well qualified senior managers come for five- or eleven-week courses in general management. They all come from developing countries, almost all from Africa. They work in groups of five or six throughout the programme, meeting for one period each day, so each of them will know each other's country, organization, job and personality quite well towards the end. We then convert the groups from integrated task groups working on exercises and assignments in the programme to sets ready to work on action planning.

Each member of the set presents a real problem (not a puzzle – these should have been dealt with in 'Options') he or she is particularly concerned about. Reflecting on the work he has done on the programme, he now wishes to prepare a plan to progress it. The set works in the normal way for (say) one-and-a-half hours on each problem and after the session the member goes away to sum up all the new ideas. These are represented and examined in the set, and each member takes a last look at the revised version of the action plan in the same way just before the members leave the programme. All the work is done in the sets, the same groups in which they have worked together for many hours throughout the course. The work seems valuable and is regarded as an extremely useful part of the programme. The staff have now incorporated this process in all their programmes.

But this action planning in the set cannot, because of a geographical spread of thousands of miles, be concerned with *implementation*. There is a hope that 'things will happen' and support by letter, telex and telephone is available from the centre and from set colleagues, but the invaluable working through implementation step-by-step with the support, analysis and evaluation of the set cannot be experienced. As the group leave, we wonder about the future course of action actually to be pursued by a manager who has to tackle keeping a secure boundary round his research centre, with squatters seeking life-giving water from his water source; or another who must tackle the nepotism from above him which ensures that one of his four divisional managers who does not perform (or even arrive for work very regularly) cannot be moved – and the set's analysis here was extremely imaginative! Or the one whose responsibility is to provide the government with the income from the farmers on his coffee project, but who knows that the money is demanded from the farmers by the 'patriots' or 'terrorists', on the border, on pain of death – and he is equally at risk if his own demands are too harsh! Managerial problems take on a new dimension, and the lack of support during early implementation stages, a new importance.

Action learning requires this testing of the pious hopes and 'case study' solutions arrived at in the early stages of the sets. However well done, however discriminating the questions and the analysis, we know that the really significant challenges will occur *as we move to change things*: vested interests will be threatened, someone's *amour propre* upset, the dominant power culture will react, and the resulting processes have to be carefully managed. Powerful people will have to be convinced of the value of the plan, persuaded to cooperate, or be overpowered by the carefully selected band of allies the project champion has collected together.

In many sets, it is in this area that most insights are gained – not necessarily mind-blowing revelations, but a growing understanding of how the power system works (and how it can be worked with) to achieve change. One's own immediate structure and the system within which it is embedded often seem quite invincible, but others in the set can, by careful persistent and sympathetic questioning, identify chinks and open up new pathways. Checking assumptions and testing boundaries can have surprising results. Unfortunately, little of this valuable questioning, persuading and risking is available within the supportive environment of a programme that cannot include implementation.

THOUGHTS ON ENDING

As I have struggled to write this chapter responding to questions remembered over the years, such clarity and insights as I have experienced have come (as they always seem to) in two different ways. Sometimes we see a simple new way to look at something – an incremental eye-opener – which helps learning. Members of a set have called these the 'nuggets in the gravel', others say they take home from each set meeting one or two ideas they can apply next week. At other times, the simple nudge of a question occurring as one responds to another can change the way we see ourselves and be a permanent, unrepeatable eye-opener! Questions always lead to more questions: and perhaps more discriminating questions! It seems unlikely we will be able to make progress on the vast organizational problems in businesses, governments, and society without developing the skills of asking and responding to more and more discriminating questions. It is certain that we will not find in any book an answer on how to distribute food to the starving; how to enable computers to arrange to do the heavy, dangerous and repetitive work without causing hardship to people; how to ensure that we give adequate health care to all new-born babies; or how to house even our present population.

NOTES

1. Revans, R. W. (1971), pp. 54–5: a distinction underlined in the often ignored chapter on the theory of action learning.
2. Letter to the author: re Consortium programme, from John Bird, then Chief Executive, Private Systems Business, Cable and Wireless Ltd (14 October 1976).
3. Many others refer to the processes in sets, often while discussing the set adviser role (e.g. Casey, 1976, adapted in Pedler, 1991, pp. 261–75).
4. Also my early personal exploration (Casey and Pearce, 1977, pp. 96–7).
5. Mike Bett, then Personnel Director, GEC, wrote of the need for improved communications: 'probably the most important lesson those involved have learned' (Casey and Pearce, 1977), and specific actions were taken.
6. In Revans (1982), Chapter 31, he writes of choice of Projects, Clients and Fellows (participants), and I see he uses a 'questioning approach' to start the chapter!
7. Garratt's Chapter 4 in Pedler (1991).
8. A list of the projects and the way they were tackled is given in Appendix III (pp. 139–44), the variants discussed (pp. 19–20) and summarized to nominators (pp. 132–3) (Casey and Pearce, 1977).
9. 'The Self-Developing Manager', a description of the Consortium programme printed by Cable and Wireless, a participating company, to help recruit other organizations (available from International Foundation for Action Learning, 46 Carlton Road, London SW14 7RJ).
10. The 'Management Action Group' was originally spawned by the Management Action Programme, sponsored by the MSC and operated by EMAS Ltd.
11. David Carr's Chapter 7 in Casey and Pearce (1977).
12. Appendix 1, 'Getting Started – an Action Manual', by David Pearce in Pedler (1991).

REFERENCES

Braddick, W. and Casey, D. (1981) 'Developing the Forgotten Army: Learning and the Top Manager', *Management Education and Development*, 12 (3), pp. 169–80.

Casey, D. (1976) 'The Emerging Role of the Set Adviser in Action Learning Programmes', *Journal of European Training*, 5 (3).

Casey, D. and Pearce, D. (1977) *More than Management Development: Action Learning at GEC* (Aldershot: Gower).

Owen Report (1971) *Business School Programmes, The Requirements of British Manufacturing Industry* (London: BIM).

Pascale, R. T. and Athos, A. G. (1981) *The Art of Japanese Management* (New York: Simon and Schuster).

Pedler, M. (ed.) (1991), *Action Learning in Practice*, 2nd edn (Aldershot: Gower).

Peters, T. J. and Waterman, R. H. (1982), *In Search of Excellence* (New York: Harper & Row).

Revans, R. W. (1971) *Developing Effective Managers – A New Approach to Management Education* (New York: Praeger) (includes a full report of the Belgian Programme).

Revans, R. W. (1980) *Action Learning, New Techniques for Management* (London: Blond & Briggs).

Revans, R. W. (1982) *Origins and Growth of Action Learning* (Bromley: Chartwell-Bratt).

Revans, R. W. (1983) *The ABC of Action Learning*, 2nd edn (Bromley: Chartwell-Bratt).

GUIDANCE TO READING ON ACTION LEARNING

For basic ideas and practice in the UK: Casey and Pearce (1977); Pedler (1991); Revans (1983).

For a comprehensive guide to thinking about wider applications of the principles, with examples of practice worldwide: Revans (1982) and (1983).

15 Learning design for effective executive programmes

Jim Butler

Since 1975, much has been written, if not practised, about the most effective ways of training and developing managers – particularly experienced people: those who have already had, if not basic management training, then some practical exposure to managing.

There have been so many persuasive arguments to suggest that although many adults working in business organizations need formal management training (and this usually refers to the technical areas of management – i.e. marketing, finance, business planning, etc.), the most significant learning can come only from *doing the job* – that is, running a project, function or business unit and being held accountable for doing so. Experiential learning, it seems, can only be defined within the domain of the workplace – learning by doing is the only way. Few of us who have worked in management development for a number of years would doubt that the workplace is the only really legitimate arena for applying managerial expertise; it may, however, not be the best place to learn all the skills (or certain of them) that have to be learned, particularly skills in developing new *behavioural competences* for 'experienced' individuals, and the action skills required for implementing business strategies and bringing about organization change.

This point is particularly pertinent to able young middle managers who may already be operating at an acceptable level of competency within their own function or discipline and who have been identified as managers with potential to effect improvements in their company's performance and to fill key senior positions in the future. Such managers have already learned 'by doing' and have 'concrete' (in the sense of Kolb, 1976, see Figure 15.1) in-company experience but are required to go on learning and to acquire new and perhaps 'better' experiences in order to progress their careers and take their companies forward. In a very real sense managers with in-company service bring 'concrete' experience with them when attending off-the-job executive

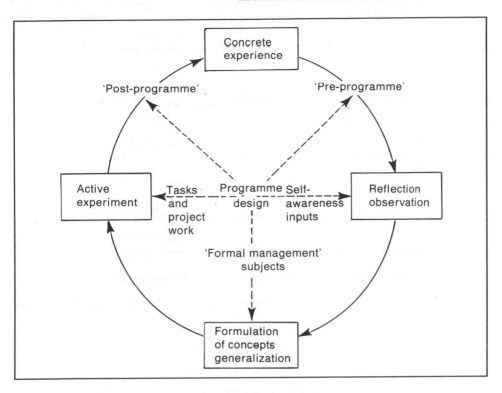

Figure 15.1   The learning design for executive participants

programmes. They have already had hard experience in 'live' business environments and their early days on a formal programme (whatever subjects are being taught at the time) are likely to provide the opportunity for reflection and observation. These 'cognitive additions' can add real value to experiences on the programme itself, especially when accompanied by experimentation (and off-the-job venues provide 'protection' for experiments). The cycle to learning can be assisted, if not perfected, on a formal programme for any one individual by the effects of timely tutorial interventions and the availability of peer group support.

The principal proposition of this chapter is that, although I would certainly not deny the importance of practical experience, my work (and that of many others) shows that so-called 'work experiences' are not the prime source of all (and perhaps the most significant) experiential learning for managers. A great deal can be learned (in addition to abstract concepts and generalizations about management) on formal programmes, especially if the design of such events takes into account the existing level of experience, knowledge and skill of participants and treats it as a *potential barrier* to certain modes of new learning as well as a *possible foundation* for further development. Such design must move away from the conventional dichotomy (see Figures 15.2 and 15.3) that separates management *training* from management *education*, and move towards a much more dynamic perspective that recognizes that in practice   *237*

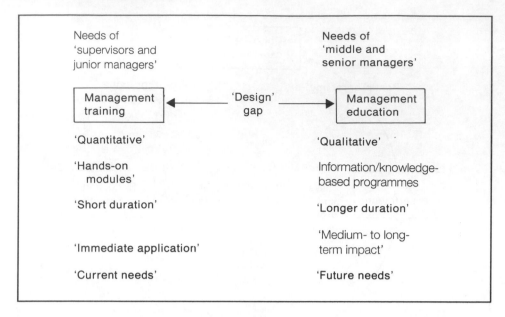

Figure 15.2   The conventional design dichotomy

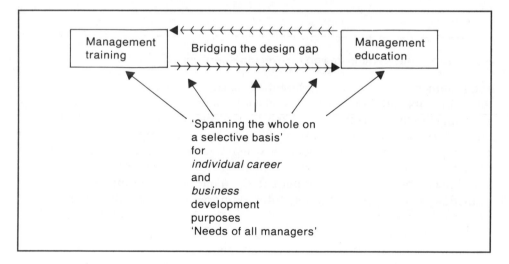

Figure 15.3   Dynamic perspective for managing change (skill and organization)

management training and education overlap, and that learning events should be designed to ensure that the learning process links and combines theory with practice, knowledge with skill, and insight with action, thereby enabling individuals to make *transformational learning leaps* as well as *incremental learning steps* (see Honey and Mumford, 1989).

What follows is a description of two very different formal programmes, within which there are design features that provide unique learning

238

opportunities for international senior and middle managers, run at BAT Industries Residential Group Management Centre, Chelwood Vachery in Sussex.

MANAGEMENT DEVELOPMENT PROGRAMMES (MDPs)

The MDPs run at Chelwood are industry-specific general management programmes. They cover the main business interests that make up BAT Industries Group Plc – tobacco and financial services. The current programmes are for functional managers (in marketing, finance, production, etc.), with potential for development as general managers or senior functional heads. The principal aims of the programme are to enhance the delegates' understanding of how management functions and disciplines are integrated to meet current and future business needs of 'whole businesses', and to assist them to develop effective learning strategies and tactics for self- and career-development purposes.

The first of these aims is addressed by a design feature that comprises three main stages. The first is a *preparatory assignment* which takes place in the delegates' own company: note that they are not referred to as 'participants' or 'programme members': they are nominated rather than sent to Chelwood programmes, and arrive with a real sense of representing their company.

The Chelwood part of the programme lasts two–three weeks and represents the second stage, the fulcrum of the whole programme, followed by the third *stage, re-entry and debriefing*, when delegates return to their companies. A fourth and unscheduled stage is the all-important *continuity of learning and development phase*, which of course depends on the success of that which has gone before, as well as the business environment to which the delegate returns.

Some 25 to 30 delegates for the MDP arrive at Chelwood from all parts of the globe (sometimes as many as twenty different nationalities are represented) with high expectations derived from both the accolade of being selected and the reputation of the programme passed on by colleagues (i.e. Chelwood's worldwide alumni). Programme tutorial staff are much influenced by the notion of 'The only man who is educated is the man who has learned how to learn . . . how to adapt and change' (Rogers, 1969), and they aim to fulfil not only these expectations but also to help maximize the accompanying 'readiness to learn' by encouraging *proactivity and self-development* from the very start.

The design of the programme affords the opportunity for delegates to gain some depth of knowledge in the principal management disciplines, while at the same time promoting a breadth of understanding of the management task of running business organizations. It is my belief, after running many international general development programmes, that some managers demonstrate a predisposition to learning in an integrated way (perhaps another indicator of general management potential and quite as reliable as current performance appraisal and assessment centre test results). This *239* propensity can be supported and developed, but management subject speakers, however competent in their own specialism, find it extremely difficult to teach in an integrated fashion.

The initiative to develop management teachers and teaching materials for integration at IMI Geneva (1986) (now IMD in Lausanne) is welcomed, but has yet to reveal exactly how management subjects can be taught in an integrated frame. We know from experience that some managers can (and do) learn in an integrated way, and that we should perhaps therefore direct our efforts in management education to designs that facilitate the self-learning process.

Self-development within the MDP design

To facilitate the integration of the MDP sessions further and to address the second main aim of the programme, delegates are introduced early on to the notion of self-development and are reminded of their own responsibilities for identifying and making the most of different learning opportunities that are likely to arise during the programme. This process is initiated by the formation of a number of *learning teams*, each consisting of six or seven delegates (this learning teams concept is much influenced by the work of Reg Revans and his disciples of action learning). A member of the resident tutorial staff is assigned to each team to advise and support them throughout the programme.

What now follows is a detailed description of five sessions designed to help delegates generate *self-awareness information* that will enhance their understanding of *existing behavioural identity*: as an individual (personality), as a learner (learning style), as a team player (role preferences), as a manager of others (management style), and as a professional careerist (in the sense of making career choices). The whole self-awareness process comprises a series of sessions that make up 'a course within a course' and is called Managing Your Own Learning and Development (MYOLD).

MYOLD Part I: personal learning objectives (first day of the programme)

The first session in teams provides an opportunity for delegates to get to know one another while working on a real and valuable task. Delegates are asked by the team tutor to 'scan' the programme contents, make a note of those subjects that are likely to be most important, and to describe briefly for themselves what they hope to learn. As readers will know, it can be difficult to determine one's own learning needs, especially when faced with the daunting prospect of surviving a two- to three-week programme. Many real needs may be suppressed either consciously or sub-consciously because they are 'painful' to remember; individuals who have been criticized for their mistakes or inabilities will have 'learned' how to avoid exposing their learning difficulties to others, and will almost certainly prefer to 'learn in secret'. The objectives noted by delegates at this stage are usually sketchy, but a great deal of significance is placed on the discussion that arises – on concerns as well as expectations. The notes produced form working guidelines for delegates' own use during the programme, and indeed a useful basis for *review and action planning* at the end.

Health and learning

At this early stage of the programme, delegates are also offered a voluntary 'Keepwell' course (devised and led by Dudley Cooper). This course consists of a brief assessment of health and physical fitness status, followed by a presentation where delegates are able to compare their individual performance against health risk analysis. An exercise course capable of adaptation to all age and fitness levels is explained and delegates are encouraged to follow the course during their free time. An interim fitness assessment is carried out mid-way through the course to encourage and motivate, and another assessment is carried out at the end of the course. This demonstrates the significant improvements which can be made during a three-week programme, and seeks to encourage delegates to continue with an exercise routine when they leave Chelwood. Originally designed as a counter to the enforced physical inactivity experienced during lectures and syndicate sessions and to the effects of the social side of the programme, the 'Keepwell' course is now perceived as contributing rather more to the wellbeing of delegates than had previously been envisaged. Consistently positive feedback from delegates and high levels of participation indicate that managers are not only well aware of the health risks associated with their lifestyles, but also enjoy the enhanced feelings of wellbeing which can derive from participation in a relatively modest exercise routine.

Frequent comments made about more positive attitudes to themselves, improved sleeping habits and better powers of concentration strongly support the contention that this must be conducive to more effective learning; the design of the 'Keepwell' programme also reinforces the Chelwood 'message' that individuals have a responsibility for their own development and focuses their attention on a *behavioural model of health*, rather than on the traditional medical model.

After the introduction to the 'Keepwell' course and the first session on MYOLD, the programme continues with more formal management subjects of business and political environment, information technology and strategic planning, and delegates tend to take up the stance of pupil-student waiting to be taught. They are shaken by the second input on MYOLD timed for the mid-point of the first week: this session is designed to promote *self-awareness on personality differences* and *learning style preferences*.

MYOLD Part II: individual learning styles (mid-week, first week)

A number of questionnaires and inventories are used including the Pentagon version of Saville and Holdsworth's Occupational Personality Questionnaire (OPQ) and Honey and Mumford's (1992) Learning Styles Questionnaire (LSQ). The questionnaires can be completed in 60–90 minutes, and are self-marked; *241* questionnaires are completed in learning teams but interpretation and discussion of the results take place in plenary.

Interpretation is handled in a very descriptive non-evaluative way, with the speaker using an example of the residential tutorial staff's individual profiles to make points on differences. This usually works very well, with the delegates feeling that there is no obligation for them to share their own profiles in general session at this stage, but simply to observe differences and to understand what the indicators are purporting to say about themselves and others. The results of OPQ are related to an 'optimistic' model of personality make-up and personality development at work; the model does not ignore or deny that 'fixed' innate traits exist, but stresses that they are only part of an individual's overall personality and in work situations, and assuming optimum development of other 'developable' traits and behaviours, probably become less significant over time.

In the context of managing one's own performance or behaviour at work, personality traits are treated as a 'knowable' characteristic for an individual, and therefore an important part of 'information about self'. Once raised to an accessible level of consciousness, personality becomes part of one's own self-awareness and can lead to *proactive strategies* in making changes and taking advantage of different learning opportunities. LSQ results are also examined in plenary, again in a descriptive manner; general norms and BAT Industries managers' worldwide norms tables are used and explained. Delegates are then issued with Honey and Mumford's *Using Your Learning Styles* (1986) and encouraged to read it thoroughly before the next MYOLD session.

Before MYOLD Part III input, delegates have completed more than a third of the programme, working through formal subjects including three days of finance in the latter part of the first week and a day of 'Effective Marketing Management' early in the second. By this time they have usually established rapport with colleagues and tutors, particularly in their learning teams (some meet informally between sessions) and are more ready to discuss and share their feelings about their assumptions and preferences on learning effectively. Some are already raising questions of 'best fit' regarding their own learning preferences, the design of the programme and subject tutors' teaching style.

The raving activist (albeit we do not seem to have many among our delegates) begins to wonder whether he or she should have come on the programme at all – too much lecturing, too much reading and not enough time for 'action'; whereas the strong reflector is questioning the merits of the frequent syndicate discussion in different subject areas, and the lack of time to complete exercises satisfactorily. We have found that the reflectors and theorists do in fact seem to prefer the lecture-room sessions with clear conceptual visual aids and the methodical working through of formulae and data.

The pragmatist (and they seem predominant on MDPs) has a different 'carp' – he or she is concerned with the practical value of MYOLD as we have developed it thus far: 'When are we going to get the chance to practise and try out some of the suggestions in *Using Your Own Learning Styles*?' is the question asked. These reactions are fairly common at this stage of the programme and are a reasonable sample of the more extreme cases of 'complaint', 'observation' and 'concern' raised at the beginning of Part III.

Very rarely do delegates cast doubt on the validity of the OPQ and LSQ results (and we have now had 300+ managers from all parts of the world participating). No cultural difficulties have arisen save on interpreting some of the colloquial phrases used for certain questions in the questionnaires. Indeed, the majority express the view that they believe the OPQ and LSQ profiles have reported accurately and fairly. (The notion of 'fairly' derives from what many believe to be good and bad profiles; however hard tutors try to explain that the trait descriptions of these instruments are not value-loaded, delegates still attach their own values to the results, usually with reference to certain 'managerial types' who they know and believe to be successful.)

MYOLD Part III: effective team working (end of first week)

The aim of this session is to enhance delegates' understanding of their own team role preference when working with others. Belbin's Self-Perception Inventory (SPI), a much simplified and shortened version of the battery of instruments (now incorporated in his computerized package 'Interplace') he used in his earlier work (1981) has proved to be a reliable indicator of team role preferences (Belbin, 1981). I was involved in some of Belbin's work some years ago, and underwent the full battery of psychometric and psychological tests. My primary team role preference was strong Resource Investigator; the SPI version reliably renders the same propensity on a test–re-test basis. Delegates using this instrument acknowledge its usefulness in providing self-awareness on their psychological positioning and stances when working with others. The instrument is easily self-marked, and has strong face validity for the user.

The results of the SPI are discussed in relation to management team effectiveness, and delegates are reminded that they have been placed in learning teams using the 'usual criteria' of professional discipline, with the additional criteria of national and industry group company differences, but without reference to any personality difference. (In the business world, management teams are brought together or emerge because of their professional and functional expertise; rarely are such teams selected and 'balanced' according to personality or psychological dispositions; we therefore resist the temptation of selecting teams according to team role preference inventory results.) It is also explained that they will, later in the programme, be asked to work in the same teams on a live business project.

MYOLD Part IV: managerial styles (beginning of second week)

Managerial styles are treated as another part of 'knowable' data, and self-awareness is promoted by using managerial style questionnaires (MSQ) (McBer) based on the original research of David McClelland (McClelland *et al.*, *243*

1976 – see note 1 at end of chapter). This also is an extremely 'user-friendly' instrument in the three parts we offer. Part 1 is a subordinate version of the respondent questionnaire, and this is sent to delegates before they leave their company with a request to choose a 'trustworthy' subordinate to fill out the questions related to how he or she perceives the management style of the delegate. Part 2 is the respondent questionnaire, and is filled out by the delegate manager himself or herself. The results are compared and interpreted by using the third part, a short but comprehensive profile–interpretive booklet.

Dominant managerial styles are described on six descriptive dimensions: Coercive, Authoritative, Affiliative, Democratic, Pacesetting and Coaching. There is of course no 'right' style for all managers in every situation; each style has different effects in varying circumstances. The interpretive notes are fully descriptive, with guidance and suggestions for practice and application. The whole package provides the delegates with a tangible piece of information on themselves and has good face validity.

Two or three weeks is just about long enough for delegates to get to know one another sufficiently to give some, albeit qualified, feedback on their own perceptions of the validity of MSQ profiles in describing their fellow delegates: remember that delegates work together on syndicate tasks in all formal subject areas as well as completing a business project together, and tend to reveal how they are likely to respond to subordinates, especially when deadlines for completion are looming large and someone believes it necessary 'to take charge'.

MYOLD Part V: career and self-development (early in the third week)

This MYOLD input is just prior to the commencement of the project work, which takes much of the final three or four days of the programme. This input is concerned with individuals' perception of their past work experience, and how they might 'choose' to progress their careers further. The whole emphasis of the MYOLD thread through the programme thus far has been to help individuals become more competent in both identifying and realizing learning opportunities that will help them improve their *current performance*; the emphasis now shifts to the medium–longer-term consideration of *career development*. It would appear that most delegates attending the MDP have not given very much thought to their career since joining their company – at least, not in the sense of actively thinking through what *realistic options there are for meeting their own aspirations*. Although some managers on our programmes have definitely demonstrated a very proactive stance to their own career development, others seem relatively passive and prepared to rely on their companies' succession-planning systems. I have no evidence that BAT Industries Group's operating managers differ markedly in their attitudes to careers from other business organizations' managers.

An instrument developed from Schein's Career Anchors questionnaire (Schein, 1978) is introduced here to generate self-awareness data on *occupational identity, aspirations* and *career choices*; the questionnaire is a self-marking inventory that takes about thirty minutes to answer, but rather longer to interpret. Initial interpretation of results takes place in plenary, but this can be of only general assistance to most delegates as they come from different national as well as organizational cultures, and there are therefore obvious variations in perception of what is (and is not) possible for them as individuals. It is recognized that a single session on career development can never be complete, and delegates are left with many questions to address and seek answers to for themselves. The very nature of self-development in the context of looking at one's own career is that it is a *continuing process*, and that individuals need to consider all factors – family and personal circumstances as well as work and vocational opportunities.

The session ends on a positive note with the distribution of Dave Francis's excellent little workbook *Managing Your Own Career* (Francis, 1985). This handout provides delegates with a really tangible aid to helping them think further about their own achievements, personal circumstances and career aspirations beyond the programme and into the foreseeable future.

Live business projects: active experimentation (last four days of the programme)

The grand finale to the formal subjects on the programme is the completion of live business projects. Projects are introduced early in the programme, and dedicated sessions are then scheduled at intervals over the duration of the entire three weeks. The last two days are usually devoted almost entirely to completing projects. *Learning teams* (having worked together on MYOLD inputs for the last two-and-a-half weeks) become *project teams* and are presented with terms of reference on substantial business projects. The sponsors of projects are senior managers from BAT Industries Group companies, and will already have worked with Chelwood tutors in putting together the principal issues to be addressed in project briefs. The sponsors understand fully the aims and objectives of the MDP in using their projects as a learning vehicle for delegates, but nonetheless are primarily interested in answers to their problems.

Chelwood tutorial staff are careful not to involve sponsors in the possible and potential 'learning' benefits for delegates as this would confuse roles and possibly detract from the realism of the projects themselves; it is our experience that if delegates on programmes are presented with projects and told that they are real, alive and owned by business managers really looking for answers and solutions, then it is imperative that this is so, and is seen to be so.

Managers on training programmes are discernibly perceptive when it comes to recognizing what is 'real' and what is contrived; if they are asked to work on a case study or syndicate task, they usually oblige in the knowledge that it may well render some interesting learning for them. With a live project, however, they become as much involved with the sponsor and his perceptions and *245* views about the problems as they do with actual data. In this sense they are highly sensitized to the concerns of people involved in the exercise, and if it is really a 'real' project, the sponsor also had better be really interested in the outcome, otherwise delegates are liable to play a very different game. Many of the projects are personally owned by sponsors who may be just about to launch a new venture for their company, or present a business project plan to their board for investment capital purposes. Occasionally the sponsors have already launched or presented their projects and are looking for confirmation or refutation of certain strategies and tactics. Provided, however, that the actual situation and state of the venture is explained fully in the project brief at the very outset to delegates, this does not detract from the importance and realism of the exercise.

Project teams are supported by *project advisers*, whose role it is to ensure that the teams organize themselves effectively and involve all their members. At this stage of the proceedings, the teams are reminded that they were put together at the beginning of the programmes using the 'usual criteria' for management teams where selection (or, perhaps more often, emergence) of a management team is based on some functional or professional expertise. An added criterion for the learning team formulation was used, that of nationality and industry–company sector, rendering *balance and spread* in the teams on at least *three significant dimensions*.

Tutors encourage the teams to reflect and share again the information they have on team roles generated during MYOLD Part III, and to consider their *role preferences* in the context of organizing themselves to complete the project. This way, the team role data are treated in a practical rather than an academic mode and delegates can really test out their preferences. Revelations come for those genuinely moving across professional boundaries: for example, an accountant in one of the groups working through the marketing data understood for the first time the difference between a profitable segment of a market and overall profitability across total market share. Similarly, a marketing man in the same team really learned why accountants 'get all steamed up' about slow stock-turns with financial resources tied up in working capital, by actually having to work through the client company's accounts and identify the elements that influenced the declining return on trading assets.

Learning continues, I believe, right up to the presentations to sponsors at the end of the programme, as delegates are usually totally absorbed in their team's performance. They usually share the task of giving the presentation, but to explain the details of their final reports revert to their own disciplines, supported by colleagues who have also contributed to the 'whole analysis' and formulation of the recommendations. Live business projects create energy and excitement in a way not possible with 'case material' and case studies, exposing the project team to organization, business politics and data owned by the sponsoring company. Vested interests and power relationships are very difficult to simulate in case studies but virtually impossible to eradicate from live projects, even if the script writers have tried to do so. Business projects form an important part of the MDP, and provide a challenging, rewarding and insightful learning experience for delegates in their learn-ing–project teams.

MYOLD Part VI: preparing and presenting action plans (more 'reflection in action': penultimate session)

The penultimate session is concerned with *action planning* in readiness for disengagement from the MDP and returning to the 'real world' of the delegates' working environment. Continuing in their learning–project teams, delegates exchange views on the most salient features of the programme for themselves, and how they plan to *progress important areas of new learning* 'back at the ranch'. Tutors work with the groups in providing an outline checklist to help delegates focus their attention, and make reference to their notes on personal learning objectives, prepared on the first day of the programme.

The important thing about this session is that individuals support one another in working through *practical ways of implementing change* and/or *improving some area of their expertise* back in their own company environment. One person in the group is asked to summarize his own principal action points, together with those of his team colleagues, for presentation in plenary to the whole group at the end of the programme. This *programme exit planning exercise* ensures that delegates remain active in their recall of important subjects covered ('important' to each individual) to the very end of formal proceedings.

Presentations are usually a mixture of serious points for action tempered with humorous (though rarely facetious) comments on the performance of certain team members during the three-week MDP. This session is right at the very end of the programme and after completing project work, delegates are feeling more than a little fatigued. Humour should not be taken as a sign of casual and uncaring behaviour in this context. It often indicates 'tension release' and reveals real concern for certain areas of difficulty, areas that may have occupied an individual or the whole group for some time but have almost certainly rendered new learning experiences.

It is difficult for many managers openly to articulate and admit to progress *at the time it happens*; there is often a 'distancing' of overt recognition by both the recipient (the individual or individuals benefiting) and other participants (colleagues who may have positively contributed to improvements and also learned from the experience themselves). A joke or funny story as an account of the experience becomes a safety valve for 'pent-up' anxieties and genuinely-felt embarrassment, either for the story-teller or his colleagues involved in the plot, depending of course upon his or her own, or their, prediction of audience response and assessment.

On one programme, for example, the spokesman for team *A*, in explaining benefits which may accrue to one or two participants or perhaps the whole team, told a story about how an exchange between a tutor and one of their group had led to confusion in their team over the understanding and application of a financial performance indicator 'Return of Net Trading Assets' *247*

(RONA). The incident was elaborately explained by poking fun, albeit in good taste, at the tutor for seemingly becoming impatient with the person and resorting to the use of some choice North of England adjectives to illustrate the point. The ensuing laughter from team A, and reinforcement from the rest of the audience, indicated that everyone had remembered the incident. The interesting observation from a learning point of view was that the individual most affected by the incident acknowledged the value of the support of his colleagues by joining and sharing in the story and overtly claiming ownership of the 'new' and accurate understanding of the term RONA. The exact nature of the interaction in team A just after the exchange between tutor and delegate can only be conjecture, but almost certainly such interactions were supportive of one of their team requiring help, and who knows how many others benefited from the discussion that took place? The work of Reg Revans (1971) has shown that when a genuine peer group is faced with 'uncertainty, threats and sanctions' from not 'knowing', the minds of individuals become concentrated, which can lead not only to consensus on common problems but also to managers supporting one another in finding solutions. There was certainly learning for the main actor in this example and for his team – and, indeed, perhaps the whole 'audience' in the plenary session. The novelty of the explanation and detailed account of 'coming to grips with dear old RONA' gave all present in the plenary session the opportunity again to check out their understanding, and at the same time also provided an enabling vehicle with 'protection' and 'safety nets'.

LEARNING TO IMPLEMENT BUSINESS STRATEGIES

A very different design from the MDP described above has proved successful for groups of managers determined to be more effective in formulating their *company's business plans*. In large multinationals like BAT Industries there are bound to be many (perhaps never enough) intelligent people striving to be personally successful whilst at the same time genuinely working hard to keep their company ahead of their competitors. But being intelligent and trying hard is never enough in fiercely competitive and changing business environments.

Conventional management education courses and programmes have always been designed to reduce unintended error and to eradicate hitherto unrecognized ignorance, and of course this must continue to be important in management education, particularly for new entrants to management jobs, and for junior and inexperienced managers: facts and figures, systems and techniques in key areas of production, finance, marketing, sales and distribution and personnel have to be learned. However, such conventional management education is of only partial benefit to the already experienced manager who seems to understand the concepts and techniques of business operations, but still frequently demonstrates difficulty in designing and implementing *effective action strategies* to achieve new objectives and change. It is not more learning of an esoteric nature that will help him or her here, but

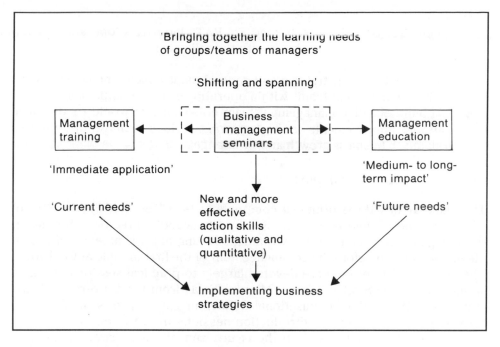

Figure 15.4   The design spectrum perspective

a new experience that first enables him or her to become aware of the absence of certain competences and skills, and secondly the opportunity to practise and perfect some kind of new expertise.

In order to address this issue, the management educator must consult the more dynamic learning spectrum of design mentioned earlier in this chapter (and see Figure 15.4); for there is no other area of management where the overlap of management training–education – and therefore the interaction of knowledge and skill, theory and practice, insight and action – is more critical than in implementing new business strategies.

Learning to turn business strategies into operational reality: the Business Management Seminar (BMS) – a new design

During 1986 we at the BAT Industries Group Management Centre, in close consultation with senior directors from our operating businesses, decided to experiment with an approach that would attempt to integrate management education and new skills learning for selected teams of managers, whilst at the same time actually 'getting their jobs done more effectively'. Their 'jobs' in this case refer to the implementation of some strategy of medium- to long-term importance in achieving part of their company's business plan. Selection criteria for those taking part was carefully described to our operating businesses so as to ensure we really attracted individuals (together with their teams) of requisite seniority and responsibility for implementing business   *249* strategies.

The new design BMS was offered to BAT Industries operating group companies on a very selective basis with the following aims:

- To strengthen the strategic and general management *competency skills* of key management teams within operating groups–companies
- To build effective management team cohesion that would render measurable improvements in *implementing* various *managerial strategies* related to business growth and/or change.

Content and tutorial support

The seminar has three principal components (see Figure 15.5), the first of which is a *pre-seminar briefing* session by Chelwood's Director of Studies in the delegates' own company environment lasting approximately half a day, ideally one month before the commencement of the first module at Chelwood. The six days at Chelwood are devoted largely to practical sessions in teams supported by the Strategy Tutor (Maurice Saias from the University of Aix-Marseilles III) and the Organizational Behaviour expert (Chris Argyris from Harvard). There are formal introduction sessions from tutors, but all other sessions are directly focused on the issues and problems concerning each team.

The third principal component is a four-day module follow-up/progress meeting at Chelwood some eight months later, again led by Argyris and Saias. The main objective of this session is to address *practical implementation problems* that may have arisen during the interim period.

The original teams also invite certain of their colleagues to attend this follow-up session (i.e. 'significant others' identified as key players in implementing business strategies). New delegates identified in this way for the second module only are invited to complete the full four days, the first two of which are spent in tutorial sessions with Saias and Argyris to familiarize them with what has gone before. They then join their team colleagues for the remaining two days of this second module.

Impact of the BMS design – individual and management team learning

By 1990, four years on from the first pilot programme, we have had eight teams participate on the BMS from five very different businesses. The seniority of the team leader has been at an Operating Group/Company Director level, or just below. Our Operating Groups are sizeable businesses in themselves; the subsidiaries of these large operating groups we refer to as Operating Companies, and they trade in many countries throughout the world in businesses as diverse as insurance and tobacco.

Some teams have been led by operating company directors: for example, we have had two operating company board directors; one was from a

manufacturing and merchanting-based business who led his team in looking at

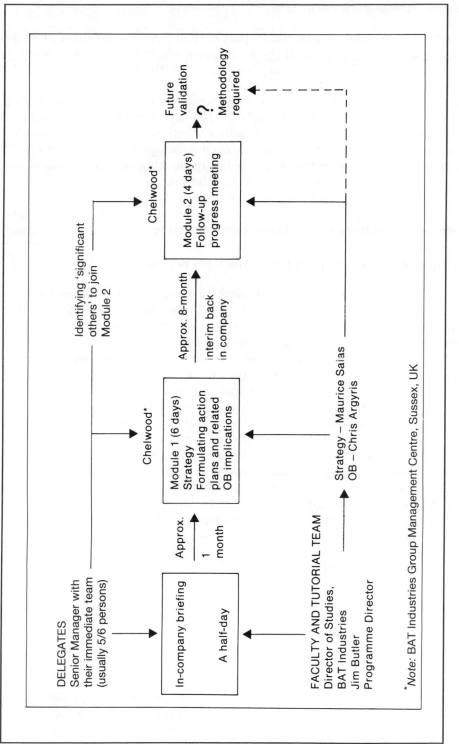

Figure 15.5   BMS programme design

their marketing strategy as a crucial part of their five-year business plan; the other was a sales director from an insurance-based business looking at organization and sales–marketing strategies for their immediate planning cycle.

The important similarity of each of the team leaders involved is that they were directly responsible for the implementation of strategies to achieve part of the company's business plan, and were collectively accountable (together with their peer group directors) for the *overall company business plan results*. We have some evidence that each of the teams that has participated has subsequently implemented new strategies, the success of which has yet to be fully validated. In the meantime we and our client companies were sufficiently confident of the benefits to schedule two programmes for 1990, each of which sought to attract three or four teams per programme.

Example of new skills learning in the BMS design

The immediate impact of the seminars is clearly visible for each team participating during the first six-day module. The effects on individuals and teams as a whole when real 'breakthroughs' are made are clearly discernible: such breakthroughs often come after the team has become 'stuck on' key issues of strategy formulation, and one or both of the seminar tutors intervenes. For example, the merchanting team looking at marketing strategy during the first module of the BMS had debated the merits of applying a particular technique of competitor analysis, the outcome of which could result in changing their pricing policy. There seemed to be a shared understanding of the technical features of the approach and consensus on the advantages of applying it to the job in hand, and yet a marked reluctance to commit to implementing the strategy by some (or a majority) of the team. The interesting thing here was that the 'blockage' was obviously not due to ignorance or lack of skill, in the sense of not knowing what technical device(s) were available and how to implement them (indeed, this had been effectively covered by the strategy tutor early in the session), but more to do with the very 'skilful' way that some team members managed the potentially embarrassing and threatening (principally to the architect of the existing pricing policy – i.e. the director and leader of this team) prospect of changing current practice. The high level of skilfulness in avoiding threat and embarrassment (Argyris, 1982, 1985) was resulting in the maintenance of existing governing values and assumptions, and was not only a block to learning *new ways of solving strategic problems* at hand, but was also a block to learning *new human interaction skills* that reduce potential embarrassment to individuals personally and threats to organizational norms.

Those team managers 'covering up', in this example did so very competently (i.e. it was difficult to detect the cover-up and certainly almost impossible to discuss it in the group, hence the need for the tutors to intervene). The team members, in other words, were skilful in protecting their boss from an embarrassment that they attributed to him (without any articulation or testing

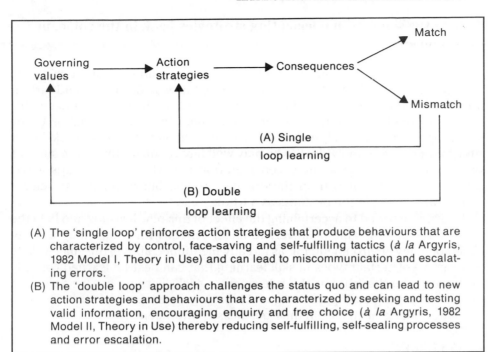

(A) The 'single loop' reinforces action strategies that produce behaviours that are characterized by control, face-saving and self-fulfilling tactics (à la Argyris, 1982 Model I, Theory in Use) and can lead to miscommunication and escalating errors.

(B) The 'double loop' approach challenges the status quo and can lead to new action strategies and behaviours that are characterized by seeking and testing valid information, encouraging enquiry and free choice (à la Argyris, 1982 Model II, Theory in Use) thereby reducing self-fulfilling, self-sealing processes and error escalation.

Figure 15.6   Double loop and single loop learning

of such embarrassment), because he was the original 'perpetrator' of the current pricing policy and, as a member of the team later explained, had been overheard on many occasions confirming his commitment to it.

Concern, surprise, perhaps even shock could be used to describe what these same managers experienced when they for the first time *illustrated* and then *tested* by open *enquiry* this *attribution*, and found that the director was anything but embarrassed or hurt by the suggestion that they should consider fundamental change, especially over pricing policy! His lack of awareness of 'cover-up' tactics was not due to any personal inability to recognize what may appear obvious to the reader, but because of the high-level skills his colleagues were applying and sharing in their inferences.

This was just one example of one team making a real breakthrough into what Chris Argyris (1982) has called 'double loop learning' (see Figure 15.6), moving from a predominantly *status quo* defensive–control stance of operating to a more open exploratory mode of performance by *challenging the governing variables* of how things are 'normally' understood. Permitting free and informed choice on real options, gaining real commitment which leads to action strategies that are subject to *enquiry* and *testing,* will thus subsequently result in the implementation of more effective *problem-solving.*

Beyond the seminar: implementing strategies back in the company environment

Certain progress was made by each of the participating teams during the interim between BMS modules and, of course, this was discussed and further advanced in the follow-up progress meeting. What we have not yet been able to do is to validate the effects of the new learning after the completion of the two modules and, indeed, test whether or not the new learning 'sticks' over time for *individuals*: individuals who may well have contributed to the success of the current strategies under consideration but who later perhaps leave, move on, are promoted from the original groups, but nevertheless remain significant players in the business as a whole.

We are committed to ascertaining the effect of this new learning and how the original recipient is able positively to affect others with whom they work in their company environment: for, as already mentioned above, this may well be an example of certain types of skill learning that can best be learned (or only be learned) off-the-job, but the relevance of such learning can be validated only by practising managers doing real jobs, implementing real strategies and bringing about real change in their business environments.

CONCLUSION

As I have attempted to argue above, with some practical illustrations and examples, not all of what has to be learned by managers can be learned on-the-job in the workplace. There are certain areas of theory and practice, insight and action, that are critical to managers in developing new behavioural competences and managing and changing their business organizations, and these perhaps can be learned *only* on formal programmes, away from their normal place of employment. If it is necessary for organizations to change drastically to meet the challenge of today's environment, and if in one way such changes as listed by Peters (1988) (most of which require radically new behaviour on the part of managers) are to be achieved via formal training programmes, then an immediate paradox arises: 'the programme' is necessary only because the required behaviours are not a normal outcome of existing practice and procedures, otherwise there would be no need to develop them in programmes and seminars. Yet if they are not a normal part of organizational procedure, managers may sense a disjunction between programme content and everyday organizational life, be cynical about programme exhortation, and resist change.

The problem is thus not that experienced managers cannot learn, or that they resist learning on formal programmes, but that they have learnt too much and too well already: they have 'learnt the ropes' and these lessons about how their organization works may obstruct their openness to *further learning* – further learning that will almost certainly be more important to survival and success in the future than existing ways of doing things.

Although there may initially be conflict between a value being advocated in formal training and the structure and culture of the 'learner's' organization, it is essential to help the learner persist with this 'new experience'; within the normal workplace it is of course hardly possible for an individual to persist in such circumstances: it would take not only exceptional courage and energy but in some businesses a strong propensity to commit professional suicide. A formal programme can, however, effect learning design that provides 'legitimacy' and 'protection' for the practice of new actions. We now have evidence that these new and more effective actions/behaviours can be transferred to the workplace provided that the programme *design* encompasses groups of managers that share part of the same organization culture, as with the example of our BMS above and/or extend beyond the programme (both pre- and post-programme *links*), as with the other example in this chapter, the MYOLD course within the BAT Industries Management Development Programme.

I have argued elsewhere (see Butler, 1988) that the able manager selected for the appropriate programme at the right time in his career can experience an immeasurable boost to improving his individual performance. In the light of new personal experience, I would add that business organizations can also benefit considerably from the initial investment of selecting and nominating their experienced middle and senior managers for executive programmes: provided the design of such programmes addresses 'learning issues' for individuals and their organizations and moves them beyond *insight* (many conventional education events provide this) and towards *new strategies for improvement and change.*

NOTE

1. Questionnaires published by McBer & Co. (137 Newbury St, Boston, Mass. 02116, USA).

REFERENCES

Argyris, C. (1982) *Reasoning, Learning and Action: Individual/Organization* (London, New York: Jossey-Bass).

Argyris, C. (1985) *Strategy, Change and Defensive Routines* (New York: Ballinger–Harper & Row).

Belbin, R. M. (1981) *Management Teams: Why they Succeed or Fail* (London: Heinemann).

Butler, J. E. (1988) 'Learning More Effectively on a General Management Programme', *ICT*, 20 (4) (July–August).

Francis, D. (1985) *Managing Your Own Career* (London: Fontana).

Honey, P. and Mumford, A. (1986) *Using Your Learning Styles* (London: Honey).

Honey, P. and Mumford, A. (1989), *The Manual of Learning Opportunities* (London: Honey).

Honey, P. and Mumford, A. (1992) *The Manual of Learning Styles*, 3rd edn (London: Honey).

IMI (Geneva) (1986) *Report of the Commission of the Year 2000: Integration of Management Education* (Geneva: IMI), pp. 9–13.

Kolb, D. (1976) 'Management and the Learning Process', *California Management Review,* 18 (3), pp. 21–31.

McClelland, D. C. and Burnham, D. H. (1976) 'Power is the Great Motivation', *Harvard Business Review*, 54 (2).

Peters, T. (1988) *Thriving on Chaos – Handbook of Management Revolution* (London: Macmillan).

Revans, R. (1971) *Developing Effective Managers* (London: Longman).

Rogers, C. R. (1969) *Freedom to Learn* (Columbus, Ohio: Charles E. Merrill).

Saville and Holdsworth (various years). Publications including the full range of the OPQ instrument, developed in conjunction with over 50 organizations in the UK and Europe (Esher, Surrey).

Schein, E. H. (1978) *Career Dynamics* (Reading, Mass.: Addison-Wesley).

FURTHER READING

Argyris, C. (1987) 'A Leadership Dilemma: "Skilled Incompetence" ', *Business Economics Review* (Summer) (University of Wales).

Argyris, C., Putnam, R. and McLaren Smith, D. (1987) *Action Science* (San Francisco, London: Jossey-Bass).

Boyatzis, R. E. (1982) *The Competent Manager* (London: John Wiley).

Butler, J. E. (1990), 'Beyond Project-Based Learning for Senior Managers and Their Teams', *Journal of Management Development*, special issues, 9 (4), 'The Executive Learner'.

Casey, D. (1976) 'The Emerging Role of the Set Adviser in Action Learning Programmes', *Journal of European Training*, 5 (3).

Janis, I. L. (1972) *Victims of Group Think* (Boston, Mass.: Houghton Mifflin).

Mumford, A. (1980) *Making Experience Pay* (London: McGraw-Hill).

Mumford, A. (1988) *Developing Top Managers* (Aldershot: Gower).

Pedler, M., Burgoyne, J. and Boydell, T. (1988) *Applying Self-Development in Organisations* (London: Prentice-Hall), esp. Parts I and II.

Prospect Centre (1988) *Strategies and People* (Kingston: Prospect Centre).

Rogers, J. (1971) *Adult Learning* (London: Penguin).

Salaman, G. (1986) *Working* (London: Ellis Horwood/Tavistock).

Scheffler, I. (1985) *Of Human Potential: An essay in the philosophy of education, human nature and value* (London: Routledge and Kegan Paul), esp. Chapter 1, pp. 10–40, 76–7.

Schon, D. A. (1983) *The Reflective Practitioner: How Professionals Think in Action* (London: Temple Smith), esp. Chapter 8, pp. 236–66.

Smith, R. M. (1983) *Applied Theory for Adults* (Milton Keynes: Open University Press).

16 Using the outdoors

John Teire

In recent years a growing number of companies have been making use of the outdoors as part of their management training and development; they are finding that courses with projects based on physical activities present their delegates with a challenging variety of managerial situations which cannot be matched in the lecture room. Those taking part soon realize that they are learning quickly and directly from their own experiences: the outdoor projects demand qualities of leadership, teamwork and managerial skill, and when combined with review and discussion are a powerful training medium; the lessons learnt can soon be applied back in the workplace.

Yet, to be effective as a training method, the outdoors must be used appropriately. The activities themselves – be it climbing, canoeing or any other – are a *means to an end*: they need to be linked with theory, discussion and review to make the most of them.

Course design is also important, and depends upon the *training objectives*. What are you setting out to achieve? How does it relate to other company development activities? How will you follow it up in the workplace? As a way of answering some of these questions and sharing information on the use of the outdoors, this chapter is written as a case study on the development and running of such a course for a particular company. It covers the background, the course itself from a participant's point of view, and subsequent follow-up in the company.

THE BACKGROUND

Like many others the company is experiencing changes in markets, technology and traditional ways of doing things. Product life cycles are shortening and there is a need for greater flexibility. Not surprisingly, this has had an effect on the people and on their training and developments needs. The company has evolved a management training programme to cope with these changing times. This has aimed at broadening management understanding, increasing the awareness of working with and managing others, and developing specific skills and knowledge for the industry. After a while it became clear that the managers who received a grounding from the programme were now ready and eager for a next step which would take their learning further. With this in mind, the training manager and I sat down together to explore the possibilities.

THE OBJECTIVES

The next step for us had two main objectives. The first was to build on previous courses, particularly in the area of taking *personal responsibility* in management, and understanding and working effectively *with other people*; the second was to look at the process of *change*, and how individual managers were coping with it. It was also our objective that any further development activity should be a participative one, and should give delegates a practical and relevant challenge from which they could learn.

The many ideas we generated just did not fit together into a neat jigsaw puzzle; they kept moving around as we tried to get hold of them. But we realized after a while that this was just the same in any company: it is impossible to have a complete and unchanging picture of what is going on. We found that we had ended up with a set of concepts which we felt were important and which we wanted to build into a week's programme. To do this, we needed a basic structure and a range of activities which would highlight the concepts in an experiential way and show how they were interrelated. At this stage we had more or less decided on a residential week somewhere off-site.

THE DESIGN

One of the first concepts we wished to make use of was the relationship between a manager's *thoughts, feelings* and *actions* (Figure 16.1).

Many training courses concentrate on the delegate's thoughts by presenting a series of concepts and ideas; a few (but not many) take into account the manager's feelings and deal with personal motivation and attitudes; a growing number are looking at 'action' by using outdoor projects and physical skills. We wanted to bring these together in a more balanced way which would also show how all three *influence each other*. This was particularly important for helping the manager understand his own *reactions*: one of the problems which many of us have in managing is *ourselves* – our set patterns of behaviour, our fixed ideas and our conditioned feelings about things.

We needed activities which would be unusual for the delegate and would challenge the elements of thoughts, feelings and actions; through the challenge he might see and understand his own reactions better. We decided to make use of outdoor projects incorporating sailing, canoeing, rock-climbing, horse-riding, orienteering and trekking. But the outdoors itself was not the only objective. We also decided to use the 'great indoors', and to learn   *259*

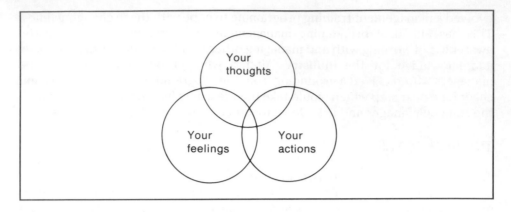

Figure 16.1   Relationship between a manager's thoughts, feelings and actions

from how one planned and reviewed the projects. Many of these would challenge the manager's preconceived ideas of what he could and could not do, as well as allowing him to see how his feelings affected his actions. We all have unused potential: often unused because of the *unnecessary constraints which we impose upon ourselves.*

Another concept we wished to use was the *interdependence* that the individual manager has with both his work team and the company organization (see Figure 16.2). So many times these are taken in isolation from each other, and the ways in which the needs of each are related are not seen at all. This is particularly so when we add the third of the concepts, that of the *task* and the *process*, where the 'task' is what we are doing, and the 'process' is how we are going about it, often with little awareness. Both of these concepts, we felt, were important for understanding and working effectively with other people.

Any increase in the manager's awareness of these concepts would not be a bad thing! It occurred to us that the most direct way for those taking part in the programme to learn would be for them to have some responsibility for the *organization of the week's structure* as well as for the *daily tasks of living together.* Within the limits set by the resources available, the delegates could have the task of designing part of the week's programme and balancing and coordinating the many different (and often conflicting) needs; this would include planning the week's menu and buying and cooking the food each day: the course would have a budget to do this.

It was important for us that the delegates be given a choice in what they *did* and in the *roles* they took. This meant that although there were many activities and projects available, no one delegate would have to do them all, and different delegates would have done different things during the week. Some of these were group activities, some were individual, and some involved everybody. By giving the delegates a range of tasks and activities from which they could learn but also giving them some responsibility for organizing *260* and managing themselves, we hoped to create a realistic and challenging

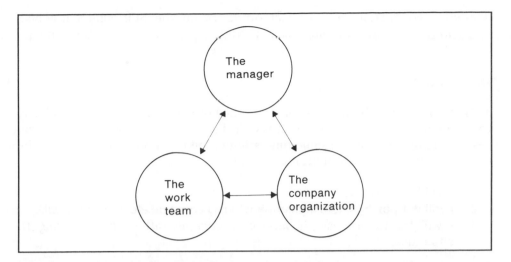

Figure 16.2   Interdependence with work team and organization

environment.

So, as a basic structure, we decided on a residential course of six days' duration with twelve to fifteen delegates at a training centre in North Wales; the choice of place was important but only in how it fitted in with what we wished to achieve. Taken together, we thought, these parameters would give ample opportunity to explore the last of our concepts, that of managerial *responsibility*: in so many cases, we can see when things are going wrong, but we are not prepared to do anything about it *ourselves*; it is easier to blame someone or something else, than to take a little risk and have a go ourselves.

THE EXPERIENCE

The theory has already been stated. But what actually happened? The personal account which follows is by Dave, a participant in the programme, reflecting his own experiences. Right at the beginning he had decided to keep a diary of the events, and extracts from this are given here.

Before the residential part of the programme a meeting was held at the company for the training manager and me to introduce it to the delegates and to start them off; we explained the thinking behind it, the range of possible activities and the need to do something about food for the week! They held a second meeting by themselves two weeks later.

Although twelve delegates shared the week, and took part in many common tasks, there was also opportunity for individuals to select options relevant to their own needs. Most days there were two to four groups doing different projects and coming together to take stock, review and reorganize as necessary. To put the diary into context, bear in mind that the Monday morning was set aside for detailed planning and organization of the week (started a number of weeks earlier at the two meetings on the company site).   *261*

Thursday was a full day's project outdoors on the hills which involved everybody, and Friday evening was reserved for some creative entertainment. The rest of the time was organized by the delegates.

DAVE'S DIARY

This first meeting is held to discuss what the course is about and what is likely to happen. We make little progress. It has a debilitating effect on my responsibility cells, at the same time stimulating my mouth cells. During the meeting I make a number of promises to myself. These are that:

1. I will keep a diary.
2. I will not put myself in a position where I could be elected as the MD.
3. I will try to practise the art of *responding* rather than *reacting* to situations.

The meeting goes on and we talk about food (my subject!). There is an overwhelming apathy about this. I quote: 'Don't bother, beans is fine.' This strikes at my very parts. I offer to be quartermaster (my mouth again). Again there is overwhelming apathy, but an acceptance upon my threat of withdrawal. Things begin to look up as the meeting continues. Stan asks, 'Who wants to go sailing?' This sounds more like it. We provisionally organize a sailing party. After more talk we agree to meet again in two weeks.

A very different atmosphere at this second meeting; lots of talk. I had circulated a menu and a shopping list but there is no response from anyone except Bob who says 'Why can't we have fresh meat?' Despite the three commandments I react, and instantly wish that I had not. Not as easy as it sounds, this responding thing. Suspicion is rife that the whole course is a big 'con' and that any arrangements we make will be reversed and we will be told to 'get out of that'. I begin to believe this. It all sounds too good to be true. I receive lots of help and enthusiasm from people outside the course who do not see the black cloud. Maybe there isn't one.

I think of some activity and prejudge it, for example canoeing – there's no way I am going in a canoe. Conversely, I think of an activity which I would enjoy and my imagination pictures me climbing impossible cliffs or canoeing in fast-flowing mountain streams. I must admit I feel somewhat frustrated at not having a finite situation to unravel, and problems to overcome. Others are in a similar frame of mind but are prepared to tackle the situation as it happens.

After our second meeting the suspicion deepens. Why don't the garage know anything about the hire cars we shall need to get us there? Why are the catering people delaying our order? Why is there such a large queue at Tesco?

Sunday

The sun shines. We arrive in good order and, first of all, pick the best beds. A touch of remembrance of thirty years ago at school. John and George do not arrive, although the others do. Is it all a con? We eat, we lock up the centre, and we go to the pub like schoolgirls whooping. We say we don't care. I think that we do. We get back and they still haven't arrived. What next, I wonder. Then they do arrive. There is lot of duvet stuffing, pillows, laughter and silliness. Did we know that they would come? Of course we did. The very idea!

Monday

We have an 'unstructured breakfast' and it is a huge success. Brian has been doing an imitation of a Kamikaze pig all night. He and I will not last the distance, I swear. There will be an unexplained accident...

When the range of projects is announced I feel dread at the thought of undertaking some of them and a thrill of excitement towards others. This is crunch time. Do I go for what I feel I would get something from, or wait and see what the majority split is?

I choose the latter and then realize that this group appears to have forgotten all the advantages of group discussion. I become aware that there are definite sub-groups, those prepared to go along with the majority without any input, and those anxious to get on with it. I try to respond to the situation but find I cannot find anything to respond to. This task is more difficult than I thought. As I look out of the window I can see a man over the wharf from me. He stands, building a fire in an old ship ventilator in the autumn sun. It is Monday, 10.30 a.m. I do not envy people but I might envy him. I expect that he thinks that 'process' is what you do to peas. I think that he is right.

I lose interest in the proceedings but, noticing that others are the same, I decide to make a suggestion. This time a pen lands in my lap with a voice saying, 'Get on with it, Dave.' I feel relief. At last I can do something useful.

Once at the board things move. Suggestions are constructive and the situation assumes one of order. People air their views and a programme materializes. It is evident that some are unable, or unwilling, to make decisions. It also appears that certain activities are under discussion, but the less appealing ones such as cooking and washing up are not mentioned . . . Perhaps they think these will go away if ignored. A separate chart is drawn up for each day and individuals enter their requirements under specific projects. This saves a lot of argument and debate, and I feel that I have achieved something.

The afternoon's project of problem-solving based on orienteering is a chance to achieve some concrete objective. Everyone is involved, in small groups, and we need to give attention to target-setting, communications, and dealing with limited information. We also have to judge the capabilities of each team member.

The exercise benefits everyone. My colleagues take it in turns to direct, and we progress at a cracking pace. Mistakes are made and assumptions prove incorrect, but overall we all feel a sense of achievement.

We get back having correctly completed the task. One group, considered to be expert, comes in one hour after everyone else. Until they arrive we all have a laugh at their expense. When they arrive, we say nothing, and mumble about 'having to go round the course anti-clockwise is difficult'. We are two-faced and charitable. We return and have a good meal. It occurs to me that it is the same ones who are charitable who also say that the meal is good. I cannot unravel that.

The evening discussion is very similar to the morning session. However, the division of the larger body into the smaller sub-groups is an interesting exercise. We divide ourselves into discussion groups to review the events of the day. I bend the resolutions that I had made and change groups three times. Does this mean that I am trying for selection rather than being selected? Some of this is gratifying, but not all. I think this only applies to me. I do not care. Yes I do. Why? I end up with three people I know and like. Fine. The different groups separate and we talk and laugh.

I feel happier in this closer environment, but nevertheless, I am finding difficulty *coming to terms* with some of the statements being made. After some time it becomes apparent that the group need help, but can I offer the kind of help that would be constructive, and would the group benefit? I decide to soft-pedal, concentrate on two members and then to meet the obstacle on my own ground at a more opportune moment. This works and a *relationship* is beginning to form, to which I can offer a useful *contribution*. It is getting late. The door opens and Ken comes in in his pyjamas saying, 'What's all the noise?' He says he can especially hear my voice. If only he knew that two hours earlier I would have apologized. I say, 'Hard luck, mate', and I am ashamed later. But at that moment I can justify what I say as a response. I ought to make efforts in this direction, but suspect I will not.

We go to bed, giggle at the snores leaking from next door and fall asleep. Brian and his pig gain the benefit of divine intervention. He lives till morning.

Tuesday

Sailing today. I am up alone at 6.40 a.m. and listen to the shipping forecast: 'Irish Sea, gale force 9 is expected soon. Good.' Bad, it is cancelled. First thoughts, let us go quickly, we are all packed up for the day. Too late. We have breakfast and then meet to replan. I find myself trying to establish a *consensus* and then remember my promises. I stop and observe.

We are doing better. People are making an attempt to *listen*. How are we managing this *change of plan*? Some *adapt* easily, others are stuck. Is this a time to respond? No, not now. Peter is doing fine. Do not cramp his style. We do not need two leaders. Good stuff, this self-management, when we do it well.

I take on the *challenge* of a canoeing project with a team of four. Do what you are unsure of, said the tutor. It is better for your learning. Well, here goes. What an eventful day it turns out to be. There is no handholding with this one. In at the deep end, so to speak. We are given three possible projects with information on weather conditions, tide times and a guide to the progress we could make if we work well together. None of us has had any canoeing experience before. We set to and sort out our objectives for the day and select a project which we feel will give us a challenge.

During the day my ideas about canoeing are turned around. How *fixed opinions* can get in the way! Watch out for this. I find that I can do much more than I would have dreamt. We have lots of *problems to overcome as a team*, and spend as much time on dry land, *discussing and deciding*, as we do in the water. My problem person from last night is in the team, and I make a special effort: it works.

A pity we miscalculate the falling tide and can only get back to the centre by carrying the canoes through the wood. We do look silly.

My return is met with a headache. A belaboured cook is panicking over supplies. I *respond* easily and fix it. Am I improving? I take time to write to the kids. There is lots they do not know about me (and the reverse). Will I live long enough? Wish my dad had. I write to Joan; warm feelings. Good.

Another good meal. Did I misjudge the feelings and capabilities of my colleagues? How could I have found out? That is something else to ponder on.

After dinner we discuss the day in our small groups and I find that my fears of the impression I give are well-founded; I think this is my major task – to take a 'step back', to be *aware* of its effect.

We go to bed, and I find that I am also a Kamikaze pig. Am I on the start of a *learning curve?*

Wednesday

A sound night's sleep and I awake feeling refreshed. Will my legs work when I swing them out of bed? They do. Relief, and I get as far as the showers to wake up the rest of my body. The breakfast group has been up already, and smells of bacon and eggs come drifting up the stairs. At breakfast there is much talk about yesterday's activities. I hear a lot from the group that went rock-climbing. This is my project for today. I listen and take it in, being aware of forming ideas which would only cause problems. What comes across clearly is the extent to which people become *involved* in their projects and how this *practical approach* sorts the theory out and brings us face-to-face with our own *abilities*. The tutors seem to be there for *guidance, safety* and *advice* when *necessary*, but most of the time we are having to sort ourselves out. What things have I *avoided in the past*? More importantly, what things am I *avoiding in the present*?

Rock-climbing today. What a surprise – we all enjoy it. A different team and different personalities to contend with. And different skills to take into consideration. Paul is 17 stone, and with his positive attitude is turning out to be the star of the course. He causes us to slow down and pay attention to each other. Do I ignore others at work? How am I to know? Am I learning to stand back a little more, instead of rushing in? Our day is one of working closely together, while pushing through fears which come from our minds. I see similar fears getting in my way at work. Are they in my mind? Must investigate further when I return. One incident in particular strikes me. On one section of our climb, Brian sits down and refuses to go on. We spend twenty minutes with him, giving support. With no effect. It is only on our way back that he says he needed a kick up the backside to move him. Remember not to be stuck with just one style of dealing with people. *Be adaptable.* Also, we can learn from *what we do not do* as well as from *what we do.*

In the evening we review the day's projects and then change the groups around to discuss the 'entertainment' for Friday evening. I catch myself falling into the lead. Before bed a small group do some relaxation exercises. Not for me. I go to bed very tired and try to learn my monologues for Friday evening, but never get beyond 'Now Pa, who had…', because I fall asleep.

Thursday

Today is our all-day project for everyone. We wake and I just know that the preparation of the packed lunches will be left to John and myself. How wrong I am. All hands set to. There is no 'organization', but everything is completed swiftly and effectively.

There has been a build-up to Thursday as the highlight of the week. As a result there is considerable *enthusiasm*, and judging by the alacrity with which we leave the centre, everyone is *determined* that we are going to do our utmost to *succeed*. But to succeed in what?

We set out separately in the discussion groups used in the evenings. Good. Our group follows the rules and enjoys a self-righteous feeling. Soon, Bob becomes impatient with John's map-reading, but we get on well and arrive at the first rendezvous point with another group and everything is going well. Bob asks us to *monitor* the way in which he interrupts people. We do so in style.

We manage to rearrange the groups quickly as required for the task, and I launch a brief sermon on 'no competition'. I just do it and enjoy it, but as I seem to be banging on, I shut myself up. Everybody is *confident*. We pick up more gear and flog on back up the hill. John cannot manage going up hills. Smoking? I carry his bag and try not to feel smug, and I believe I may need similar help later. From then on I carry double packs to *assess capability*.

Wales is like a documentary; it shows all the best bits. Super, I fall in a bog! I'm very wet, and I imagine the rest of the group thinking, 'Go on, make a joke out of that!' I do; it is not always easy. At lunchtime we meet up with the other group and all are happy. It is only when the majority of people are formed up that I realize one is missing.

Leaving the others, I retrace my steps to find a member of the team sitting at the bottom of the hill. He has severe muscle cramp and does not have enough strength to climb the hill. After some discussion I carry him piggy-back, taking care to put him down before we come into view of the others, to save embarrassment. Neither of us speaks, but words are unnecessary. Then I go back for his kit. This is another of those instances that the memory retains for the rest of your life. Words are inadequate to describe how I feel. Perhaps I am too sensitive.

Later, during the 'rescue', *tempers fray* and we manage in a totally *uncoordinated* way. Wetness dampens the spirits and puts people *under pressure*. The heavy pack reminds me that I am *coping*. I realize that my pressure is not knowing whether I can manage, and I try not to be boastful when I can. We arrive with some steam left and our original group are so *elated* we decide to walk back. We enjoy it, but wonder what effect our behaviour has on the others. I hope they understand. We all arrive back and everybody is happy again. It *worked well*.

There is more panic in the kitchen, over milk this time. Steve does a Dave and fixes it. Is the pleasure it gave me the same for others when I do it? I hope so.

At the evening *review* we come back to our *disorganization* at the 'rescue'. It is bad news. On reflection, if I had not been determined not to take on the 'MD' role and overpower the situation, things may well have been different. I conclude that this was neither an honourable objective nor a very sensible one. It must have contributed.

There is a certain contentment to be found in letting things happen all around you, and spending time *observing* while the *now* spirals into chaos. But during *reflection* the contentment fades away. Worse still, we cannot relive this afternoon.

Friday

I wake up with yesterday in my mind. How our *understanding* of a situation can change when we stand back! For me, yesterday was all about groups working together, and the *responsibility* each of us has. I can see it going on at work amongst the different departments, and how we blame each other instead of doing something about it. There is a lot to learn here.

Sailing today, rearranged from Tuesday because of the weather. Stan is a man transformed. We are due to be out for the morning only, and the others are expecting us back at the centre for lunch.

Yet at lunchtime when the question is asked 'Do you want to carry on?', we live the biggest lie of the week. In the afternoon, discussions are planned to finalize the evening's entertainment. Steve and I have put together a couple of sketches, but these need rehearsal and polish; also, we have not *consulted* any of the other groups. If we stay at sea, these *discussions cannot take place*. We debate as a group, and come to the conclusion that we will stay at sea but inform the centre via ship-to-shore radio. What have we done? We are enjoying ourselves, the evening's entertainment has taken second place, and perhaps the other groups will put something together without us. More to the point, we have *avoided the responsibility of involvement* and *put our own interests before that of the others.*

The sailing is of great value and brings out qualities in people which I had never suspected. We see each other in a new light and are amazed at what we achieve in a short space of time. It is not until we approach the centre in the evening that unspoken thoughts of apprehension are apparent. In the centre we narrate our day's experiences, carefully avoiding the evening's entertainment. There is a disgruntled atmosphere and I am aware of *267 annoyance* about our absence during the afternoon.

The evening meal is superb. The cooks have put in a terrific effort. The organization as well as the quality cannot be overlooked. I think that if a small number can organize themselves, why are larger numbers incapable of the same?

The evening approaches and I can see that everyone is conscious of not having *fulfilled the suggestions* put forward earlier in the week. As groups chat, most people are hoping that by *ignoring the situation* it will go away. However, as we know deep down, there is *no avoiding the inevitable.*

Someone has a few direct words with Stan about how the sailing trip, which started at the first meeting many weeks ago, has had an effect on this evening. Stan is quiet and thoughtful. This leads me to offer him the monologue I had prepared. We go into another room and Stan is very *nervous* but *willing to have a go.* He does, and it is magic. He is very good and I am pleased afterwards when he thanks me. This changes the mood, and the 'entertainment' gets under way. I do a hastily put together sketch with some others about the week; we play some games and enjoy the general air of relaxation which develops. I regret that I am the first to crash out. I do not want to break up the party but I go limp from my head downwards. Good sleep.

Others have the stamina to stay on into the early hours discussing many matters of a personal nature which have come to them during the week. There is a good *feeling of togetherness.*

Saturday

Everyone is busy cleaning, scrubbing and getting everything shipshape. The remarkable thing is that *none* of the activities is *pre-planned.* We all know *what wants doing* and, when one job is finished, people look to see *what else is required.* This is what it is all about – *working as a team.*

When the work is complete, group photographs are taken, we say our goodbyes and offer thanks before leaving. Each of us is deep in thought as we travel many miles without talking, each remembering the week as each wants to remember it.

REFLECTIONS

On the journey back, the training manager and I had many thoughts buzzing around. Had it worked? Did we get the right balance? Had the delegates seen the underlying reasons? What will be the effect in the coming weeks? One thing we were sure of – it had been a full and rich week with many experiences for the delegates to learn from.

By the time we arrived back, we had talked ourselves into a few early conclusions. First, we were surprised and pleased that the delegates had taken to self-catering and had produced such a high standard of cooking; giving them the *responsibility* for this had been the right thing. Secondly, the decision to leave the *choice* of projects to the delegates had been right. We had not wanted to force them into anything, or to organize the week for them. Giving them this responsibility had thrown up many valuable *organizational* problems. Thirdly, not seeing the outdoors as the main reason for being there, but making use of it as an aid to learning. Finally, on the overall structure of the week, we felt that we might have achieved a better balance by restricting certain activities to particular days. Surprisingly for us, the conclusions from the delegates were that we should not change anything. The point they made was that *to learn*, they had *to struggle, make mistakes, create their own problems,* and *enjoy their own successes.* If only, they said, they had *believed* at the time that we really were giving them the opportunity which we said we were! However, these are my thoughts. What about Dave's?

'My first reflections after the week were about how we all anticipated problems and assumed that these would be created by interference from the outside. This turned out to be completely unfounded. Most of our problems were self-generated! Far worse than the real thing. How much of the time are we doing this?

'Of my *longer-term reflections*, one thing has become very significant. This is about the three promises I made. The first was to keep a diary – which I did. The second was not to get elected MD. This proved to be particularly *selfish* during those times when I could have *contributed more*. I tended to listen and watch. *A balance* between the two is *more desirable*.

'Promise number three, to *respond* rather than *react*, proved difficult. However, with practice, this has become easier and has had a *significant effect* on those around me *at work*.'

SOMETIME LATER

SInce the course which Dave wrote about, we have brought together delegates from a number of courses to share views and experiences. The structure of this day was for the participants to work in small groups and then to present summaries of their discussions with flipcharts. These fell naturally into the three areas of before the course, during the course, and after the course, and the charts (Figures 16.3, 16.4 and 16.5) give the main points of general interest which emerged.

One thing which struck me about them was the absence of the activities which the delegates were taking part in on their courses. Many people who are considering a course which makes use of the outdoors have a natural concern that it should be relevant to the manager's job and to the company. Often, they have difficulty in appreciating the link between, say, an orienteering or a sailing activity, and the day-to-day problems back in the company. Here, the delegates have *concentrated on the learning* which has *come from the activities*, rather than on *the activities themselves*, which indicates that it is the resultant learning which is important and relevant.

The flipcharts here are like most flipcharts produced by syndicate groups for presentations to other delegates. They give the essence of their discussions, and the presenters fill them out with examples. Perhaps you   *269*

<u>BEFORE THE COURSE</u>

<u>FOR OURSELVES AS INDIVIDUALS</u>
* WE HAD A MIX OF FEELINGS AMONGST US ABOUT THE COURSE.

* THERE WAS ANXIETY ABOUT THE UNKNOWN, WHAT CHALLENGES WOULD THERE BE? WOULD I BE ABLE TO COPE? WHAT ROLE SHOULD I TAKE?

* THERE WAS EXCITEMENT ABOUT THE OPPORTUNITIES IN STORE, WE WANTED TO MAKE THE MOST OF THEM.

<u>OUR PRECONCEPTIONS OF THE COURSE</u>
* THESE VARIED FROM PERSON TO PERSON.
* SOME OF US WERE SUSPICIOUS AND THOUGHT WE WOULD BE 'SET UP' DURING THE WEEK.
* SOME OF US SAW IT AS A 'PRACTICAL' FOLLOW-ON FROM THE PREVIOUS COURSE.
* OTHERS WERE ANTICIPATING INTERPERSONAL, LOGISTICAL AND ORGANISATIONAL PROBLEMS TO DEAL WITH.

<u>AS A GROUP</u>
* WE FOUND THE PRE-COURSE PLANNING MEETINGS WE HELD OURSELVES TO BE VERY VALUABLE.

* IT WAS NOTICEABLE HOW WELL WE ALL GELLED TOGETHER – GROUP EMPATHY.
* THERE WAS A FEELING OF WANTING TO 'GET IT RIGHT' AND MAKE IT WORK.

Figure 16.3   Summary chart: before the course

<u>DURING THE COURSE</u>

<u>MOTIVATION</u>
* THERE WAS A HIGH MOTIVATION BY INDIVIDUALS TO 'HAVE A GO' AND ACCEPT CHALLENGES.
* INDIVIDUALS AVOIDED THOSE ACTIVITIES WHICH THEY CONSIDERED TO BE TOO HIGH A PERSONAL RISK.
* THERE WAS AN UNSELFISH, SUPPORTIVE ATTITUDE. AMONGST ALL THE DELEGATES.

<u>LEADERSHIP</u>
* WE WERE HOPING FOR 'LEADERSHIP' TO EMERGE.
* THROUGH THE WEEK WE SAW EACH OTHER IN VARIED AND CHANGING ROLES WHICH WE HAD TO MANAGE.

* INDIVIDUALS WERE ADAPTABLE IN THE DIFFERENT ROLES THEY TOOK....

* .... AND THERE WAS A NATURAL AND SOMETIMES SURPRISING SELECTION OF LEADERS AND FOLLOWERS IN DIFFERENT SITUATIONS AT DIFFERENT TIMES.

<u>TEAMWORK</u>
* AS THE WEEK PROGRESSED WE BUILT UP TRUST AND SUPPORT WITH EACH OTHER.
* THIS LED TO GOOD TEAMWORK AND MORE WILLINGNESS BY INDIVIDUALS TO HAVE A GO.

<u>.OTHER THINGS OF VALUE</u>
* OUR REVIEWS AND DISCUSSIONS BEFORE AND AFTER THE ACTIVITIES.

* THE WIDE CHOICE OF ACTIVITIES WE HAD.
* HAVING TIME AND SPACE TO ONESELF PERIODICALLY - RESPECTING THIS NEED IN OTHERS.
* LEARNING TO RECOGNISE OUR LIMITS.

Figure 16.4 Summary chart: during the course

<u>AFTER THE COURSE</u>
(A NUMBER OF MONTHS BACK AT WORK)

<u>FOR OURSELVES AS INDIVIDUALS</u>
* IT HAS CLARIFIED AND REINFORCED THE PREVIOUS COURSES.

* THERE IS AN INCREASE IN OUR SELF-CONFIDENCE.

* WE HAVE A BETTER UNDERSTANDING OF OUR OWN ABILITIES.

* IT SHOWS THAT A POSITIVE ATTITUDE CAN LEAD TO SUCCESS.
* OUR MANAGEMENT OF TASKS AND DECISION MAKING IS IMPROVED.

<u>FOR OUR RELATIONSHIPS</u>
* WE HAVE MORE UNDERSTANDING OF, AND PATIENCE WITH, OTHERS

* THERE IS AN IMPROVEMENT IN THE METHODS AND ABILITIES OF MANAGING OTHER PEOPLE.
* WE NOW BRING SITUATIONS OUT INTO THE OPEN TO RESOLVE THEM.

* WE HAVE AN INCREASED AWARENESS OF THE RELATIONSHIPS IN A TEAM (INCLUDING THE FAMILY AT HOME)

<u>FOR THE COMPANY</u>
* DIFFICULT PROBLEMS ARE NOW TACKLED AS A RESULT

* THE SHARED EXPERIENCES AND COMMON LANGUAGE ARE LEADING TO BETTER COMMUNICATIONS.

* IT IS POSSIBLE TO SEE HOW A COMPANY STRUCTURE CAN AFFECT PEOPLE'S BEHAVIOUR.
* THERE IS A REALISATION THAT WE, THE PEOPLE, ARE THE COMPANY.

<u>RESERVATIONS</u>
* SOME PEOPLE MAY 'MISS THE POINT' OF IT ALL
* OTHERS MAY TREAT IT AS A HOLIDAY.
* THE OUTDOOR ACTIVITIES MAY NOT SUIT CERTAIN TYPES.

272   Figure 16.5   Summary chart: after the course

could use your own experience of similar situations to see the meanings behind the words.

IN ADDITION

In addition to the comments which emerged about the course and about the value which people found it to have afterwards, the review day itself was well received. The delegates said that it acted as a refresher and gave them further insights from each others' experiences back at work. From this meeting and from a questionnaire we sent out, a few observations about using the outdoors came into my own mind.

Why the outdoors?

Potentially we can learn from all situations, so what is the particular value of the outdoors for management training? Three things emerge. Firstly, it is realistic. The problems, decisions and experiences are not hypothetical. Secondly, it is a challenge to our conditioned ways of thinking and seeing. The unusual circumstances (for most of us) can shake us out of our ruts and cause us to see things more clearly. And thirdly, it involves our actions and our feelings, as well as our thinking apparatus (which often only gets in the way). The *learning* is not *about* the outdoor activities. *It is about ourselves*, individually and in teams, and about how we *react* in these *different circumstances.*

What is your purpose?

The design of a course like this depends upon your reasons for doing it. Is it *team-building*, do you want to improve an existing team, or perhaps gell a new project group? Is it *individual development*, drawing out the potential of the manager and giving him understanding and confidence? Is it *organizational understanding*, seeing how people can learn to work together effectively? Or is it for the *improvement of relationships* amongst departments; for *developing leadership skills*; for *understanding change*? *Knowing your purpose is important* for knowing how to design your course at the beginning. Each of these objectives is possible, but the way in which the activities should be used will vary. The activities are not an end in themselves, but are a means to an end (or even a means to a beginning!).

Where does it fit?

The purpose and design of a course also depends upon your other training and development programmes. Is it a first-off for the delegates? Does it follow on from another course? Does it lead into another phase?

The course described here was designed to build on previous courses which develop *awareness, understanding* and *skills of managing* and *working with*   *273 others.* It was because of this that we gave the delegates *responsibility* for their course and their learning. For other situations, the initial design could well be different. In this case the participants seemed to take up the *opportunity* readily.

Keeping a perspective

Lastly, keep it in perspective and do not get carried away with the physical activities alone. Although we have made use of the outdoors here, we have also made use of other things for learning too. There were the *pre-course meetings*, the *self-catering*, the *indoor activities*, the *delegates' time alone*, the many *one-to-one talks*, the *group discussions* and the timely *reviews.*

All of this certainly does not mean that everything ran like clockwork on the courses. You may remember from Dave's diary that at many times just the opposite was the case. But really this does not matter. The purpose is not to *'get it right'.* Again, I should like to leave the last words to Dave.

'Life is not long enough to keep retracing the path and discussing where we should have gone. *The experience of going is the real lesson . . .* Perhaps the greatest gift is the ability to stand away and view yourself and the situation from the outside. Being self-critical achieves little on its own. Changing the criticisms into actions is satisfying and reaps its own rewards.'

FURTHER READING

Bank, J. (1994) *Outdoor Development For Managers,* 2nd edn (Aldershot: Gower). Bank discusses the what and how of OMD as well as presenting a number of company case studies and an outline of the work of many of the providers.

Beeby, M. and Rathborn, S. (1984) 'Outdoor Management Development: Choices About Use', *Management Education and Development*, 15(3).

Creswick, C. and Williams, R. (1979) *Using The Outdoors For Management Development and Teambuilding* (FDITB) – is one of the earliest reviews. They discuss the range of applications and explain the progression during a typical course.

Honey, P. and Lobley, R. (1986) 'Learning from Outdoor Activities', *Industrial and Commercial Training* (Nov/Dec).

Mossman, A. (1985) *Personnel Training Bulletin* (Tapes), Issues 21 and 22 (January/February), Didasko, Huntingdon, Cambs. – talks to providers and users of Outdoor Management Development.

Mossman, A. (1983) 'Ways of Using the Outdoors For Manager and Management Development' *Management Education and Development*, 14(3), pp. 182–96 – differentiates between manager and management development in the outdoors and describes the differences between the management training and self-development approaches. This paper concludes with a fairly comprehensive bibliography of good and bad reports on OMD.

17 Business strategy and international people development in ICL

Andrew Mayo

It is becoming rare today for commercial organizations to have no interests outside of their own country. For those based in the UK, the membership of the Single European Market itself demands at the very least an awareness of what is happening in the relevant business sector. A key question organizations face in human resource management therefore is: 'What *needs* do we have for developing international capability in our people?'

The term 'people' rather than 'management' is used deliberately. It embraces management of course, but it is insufficient to concentrate only on that – diminishing – sector of our populations.

International development in whatever form is expensive. A job assignment abroad is generally reckoned to cost some two to three times the cost of employing a local; bringing people to multinational training events is heavy on travel and other costs. An organization needs therefore to consider carefully its needs, and have a strategy to meet them that is appropriate.

In this chapter, we will look at how to go about analysing those needs and illustrate how ICL matches such analysis, and responds practically to it.

ICL

ICL was created in 1968, merging together the primary computer manufacturing interests in the UK at that time to form International Computers Ltd. Traditionally strong in 'Commonwealth areas', it received a significant boost in the USA and Europe by the acquisition of Singer Business Machines in 1976, and in 1984 it merged with STC. In 1990 STC sold 80 per cent of ICL to Fujitsu, and shortly afterwards STC was bought by Northern Telecom. Pursuing consistent strategies of market focus, open standards and collaboration for several years now, ICL has an overriding objective to become one of the leading European IT companies.

The relationship with Fujitsu is very much at arm's length, and ICL operates autonomously. There are exchanges of staff at the technical level, and some trainees but, this apart, it would be difficult to see the Japanese connection in day-to-day contact with the company.

ICL and its predecessors have operated internationally for over 50 years. Naturally the needs have changed over that time, as non-UK operations have matured – and particularly as a result of mergers and acquisitions. In recent years these have included the retail company Datachecker (USA-based) and the PC and specialised terminal company Nokia Data (Nordic-based), plus numerous other smaller ones. In 1994 ICL employed some 24 000 people spread across 70 or so countries, with 22 000 of these in Europe.

Fujitsu's business philosophy is to operate through a family of strategic alliances, a global approach that respects local cultures, methods and strengths. It wishes to learn from and pool the strengths of its family members. For ICL it is imperative to be seen as truly European, to be competent in what that means, and to be able to respond better than our competitors across the borders of Europe.

THE DEVELOPMENT OF INTERNATIONAL OPERATIONS

There is no single recipe for international development needs, because many factors come into play. International companies develop through either organic growth, or – more commonly today – through mergers, acquisitions and alliances. Growth typically has the following stages:

- First, the mother company *colonizes* – sending out brave managers to get operations going and build up local capability
- Secondly, it *localizes* – hiring local managers and passing over control
- Thirdly, it *internationalizes* – regarding all its management talent as in the service of the group and utilizing it across borders
- Fourthly, it *globalizes* – it is integrated strategically but operates parts of its business from the most effective point in the world.

Whereas the first three may be achieved organically, the fourth stage is more likely through mergers and collaborations. Human resources (HR) strategies and policies clearly change and develop as the stages mature. It is a constant challenge to ensure that management capability can keep pace with business development. Costs, cultures and the domination of the homebase nationality form potent resistance forces to progress. The pace of progress can depend on the homebase culture; whereas most Anglo-Saxon companies generally seek localization as quickly as possible, the Japanese are extremely reluctant to allow subsidiaries to be locally managed. Part of the reason is that Japanese companies value highly the development opportunities that overseas assignments give to their management.

Some measures of realization of this stage might be: the number of non-nationals in senior positions in the homebase; the number of managers who 277 can acceptably operate in any country as needed; and the recognition of an equitably treated executive group across the whole organization.

Whereas Fujitsu is at the *global* stage, ICL is at the *international* stage. With the exception of several developing countries, it would be unusual circumstances that forced a British general manager to be appointed in another country. This has been so for several years, and slowly nationals are taking over the developing countries also. However, we cannot claim to have consolidated the third stage. There is still a too small minority of non-UK people in key positions outside of their home country.

International mergers and acquisitions can force an organization to come to terms with new cross-border scenarios very quickly! Many fail to do so and lose key staff and managers through disenchantment. There are many fascinating case studies that illustrate success and failure in this area. ICL has learnt some interesting lessons here also, some of which will be referred to below.

Factors affecting development needs internationally

The following factors seem relevant in considering the needs for international development:

- The geographical structure
- The business structure
- The management structure
- The corporate culture.

The answers will point to the areas of needs we might have, such as:

- The transfer of technical expertise
- The needs for training in the homebase for other-country staff
- International coordination
- Sharing of scarce skills
- Career management
- Cultural change programmes
- Corporate representation

and so on.

The geographical structure

Development needs vary considerably depending on the part of the world we are looking at. One way to classify these needs is whether a particular country is:

- A *developed* or *developing* country
- What the *language* of business is

- Whether it has Eastern or Western *cultural values.*

The characteristics of 'developed' are those of an OECD economy, convertible hard currency and sophisticated infrastructure. In the 'less developed' group, of course, a great range exists – with countries like Brazil, India and Taiwan on the margin from an economic point of view, but not culturally.

The language of business is especially important for native English speakers, where capability in other tongues is frequently quite limited. This gives rise to a particular difficulty with Europe, to which we will return below.

Japan is a special example, being the only highly-developed country that does not have a 'Western' culture and language.

This split is important because it affects:

- The nature of opportunities available
- Selection of individuals for cultural match; independence required; resilience
- The knowledge, skills and attitudes needed for people development
- Costs of package, security, hardship, etc.

For example, depending on the maturity of the foreign subsidiary, the local need for experienced management staff in the well-developed countries may be very low. The main rationale for an international move is likely to be for the personal development of the individual. However, in, for example, an African developing country, several members of a management team may be needed as the local people are steadily developed.

ICL operates primarily in areas where English is the normal language of business, both developed and developing, plus of course all the European countries. Naturally, with the Fujitsu connection, some people are also being sent to Japan, and we would say this provides the greatest challenge to individuals in the extent of learning and adaptation needed.

The business structure

There are many different forms of business structure, and today's networks of alliances and partnerships produce extremely complex variations. To illustrate the point of how people development needs may be affected, consider the following options:

- A holding company with separate distinct subsidiaries.

Here there may be very few business reasons for international people development if subsidiaries are local and self-sufficient, and consistent 'corporate' culture or branding are not seen as important.

- A network of dependent constituents of world-wide businesses, of which there are several.

This structure is typified by the Swiss–Swedish company Asea Brown Boveri (ABB). Here, each business needs international expertise exchange and coordination, although the company headquarters may be in any country. Within a country, several ABB businesses may exist. There is, then, the question as to whether a common 'ABB' image and set of values is desired, both globally and locally, in which case a complex set of needs arises. ABB is an example of a company that works hard to achieve a true internationalization of its businesses through managed appointments and international education events.

- A multi-national network of sales subsidiaries supporting one or a few centres of excellence in development, manufacturing and corporate services.

This is the ICL case: a one-business focus – in computer systems and services – and a network of subsidiaries and partnerships supporting that. ICL has factories and development in the UK, Sweden, Finland, the USA and India. Otherwise operations are essentially sales and service.

Such a business structure calls for significant international understanding, experience and sharing. If products and services are to be appropriate for a wide variety of markets, those concerned with designing and producing them need to understand and appreciate the variety of needs. The nature of the business is complex, so that needs for the sharing of special skills are frequent.

Clearly there are important secondary questions that we need to ask to find out how the international capability supports the business, particularly in terms of strategic directions and the role of 'centres of excellence' in supporting the organization.

The management structure

Those who manage people development for organizations will be very familiar with the importance of the structure of the organization. It dictates the nature of opportunities available for career progression, and general development through experience.

Thus we might ask whether we have:

- Free-standing country operations?
- Matrix lines of business?
- Regional/area groupings?
- Pyramidal, flat or networked structures?
- Central support groups?

The flatter the organization, the less the opportunity for non-nationals – especially where country operations major in customer-focused activities. Regional or area groupings provide particularly useful openings for international experience on the ground, as distinct from an headquarters base. One could argue that if the business strategy calls for a significant level of international capability, then the structure should be designed to facilitate that. The Human Resources Director who can use such logic to win against the pressure to reduce costs and layers of management has influence indeed!

ICL has flattened its structures over the years. Its challenge is to identify posts which can be done by non-nationals in every country and plan accordingly – below we look at some of the processes that facilitate this.

The corporate culture

The simple definition of culture we all know and love is 'the way we do things around here'. It's the sum of the values, written and unwritten, and the processes and systems in operation. And it's always unique – a product of history, processes, mergers, personalities, nationalities, and so on. The relationship between corporate and national cultures is important, and we shall return to this.

One important question is the extent of the 'corporate umbrella' in the organization. That is, are there values and processes that are universally to be applied, that characterize and make up the core of the organization, and are not tradeable?

Like many organizations, ICL has a statement of company values. It is called the 'ICL Way', and is translated into all languages and is part of the 'umbrella'. However, in pursuit of an empowered devolved organization (and influenced by the Finnish company Nokia Data with whom it merged in 1992) it defined its core processes along with the values of the ICL Way in the booklet, *The Management Framework*. This sets out to clarify that which is 'untradeable', but this has been kept to a minimum. In Human Resources it includes processes relating to 'management for performance', 'individual development' and 'organizational development', which will be described below.

But then we need to think about the aspects of *corporate cultural values* that require and support international development. Many companies still struggle with the continuing career development of the returning expatriate; others have an understood pattern that postings abroad are essential to promotion above a certain level. The latter are mostly companies that have been long established and traditionally offered lifetime careers to their people.

A study of 130 multinational companies in 1992 showed that less than 30 per cent of the organizations were convinced their executives saw international moves as a positive career step (Conference Board, 1992).

We may ask some questions. Do we:

- Position postings abroad as part of a positive career plan, or do they happen opportunistically?
- Pay lip-service or have total commitment to international management capability?
- Believe in the value to personal development of working abroad?

- Believe in strong indigenous development?
- Have a directive or non-directive culture on career moves?

This last point is a major factor in the management of careers. On the one hand we can take the view that organizations today change so fast (and loyalty to one organization is a disappearing value), that it is pointless to invest effort in career management. Better to be opportunistic, reactive, flexible and open-minded, placing initiative primarily with the individual.

Alternatively, we can take a central planner's view: that people are resources to be planned and used like any other resource, and their careers should be planned to take advantage of the right opportunities and experience needed for future advancement.

Of course, there are variations in between the extremes, and most companies today would balance a form of succession planning and individual career planning with considerable latitude on the part of individual and recruiting managers in making their own choices.

TYPES OF INTERNATIONAL CAPABILITY

People development needs can be classified according to knowledge, skill, attitudes and experience. The category of 'attitudes' is particularly relevant when discussing international capability, embracing a particular respect for the values of other cultures and their way of doing things.

We have a range of options for meeting these needs. The lowest level are seminars and training courses which provide understanding of other operations and countries. Events, such as those arranged by the Farnham Castle International Briefing Centre, are not only used to brief pending expatriates, but can be useful to home-based staff who deal regularly with different parts of the world.

Both in-company and external executive education with international participants are valuable, not just for what is taught, but in the sharing of common experiences with people from different parts of the world and creating lasting networks. In ICL we make considerable use of specifically international schools in this respect.

But developing international capability is not fundamentally a matter for the classroom. Of course, there is knowledge of the international business environment, of the workings of the European Union, of legal and commercial systems which provide a useful background; but 80 per cent or more of the learning necessary will come from the *experience* of living and working abroad. Organizations need to exploit the opportunities they have, and create new ones, to enable international experiences to be achieved.

Such opportunities will be provided by:

- Full international assignments
- Short-term (up to six months) assignments
- International project teams and steering groups

- International coordination roles
- Involvement in cross-border mergers and joint ventures
- Membership of subsidiary boards
- Involvement in external international bodies.

Clearly, there is a range of demands for international experience and competence. Assignments tend to be to and from the 'homebase', and a mark of a truly internationalized company is where so-called 'third-country movements' are equally as common. One important policy question is the extent to which the 'mother' company wants international representation and experience in its homebase – on the board, in the main policy-making units, and in product development. Thus companies like ABB and ICI have a very mixed board to ensure international perspectives are considered.

We can classify the reasons for international assignments as follows:

Transfer of skill or knowledge

- Sharing and utilization of highly-specialized talent globally
- Local assimilation of skills from an expert
- Local need required quickly
- Ensuring international needs are built into the organization's products/services/plans
- Safeguard of the organization's assets
- Managing the integration of a merger or acquisition
- Participation in a joint venture.

Individual personal growth

- Training of young entrants in a common country, such as the homebase, to create early international attitudes
- Development of specific knowledge, skill, attitudes or experience as part of a career plan
- Deliberate provision of international exposure to high-flyers.

It is worth noting the kinds of personal growth that come specifically from working abroad:

Knowledge

This will include understanding of other parts of the organization, and their needs and values; markets and environments; contacts and how to use them.

Personal skills

The development of skills in planning and organizing, self-reliance, personal and cultural sensitivity, initiative, stress tolerance, languages.

Attitudes

Non-parochialism, appreciation of other's value systems.

Unfortunately, it is rarely the case that every job in every country is available to any national. In ICL we find the options quite limited (see Figure 17.1).

Function	Field	Business or Regional HQ
General Management	Caution	Yes
Sales/service	No	Yes
Manufacturing	Caution	Yes
Finance	Caution	Yes
Human Resources	No	Yes
R & D	Yes	Yes
Marketing	No	Yes

Figure 17.1   Options for international placements in a manufacturing organization

We find all the justifications above applying from time to time. We are particularly concerned to track the proportion that are being used for career development rather than business need *per se*. Monitoring (for full assignments only) showed an increase from 8 per cent in 1988 to 33 per cent in 1992 for career development assignments, with a corresponding drop in the proportion of technology skill transfers. The percentage classified as 'representing the mother company' remained about the same. The study referred to earlier in this chapter (Conference Board, 1992) reported an average of 20 per cent of assignments being for career purposes.

THE SPECIAL CASE FOR EUROPE – THE CONCEPT OF THE 'EUROMANAGER'

As indicated earlier, Europe is particularly important for ICL, determined to be viewed as a truly European organization rather than a British one. Is there something special about the successful international manager in Europe? A definition of the 'Euromanager' might be:

> A manager who, in any European country, is able to bridge between the global organizational culture and that which is locally national, in order to be both effective in the business and respected by staff and customers alike.

Tijmstra and Casler (1992) summarized the distinctive character of such a manager. They included these capabilities:

● Comprehending a changing and as yet uncertain political and economic entity

- Creating and leading new forms of cross-border businesses
- Managing within the context of intense competition in globalized markets, requiring a pan-European level of efficiency
- Building commitment to a corporate identity and mission that transcends national cultures
- Winning the support of national 'stakeholders' in whichever country he/she is operating
- Ability to accept and pursue a transnational career path as if Europe was 'home'
- Managing the demands of corporate culture and national culture to maximum effect.

The issue of culture is critical. It is natural that French and British and Germans and so on feel more comfortable if 'things are done their way'. Each manager brings his or her own style, which is a product of their natural way of managing and the environment in which they have developed managerial skills. Some find it impossible to adapt their style, and only succeed if they have exceptional business talent which is visible and valued.

Individuals need a very solid level of technical and managerial competence that demands respect in whatever country the person is working. Also a high level of personal adaptability, of healthy curiosity and respect for other cultures, and of more than just a willingness to learn other languages. Personal sensitivity, enthusiasm and empathy for different peoples; and the ability to balance convergence and divergence for the best benefit of the business are key characteristics. They need to comprehend a complexity of environments and legislation, operate within new forms of organization, and obtain commitment from national entities to a 'cultural umbrella' that lies above them. Acceptance of a high degree of change in one's personal life is an inevitable requirement.

Compared to many other parts of the world, there are some unique difficulties presented by Europe. The following list gives some examples:

1. Problems of acceptability of one nation in another. One can draw up a 'cautionary matrix' of where one would be wise to think carefully before putting a boss of one nationality into another; particularly sensitive are smaller countries to their large neighbours. Of course, the good Euromanager transcends his or her own nationality through personality and capability. Figure 17.1 looks at the options available for functional moves across Europe.
2. Language and nationality needs for customer contact. The variety of languages and cultural variants preclude foreign nationals from taking up many customer-sensitive positions in subsidiaries.
3. Lack of 'expatriate communities'. With some exceptions, communities of other European nationalities are not to be found as they would be in, for example, many developing countries. This can lead to a very lonely experience for spouses who are not themselves employed.

4. Resistance to the mother-company culture. Nowhere else in the world is resistance to the mother company's way of doing things likely to be so strong. A lot of local adaptation and ownership is needed.
5. Increasing immobility in many areas. Many Europeans today are very reluctant to move from where they have their roots, even for a relatively short period. Thus Monday–Friday commuting over significant distances is very common. This substantially reduces the 'total experience' of being part of another culture.

The transfer of technical skills has fewer difficulties than for managerial skills – the technical language is usually based on English, and there is often a pressing local need. It is with managerial staff that many of the above issues arise.

ICL'S VISION OF A 'EUROPEAN COMPANY' IN HR TERMS

All change programmes require an end-point to be specified, a vision of the future. What we would like to realize in ICL is the following:

- Senior management in every key decision-making area is multinational
- Having worked in another country is a requirement for promotion to a certain level
- Company problems are solved by multinational teams
- Young people from different nationalities train together
- Key specialist resources are deployed across national boundaries – shared, not guarded
- Executive training is international
- While the business language is English, capability in another one or two languages is the norm
- 'Company culture' lives harmoniously with national cultures.

It is one thing to have a vision, but one must have real commitment to achieving it and some practical programmes backing it up. It requires a sharing of the vision, attitudinal training, investment, an organizational structure supportive to secondments and assignments, smooth administrative procedures for international movements, an open appointments policy, and a career development 'framework' that is managed.

ICL AND EUROPE

ICL has operations in all the countries of Western and Eastern Europe. The former Eastern bloc is (at the time of writing) separated organizationally from the 14 operations in the Western part. The acquisition of Nokia Data was particularly significant in expanding our European operations, and gave substantial manufacturing and development capability in Sweden and Finland. A policy of localization of management has been pursued for many years. Thus, apart from the developing countries of Central and Eastern Europe, all senior management teams are locally national, with only few exceptions. Though this makes for effective and coherent teams, it limits the opportunities for cross-border assignments at management levels.

The impact of the merger on internationalization

ICL had made acquisitions before, but none with the cross-border implications that Nokia Data had. Nokia Data itself was the product of a merger with Nokia and Ericsson Data Systems in 1988, not yet finally complete in itself. In most countries outside the Nordic area, no real merger had taken place as it was a takeover and local operations just put up a new sign! But it was very much a Nordic company, dominated by the Finns. Some of the differences with ICL were as follows:

- The style and culture were very different – more aggressive, very unbureaucratic, very little strategic or 'HQ' overview, and essentially pragmatic
- Human resource management did not exist in any professional sense, except by local initiative
- A number of Finns were in key positions outside Finland, but the managing director was Italian and had brought in several European executives; therefore, the company had become more international in outlook
- Apart from these recent acquisitions, expatriates were either Finns or Swedes – and going to lower-tax regimes. Packaging was relatively simple, therefore.

One of the lessons learnt from previous such activities was the importance of dedicated and effective integration management. This is a job for mature, respected players, not high-flyers wanting to make a name for themselves. So each country had a dedicated person for this task.

In the spirit of good British fairness, we made key appointments on the basis of 'the best person for the job'. (This caused some surprise, as the acquired managers expected to be subjugated.) This policy backfired on us in one country, but otherwise gave us a good balance. In particular, we were very anxious not to destroy the excellent development and manufacturing capability which we had acquired, and we put our own PC activities under theirs – the merger of product lines has been particularly successful. We spent a long time understanding the Finnish and Swedish characteristics (totally different), and did a major cultural analysis of the two organizations, country by country, prior to the merger. We believe this investment was just as important as the legal and accounting due diligence activities. For the first year we emphasized the importance of 'keeping customers and keeping key people', and tried to disturb as little as possible. Now we are keen to build a new approach to the demands that Europe and changes in our industry place upon us, and to use executive education as a vehicle for this.

From the beginning we decided to apply our own international assignments   *287* policy, and the new diversity of the business has created both new demands and new opportunities for cross-border experience. For example, we have had many exchanges in the product development areas. Also, we have found the Nordic people much keener to take assignments than some from other countries further south.

PRACTICAL APPLICATIONS OF INTERNATIONAL DEVELOPMENT IN ICL

The following list describes some of the practical ways in which ICL seeks to meet its own needs for international capability:

1. We have experienced and professional international assignments policies and staff, and believe in having such expertise centrally even in a devolved world. It is a very complex area, and there is no way every personnel officer around the world can be expert in this area in their own right.
2. We have a policy of indigenous development, with special effort put into the developing countries – this means a number of secondments to 'developed' areas for knowledge and experience.
3. We have developed an Assessment Centre specifically for the selection of general managers for developing countries. This serves also as a 'Development Centre'.
4. Our in-house training includes a special course for newly appointed country general managers, plus a number of distance learning and CBT modules over both managerial and technical subjects.
5. We have developed a cadre of international managers experienced in the developing world, flexible and adaptable according to needs.
6. We have a number of technical exchanges between developed countries – especially UK and Japan, and particularly for young people.
7. We use multi-country graduate training programmes – for Africa, the Far East, and for Europe (see below).
8. Investment in cultural awareness programmes, and encouraging language learning at all levels even though the company's international language is English.
9. We utilize subsidiary board appointments to give understanding of different country operations to executives.

Company-wide HR processes

The above would not be complete without mention of some of ICL's company-wide HR development disciplines that are applied across all countries, and which are considered part of the 'corporate umbrella' that says 'this is being part of the ICL Group'.

Our *appraisal and development programme* is called 'Investing in People' – it consists of a series of handbooks for managers and an explanatory one for employees. It is made available in all languages and is built on objective-based performance appraisal and in-depth development planning. It is one of our few core worldwide policies as an instrument in 'managing for performance'.

We hold a common *opinion survey* each year checking the views of our people on a range of HR issues. We belong to the 'BEST' group that shares such information for the countries of Europe.

We have a process called the *organization and management review* – a line management review each 4–6 months of organization and management capability, of high potentials and international movements, of succession, and so on. It provides an excellent means of keeping the issues hot and on the agenda, and of everybody being reminded of where we are trying to get to. HR people facilitate the actions arising. ICL has a well-established *career management framework*, enabling the results of both individual and organizational reviews to be turned into career action plans, mutually owned with the individual and regularly reviewed.

And especially for Europe

We are particularly keen to get more senior managers into the headquarters from different nationalities, and to use opportunities to develop those with high cross-border potential. However, like many organizations that have devolved accountability, this is not easy. Local organizations are reluctant to part with their best people, and equally reluctant to receive foreigners. There are high costs involved, and we all are familiar with the widely differing remuneration and tax levels across Europe. Especially in these days of downsizing, many individuals are cautious about taking career risks into 'the unknown' with what may be perceived as an uncertain outcome.

We seek to combat these difficulties in various ways. Firstly we have the regular organization and management review (referred to above) which keeps the issues of people development in discussion. Secondly, we encourage all parts of the organization to identity 'development positions' which could be filled by non-nationals. Thirdly, we hold some central funds for 'strategic resourcing', recognizing the reality that financial assistance to operations for acting in the 'corporate interest' saves a lot of argument. These funds cover, for example, the expatriation costs (over and above the cost of employing local people in a post) for high-potential career moves. They also pay for the initiatives outlined below.

We have come to the conclusion that the future lies with the young people. They have an outlook unclouded by the history and reserves and prejudices of their elders. For them the vision of Europe as an entity is very real. The percentage of students undertaking part of their studies in another country is rising dramatically. The opportunity to work in another country is, for most, attractive, unencumbered as they are with worries of children's interrupted education or maintaining a particular standard of living. They are flexible, adaptable, and relatively low-cost. It is our conviction that bringing young people of different nationalities together in their early years, or providing   *289* cross-border experiences for individuals, will lay foundations for the Euromanagers of the future.

There are four elements to our approach:

1. Eurographics.
2. Young Secondee Scheme.
3. Continental recruitment for the UK.
4. Work placements.

We have always recruited graduates in major European countries locally, but the programmes have been subject to cost constraints and training left to local devices.

Eurographics

The Eurograduate programme is marketed under the heading 'New Europeans'. An English brochure is used, with local language inserts on terms and conditions, information on the country operation and positions available. The basis is to recruit in countries people who will train in the UK for 10 months together, and then return to their country. Since these are people to be 'owned' by the countries we have relied on local recruitment, but have a person designated as project manager working in ICL headquarters to coordinate all the activities in the UK.

Each recruit has individual 'on-the-job' training programmes defined according to the business need of their country, and they come together for common events. The first intake was September 1989, and the funding for the 10 months is provided centrally. Typical 'common events' include off-the-job training, a cultural awareness course, an outdoors leadership course in Scotland, and from time to time we bring recruits together to meet the senior management of ICL Europe. The aim is to build up contacts and relationships across borders, and a mentality that will give loyalty both to the country and to Europe as a whole.

As we enter our fifth year of recruitment, the signs are good, and the bonds are lasting. Less than 10 per cent of those recruited had been lost by mid-1993 – some, it has to be admitted, as a result of the cultural differences arising from the merger with Nokia. However, this is a low loss rate, and the recruits share a tremendous common spirit which is positively encouraged. Some are now on their second assignment abroad – but this is discouraged until their home country really feels ownership for them.

In 1993, some 'vertical integration' of the different entry years took place, when all four entry groups met together for a combined business and social event in Holland (mostly at their own expense). The progress and career of each of the recruits is tracked carefully by the HR division at ICL headquarters.

Young Secondee Scheme

The scheme takes trained graduates – 18 months or so in a local operation –

who have language capability and have learnt a skill that another country needs. We second these on a low-costs basis for 6–12 months to give them experience and to provide a useful skill to the receiving operation. Commencing with young people going out from the UK some four years ago, this is now established inter-country in many combinations.

Continental recruitment for the UK

The programme is designed to recruit non-British graduates into the British company – to begin to dilute the domestic powerbase with a broader European diversity. We are setting a target of 10 per cent of our recruitment needs to be from continental Europe – in R&D, in manufacturing, and in sales and support services. So we have built up relationships with a selected number of educational institutions in three or four countries, in which we promote our opportunities.

Work placements

The fourth element of our approach. In countries like France the *stagiaire* has for a long time been a familiar sight in the office, as work placements have been normal practice for many French courses. Now they are looking to the UK and other countries for this experience, and the same is happening vice versa. Not only do we regard such placements as an excellent source of future recruits where mutual knowledge of each party is very beneficial, but we find the work done for low cost of great value. We take a sympathetic view to requests therefore, and use the relationships with institutions both on the Continent and in the UK to provide regular placings for their students abroad. We subscribe to AIESEC – an international student organization that helps match-up of placements.

SUMMARY

The need to think through the levels of international capability needed in an organization increases all the time as the business world becomes global in more and more sectors – and especially in Europe. Those needs might be less or more than first impressions indicate as future strategies are taken into account. The organization, then, has to be resourced determinedly based on those needs. Like most organizations, ICL continually re-examines its needs as its demands and structures change. Progress is often painfully slow – and when an acquisition or merger is made there is a renewed and complex round of convincing and educating, and obtaining of commitment. All development is a long-term process – and it is experience, not training courses, that provides it. So stop-go policies will achieve nothing.

The Swiss are one of the best internationally-minded countries in the world. We conclude with a quote (Jakob, 1990) from an executive of Suchards on how the famous chocolate company was seeking to become European:

A successful Euro-business needs a strong Euro-management, and a strong Euro-management means a majority of managers who have lived abroad and worked in multinational teams.

It sounds simple – but it is a real challenge to management determination to make it real.

REFERENCES

Conference Board (1992) 'Recruiting and Selecting International Managers', Report 998 (New York: Conference Board).

Tijmstra, S. and Casler, K. (1992) 'Management Learning for Europe', *European Management Journal*, 10(1) (March).

Jakob, H. Jürg (1990) 'From National to European – Making It Happen', *European Management Journal*, 8(2) (June).

18 Assessing for competence at Safeway Stores plc

Mike Stringfellow

As one of the leading food retailers in the UK, the Safeway Group are acutely aware that the 1990s may well be judged by history as the most vital European decade of the century. By the end of it, Britain's standard of living will depend even more on the competitiveness of her industry and commerce. Competition will come both from within the UK itself and from the 12 different countries that form the European Union, across whose borders there will be a free movement not only of goods, services and jobs, but also, most important of all, *people*.

Due to demographic change and the challenge of a Single European Market, there will be at least 25 per cent fewer available young recruits during 1996, and viciously increased competition will surely ensue for the lesser number; crucially, staff will be in short supply and a readily available educated, skilled workforce will virtually be a thing of the past. To add to these pressures will come the almost daily changes in technology and the relentless search for ever-increased productivity.

It is against this backcloth and the need to ensure an efficient workforce to meet the company's future needs that a strategy was evolved within Safeway during the 1980s to ensure that employees and prospective employees are matched against specific competence-based specifications for each job.

To illustrate these developments in assessment criteria, the role of store manager, a position familiar to most people as a result of their day-to-day shopping experience, has been chosen. However, principles of assessment applicable to this role also apply on a general basis across the broad spectrum of management and supervision employed within the Safeway Group.

BACKGROUND

Safeway in the early 1980s was a wholly-owned American concern, operating   *293* approximately 80 stores and employing 20 000 people within the UK. Today, Safeway forms part of the Argyll Group, whose main concerns are represented by Lo-Cost, Presto and Safeway. Within Safeway, 345 stores are operated, employing nearly 68 000 people. In 1992/93 the annual sales were £5.5 billion and include working arrangements with Groupe Casino in France and Arhold in The Netherlands. As a group, Safeway consider themselves the pioneers with regard to food retailing relating to green issues.

THE STORE MANAGER

Before assessing the role of store manager, it is necessary to turn the clock back to 1983. Stores were then called supermarkets; Safeway operated 72 of them, the average floor space of each unit being approximately 15 000 square feet, with a turnover of £3.6 million per annum. Each unit employed approximately 35 to 70 people, of whom 50 per cent were part-time workers. The cost to build was approximately £2.5 million. Safeway realized from the various directives received from the parent company in the USA, together with the shopping trends which were developing there and in the UK, that the supermarket as we knew it would rapidly be replaced by the current superstore. The responsibilities and the role of the store manager would therefore have to change, being influenced by higher customer expectations and increased sophistication owing to the development of information technology resources. It became essential that Safeway staff training schemes should produce effective store managers from day one of their appointment.

Contrast the supermarket of 1983 with the superstore of today – the latter has a floor space in excess of 30 000 square feet, an average turnover of £17 million, employs up to 300 staff, and requires a unit cost to build of anything from £8 to £10 million.

STORE MANAGER EFFECTIVENESS

Following a detailed factor analysis of the store manager's role, Safeway identified 12 key areas which related directly to store manager effectiveness. In the 1980s such areas had been defined as *management dimensions*, for the word 'competence' had not yet been born – in the context in which we now use it. The 12 dimensions, or competences, identified then are still in use today. Safeway wrote them into their staff training schemes in behavioural terms to ensure that they could be objectively measured by observation. They are:

- Problem analysis
- Problem-solving
- Planning and organization
- Decisiveness
- Delegation
- Management control
- Leadership

- Human relation skills
- Personal effectiveness
- Verbal communication
- Oral communication
- Stress tolerance.

A store manager's effectiveness can be measured by use of these 12. For example, 'competence of management control' is defined as the ability of the manager to develop follow-up procedures for the review of assignments and/or personnel.

Because of the Safeway Group's commitment to this approach, a purpose-built assessment centre was designed and constructed. It provided an ideal facility, purposely isolated from the day-to-day operation to ensure a high degree of standardization from one assessment course to another.

A three-day assessment centre course was researched, developed, designed and trialled to 'mirror image' wherever possible the day-to-day role of the store manager.

It was considered that the key to the success of such assessment centre courses lay within the quality of observation which could be recorded by the assessment centre observers. Specially selected groups of store managers and area managers were trained in behavioural observation and the classification of observed behaviour under each of the 12 competences. This provided the key to the competence-based assessment procedures which Safeway operate. Each assessment centre course lasts for three days. There are six candidates with three observers in attendance. An independent member of the group management development department acts as a facilitator for the assessment centre course but does not participate in the recording of behaviours, etc.

To ensure objectivity during the assessment, the following points are applied rigidly:

1. The six candidates are drawn from different parts of the country and are not known to one another.
2. The three observers selected from store managers or senior area managers are also not known to any of the candidates.

It is an explicit requirement to be an observer that he or she must:

- Have successfully filled the role of store manager for at least four years
- Be able to demonstrate a satisfactory people development record
- Have participated in a behavioural analysis programme
- Have agreed to abide by a rigid assessment centre code of conduct.

It is required of each observer that they:

- Observe approximately one-third of the candidate's work (to ensure   *295* impartiality each third of the candidate's work varies from observer to observer)

- Are capable of classifying observed behaviour into the key competence areas
- Can meet in debate and agree an overall rating as to the degree of demonstrated competence
- Are able to record and formulate a comprehensive factual report and discuss the document with each candidate when required.

And, finally, can:

- Rate an individual's potential for carrying out the duties and responsibilities of a store manager based on the overall evidence gathered from the complete assessment centre course.

Following the assessment course, each candidate (in conjunction with his/her supervising manager) is provided with a copy of the observers' report and a complete feedback which is also supported by evidence gathered from a selection of psychometric tests.

From the above report candidates determine how to enter into personal development plans, covering any areas highlighted at the assessment.

Within the Safeway Group, 87 per cent of store managers have now been selected by this method.

APPLYING A COMPETENCE-BASED APPROACH

Once this assessment process had been established, Safeway reviewed their various training programmes and selection procedures. Those for management trainees were found wanting, and therefore a competence-based approach was applied.

The starting point was the interview – the initial contact that a prospective retail graduate management trainee has with the company. Each personnel professional responsible for carrying out interviews of this kind is now trained in competence assessment processes and observation techniques and, more importantly, in the recognition of behavioural indicators.

As part of the interview process, structured questions are introduced, the candidate's reply analysed and any behavioural indicators recorded as evidence. The competence traits and behavioural indicators are then compared with established competence profile bands and selection made for the second-stage interview. The process is highly objective and ensures the standardization of candidates progressing through to a second interview which is carried out over a day at an assessment centre, complemented by the use of psychometric tests.

Second stage assessment

The selected candidate is then placed on a training programme which can range from 12 to 24 months, the programme itself being competence-based. Within each store location Safeway assessors, trained in assessment and observation techniques, ensure that trainees regularly undergo assessment reviews. The trainees' application of skill and knowledge is also independently assessed by a review committee. Trained observers are used in the make-up of these committees, each of which is carefully structured to ensure that an objective assessment and associated recording procedures are standardized against agreed company requirements.

This second stage of assessment, which is part written and part oral, provides an opportunity to reassess competences by an alternative method, so overlaying and endorsing the candidate's ability to demonstrate competence on an ongoing basis.

The trainee's final assessment, for example in the role of store manager, is noted by the company. He or she is awarded a certificate, endorsed by the MCI, thus confirming the individual's ability to carry out the duties and responsibilities of a Safeway store manager to national standards.

The application of competence criteria within Safeway has now been applied more widely. We have now established major competences for the whole of our company, which are:

- managing within the Safeway environment;
- management of people, finance, information and assets, and personal effectiveness.

Major competences are used as the basis of a behaviourally-based appraisal system. The competence-based appraisal review focuses on the behaviours under the various job competences, and matches them against stated performance criteria. Operating results – so often key to the majority of appraisal schemes – do not form part of the discussions and are handled by establishing key result areas with the appraisee on a separate occasion. By carrying out appraisals along these lines, a non-threatening environment is created between manager and subordinate, high levels of objectivity are achieved throughout and a high degree of standardization of appraisal is maintained. Appraisal results are readily taken on board by the subordinate, and, more importantly, *acted upon*. By entering into such systems it has enabled a database to be established which provides the personnel professionals operating within the company with an objective assessment of management potential.

Linking Safeway competences with the national standards

Running parallel to Safeway's development of competence assessment procedures were the Government's own proposals for NCQVs and the   *297*

Management Charter Initiative. Eventually, to the relief of the majority of management development specialists, MI and MII standards were agreed and published.

The opportunity immediately presented itself for Safeway to be one of the first companies to link the competence work they had already undertaken to the *new* national standards published by the Management Charter Initiative (MCI).

It was therefore decided that the Safeway Group's management training scheme, designed to take mature people, with or without previous retail experience, down the exacting road to the position of assistant store manager, should be chosen for submission for Certificate Level (MI).

Action plan to gain national recognition

Safeway's application for participation as a pilot on the MI trials was accepted by MCI and work commenced to implement the standards into existing assessment procedures. Using the graduate recruitment programme, an assessment centre to measure previously gained competences was researched and designed. This was done by carefully selecting the appropriate psychometric tests, use of collective bio-data, introducing structured interviewing techniques, application form redesign and analysis, and introducing a carefully monitored one-day competence-based assessment centre. Through this Safeway are able to match an individual's competence profile against their own store management profile and carry out the appropriate 'mapping' exercise against the national standards.

To support the management training programme and to monitor the trainee's progress, as well as 'on-the-job observation' and review of the trainee's 'log book', three key periods of assessment are carried out 'off-the-job', with a trained observer acting as the assessment panel's chairperson.

Following the completion of the programme and the signing-off of the individuals into retail, it was initially thought that this would be the appropriate time finally to review the individual against the competence criteria to the level of certificate.

The pilot scheme outcomes

As the pilot for the Certificate got under way, realization dawned that the original training programme issued to management trainees was too work-related and did not reach the Certificate levels required in reflecting the demonstration of generic managerial competences. This was finally highlighted when in June 1991 the final version of the Management I and II competences was published and the performance criteria studied. As a result, training programmes were rewritten in order to ensure that managerial competence could be practically demonstrated throughout the programme. Procedures were introduced so that a trainee was given the responsibility for the management of people and various departments. Assessments of each individual's progress was carried out during this period and reporting procedures on the assessments and feedback modified to ensure that the individual was able to gain maximum benefit from the experience. Assessment committees became known as the 'ASK Committees' – the Assessment of Skill and Knowledge.

Personal development journals were introduced to all trainees as a key mechanism to allow the trainees to record situations which reflect their ability to demonstrate specific managerial competences against the laid-down performance criteria. The introduction of such journals requires a lot of forethought, planning and careful instructions, both to assessors/mentors and trainees alike.

A formal 'two-stage' mentoring system was introduced to support each trainee. Initially, when a trainee starts on the programme their mentor is the personnel officer who, after introduction and initial basic training, hands over to a senior store manager.

The mentor not only looks after, directs and helps the trainee, but also advises on such things as personal development journals, approach to assessments and, through other senior managers, is able to make recommendations for modifications to individual training programmes which help and support the trainee's progress.

Finally, it became obvious during the Certificate Trial that Safeway's original intention (which was an award at Certificate Level, once a trainee had completed his/her training programme) was not going to be achieved in many instances. So now, when a trainee finishes his/her training, they are required to carry out the duties and responsibilities of a junior assistant manager for between three and six months. The individual's day-to-day operating performance is finally assessed against the Management I standards. Only at this stage is the trainee then finally 'signed off' as being competent to Certificate Level.

The changes Safeway have introduced – and the steps they have had to take, as additions which they themselves have implemented to ensure the objective measurement of management competences – have greatly enhanced the quality and delivery of staff training programmes.

The key success factors of a competence-based development programme may therefore be summarized as:

- A competence-based training programme
- Existence of a highly-trained team of competence assessors who, if possible, are able to express the measurement of competence in behavioural terms
- A commitment at all levels within an organization to the use of some form of personal development journal
- A commitment to the introduction of a mentoring system
- A mechanism for the objective assessment of prior competence levels already achieved before the commencement of the development programme
- And, most importantly of all, commitment from top management down

towards making the whole thing work.

The lessons Safeway have gained from Certificate Trials have added to the company's ambitions and aspirations to be known as one of the best in the industry for the training and development of its people. In addition, the company's participation in the Certificate has resulted in a great awakening and awareness relating to quality training initiatives which produce measurable outcomes.

An air of professionalism prevails concerning the development of people. Turnover amongst trainees participating on the Certificate training scheme has reduced. At a recent round of graduate recruitment, one recruit was asked by a prospective young hopeful: 'Are your training programmes competence-based?'; 'Will I receive satisfactory levels of assessment?'; 'Is your programme nationally recognized?'

Safeway's answer was a resounding YES!

THE FUTURE

Competence-based assessments are now being introduced within the Safeway Group to such areas as trading, IT, marketing and personnel. The aim is that eventually MI and MII Standards will be embodied within all the Group's management development programmes. Safeway will therefore be living up to the commitment made to its people through its mission statement:

> We value our people . . . We will create an atmosphere in which our people can develop their talents and contribute as part of an energetic and enthusiastic team. We will invest in recruitment and training. We will reward them for achievement through the resourceful application of knowledge and skills.

19 Making it happen

Ed Moorby

A cynic might be forgiven for describing management development as the application of inadequate resources to intractable problems in order to produce irrelevant results. One of the key considerations in achieving some measure of success is to recognize the complexity of the human resource development process. This of course means taking a very hard look at what is possible and what is not possible. A clear-sighted view is essential because in today's highly competitive world the quality of human resource development is often the best way to achieve competitive advantage.

This chapter sets out to illustrate and contrast the process as described in the text books and experienced in practice. It will illustrate the political, technical and financial aspects of operating management or career development. Short incidents will be described, taken straight from the diary of a management development adviser. The details and names have been changed in the scenarios to protect the innocent.

This book contains a wealth of information contributed by writers who are often at the leading edge of management development; therefore, in this chapter there is no need to repeat in detail material contained elsewhere. It focuses on the strategic issues in achieving success and the obstacles and realities sometimes encountered.

MANAGEMENT DEVELOPMENT IN THEORY

The route map for making management development happen as a corporate system has long been available. The main steps along the route are discussed in the following sections.

Define scope of the strategy/system

This step involves deciding who should be covered. A common way is to define coverage by organizational levels. Thus a strategy might cover top management, middle management, departmental management, supervisors, all professional staff, graduates, high-flyers or some combination of all these. Rather than using hierarchical levels, the scope might be defined by identifying key jobs and the availability of successors for them.

The scope of the strategy will affect the implementation, cost and approach used. For example, a system covering 100 professional staff spread across the world would need different resourcing to one concentrating on 20 senior posts all on one site.

Specify future managerial requirements

The specification will include three essentials: link with planners; identification of competences; and a focus on results.

Link with Corporate Plan

The human resource development strategy needs to be closely integrated with the organization's strategic aims. This requires the HR director to work with the strategic planners to identify the anticipated growth and future direction of the business. Business needs will give important clues to the direction of career development required.

Extracts from a Management Development Adviser's diary

Monday 9.00–10.30 a.m.
Attended meeting with strategic planning manager to discuss the 1994–1999 Corporate Plan. The bank's strong move into insurance was becoming even clearer with profit contribution projected at 30 per cent of total profits by 1997. The SWOT analysis (Strength, Weaknesses, Opportunities and Threats) showed a clear need for more branch managers with insurance sales management experience than we had previously anticipated. It was agreed that employee development would provide more sales management training courses and feature selling experience more positively in junior management career development.

In the car on the way back to the office we discussed how quickly the branch manager role had changed. As little as five years ago none of our managers had any real sales management experience. Now we are competing head-to-head with the insurance companies. Our links with the strategic planners were becoming more and more helpful in keeping up with the game. On returning to the office I rang one or two people in the insurance industry – you never know, and it's cheaper than head hunters.

Identify competences required

This step covers the identification of what the organization could need managers to be able to do or achieve in the future. It will usually involve the use of data to describe the competence, skills, knowledge or experience that will be required. The data will be a mixture of existing information such as personnel specifications and the creation of new data through the competence approach. Generic material such as that marketed by the Management Charter Initiative (MCI), job evaluation data such as that produced for Hay Job Evaluation, Bench Marking and recruitment specifications, may all play their part. The main thrust of this step concerns future direction. It aims to describe what it is that managers need to be developed to achieve, or do. In the early 1990s there has been increasing focus on values in many organizations and the value statements developed (e.g. to be more open in communications) may need to be built into any description of future competence requirements.

Tuesday 3.00–7.00 p.m.
Carried out interviews with two general managers – nursing and finance – to identify the key competences that will be required of third-tier managers over the next three years. Lots of conflicting views. The need to improve understanding about service and caring and control and cost-effectiveness seems immense.

Wednesday 10.00–1.00 p.m.
Wrote up the results of the key competences meeting held yesterday. Arranged for these to be circulated to the competence steering group. I am quite concerned about how to reconcile the widely conflicting views. Made a mental note to discuss the issue informally with the chairperson when she visits on the last day of the middle management course. Looks like a topic to raise rather later in the evening.

Focusing on results and current contribution

The identification of management development needs relies heavily on the clear identification of what is expected of managers. The introduction of performance management systems in many respects represented a considerable advance on earlier job specification or objectives based approaches. A comprehensive performance management system will identify managerial competences needed with a specific description of results required such as sales output that is satisfactory, or service levels that should be achieved (e.g. 95 per cent of trains arrive on time). The more sophisticated schemes will identify the level of difficulty of the task and adjust results accordingly. Thus, it might be ten times easier to sell or achieve targets for currency exchange turnover per 1 000 passengers at Heathrow, than it is at East Midlands Airport. It might be twenty times easier at East Midlands than to achieve currency exchange turnover targets at Liverpool Airport.

By weighting the results achieved, performance management systems can provide a very sophisticated basis for development information. They can identify 'soft' results such as coaching contribution or contribution to team results as well as producing very realistic performance measures.

Audit the performance of job incumbents

Decisions made about an individual manager's development are usually very *303* dependent on the quality of information available. This data may be 'hard' and factual or 'soft' and subjective. The former needs to be accurate and up-to-date, and often is not. Soft data has to be used with care. However, opinions and prejudices are essential factors in the equation. Managers really do miss out on development opportunities through wearing suede shoes or having long hair or even telling tiresome 'jokes'.

The range of data available might range across the managers' original CVs, a computer-based CV system, the results of performance appraisals, performance at assessment centres, psychometric test results, qualifications, reputation, superiors' views about performance and personality. Specialized analytical techniques such as the SRI (Selection Research Inc) approach to the identification of motivational patterns necessary for success or the SIMA approach to identifying individual motivational patterns can provide invaluable additional perspectives. In addition, technical reports such as a bank's inspection reports, a review of lending performance or an internal audit of skills could be used.

In the following sections we look more closely at some of the key issues involved in the more common of these audit techniques.

Career summaries or CVs

Mechanisms need to be set up to ensure continuous availability of current and accurate career information. In essence, the CV data above should contain all the information necessary to assess the probability of the organization having the skills and experience necessary to meet its predicted requirements. There will be a need for an accurate and up-to-date summary of educational qualifications and experience, professional qualifications and career experience. The latter should be sufficiently detailed to assess the real job responsibilities in terms of results and accountability. Specialist data should be identified (e.g. branch of medicine in which the individual practised, or types of aircraft squadron commanded).

Performance appraisal

A history of performance ratings can help to build up a more complete picture. Most appraisal schemes, including the more modern performance man-agement systems, will identify and grade performance. Clearly, problems in achieving the desired performance or a fall in achievement at a comparable job level would need further examination from a management development perspective. Traditional performance appraisal approaches, where per-formance is rated against achievement of agreed objectives, can be nevertheless subjective. They should only ever be used as one element of a decision making process and treated with care.

Wednesday 9.00–10.30 a.m.
Received a note from the personnel director asking for my view as to whether the

southern area director was being too generous in her performance appraisal ratings for current performance. She has eight direct reports of whom six were rated as superior performers and two were rated as excellent.

I carried out a comparison with the other eight regions and three head office functions. Bearing in mind that the southern area was our best performing region with sales in excess of £100 million and that few regional directors gave less than satisfactory ratings, the ratings seemed reasonable. I advised the personnel director that two of the superior ratings might be a shade generous, but both of the individuals were long-serving area managers, and the ratings could have little impact on their salary review as they were at the top end of their ranges. Neither took part in any promotion decisions and were in fact contributing very positively as mentors on the middle management course.

No action was necessary on the performance ratings awarded.

Assessment

The assessment process involves coming to a view about development needs. At its simplest it may be highly subjective. In more complex form it may involve tests, simulations, exercises and psychometric assessment. It may range from assessing who should play the lead in a musical to assessing if a candidate is competent to act as captain of an aircraft. Assessment can be carried out on a self-assessment basis, by peers, by operational superiors or bosses, by subordinates or by a panel of assessors in an assessment centre. The key elements are the relevance of the task for which performance is being assessed and the competence of the assessors for assessing the task. This basic judgement process is crucial to the success of making management development happen.

> *Friday* 10.00 p.m.
> All the assessment exercises had been completed and we had had a good dinner. The discussion turned to the exercise which had required the candidates at the assessment centre to produce a strategy for lending to Eastern Europe. At the briefing the link between the exercise and the need to identify competence in strategic thinking had seemed clear. But I could not answer the branch manger from Market Harborough who felt his head office colleagues had been given an unfair advantage. Fortunately, he had been accepted as a high-flyer.

Superiors' views

These are crucial in the audit of incumbents. The views may be expressed formally or informally. They may be recorded or not. However, for management development to happen effectively, they must be incorporated into the decision-making process.

Individuals generally see the world through their own perspective. They are typically more comfortable with people they know they can relate to. Few managers want their subordinates to threaten their position. They will almost certainly use their positions to gain their own ends. In some cases it may not suit them to lose a subordinate by singing his/her praises too loudly. There is some evidence that many managers are unable to be objective because of their personal make-up. Thus a manager who is predominately concerned with detail and procedures and who is risk-averse, may have little time for the visionary who creates exciting word-pictures of the future and takes risks to achieve them. A sensitive recognition and handling of these issues is needed if the approach to management development is to have any chance of success in the real, hard world of personal development.

The view which you see depends very much on where you stand, and what you are looking for. Accommodating this simple fact is one of the great challenges of making management development happen successfully and to the satisfaction of senior management.

Discussion with senior executives

All the information generated needs to be assembled and presented to the chief executive and the executive directors of the organization. It is advisable to do this by assembling the information as described earlier. An informed discussion of the strengths, weaknesses and development needs of the chief executive's direct reports then needs to take place. This discussion should cover careers to date, likely future moves, any performance or personal concerns and development needs and plans. A clear indication of high potential or the need to redeploy or remove individuals should also be sought. Ideally this discussion should be written up and signed-off by the chief executive as representing a fair and accurate record of the discussion. In a large organization this information might then need to be considered by a group chief executive or the head office board. The information is clearly highly sensitive. It must remain confidential to one or two senior human resource executives and senior line managers.

The chief executive's values are particularly crucial at this level as they will colour judgements about individuals. (For example, media reporting of clashes about such values at British Petroleum, British Airways, Tottenham Hotspur and even within Mrs Thatcher's Cabinet, all in the early 1990s, illustrate the point well.) Success in long-term development requires the ability to cope with major changes in this area.

Identify succession plans and threats

One of the essential ingredients of succession planning is to review the probable shape and mission of the organization over the next three to five years. From this the likely senior posts and roles can be projected and then subordinate posts can be identified by extrapolating downwards. Present incumbents are then entered onto an organization chart and succession needs can be highlighted and agreed. These may arise from projected retirements, planned redundancies or planned reorganization. Key jobs or roles can be identified and the available managers proposed for key roles. This enables a focus to be created and maintained.

The process then is to agree the demands of the roles and who might be appropriate contenders for promotion and in what timescale. Thus, a manager who may be identified as a budding chief executive in ten years' time, will need senior line management experience overseas during the next five years. In reviewing the shape of the future management for the whole organization much will depend on sponsorship. Powerful managers will argue for career moves for particular individuals whom they favour for some reason.

The process of identifying threats, and opportunities, is important. At its crudest, the threat of losing a senior manager can be the motivation for promoting him/her. The threat may be financial, motivational or personal – the manager may be worth more (e.g. a successful young research manager) or bored and therefore losing an edge, say, in sales or advertising; or, the manager may be a thrusting entrepreneur working for a time-serving bureaucrat.

Threats need to be carefully assessed. It is in these areas where the judgement of the senior management becomes crucial. Opportunities for development can be provided on reorganization and through career management for succession. The quality of the information available in large organizations becomes crucial.

All the discussion and data is usually recorded on succession charts, and the progress of key individuals should be monitored regularly by the board or by a senior staff committee. The same process is cascaded down the organization when management development is happening effectively. Individual general managers may undertake the function of the chief executive, and the management development adviser or personnel director may have an important role in achieving cross-functional moves. It is sometimes necessary for a manager to forego the services of a good high-potential graduate – who needs experience elsewhere in the organization to achieve his/her full potential – in deference to the overall needs of the organization itself.

SOME REALITIES OF MANAGEMENT DEVELOPMENT

Achieving commitment to, and implementation of, a formal or systematic approach to management development can require considerable energy and skill. Some will see any management development initiative as interference in the natural order of things. Others may resent what they see as the intrusion of the human resourcing function. The scope for demonstrating the contribution of the development activity in a short-term focused environment may be limited. Assertions about the contribution of the development activity, especially when it takes the form of an external training course at some expensive but academically driven management college, may be less than convincing.

A one-week training event for 15 managers could easily cost in excess of £25 000. An investment of £2 000 for a week for just one manager would require careful consideration in a smaller organization or one facing cash-flow difficulties. Time spent away from the job may be difficult to cover with other staff.

Time and effort to plan managers' careers through succession planning and   *307* career development meetings will have to be allocated in the face of competing demands for management time. It is not surprising, therefore, that the process of making development happen involves tackling many difficult areas. Some of these are outlined in the following sections.

Inertia

There can be many reasons for inertia. One of the most common is a vested interest in preserving the *status quo*. The thought of developing managers who have different and opposing views to your own is not universally attractive. Few companies would deny the desirability of creating ever more committed and thrusting managers with more and more competence. Equally, some senior and middle managers base their retirement plans on an anticipated age of sixty years with a high final salary. They clearly can have a lot to lose to their younger competitors.

There are many other reasons for inertia. One might be the wish to negate the personnel director's influence, without being too explicit. So, when corporate proposals are made they are regarded as being at the wrong time – 'the summer/winter is our busy time and we cannot release managers'. Or, 'the business is in the process of identifying its own competence requirements for the next five years and cannot buy into the corporate approach just now'.

Delay is sometimes the classic inertia tactic and making development happen will often require a strategy to create the dynamics necessary for success. This will require energizing activities such as finding out the sometimes covert agendas of the senior managers involved, getting their commitment by discussion and involvement, and showing that the approach to development can help them personally either by providing personal development or advancing the careers of their protégés.

A simple analysis of which influences or individuals are obstacles to successful implementation can help. This should identify where and why progress will be difficult to achieve. Inertia may spring from lack of familiarity with the ideas, lack of funds, cynicism about development, fear of threatening younger managers, conservatism and many other reasons. A risk-averse bureaucracy with a penchant for precedence and the *status quo* has little obvious inclinations for a pro-active approach to the future. It should be no surprise if the initial reactions are very much about not actually doing anything – certainly before it has been thoroughly analysed, compared with other organizations and tested through a pilot scheme. The likely reactions themselves indicate how the approach would need to be sold to overcome the natural institutional inertia.

Political influences

Management development is probably the most politically sensitive area of human resource management. It can affect directly the status and income of the most powerful individuals in any organization. In theory, senior managers should act in the best interests of the shareholders. Sometimes, however, they act in their own best interests. Politics has been described as the art of the possible. It is of course more than that. It is about opinion forming and understanding at any particular time who has the ability to award or take away the power to act.

Events in the Conservative Party demonstrated this well. Margaret Thatcher was an elected prime minister. Elected by her party which in turn was elected by the electorate. But she lost the support of her party and consequently the power to act. She had to resign. Opinions, prompted by Sir Geoffrey Howe's resignation speech, had turned – or more probably had been turned – against her.

A somewhat different kind of example occurs fairly often in organizations. The chairman or chief executive who loses the support of the board will often be prevailed upon to resign. The 1990s have provided many examples, the Guinness Trial being one of the more spectacular. These cases usually involve a shift of political opinion on the part of the key players. They often impact directly on succession and development issues and are sometimes motivated by the ambitions of the prime movers.

The key issues for survival for the management development executive are to identify in each area of the organization who has the power to make or break a development strategy. All the political levers then need to be used to generate support. Political alliances change with changes in personnel. One of the most difficult tasks for the HR executive is to maintain his/her political position in the face of changing management teams. One saving grace is that the access to information about future succession plans should at least give some clues on who should be targeted – to help maintain the HR executive's political influence and survival into the future.

Thursday 5.00–7.30 p.m.
It was a very tense meeting. Jim White the deputy sales director had moved with his family from Glasgow just six months ago. He had eventually found a house and moved his family – a week before Rob Evans had his fatal car crash. Rob's successor as sales director, Paul Green, was in the middle of the annual performance review. Jim did not like the blunt way that he was being told that he did not fit with Paul's future plans. He had uprooted his family on the promise of succeeding Rob Evans as sales director. He had done everything Rob had asked and had been told that he was a front runner for the director role. Unfortunately, he had not had time to prove himself and Paul Green has been moved across from the American group office.

It seemed to Jim that his reputation was now to count for nothing. Paul felt he was too concerned with pushing sales and not sufficiently concerned with the profitability of the business sold. All Rob had wanted was more sales, and Jim had worked with him for ten years to build the company's market-share up to 60 per cent. Here he was, at forty years of age, living in the south-east and with no real future while Paul was sales director. So much for his career planning. He had a long chat with the employee development manager after the meeting. Both he and she were now looking at alternative options for Jim's future.

Personalities

A further fact of organizational life is that some people just are not able to get on together. What is sometimes referred to as chemistry can be a major feature. Individuals may be:

- Domineering
- Cautious and risk-averse
- Detail-conscious
- Visionary
- Expansionary and bold
- Sociable and team-players
- Loners and independent
- Bullying and dishonest
- Power-centred
- Pursuing excellence
- Competitive
- Profit-centred.

Clearly, any individual will have one predominant and/or a combination of these or other personality aspects. Thus a domineering visionary who is profit centred and a chief executive might have difficulty working with a finance director who is a cautious loner, risk-averse and motivated by power. Equally, a finance director who was pursuing excellence might have difficulty working with a detail-conscious and risk-averse chief executive.

The impact of personalities is crucial in considering selection and succession issues. They rarely appear as clearly as expressed here in management development data.

A view of an individual's personality can be built up by comprehensive psychometric testing and supplemented by assessment and appraisal data. Interviews or discussions between senior executives and senior HR development staff can provide powerful supplementary data on individuals.

It is of course necessary to take into account the personalities of those expressing the views. An expansionary and bold marketing director might see a subordinate as cautious and risk-averse whereas an actuarial colleague might see the same person as quite adventurous. To make management development happen, the HR executive needs to be sensitive to and competent about these issues. He/she also needs to have created an atmosphere of trust whereby the personality of any manager can be discussed and dealt with as development issues. One of the great Achilles' heels of the management development process is that the data used is essentially so subjective.

Subjectivity

Practical management development is a human activity. As such it is basically subjective. No matter how much analytical or objective data is obtained, decisions will be made on a subjective basis. The analytical personnel director will tend to prefer certain stereotypes. Equally, the classic extrovert will rarely be truly comfortable with the more introverted analytic. Those more comfortable with people do not always relate well to those highly focused on ideas. A great deal of effort is used to reduce the impact of subjectivity in the operation of management development systems. Typically, appraisals are reviewed, and the 'halo' effect may be allowed for by adjusting or qualifying the data. Assessment centres use panels to seek to achieve objectivity in the observation of behavioural performance. More recently, some believe that competencies can objectively describe what is required to perform a task.

The key skill in operating management development is to keep attention focused on the business results required. The HR executive will necessarily take a personal viewpoint. This subjectivity should be continuously reviewed and monitored against the views held by senior executives.

As much relevant information and debate as possible should be generated and weighed to improve the vital task of promoting the correct types of skill for the future. Success in strategic planning – such as making the National Health Service more patient-centred or the Post Office more cost-competitive – will depend greatly on the correct subjective decisions being made about managerial appointments. An interesting, and illustrative, example can be taken from the world of sport. The England soccer manager has access to fit and skilled players. Subjective judgements about individuals, style of play and the strategy and tactics of competitors clearly can impact directly on results. In the final analysis, the results, either in sport or business, demonstrate the success or otherwise of the competence deployed.

> *Saturday* 9.30–12.00 noon.
> An interesting round of golf. At the nineteenth hole I sat with the sales director. She was in the frame of mind to talk about succession, so I listened. The first point she made was that I should not take too much notice of the formal system. She stressed that she knew her people and could enhance or destroy their potential. Few senior consultants would show good results – and thus potential – if assigned to Merseyside or Tyneside; business was very difficult to come by. By allocating poor support teams in difficult areas she could easily destroy a career. Her view put me in mind of 'the leper colony' aircraft in the film 'Twelve O'Clock High'. I made a mental note to watch the film again.
>
> Driving home, my mind kept returning to the talk I was due to give in two weeks' time. Should I really promote the success story of my organization's competence and assessment approach? I know full well that the next three area directors to be appointed had all worked for the sales director in the north-west ten years ago.

Lack of talent

Lack of talent can manifest itself in many ways. It may arise from earlier inertia or an inappropriate strategy pursued by former managements. The historical culture values, such as a cradle-to-grave approach to careers or a refusal to recruit at any level other than the basic task (e.g. insurance sales representative, bank clerk, police constable, railway engine driver), can create talent problems. A good home-beat constable or primary school teacher may or may not have strategic management skills. In the increasingly competitive world that now exists, a *laissez-faire* approach to attracting talent is unlikely to work. The insurance companies and banks began to realize this in the early 1980s, as have the police, railways and similar institutions. The classic responses were to recruit middle and then senior managers from competitors or closely related markets. Graduate recruitment schemes were the medium- to longer-term response. A further strategy, employed particularly by international companies such as airlines, car producers and pharmaceuticals manufacturers, has been to recruit senior management from the international labour market. This has often meant North American born or developed executives, such as Sir Graham Day or Sir Colin Marshall, running major UK organizations.

Monday 3.00 p.m.
Returning from my meeting with the strategic planners, a note from the chief executive was waiting for me.

'When we meet tomorrow would you please arrive prepared to discuss who we should appoint to run our new estate agency business.'

I rang the strategic planners to get a view on projected size and rate of growth. A brief meeting with my management development manager got the work started on identifying in detail any internal candidates we might have.

I asked for details on three options:

1. Who was available internally?
2. Who might we attract from other financial services organizations?
3. Were we planning to buy, or could we buy, any estate agency business which already employed a potential chief executive?

I met with my staff at 8.30 a.m. next day. We concluded that we needed three main skills – in the areas of marketing, building profits, and setting up a large organization from small beginnings. The only possible runner we had internally was already earmarked for something else. The people in the other financial services organizations, with one exception, did not look very promising.

We would have to buy the talent either by attracting this one person or by buying one of three large estate agency groups known to have a capable chief executive. Fortunately, no one blames me for not anticipating the rush into acquiring estate agencies.

POINTERS TO SUCCESS

Making management development happen can be demanding, satisfying, threatening, exciting, stressful, intellectually stimulating and very exposed – all at the same time. The casualty rate seems to have accelerated somewhere ahead of the rate of change in the 1990s. Some pointers on surviving and achieving success are listed below.

1. Ensure that you as management development executive understand and provide what key senior colleagues want.
2. Provide a well-recognized and distinctive expertise spanning the skills of counselling and individual personal development and those of operating the management development routines.
3. Create a situation where you are trusted at all levels. Remain as politically neutral as is possible and realistic.
4. Attract subordinate staff who can operate independently and gain personal credibility as committed developers.
5. Promote commitment and understanding of the management development process from the most senior levels and throughout the organization.
6. Encourage as much line ownership as possible. In reality, senior line managers have the final say on who is promoted or developed: their immediate superior will usually be reluctant to suggest that they appoint someone against their personal wishes but on the advice of the HR director.
7. Create situations where you are invited to be involved in decisions on development issues and promotions.
8. Continuously develop your personnel expertise through networking, conferences, professional activity, and increasing awareness and proficiency about development strategies.
9. Promote what you are doing both within and outside the organization through articles, presentations and seminars.
10. Ensure that the results of your activities are fed into and recognized by senior managers. These results must be in terms which are relevant to key managers.
11. Regularly review the political situation and any political alliances which affect you. This will require ethical or value judgement at times. It may not always be possible to resolve some situations positively.
12. Be prepared to recognize when it may be necessary to trim your aims or even to cut and run. A realistic view of situations should include the possibility that the HR function will at times not have sufficient power to persist.
13. Remember Machiavelli's advice:

   > The innovator makes enemies of all those who prospered under the old order and only lukewarm support is forthcoming from those who would prosper under the new.

14. Continuously update and strengthen internal support and alliances.
15. Have clear values about development and communicate these.
16. Recognize that longer-term strategic activities are vulnerable to short-term turbulence.

FURTHER READING

For those who are interested in a deeper view of the political and practical issues, the following short recommended reading list may be found stimulating.

Jay, Antony (1967) *Management and Machiavelli* (London: Hodder and Stoughton).

Machiavelli, Niccolo (1961) *The Prince* (Harmondsworth: Penguin Books).

Moorby, Ed (1991) *How to Succeed in Employee Development* (London: McGraw-Hill).

Part V
ISSUES IN MANAGEMENT DEVELOPMENT

20 The cultural contexts

Bob Garratt

'When I hear anyone talk of Culture, I reach for my revolver.' Such strong sentiments are not restricted to Goering alone: many of the managers I meet in the course of my work have similar feelings, but these are changing and for the better. They are coming, sometimes grudgingly, to the realization that 'culture' is an area of growing importance: it seems to be what links organization strategy and structure, through vision and energies, with the values and behaviours of the people comprising the business and delivering its targets.

This chapter is a distillation of my recent work. In it I have tried to do two things: first, to tease out the meaning of the word 'culture' in the very different contexts of the (specialist) department: the organization, and the international environment, and then the management of the total concept. Second, to stress that most of the tools needed to measure and manage the cultural dimensions are already easily available and ready to be applied to the increasing range of 'cultural' problems. What is needed is a conscious effort on the part of the managers to *give priority to managing them*.

I shall define 'culture' as 'the way we do things around here': it is a combination of the values, behaviours and history of an organization which define (often tightly) the limits to thought and behaviour in the organization. New entrants hit it when they do what they think is right in their job, only to find others saying, 'Oh no, we don't do things like that round here!' (See Chapter 17.) Such a simple definition gives too uniform a flavour to the subject; it hides the complexities of different levels of culture and their interactions in and between organizations. However, it is a good start when working with directors and managers.

The idea that culture can be *designed, directed* and *managed* is so seductive that managers can get quite excited and energized to 'do something about our culture'; being typically action-fixated, they will then demand to start the change process. This often causes problems for management developers who are as ill-informed and ill-equipped in this area as their managers. Both need training and development since culture is, literally, central to creating and maintaining an effective organization. I hope that this chapter gives some clues to the ideas and processes that can be used.

A CULTURAL HEALTH WARNING

'Culture' has become a particularly fashionable issue with directors since it was legitimized, initially through *In Search of Excellence* (Peters and Waterman, 1982). The possibility of integrating the three 'hard' areas of business (systems, strategy, and structure) with the three 'soft' areas (staff, skills and style) via shared values, has made possible the discussion of culture and values at the top level of organizations in a way that has not been possible for twenty years or more. But 'culture' is in danger of losing its meaning if those who are so eagerly embracing it use it in too profligate and ambiguous a way. Moreover, many new converts see culture as the new cure-all which it patently is not. If it can be said to be anything at present, it is the thin film of lubrication which enables people to *work together within their organization structure* for *common ends*. This notion of culture helping alignment and attunement in an organization is central to understanding it.

Most companies with which I have worked see culture as a unitary thing; I initially annoy them by saying that it is a series of different things at different hierarchical levels of an organization – and that directors need to handle each level differently. However, there are strong stereotypes about the unitary nature of culture which can lead an organization to some very basic problems of profitability. For example, it is accepted in most multinational businesses that I have interviewed that their company culture must – and should – transcend national and all other cultures. Such a notion of culture is implicit in the planning of most executive directors and in their subsequent behaviour; yet the results regularly contradict their assumptions and behaviour. They ask, 'How can the same sort of people with the same sort of education in the same sort of job in our global organizational structure, do such different things?' The question is usually set emotionally in terms of frustration, anger, and despair, often because the questioner is aware of the varying levels of profitability and complexity that will be needed to manage what is being uncovered.

This is typical of the problems many companies face in trying to direct the international cultural dimensions of their business. It is not a particularly British characteristic; there is evidence to show that US and Japanese corporations have considerably more problems in coping with international cross-cultural aspects than, for example, North Europeans and Overseas Chinese (March, 1980). It would be a mistake, however, to think that managing cultures is a problem only for organizations who have to trade across national boundaries. The *internal organizational culture* is being seen as of increasing importance as companies face up to radical and structural change. Coming to grips with the internal dimension alone is enough for most managers, but few have this luxury nowadays. Increasingly managers, particularly top managers, have to cope simultaneously with both the internal and international dimensions. How they cope with this is of great interest.

My experience of working with companies across cultural boundaries has been that the problems are often felt but then hidden, rather than exposed and managed. The reasons for this are complex but amongst them is an awareness that to confront them would force a radical change in the board's ability to think about the multicultural dimensions of their work; this, in turn, would force reconsideration of their *present allocation of time* – and this is often treated as sacrosanct 'because we are busy enough already'.

This is true but, as an Institute of Directors report (1990) has shown, most directors are untrained for directing and so tend to focus their use of time on the operations cycle of work and learning (where they have trained and been comfortable), rather than on the strategic cycle in which such 'soft' subjects as culture lurk. It is patently most effective to start any re-evaluation of the role of culture in management with the board. That this is not always possible is accepted, and very useful pilot projects can be started and measured without board involvement; however, they need to be built into the overall organizational learning process, or such projects may be seen as setting up alternative power bases within the business and will be resisted by the board, demeaning culture in the process.

The subtleties and differences of thinking about the cultural dimensions needed will rapidly show up a lack of knowledge and skills in many directors; such lacunae are difficult for any individual at board level to talk about so progress is rarely made – unless there is team commitment to do so. This is usually not the case, and so the issue is hidden again, whilst the already inadequate corporate culture is brought to bear once again on a problem which has regularly proved intractable. Yet the board knows that doing 'more of' or 'less of' the same thing will not change the problem. How can they *re-frame the cultural issue* so that it is resolvable within their own resources?

SETTING THE CONTEXT

My experience has been that the very act of saying that it is legitimate to talk of cultural difference at board level, and get people used to so doing, is sufficient to allow the re-framing of the problem so that constructive change can happen. There are often audible sighs of relief around the table when some basic vocabulary, concepts, and measures are introduced to help define and explore the area of 'culture'. Often the analogy of 'it felt like a boil being lanced' is used. I have learned to curb my didactic tendencies on such occasions and to work from the board's existing positions on one fundamental issue – *difference,* and how to value it. Around the table it is usually easy to get agreement that there are physical, social, and psychological differences between those present; it is then not difficult to get agreement that the reason this particular group is charged with giving direction to the organization is that they represent the synthesis of the various specialized functions needed *319* for the organization to sustain and develop itself. As such, they must subscribe (albeit subconsciously) to the idea that such amalgamation allows for *synergy* amongst them – that the individual inputs give an output that is *quantitatively and qualitatively better* than the simple sum of the inputs.

Such statements are usually met with acclamation. 'So why then', I ask, 'do you as a board who obviously value the differences between you, behave in a way that tries to eliminate rather than celebrate and use the differences in your operating units and with customers?' This is the time when some resentment can erupt. Then a dispassionate review of strategic problems – business and people strategy – will usually gain support for my plea to develop thinking and procedures in the cultural context. It is at this point that a start can be made on coming to grips with the paradox that the more an organization tries to impose a unitary 'corporate' culture on its disparate parts, the more the differences become magnified and difficult to manage. If this does not work, then a quick study of the main reasons for corporate collapse (Argenti, 1976) – too many people of the same sex, age, education, and nationality at the top, with too little authentic information about the changing environment, and few managerial information systems – usually makes the case adequately for 'sufficient diversity' of personalities and cultures (see Ashby, 1956).

SOME WORKING DEFINITIONS

With line managers, I use at first the notion of 'culture' being 'how we do things around here', and get them to give examples of how they ran into this organization's culture when they joined it; this elicits great passion and merriment and helps make the profound point that unless people are psychologically 'included' in their work-groups and the organization then they can never be seen as 'competent' in it, no matter how well-qualified. As we get into the deeper comments coming from this, we can take a deeper look at culture itself.

The word 'culture' is loaded with ambiguity and complexity. For the sake of this chapter I will use a single definition:

> An historically transmitted pattern of meanings embodied in symbols, a system of inherited conceptions expressed in symbolic forms by means of which men communicate, perpetuate, and develop their knowledge about and attitudes towards life…man is an animal suspended in webs of signification he himself has spun. I take culture to be those webs, and the analysis of it to be therefore not an experimental science in search of law but an interpretive one in search of meaning (Geertz, 1973).

But I do not say that initially in the boardroom. The cultural divide would be too great!

There is significance in the vocabulary that any operating group uses, and the above quotation is so far outside that used by business or organizations that it invites initial hostility and rejection – made manifest in such comments as 'stupidly academic', 'psuedo-science', 'soft', etc. In that form, it has no significance for the board. This does not diminish its conceptual value, but it does make it indigestible when presented in unadulterated form. That is why it is important to use the 'empathetic' approach of starting from where the line managers are, and *using their experience to create the higher concepts* – the move to the 're-framing cycle' (Watzlawick *et al.*, 1974) of learning which allows them to explore recurrent organizational problems by using a cultural perspective to re-frame the problem. This is necessary to gain board awareness of the 'webs of signification' which they have spun themselves. An awareness of the organization's symbols – logo, predominant colours, furniture and furnishings, equipment, etc. – and the ways in which a new entrant becomes 'included' (Smith, 1986), often through subconscious behaviour and semantic modification created by the existing staff, is crucial in opening up the cultural dimensions so that organizations may develop constructively.

Present perceptions, behaviours and values can be measured by such processes as the Handy Organizational Culture Questionnaire (Handy, 1985), the Organizational Climate Survey, and Neuro-Linguistic Programming. In so doing, a veritable maze of dead ends and diversions can be constructed; it is not my intention to do so, and I have to contain myself from following those seductive idiosyncrasies and differences found in organizations, and use them only in those dinner party conversations where one can add the tag 'not many people know this'. What concerns me much more in my consultancy role is to get the board to find and focus on those aspects of the cultures within which they work that affect and determine the *effectiveness* and *efficiency* of their organization.

A WORKING VOCABULARY

To do this it is necessary to try and give more definition to our use of the word 'culture'. In a small working group, 'culture' can be taken to refer to national characteristics, political beliefs, organizational style, individual attitudes, historical progression, and the fine arts. Little wonder that confusion can reign even between those who work together each day! I have developed my own categorization of 'cultures' which I use when working with an organization. This involves four levels of cultural differentiation:

Micro-culture   relates to the world of the *functional specialists,* and *work-groups*

Mini-culture   relates specifically to the *organization* and its *social structures* (a sociological notion), otherwise known as the 'corporate culture'

Macro-culture   relates to the wider, *national, multiracial and international contexts* (an anthropological notion)

Meta-culture   relates to the transcending of mini-, micro- and macro-cultures by those *giving direction* to the organization (i.e. the   *321* management of the other three levels of culture – an integrative notion).

How do these very different levels of culture work in practice in an organization?

'Micro-culture' is usually the best understood as it is the most personal; it is where we spend our daily lives. This is the most basic (some would even say 'tribal') level of culture (see Chapter 9): it is where you are accepted or rejected as an individual. Because of this there are often complex 'rites of passage' for acceptance, usually involving you in proving yourself through some emotional and/or physical test. If inclusion happens, then all is well; if not, the individual becomes a social isolate. This can happen at all levels of an organization, and in my experience is very common in the senior and top management positions. It is rarely managed well in organizations and yet, if not managed, can create massive problems as the micro-culture is the foundation on which all the others are built. Micro-culture is measurable by a wide range of group and team psychometric tests.

'Mini-culture' is the level commonly known as 'corporate culture'; it encompasses the social composition and history of specific departments and divisions within the corporate whole. How they started, who was involved, and for what reasons, are key indicators of mini-cultures. Who holds power now, and what values do they espouse – raw divide-and-rule power, or stability and continuity, or professionals coming together to run high-quality projects, or very personalized activities nearer to a group of high-powered colleagues? What is the prevailing 'party political' flavour? Are there strong religious tendencies at board level, or are there particular ethnic characteristics which predominate? These are typical of the types of questions which reflect the mini-cultural aspects I would want mapped and debated. To this can then be added some of the more management-orientated mini-cultural analyses. What is the organizational culture? Which stage of the product lifecycle have the various units reached? Which functional specialism is dominant in which parts of the company? In process terms, it is usually much easier to begin mapping in the technical areas and work towards the 'softer', less appreciated, aspects rather than vice versa. The board then starts from what it knows, and can ease itself into the more difficult areas. These are measurable by, for example, Handy's Organizational Culture Questionnaire.

Interest in the mini-culture or 'corporate' culture is growing as top managers take more interest in strategy and find the complexities of implementing their strategic ideas need more than just instructions to the operational people. A picture of the future, a way of getting there, and a way of getting aligned to get there, are all needed and I shall say more about this at the end of the chapter.

'Macro-culture' analysis and mapping is a more difficult step to take in the move towards an organization's understanding and management of culture. Most boards accept that there are the mini- and micro-cultural aspects to the process of managing, even if they would prefer not to express it in that way. They are usually more comfortable with terms like 'Managing the human side

of enterprise', 'Motivating and maintaining morale', or 'Proving that people matter around here'. However, they do understand that their organization operates in a wider political, multiracial, and international context. This is characteristically much more unpredictable and disruptive and much more difficult to manage. Macro-culture can be measured on such dimensions as Hofstede's cross-cultural maps (Hofstede, 1980).

Managers are unlikely to grace this domain with the term 'political science' or 'anthropology', but these are the areas into which they are moving. Considering the narrow educational backgrounds most managers have it is hardly surprising that they have difficulty coming to grips with macro-culture; but come to grips with it is what they will need to do – a troubled US manager working for a British multinational in Hong Kong facing a problematic Taiwanese member of staff is not so unusual a problem nowadays. Nor is negotiating across a table on behalf of an international consortium with backing from a range of overseas financiers whilst facing your opposite number who, in turn, represents a newly industrialized country's minority government being backed by the World Bank for a new infrastructural project. It is no good in these circumstances insisting that there can be only one culture around here, and that is our corporate one; it just will not wash. Acceptance that the game has risen by at least one plane, and that the roles of all players become much nearer to that of diplomat–negotiator and international troubleshooter, is the only way out. This requires training and development, if only to ensure the clearing of diaries of operational impedimenta to get seriously into the management of the macro-cultural role.

I have argued elsewhere about the characteristics of boards (Garratt, 1987), of their tendency to keep their eyes and hands on daily operations, rather than on policy and strategy, because this is how they have behaved over a long period; and of their rarely being able to retrain to cope with the less tangible world of macro-culture which they are expected to inhabit when they join a board. Ideally, there is a strong case to be made for directors being properly inducted and trained in the *art of directing* – of managing the boundaries between their inherently controllable organizations and the inherently uncontrollable and unpredictable world outside. Because this is rarely done, it is hardly surprising that most directors show signs of great stress when asked to attend to such environmental monitoring, analysis, and prediction. They usually take the comfortable route and return unofficially to their old job whilst keeping the perks of their elevated job title. For the organization such behaviour is disastrous, as the external boundaries are not manned, and so it loses touch with the outside world.

In an ideal world, directors would add to their range of disciplines political science, anthropology and design as key tools in their directoral kitbag. But as these are not only not offered by the business schools, but are actively rebuffed by them, some quick and dirty methods are needed to help transform current problems into useful practice.

Macro-culture is for me about the broader national and international contexts in which the organization operates. It can be regional, but is typically *323* national – and, increasingly, international – in scope. It encompasses the issues of nationality, religion, politics, language, and combinations of these which boards find often opposed to their organization's micro-culture – and its assumed primacy when the micro- and macro-cultures are in opposition.

CHARACTERISTICS OF META-CULTURAL MANAGERS

It is the act of rising above the three levels of culture and *re-framing them to make good business and organizational sense* that is required of the meta-cultural manager. It is here that the wheat of the effective strategic manager is sorted from the chaff. Managers with only a 'binary' thinking style (either something is good, or else it is bad; it is either right, or it must be wrong) cannot cope with the macro-cultural level of complexity. They are comfortable with single cultures once they know how to manage the deviances from them, but find the management of the continuous differences and disruptions involved with macro-culture unacceptable to their binary style. When the macro-cultural factors combine on an n-dimensional matrix, who is to say what is right and wrong? There is no simple choice, no time to get totally accurate information, and each choice made will affect all the others in ways that are not always predictable. Moreover, the whole picture is liable to disruption from other people apparently way beyond their control. When these other people are significantly different from their board's culture and powerbase – northerners against southerners, westerners against easterners but, worst of all, foreigners against us – then the trouble will follow. This is the point where the meta-culture can be brought into play for the benefit of organizational effectiveness: unfortunately, it rarely is.

'Meta-culture' is for me the synthesis of the organization's mini-culture and the environment's macro-culture into a workable whole which transcends the cultural aspects of both; it is not a permanent and binding notion, rather a way of understanding and valuing the differences and making the most from them – a *design* notion which gives both parties common meaning and common objectives for a period of time. To achieve this requires styles of thinking and learning amongst the directors which are far removed from the binary stance. A combination of the ability to value differences, and to use the energies of apparently opposing forces to your own creative ends, has to be the target for the board – the design and management of their meta-culture. But, again, the skills needed are in short supply in management and management education. The use of opposed forces to achieve creative ends is very much the province of the designer; valuing differences whilst seeking common grounds on which to build is the province of the statesman–diplomat. Neither are commonly found on executive boards, and yet the future of business through the exchange of learning, know-how, and technology would seem to involve more and more the crossing of national cultural boundaries in a manner sympathetic to those boundaries.

It would seem that significant reconsideration needs to be given to the *selection processes* for a board. If what I am finding is transferable, then it will be necessary to select those who can tolerate ambiguity, cope with uncertainty, think creatively, determine policy, manage cultural boundaries, implement strategy, and delegate effectively. As many of these are 'right-brain' functions (see Wonder, 1984), outside the usual managerial areas of logic and certainty, careful selection must be made on the potential for such skills and not as a reward for previous good performance in 'left-brain' functions. It seems normal for boards to reward long-term left-brainers by asking them to join the board; that they are usually incapable of coping with the right-brain functions necessary for their new role is rarely addressed. The consequences in organizational effectiveness are often profound, and lead over time to corporate collapse. In many of the less effective and efficient organizations I think that we are now seeing the consequences of twenty or thirty years of 'brainless' thinking by their boards and top managers. This seems to be particularly so when the organizations have been run entirely by engineers and/or accountants.

This sits in uncomfortable contrast to the idea that in future it will be necessary for organizations to invest in, rigorously codify, legally protect, and then actively diffuse to the customers their products or services. Behind this lies the idea that learning is central to business survival and growth; the notion that for an organization to survive its *rate of learning* has to be equal to – or greater than – the *rate of change* in its environment and is a key to creating a healthy organization.

Most businesses are not organized to create a climate of learning and a culture which celebrates and uses learning as a key organizational output. Yet people learn – or, in an unhealthy organization, fail to learn – all the time they are working. A key question for me is: How well does the board appreciate and encourage this? If not, they are on the road to corporate collapse. If so, then they need to review their corporate strategy, people strategy, vision, values, and cultures to reinforce the ability of their organizations to learn and turn this into product or service.

There are some very human problems here which reflect back particularly on macro-culture. A company engaged in, for example, research and development, will have substantial investment in assets which are largely uncodified or semi-codified (i.e. it will be in the heads and hands of its researchers rather than neatly compiled in instruction manuals). It will transfer this to its customers through turning its learning into goods and services to sell. However, around the world customers increasingly insist that they manufacture their own goods. What they wish to do is to buy the *essential investment in learning* that goes into those goods – the 'intellectual property rights' – through licensing or joint-ventures. This creates problems of ownership and access to its learning for the originating company; and the essence of those problems are mini- and macro-cultural.

For example, many newly industrialized countries and Third World countries have governments who insist that they buy 'the best' from the Western world: 'the best' is usually translated by both sides as 'state-of-the-art'. There are ethical questions here about whether, for example, to sell the latest 'glass cockpit, fly-by-wire' airliner to a country which does not have many basic electronic landing aids. There are also commercial questions: if you do so, you will in some way be 'giving away your carefully won commercial secrets'. This has gone as far, in my experience, for defence companies to discuss seriously building into their product (with proper warning) a small explosive device which would trigger if the customer tried to investigate the key component.

Culturally speaking, this is the antithesis of the (often unspoken) aspiration of the customer who is hoping to be at the leading edge of his field by emulating the leaders. A joint-venture of a French and Arab company on a high-tech product led to cross-cultural misunderstandings of a high order. The French thought they were basically selling on an existing technology and helping the Arabs to manufacture it well; the Arabs thought that by joint-venturing they would get into the inner research secrets of a company they aspired to overtake. Both were puzzled, then angered, when their aspirations were not met. Both became angry when each accused the other of cheating on the joint-venture contract. In the end the project broke down with great organizational and personal bitterness on both sides.

This brings me back to the need to be very clear, particularly at the macro-cultural level, of the roles of people in, across, and above the national cultural levels. One needs to build these into *job descriptions inside the organization,* and *contracts between organizations* in the initial stages. Then, as the work matures, the top managers need to create a working climate which can cope with the creative ambiguity of both having structure, yet also the flexibility to deal with the many different personalities and cultures involved. This is often referred to as having the strategic skills to create a 'loose/tight fit'.

NECESSARY ROLES

When John Stopford and I started looking into these issues in 1978, we produced a list (Garratt and Stopford, 1980) of the different types of manager who seemed to be operating at the macro-cultural level.

Ambassadors	senior general staff of peripatetic missions outside the organization
Diplomatic technicians	senior functional specialists on visits or short-term secondments
Expatriate residents	medium- to long-term-stay career-builders living abroad
Home country nationals	indigenous local managers of national or multi-national companies
Third country nationals	managers in international organizations who are neither from the headquarters nor the local country
Home country hosts	managers who receive guests and foreign clients, and ease them into the local social and business environment.

This list is neither exhaustive nor exclusive and managers can hold a combination of these roles; it was an attempt to help define the *strategic boundary* managers and *operational boundary* managers. To be explicit, the board are the strategic boundary managers – monitoring the external environment, analysing and predicting disruptions from that environment, and trying to give the 'business brain' a good chance of being able to *design* the future rather than simply *react* to it.

Tension does arise from conflicts between the mini- and micro-, and the macro-cultures. The mini-culture is trying to maximize its internal return and tends to discount macro-cultural considerations as outside its remit. Its members are right on the last point; this is where the top managers need to take up their *meta-cultural* role. Boisot (1987) has shown that the amount of time needed to design a project from the macro-cultural viewpoint is relatively large; this can rarely be done before or during the tendering process so it often needs to be done immediately afterwards. There is some evidence that if you can be seen to be operating in full an ambassadorial, meta-cultural role, there are ways in which the personal contacts established mean that you may never have to go to tender at all.

THE ROLE OF MANAGEMENT DEVELOPERS IN DEVELOPING CULTURE

Those who are essentially trainers will find the lack of material in the cultural area deeply frustrating. Currently culture is not an easily trainable area; it is more an area for *developers* – who can work with managers from where they are, relate this to a vision of the future, and the necessary business targets, and find an appropriate process for developing themselves and their work whilst also ensuring the redundancy of the developer on the way. This is easily said, but most developers do not have easy access to their directors or line managers affecting 'culture' at any of the four boundaries mentioned above. Yet they are often more sensitive to the problems and possibilities of effectively managing culture than their top management. The question is: 'How to connect?' Part of the answer is potentially painful, in that it involves emotional and financial risks – specifically, successful developers who have made a major impact on helping develop an appropriate range of cultures for their organization have put themselves forward to become a member of one or more senior management teams creating and managing strategic change in their organization. They take on what is effectively a line responsibility for delivering the organizational culture and climate which delivers the business results whilst making the best use of the individuals involved. This can feel quite daunting at the start. But, as I have said before, the tools to measure where the organization is on each dimension are available; they allow top managers to know where they are starting from with their people strategy and this, in turn, allows them to see how they are progressing as later measures are taken.

The research of Campbell and Devine (1990) gives a useful model (see Figure 20.1). They have been investigating aspects of mission statements and see the   *327*

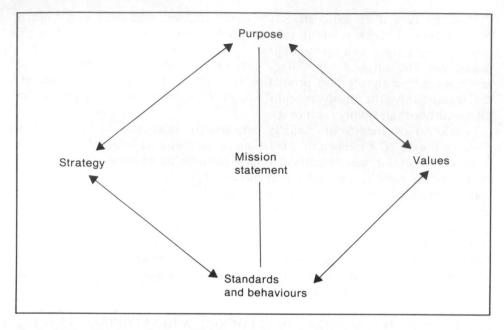

Figure 20.1   The Campbell and Devine sense of mission model

need to develop a model which links an orientation to the future – *purpose* – with a way of implementing these – *strategy* and *values* – whilst valuing and rewarding the past and present – *standards* and *behaviours*. They argue that all of these are made manifest and coherent through the mission statement. To a greater extent I agree with the tenor of their research. I argue that management developers need to be as conversant with business and people strategies as they are with behaviour and purpose; I feel that this is the challenge for management developers in the 1990s – to be able to work on the same terms as their strategic managers and be able to develop them in all the key areas: individual, team, organization, and inter-organization. The only point on which I would argue with the Campbell and Devine model is that I think that the pivotal position is not held by the mission statement but by the *management of cultures* (see Figure 20.2). This is what both bonds and energizes the organization; it creates the climate in which people can cooperate for specific ends. I commend the management of cultures as a key challenge for management developers and directors over the next decade. Handled constructively, it should make a beneficial difference to their effectiveness and efficiency; handled badly, it will lead, in an increasingly multicultural world, to corporate collapse.

A CASE STUDY OF CHANGE AND CULTURE (To preserve anonymity this is a conflation of my work with various clients)

A financial services group was keen on expanding overseas, specifically in the

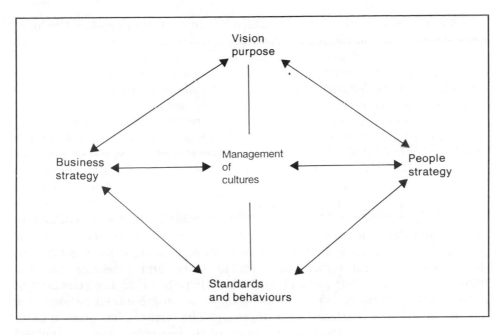

Figure 20.2 The pivotal role of the management of culture

Far East. When asked to advise them on the business and people strategy I made myself fairly unpopular by insisting that before we rushed off to 'become more international', as was their wish, we established first where we were. Given that information, it should be much easier to know how to get where we wanted. Coordinates are essential on what can otherwise be seen by top management as a 'soft' issue, and therefore of secondary importance. Once my point was accepted we set off to measure what we could in a brief time. We undertook an organizational climate survey through a sample using a diagonal slice of people in the organization. This looked at the *actual* and *ideal* perceptions of such issues as standards; responsibility; conformity; non-financial rewards; financial rewards; organizational clarity; warmth and support; and leadership. Analyses of the responses, using parametric and non-parametric statistics, exploratory workshops built around the anonymous verbatim responses, and neuro-linguistic programming techniques, teased out the organizational issues, values, reward systems, 'webs of signification', and organizational myths and folklore from which we could start the process of creating the new mini- and macro-cultures.

When the information was received along with the business strategy it became clear that, however strong the wish of the directors to expand abroad, there were some fundamental business and people issues in the UK – particularly of vision and clashing cultures – which needed to be tackled if the expansion overseas was to be built on solid foundations. These were achieved through workshops and in-company action learning programmes for the top teams to get them into their directing roles, and to create a 'performance- and   *329* behaviour-based appraisal system' which became a key to creating the 'new' consistent culture they wished to grow across all levels of their business. This went surprisingly well, and took some two years – cultural change happens in years not months: in well-established cultures it can take a decade to change fully – before it was felt to be working. The Far East market was growing rapidly and their preferred merger target was still interested.

We are now moving into the more complex directoral and managerial task of trying to cross macro- (national) cultural boundaries whilst maintaining a consistent mini- (organizational) culture. We started by working with key groups who will have to learn how to work together if the new business is to have any hope of success. This involved personal psychometric testing, the Handy Organizational Climate Survey, as well as further organizational climate surveying on both sides. This led on to an introduction to the area of macro-cultural analysis, using such work as Hofstede's cross-cultural maps of major trading nations. This was first to make it legitimate amongst the managers to debate cross-cultural issues, to learn to value and celebrate national differences, then to find ways of working which played to the strengths of both. (To say 'both' is too simplistic – there are some fifteen nationalities already involved in a relatively small group.) The analysis has given a quite different dimension to the work of many of the managers and has helped managing across macro- and micro-cultural boundaries in a way which is acknowledged would never have happened if each business had fought to get control, then imposed their culture on the other.

As business faces up to a future that involves the *constant* crossing of cultural boundaries, it will be essential for managers and management developers to prepare themselves for what is going to be one of the most exciting challenges to their skills.

REFERENCES

Argenti, J. (1976) *Corporate Collapse: Causes and Symptoms* (New York: McGraw-Hill).

Ashby, W. R. (1956) 'Self-Regulation and Requisite Variety', *Introduction to Cybernetics* (London: John Wiley).

Boisot, M. (1987) *Information and Organisations: The Manager as Anthropologist* (London: Fontana).

Campbell, A. and Devine, M. (1990) *A Sense of Mission* (London: Economist Publications).

Garratt, R. (1987) *The Learning Organisation* (London: Fontana).

Garratt, R. (1990) *Creating a Learning Organisation: A Guide to Leadership, Learning and Development* (Cambridge: Director Books).

Garratt, R. and Stopford, J. (1980) *Breaking Down Barriers: Practice and*

Priorities in International Management Education (Aldershot: Gower).

Geertz, C. (1973) *Interpretation of Cultures* (New York: Basic Books).

Handy, C. (1985) *The Gods of Management* (London: Pan).

Hofstede, G. (1980) *Culture's Consequences* (Beverly Hills, Cal.: Sage).

Institute of Directors Report (1990) 'Professional Development of and for the Board' (London: Institute of Directors).

March, R. M. (1980) 'Manpower and Control Issues', in Garratt, R. and Stopford, J., *Breaking Down Barriers: Practice and Priorities in International Management Education* (Aldershot: Gower).

Peters, T. J. and Waterman, R. H. (1982) *In Search of Excellence* (New York: Harper & Row).

Smith, P. (1986) 'The Stages of a Manager's Job', in Hammond, V. (ed.), *Research in Management* (London: Frances Pinter).

Watzlawick, P., Weakland, J., and Fisch, R. (1974) *Problem Formulation and Problem Resolution* (New York: W. W. Norton).

Wonder, J. (1984) *Whole Brain Thinking* (New York: Morrow).

21 Handling cultural diversity

David Ashton

The impact of cultural differences on work organizations, their operations and effectiveness, has become a popular subject during the last few years. Some of the reasons for this increased interest may lie in a more general trend which recognizes the importance of 'soft' data as a basis for explanation of differences in the performance of organizations. Interest may also have grown because a number of practitioners have been able to develop approaches which have made progress on real problems associated with cultural differences in work organizations.

In this chapter, we are going to start by defining 'culture' and 'cultural differences', and then look at the key ideas that have been developed in this field since 1975. With these key definitions and concepts in mind, we can then go on to examine the relevance of such approaches to learning in general, and development programmes for managers in particular. We shall consider the impact of the cultural differences both on the determination of appropriate content for development programmes and on its learning styles and strategies. The final part of the chapter will be concerned with a key development benefit which can arise when *cultural differences are present in a development group*.

KEY CONCEPTS AND APPROACHES

In this brief review of relevant concepts it may be best to start with some exclusions. By 'culture', we refer to those *national* differences which affect, among other things, the way in which people work together. There has also been a growing interest in work performance arising out of specific differences in *organizational* cultures. However, this latter body of knowledge relates to a very different set of original concepts, and will not be a subject of focus within this chapter.

Perhaps the single most important figure in the development and analysis of

Country examples: high score	Dimension	Country examples: low score
USA Australia Britain Netherlands	Individualism	Pakistan Guatemala Taiwan Indonesia
Japan Germany Mexico Italy	Masculinity	Netherlands Chile France Sweden
Nigeria Malaysia Panama India	Power distance	Israel Denmark New Zealand Britain
Portugal Uruguay Belgium Japan	Uncertainty avoidance	Singapore Denmark Hong Kong Britain

Figure 21.1   Key dimensions of cultural difference

cultural difference in organizations has been Gert Hofstede (1980a). While working within a large multinational company, he undertook a study of national differences among large numbers of employees in more than forty countries. His definition of 'culture' is based more on an anthropological approach – he describes this group identity as 'a collective programming of the mind'.

Hofstede analysed his data across all his countries in which he carried out his investigations, and identified *four key dimensions* which provide maximum differentiation between national cultures. Figure 21.1 identifies each of these dimensions and gives some examples of individual countries which have extremely high or low scores on these dimensions.

It may be helpful just to say a few words of explanation about each of his dimensions:

- **Individualism** – This reflects the extent to which a society focuses on the importance of the *individual* rather than the *group* within the society
- **Masculinity** – Hofstede has assessed this by looking at the extent to which general roles in a society are allocated along traditional *male/female* lines
- **Power distance** – This covers the extent to which *inequality* is accepted by less powerful people in a society
- **Uncertainty avoidance** – This dimension focuses on the strength of concern about *order and security* in a country.

333

Hofstede's data enabled him to 'place' countries on these particular dimensions – although it has been difficult to explain, to everyone's satisfaction, the reasons for the positions of particular countries. Careful reflection nevertheless yields some interesting points. On the whole, wealthy countries tend to have a high index score on the individualistic ethic – although there are one or two which (like Japan) are clearly exceptions. Other countries which have apparently little in common in terms of culture and heritage score highly on one particular dimension. For example Germany, Mexico, Italy and Japan all score highly on the masculinity dimension – in these countries, therefore 'male values' are likely to dominate in their organizations. Hofstede reports some general trends for all countries in two of the dimensions of cultural difference – tolerance of power distance was reducing in all countries, and concern for uncertainty avoidance was increasing in most countries.

The impact of these cultural differences, expressed in these key dimensions, is, however, not necessarily so clear-cut when we look at the level of the work organization and other factors which support or modify these cultural differences and need to be taken into account. From the point of view of the development programme, it is important to understand different societal approaches to *individual and group learning*, in order to anticipate the likely responses of an individual from a particular society to a new learning experience in his work organization.

André Laurent (1980) identified national differences among individuals' views of their *business organizations*. He found the North American and North European employees tended to take a more instrumental view of business, whereas the Latin countries of Europe took a more 'social' view. Laurent defined the 'instrumental' view as emphasizing the rational organization of tasks – and the manager's role was defined by these tasks and his or her functional responsibilities. Within this overall view, boss–subordinate relationships tended to be seen as impersonal; authority was associated with role or function in the organization. The social view, by contrast, emphasized that the business was a group of people who needed to be managed. The manager's role, therefore, was defined by social status and his authority came from personal and functional attributes. In a social organization, subordinates were expected to be loyal and deferential to their bosses – in return for more personal relationships and support.

Little has been published on culture and organizations which directly examines the impact of national differences in development and training. The work of Seddon (1985) is of particular interest here; he identified the dangers of applying a *Western organization* development approach to African business organizations. Seddon noted several contrasting assumptions, in two key areas:

- **Approach to development** – In Western organizations, the employee takes responsibility for his or her own development. African employees manifest greater dependence in relationships and hence expect all development opportunities to be identified and arranged for them. They also would not wish to lose face by encountering novel, and therefore risky, situations. Neither would they understand the Western conception of a conflict between employers' and employees' needs.

- **Tactics of development** – Western learning designs are likely to encounter problems in Africa. African employees require highly structured interventions which do *not* assume openness in relationships.

Seddon argued that the host culture was better regarded as a potential strength, rather than a hurdle to be overcome, and development approaches should take account of this.

In reviewing this work of Hofstede, Laurent and Seddon, two broad conclusions emerge: first, national differences *do* matter, and should be taken into account when constructing development programmes. Secondly, we are only just beginning to understand all the issues and problems of improving our decision-making in this area.

CULTURAL DIFFERENCES AND THE CONTENT OF DEVELOPMENT PROGRAMMES

Against this background it becomes a matter of practical concern to take account of such differences when designing and running development programmes for multicultural groups.

A first area of concern is the *content* of such programmes. Hofstede (1980b) wrote an article questioning the transferability of American theories. Given that American motivation theory is likely to focus on the *individual* employee, he argued that such an approach would be wrong if straightforwardly transferred into a collectivist society – where it will be more effective to work on the motivation of *groups* of employees. Seddon's (1985) experience in Africa would support this view.

In the design of a multicultural development programme, it is essential to look carefully at each of the principal *subject areas* of the programme, in order to understand the cultural limitations of the concepts and approaches which may be inherent in each. The extremes can be readily spotted – for example, it is unlikely that key economic concepts, and their application to the workings of the national economy, or the main structural characteristics of an industry, will vary from one country to another. At the other extreme, however, it is highly likely that the approaches to employee relations will vary – because of legal and political as well as social and cultural differences – on a country-by-country basis. Between these two extremes lie the rest of the fundamental subject areas of management. We would suggest that it is more than just the human resources field which may be affected by cultural differences.

The following contingency approach may help in the determination of subject content:

1. Identification of a *key concept or framework*.
2. Identification of *normal contingency factors* associated with the *application* of that approach.
3. The additional consideration of the *impact* that *national differences* may make upon the *application*.

Here is one example to show how such an approach might be implemented.

Productivity

Productivity is apparently a universal theme and a wide range of applications have been reported on the specific productivity approach known as quality circles. To date, however, the literature has tended to give only individual stories and to develop 'folklore' – that is, subjective and often journalistic accounts of successes and occasional failures. Clearly the quality circles approach was initiated in a specific cultural context; it seems to have been an American idea, but developed within a Japanese group-oriented context. Equally, it is clear that not every national context of employee motivation and productivity improvement is similar to that of the Japanese. Among the contingency factors to be considered, therefore, would be an identification of key characteristics of Japanese attitudes to work organization – this would take account directly of national cultural differences. These differences would then be assessed against the key features of the *other* national cultures, in which the quality circles approach might be applied or recommended.

Finally, if the approach seems to be worth examining in these new cultural contexts, then cultural differences should be part of the *application* discussions – in order to encourage awareness of their likely impact on the effectiveness of quality circles as a productivity 'solution' for the development programme delegates' own work context.

In one sense, the quality circles approach is an easy example to make – since most readers will not be Japanese and, more significantly, they will be very ready to acknowledge the cultural differences of Japan from their own societies. It is the author's experience, however, that almost *all* management and business subject areas and specific techniques should be approached on the contingency basis outlined above, when decisions are made about course content on multicultural development programmes.

CULTURAL DIFFERENCES AND LEARNING METHODS

Management development is an area which has been closely associated with innovation and experiment with learning methods. Many of these innovations have come about because of the apparent inappropriateness of formal, one-way methods (like lecturing) as an effective means for helping experienced managers to learn. But these newer methods have tended to develop in English-speaking developed countries – particularly the USA and Britain. They often involve extensive participation by the management students, including exposure of personal feelings and values, which are not usually shared by working colleagues except in the development context. It will not be surprising, therefore, that some of these methods are initially found difficult by people of other cultures, where the importance of role differences and more formal methods of education and training may be strongly stressed. Indeed, approaches to learning and social interchange may be markedly more restricted and less relaxed in some of the English-speaking countries. Such cultural differences do not rule out the use of these more participative methods in management development, education and training; but they do mean that the manner and timing of the introduction of such methods must be extended where cultural differences among delegate managers are present.

In introductory sessions, it may be important, with a multicultural group, to give everyone the opportunity to contribute – particularly in terms of talking about their own experience and the differences of their own national and business situations. Once these individual views (and some insight into these individual differences) are established, it may be relatively easier for both delegates and trainers to handle the differences and to understand the likely limitations on the contribution of individuals. Such participation by *all* delegates at the beginning of a multicultural programme becomes critical to their effective participation in later stages of the programme. But time *must* be given for all of these individual contributions to be brought out, and it must be done in a non-threatening way. The primary objective is to enable all people to *contribute,* rather than rigorously to test their ideas. Such preparation and initiation is a necessary start for effective learning in a multicultural management group.

There will, of course, be other opportunities to build on cultural differences and their impact on business as a means of learning in a multicultural group. Thus, for example, discussions about the business environment could build around *mapping exercises*, where individuals are given the opportunity to lay out their own 'national maps' which identify the important factors in their own business environment – increasing trade union power, inflation, government controls, or whatever. These 'maps' will explain what is important to enable the effective operation of their organizations in their national context.

There is also some argument for ensuring good opportunities in a multicultural programme for *small group discussions*. These must not, however, be set with such tight time limits that the predominant language group – most often the English-speakers – dominate, because the task must be able to be achieved within great time pressure. Smaller groups do make it much easier for individuals to make a contribution in somewhat uncertain circumstances.

Obviously, having realized the impact of learning methods on cultural differences among delegates, it is particularly important to judge the *pace* of the first few days correctly; trainers must also provide opportunity for individuals of all national backgrounds to make contributions, and for these contributions to be recognized by their peer delegates, as well as accepted by the teaching staff. At that point, cultural differences may become less important – individuals will have a confident and positive base on which to build their participation and response to the range of learning methods which may be involved in the rest of the programme.

CONCLUSIONS

Much of this chapter has been concerned with the differences – and, by implication, the difficulties – that cultural diversity may make to effective manager education in effective manager development. It would be wrong, however, to deal with cultural difference primarily in this negative light. Again, from the author's own experience (Ashton, 1984), for mature and successful managers of whatever nationality, comparison of themselves with other (and different) managers is a particularly valuable means of learning. The process of comparison has to begin with 'What I am' or 'What our company or system is'; this is likely to provide a basis of *self-understanding* as a starting point. This can be built on through discussion with other managers who are equally effective in their own circumstances, yet offer remarkable contrasts in the way in which they approach their work, and the goals and priorities which they set.

Practising managers are more often impressed by and learn better from others with effective but different *working models* for their own managerial roles, than they do from textbook theories – and it is right that this should be so. A multicultural group offers such richness because of the diversity of approach and assumptions of the individuals and businesses concerned that, if the communication barriers of inherent cultural differences can be overcome, then the potential plus which comes from the richer and varied bases for comparison can offer a genuine advantage and key additional feature for development and learning in a multicultural context.

Clearly this cannot be achieved quickly; programme designs must take account of lower introductory sessions and of a greater need for all to participate in the initial stages. But if that foundation can be achieved and confidence be given for all to participate, then the richer bases of comparison may provide a more effective and stronger development by the end of a development programme. The insidious assumption may be that the theories and approaches of the trainers (or of the parent company) provide the most effective universal way of approaching management and business problems in all countries; clearly this is not true, and this form of 'acculturalization' must be resisted: it will be only an ineffective form of 'colonization', which has in the past been detrimental to the effective operation of organizations in different national contexts.

REFERENCES

Ashton, D. (1984) 'Cultural Differences: Implications for Management Development', *Management Education and Development* (Spring).

Hofstede, G. (1980a) *Culture's Consequences* (Beverly Hill, Cal.: Sage).

Hofstede, G. (1980b) 'Motivation, Leadership and Organization: Do American Theories Apply Abroad?', *Organizational Dynamics* (Summer).

Laurent, A. (1980) 'Once a Frenchman, always a Frenchman . . .', *International Management* (June).

Seddon, J. W. (1985) 'Issues in Practice – The Education and Development of Overseas Managers', *Management Education and Development* (Spring).

FURTHER READING

Ratiu. I. (ed.) (1987) 'Multicultural Management Development', Special issue, *Journal of Management Development*, 6(3).

22 Cultural pitfalls of international alliances and culture-bridging strategies

Irene Rodgers

CULTURAL DIFFERENCES CAN HURT

Too many international mergers, acquisitions and joint ventures fail to meet expectations. Yet organizations that 'marry' usually have excellent strategic reasons for doing so. For example, they will almost certainly share a common mission, to which at least the top managers and shareholders can commit and will hire competent bankers, lawyers, marketing and production experts to flesh out the plans. So what goes wrong?

A recent *Business International* (1992) study points out that the two main causes of failure are the mismanagement of cultural differences and communications. Yet when it comes to mergers, acquisitions and joint ventures, differences between the personnel or corporate cultures of the two organizations are hardly ever considered at the initial stages, let alone discussed and analysed.

Those managers who have worked across cultures and have faced these problems now recognize that cultural differences strain corporate cohesiveness, delay or prevent agreement on plans, inhibit managerial consistency and even block new policy implementation. Organizations are beginning to pay attention to the impact of these differences on the potential success of the alliance because they can no longer afford not to.

Managers have seen that cultural differences can have a direct effect on the bottom line. For example:

- A blue chip corporation in the pharmaceuticals sector faces lack of cooperation, if not downright hostility, from one of its recently acquired subsidiaries in a nearby country and increasing tensions between local and expatriate staff. The results: low level of trust internally, no communication, and loss of efficiency inside the company.

- A large multinational systematically loses $100 000 every time it is obliged to repatriate a manager and the family early because of inability to adjust to a new cultural environment. The result: reduced productivity, personnel and administrative overload and personal pain.
- An important negotiation between two firms collapses when the seller plans for two weeks of meetings and the buyer reserves hotel rooms for only four nights. The result: loss of a potentially profitable contract.
- A foreign company tries to impose management practices and systems that are culturally inappropriate on a new, foreign acquisition. The result: over 50 per cent of the best managers leave and the subsidiary registers large financial losses two years after the take-over.

Cultural differences can affect other organizational issues as well:

- Internationalization and increasing trends towards participative management involve people of different cultures working together more and more. The result: differences in management styles and behaviours can become critical.
- A company at the cutting edge of technology development consistently fails in its costly attempts to train and integrate engineers from developing countries. The result: an expensive 'miss' for strategic goals.
- Today's tough and competitive environment demands quick decisions and action. The result: people with different cultural and language backgrounds absolutely need to develop a 'common language' rapidly.

These examples illustrate that the advantages of international development and the accompanying reorganization and restructuring can be severely jeopardized unless the cultural assumptions and managerial behaviours of the new partners can be made to complement one another.

The challenge

This, however, is not so simple to achieve. Internationalization requires a profound change of mind-set, behaviours and attitudes – including those that previously led to success. We have found the following to be critical success factors in the international arena:

- A new mind-set
- A credible organizational structure
- Women and men who work together
- A system that can generate positive change
- Strong leadership
- Clarity of goals.

Managers, caught up in the increased work-load internationalization usually   *341* demands, rarely focus on these success factors as priorities. On the contrary. Harassed by increased demands for information, they often keep silent, claiming they do not have the answers. So much for a new mind-set. The rumour mill churns ever faster, and so much for clarity of goals. Motivation wavers, teams are destabilized, and so much for women and men who work together. Productivity suffers. Sometimes the best people leave, and so much for strong leadership.

The cultural problems can be 'micro' (at the managerial, behavioural level), or they can be 'macro' (at the organizational and structural level). Obviously the two intertwine, but it is useful to make the distinction.

Micro-problems

Cultural differences create perception gaps. Thus, what is normal, effective and rewarding in one culture may be perceived as incomprehensible, unfeasible and hostile in another. This process operates in two ways:

1. The first type of perception gap is when people from two cultures, or two organizations, share one same value. Their cultural assumptions differ.

This leads to behaviours by each party that are interpreted in terms of actually opposing values by the other side.

Let us take the value of 'trust' as an example. In all cultures, trust is an essential component of human relations and negotiations. However, because of cultural differences, behaviours that indicate the development of trust in one part of the world do quite the opposite in another. In the United States, trust develops as negotiators proceed towards the signature of a contract, and it then finds concrete expression in that signature. Once business has been satisfactorily concluded, the two parties trust one another and can get down to building a relationship. But in many other parts of the world, trust derives first from the relationship or from how close or similar people feel to one another. In Mexico, for example, trust begins to grow as people get to know one another. Unfortunately, the time a Mexican needs in order to build a relationship feels like loss of business time to an American. And the American's need to sign first and trust later is experienced by the Mexican as aggressive and suspicious (Figure 22.1). Here we have one same value (trust), very different cultural assumptions about how one goes about building that value, and thus very different behaviours.

We are presented with another example when the same type of mis-understanding preys on management practices within new international alliances (Figure 22.2). In both these examples, then, the impact of each party's behaviour is actually to decrease the potential for trust rather than build it. How successful can business be under these circumstances?

2. The second type of perception gap is when people from two cultures or organizations experience the same behaviour from the vantage point of two different cultural assumptions.

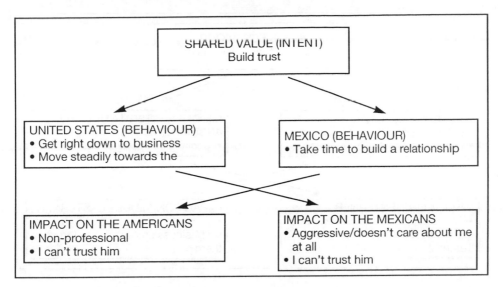

Figure 22.1   The value of trust – two interpretations

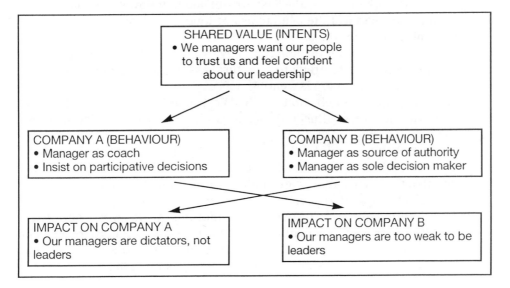

Figure 22.2   Management practices within international alliances

This can mean that the same behaviour is the visible part of a very different, sometimes contradictory, value system.

One of the most flagrant examples is giving monetary gifts for business profit. Westerners call this bribery, and it is a pejorative term, for it implies dishonesty. But in the Middle East, it is oil on the gears: a way of thanking someone for services rendered, or to be rendered (Figure 22.3). The negative connotations of the term in the West are such, however, that although most   *343*

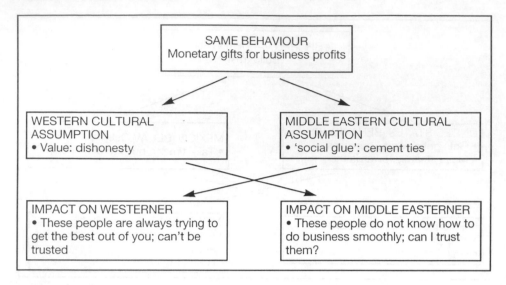

Figure 22.3 Bribery or not?

companies that work in the Middle East are obliged to follow suit in one way or another, most of them feel the need to assert loud and clear that they do not indulge in this type of practice.

Here, the same behaviour demonstrated by two culturally different people is driven by different, and contradictory cultural assumptions depending on the 'cultural glasses' each person is wearing.

The normal, expected behaviour in the West might well shock the Middle Easterner and vice versa. Business dealings clearly pay the price of these differences.

These are only two examples, but managers who have spent time overseas know that 'delegation', 'performance appraisal', and 'team work' do not mean the same thing everywhere. Greater individual responsibility, larger salaries and more challenging work might be the way to motivate performance in Northern Europe and North America; reinforcing team work and team accountability is crucial in Japan; setting up a pleasant company restaurant and allowing for better quality of life are powerful motivators in France and other Latin countries. Delegating authority works in some places; in others it is best to delegate a well-defined task.

A different kind of problem arises from the need to get results from a culturally diverse team.

International managers recognize that corporate cohesiveness, achieving goals and profitability can be strained by cultural differences, and that it is often more difficult to get results with multicultural teams (Figure 22.4).

Inter Cultural Management associates, has a process called 'Culture Bridging for Managers'. We work with managers in these situations to give them management and communications tools that help them address cultural differences constructively. Our four-step process runs as follows:

344

Some advantages	Some disadvantages
• better equipped to implement an international strategy because closer to markets • possibility of optimizing human resources through mobility • more creativity because of new approaches to problem-solving	• misunderstandings, language barriers • difficulties in gaining consensus, and longer decision-making process • greater risk of inconsistencies in implementing strategy

Figure 22.4   The use of multicultural teams

1. *With the team manager:* set objectives and success criteria for the process.
2. *Preparation:* Cultural Portrait© of the team based on interviews and a questionnaire.
3. *Two-day working session:* identify the priority issues the team faces as a result of going international. Learn tools for managing effectively across frontiers. Apply them in a work session with an expert on your priority issue.
4. *Follow-up session two months later:* strengthen the multicultural management team, review action plans and reinforce team support for meeting priority objectives.

An example: A Franco-American joint venture

A large French company signs with an American company to create a new Franco-American joint venture. Decisions about investment priorities, filling upper management positions in the new company, organization structure and where to locate are made during the top-level negotiations. On either side of the Atlantic, however, department managers who will be charged with implementing the agreement are worried about whether they will now report to a manager from the other country, and whether they will have to 'go French' or 'go American' in the way they run their business.

The human resources manager decides on a culture-bridging process with the objective of increasing synergy and building stronger relationships between the French and Americans. After getting the results of their Cultural Portrait©, the teams met for a two-day work session and decided on the following areas as priorities:

- Developing recruitment criteria for both sides of the Atlantic, to support mobility and career development
- Defining human resource management processes for performance appraisal and succession planning
- Setting training and development guidelines
- Gaining greater understanding of the role of unions in the two *345*

organizations, and how to deal with them
- Establishing a more consistent approach to remuneration
- Designing one human resource management reporting system
- Understanding different behaviour patterns and values.

Results

During the meeting, the team developed a competencies profile to which all members felt committed. This was then validated by managers in the organization. On the basis of this profile they were able to begin to develop guidelines for recruitment, development, evaluation and succession planning, as well as designing the components of a human resources reporting system that were understandable and acceptable to both sides. In addition:

- The French agreed to support the notion of 'manager as coach' and to implement individual performance appraisals more consistently
- The Americans agreed to make French-language training obligatory for their own senior and mid-management personnel
- A merit bonus was developed with enough flexibility to facilitate mobility from both sides
- The team decided to meet future staffing needs with an equal nationality mix
- The development of a common corporate culture was encouraged through a cross-training plan and a reciprocal secondment policy.

Two months later the team decided to cascade the Culture Bridging approach down another managerial level and thus strengthen their joint emerging culture further.

Macro-problems

The macro level presents other challenges. Bartlett and Ghoshal (1989) discuss two options for managing the move to becoming truly transnational. The first option involves beginning with changes in formal structure and responsibilities. We might call this the 'organizational' approach. The other option involves changes in individual attitudes and mentalities; we might call this the 'relational approach'.

The organizational approach starts with changes in the organization structure. The assumption here is that formal change will drive internal change. So, for example, new functions or operations report directly to the president; an organization by business-line replaces a geographical structure; certain staff functions are centralized at headquarters. The managers believe that the new structure will force organizational relationships and decision-making systems to change more quickly. They believe that new reporting lines will accelerate the development of new interpersonal relationships and that new attitudes and mind-sets will quickly follow.

This approach has the advantage of solving certain kinds of problems rapidly, especially in times of financial crisis. But it also carries risks of organizational trauma and human frustration.

The relational approach relies on existing interpersonal networks to carry the change. Managers are seconded abroad; international task forces and project teams share responsibility and reinforce new links. This approach attempts to win over the hearts and minds of people, particularly opinion leaders, and only then consolidates the change through structural realignment. The 'for' is surely less trauma, more motivation; 'against' is that all of this takes time, and if the shareholder is looking for rapid return on investment, this approach will surely be less acceptable.

So, these are our two extremes. The successes we have seen grow out of an intelligent blend of both, alternately stressing attitude and mind-set change and structural change. This can then be viewed as two options of a culture-bridging strategy where relative importance is given to different elements. The choice of which option to emphasize can only be made case-by-case, and we see examples of how different companies succeed when the road they choose is consistent with their own corporate culture and situation.

CULTURE-BRIDGING STRATEGIES

Let us consider the case of a French firm acquired by an Italian company. Floating in the French organization was a unit whose mission was international technology transfer and training. This unit felt threatened by the existence of a similar unit in Italy. The newly-named French president of the firm quickly decided to reduce staff numbers of the French unit and have it report directly to him, with a more highly-specialized mission, beyond Italian capabilities. This was a surgical, structural change, chosen because it was inevitable – and everyone knew it. It was a violent act that corresponded perfectly to the decision to cut quickly and rebuild differently with those who remained, rather than drag on in the face of inevitable ongoing anxieties.

The story was different for a small French, family-owned business acquired by a British multinational. The British management, newly emerging from an intensive culture change programme that had insisted on decentralization and empowerment, decided to apply these principles to the French firm. They retired the ex-owner president and left the management of the company to a so-called 'management team'. The results were catastrophic. A 'cultural audit' allowed them to recognize their mistakes and to make a second decision, still organizational, to rectify the first one. This time they were on target. The British named a new French managing director who took things in hand, remotivated the small firm and finally began to create a real management team.

In the case of a small Portuguese family company, also acquired by the British group, no structural change was made initially. The purchasing director, son of the ex-owner, continued to report to the new managing director, even though logically, within the context of the multinational, he should have reported to the production manager. This kept him, and also his *347* brother, as members of the management team, even though they were not the most competent people. In other words, nothing structural was modified in order to preserve face. The new managing director chose to build on existing relationships, reinforce these, serve as a management model (which he did brilliantly) and progressively clarify the interfaces between his direct reports. Little by little, they replaced the old 'that's not my problem' attitude with a sense of individual and team accountability. They became a real management team in the international sense of the word and adopted the attitudes and behaviours of a major multinational.

The last example concerns an American, who arrives in France as the new managing director of a French subsidiary. His team all come from the *grandes écoles* and he speaks not one word of French. Nor does he know the particular product well. Despite this – or perhaps as a result – he changes nothing. He does not reduce his management team of 17 people, a heritage of the time when the company was nationalized. He openly draws on the knowledge and experience of his French *directeur général adjoint* and uses him as an 'interpreter': linguistically, culturally and business-wise. He learns French and works at developing relationships that give him greater authority and leadership within his team. Today he is a respected management model, has reduced his team with relatively little trauma, and has developed a way of doing things that is consistent with the group but has not crippled his organization.

What we see in these examples is leaders across frontiers who succeed. They seem to get a certain number of things right:

- They accept that in different parts of the world, management styles and behaviour differ
- They keep in mind that their perception of reality is coloured by their own 'cultural filter' and they acknowledge that the other person's picture is certainly very different
- They understand that their own management style and behaviour will be perceived differently by others and that *they* will have to adapt to new cultural environments
- They recognize that managerial behaviours and expectations in international business are also conditioned by historical, political and economic considerations
- They learn basic skills for communicating with those people whose language they do not share.

As we have observed these successful international managers, we have identified a new set of competencies, 'Culture Bridging', that seem to be an essential factor in making it all happen. Culture-bridging skills build on effective communications and managerial skills, but have their own specific nature as well. Based on our individual coaching for international managers and work with multicultural teams, we propose the following check-list for successful culture-bridging:

- *Focus on process*: Focus on the process of the interaction: and make group norms explicit. These are as important as the content and they need to be monitored for misunderstandings at all times.
- *Seek increased clarity*: About the process, and about the assumptions underlying people's behaviours. This means increased clarity about intentions, and about what you see as important to the other party. It also means adjusting your language so non-native speakers can understand – avoiding complex sentences and culture-bound references.
- *Question your own negative feelings*: Differences usually generate negative reactions. Use these feelings as a signal that cultural issues may be operative rather than accept them as confirmations of previously-held stereotypes.
- *Know yourself as a cultural being*: It is a platitude, today, to say that the more people know themselves as an individual (the more he or she understands his or her individual motivations, fears, hopes, etc.), the greater chances he or she has of engaging in positive relationships. Today we need to extend this to the cultural arena. We need to understand ourselves as part of a cultural *group* (shared values, assumptions, ethics, sense of right and wrong, etc.) in order to have a greater chance of being successful global managers, working with people from other cultural groups.
- *Give credibility*: to the other person's point of view – at least to test it out. In other words, be prepared to consider that the other person's position may have validity. Once you have done that, make your decision, knowing it is not based on an automatic rejection, but on a well-considered position.
- *Trust your intuition in decision-making*: You will probably have fewer facts and less understanding than in monocultural situations. But be sure you first know and understand your own cultural biases, have questioned your negative feelings and sought for increased clarity.

Those who make it follow no pat recipes. But they are willing to learn and to listen, not only to issues concerning product complementarity, market share possibilities and financial projections. They also learn from and listen to the cultural diversity of the women and men within their organization because they truly believe that it is the only way to make cultural differences work for you.

REFERENCES

Bartlett, C. A. and Ghoshal, S. (1989) *Managing Across Borders: The Transnational Solution*. (Boston: Harvard Business School Press).

Business International Ltd (1992), *Making Acquisitions Work*, Study M184.

23 Developing women managers

Judi Marshall

When I first reviewed literature on women managers in the late 1970s, I was surprised to find so many articles asking whether women and men are *really different*. Most of the authors were trying to prove that they are not, so that women could be endorsed as suitable management material, because men were taken without question as an ideal norm. In the main the authors were able to find data to serve their purposes, for example on leadership behaviour. But this is only part of the story. It is more appropriate to see men and women as broad social groups, each highly diverse, which are both the same and different, sharing fundamental aspects of human existence but also potentially approaching issues from different bases and social positions.

Certainly research shows that women and men can behave similarly as leaders, but it also reveals contrasts in their perspectives and in how their behaviour is responded to by others. For example, women often bring different values to the workplace from those of most male colleagues (Marshall, 1984), such as valuing co-operation in working relationships and seeking to lead balanced lives. Many women favour exercising power *with* others rather than *over* them (Loden, 1985). Women are often inhibited in using position power because other people reject or undermine their authority, stereotype them in devalued 'female' roles, act dependently towards them and so on.

It is now becoming more common to accept that women managers may sometimes be different from men, and for women to be seen as equal rather than inferior in any comparisons made. But any differences now identified should not be treated as fixed, essential qualities of either gender, lest they create new constraining stereotypes. Articulating them is part of an evolving and shifting learning process. It provides us with a broader map of possible human characteristics, activities and ways of being within which we can accept more diversity from *all* individuals.

Despite much current social change we are still greatly influenced by a deeply ingrained history of sex-role stereotypes which constrain men and women, and contribute to stress for both. I therefore argue below that we now need to explore women's distinctive needs, rather than acclaim their undoubted similarities to men, as a necessary phase in movement towards true equal opportunities. In the remainder of the chapter I shall discuss the training and development initiatives currently arising from such an analysis.

POTENTIAL DIFFERENCES BETWEEN WOMEN AND MEN

There are two interlinked bases for my assertion that women and men are sometimes meaningfully different. The first involves theories of archetypal patterns, in terms of which women as a group broadly represent a different range of potential human characteristics from those of men. The second involves recognizing that because of inequalities in social power, men's qualities have traditionally been valued more than women's, and so have shaped organizational life. These frameworks help identify women's development needs and show why these are currently so important.

Male and female values

Various theoretical frameworks distinguish between male and female values as two potentially complementary viewpoints on the world, reflecting an archetypal polarity (Marshall, 1984). This is especially clearly expressed in the Chinese concepts of yang and yin, and has close parallels in Jungian psychology. Drawing on these sources, the male pole is characterized by self-assertion, separation, control, focused perception, classifications, rationality, thrusting out, and contractual arrangements. The female pole is characterized by interdependence, merging, acceptance, awareness of patterns, wholes and contexts, emotional tone, personalistic perception and containing.

Male and female values are qualities to which both sexes have access, rather than the exclusive properties of men and women respectively. But through physical makeup, social role, and social learning women are more likely to be grounded in the female archetype and men in the male archetype. As managers, then, many women draw, to varying degrees and in individualistic ways, on a distinct base of values which distinguishes them from men. Individual development involves balancing the capabilities of one's grounding with appropriate aspects of the other perspective. This offers a more flexible array of abilities than does either set of values alone. But this is to some extent an ideal picture.

Social power

In its recent history, Western society has emphasized male values, and these have shaped its organizations, cultural norms, language and so on. Female forms are relatively devalued and underdeveloped. This is such a pervasive aspect of Western culture that, until recently, it has been unusual to identify *351* ways in which women differ from men without the assumption being made that women are somehow at fault. All too easily men become the unquestioned norm against which women's behaviour is judged, and any deviations are seen as unusual and therefore to be penalized.

In this chapter, differences are not viewed as faults of either sex. Rather, they are aspects of our cultural and gender heritage which can be used either productively and creatively or inappropriately and degeneratively. It cannot be assumed, for example, that what men do in organizations is necessarily right. Their management styles and career patterns reflect a selective range of possible options. There are disadvantages of which men themselves are aware. Established ways of working contribute to job stress and coronary heart disease; hierarchical forms of organization restrict development opportunities for all but a small group of 'successful' people. (It is worth questioning whether we know what men's development needs really are.) It is possible, however, to over-idealize female values in contrast, and this too should be avoided. For example, openness to other people's views can be degenerative when it results in becoming overwhelmed, invaded and dependent.

The social dominance of male values has inhibited the development of complementary, female alternatives. This is shown culturally by an emphasis on individualism, competition, rationality and control, and limited attention to interdependence, collaboration, intuition and acceptance. Along with other commentators (for example, Capra, 1982), I see the re-emergence and elaboration of female values as a significant aspect of a current re-vision in Western society, with potential benefits for men and women alike. But unless these values are taken seriously and allowed considerable space for experimentation, they will continue to be constrained by the current pattern of culture. Women's separate development is, then, an essential element in any social evolution.

Women's development needs

Many women now want to enter employment and thereby benefit from the financial rewards, achievements and personal growth it offers. They are joining a world still largely dominated by male values. In doing so they have conflicting needs. They want both to prove their rights to membership and also to have the freedom to be congruent with their own self-images. Until recently, equal opportunity initiatives concentrated on gaining acceptance for women by emphasizing their capability to work similarly to, and as well as, men. Women's competence in these terms now seems well-proven, although they are still poorly represented in top management positions (taking only approximately 2 per cent of them in the USA, Canada and most European countries), suggesting that their acceptance has limits. So far, though, most women have felt under pressure to conform to prevailing organizational norms to prove their legitimacy. But the foundations of many women's identities as managers are different, as are their experiences of organizational cultures. Many women now want to express more of their own perspectives in the workplace and in shaping their careers. Some also want to question fundamental organizational assumptions and to incorporate more female values and more diversity into organizational life. But women – and men – who are too challenging of established norms are likely to be resisted and may be expelled.

Therefore, women engage in any development activity with an implicit, but highly charged, choice. They can adapt to male norms of management where these still prevail or develop their own notions based on a wider, combined, heritage of values. Many writers now criticize the former option, suggesting that it entails collusion with limited cultural norms which have traditionally constrained women's social and organizational participation, and so reinforces them. Gordon (1991) calls women who have succeeded through such strategies 'prisoners of men's dreams'. More women are becoming aware of this central dilemma and are seeking ways to understand and live with its challenges.

I shall now explore some of the specific implications for women managers arising from this tension of values. I am concentrating on pressures women managers experience in employment; these are balanced by many satisfactions and opportunities for achievement which women value. Also there is no common picture as women's situations vary greatly; I therefore chart a range of potential needs.

Many women managers are operating from values, assumptions, and perspectives which reflect their female grounding but are not widely represented or accepted in organizational life. This creates conflicts and pressures, and many describe themselves as working in 'hostile environments'. In their everyday work and career prospects, women are continually affected by inequalities in social power, although usually these are in the background rather than the foreground of their experience. These become apparent when women are placed in one-down positions because of their gender, find that others reject their use of authority power because it contravenes stereotypes of femininity, or they are passed over for promotion despite appropriate qualifications and experience. It is common, for example, for female managers to be mistaken for the assistants of male colleagues, to find that their opinions go unheard in meetings or to be denied development opportunities such as assignments abroad because it is assumed they will not cope. Maintaining their own self-image and confidence, and managing relationships with others thus require great insight and skill.

As female stereotypes have not corresponded to traditional images of good management, women have been encouraged to play down their femaleness and copy male management styles in order to succeed. Many have done this to great effect, and developed capabilities which would otherwise have remained dormant. But this often leads to conflict between their work and personal self-images. Some managers are currently acutely aware of the strains of working in male-dominated environments and of what they have given up in order to succeed organizationally (Marshall, 1994). They are looking for more female-compatible ways of working, and organizational cultures more influenced by female values. Their reservations are particularly reflected in dilemmas about management style. The influence-based, person-oriented management style which many favour (Marshall, 1984), is in sharp contrast to the aggressive, independent, achievement-oriented model most see around them. It can make them personally vulnerable, prove ineffective in competitive environments and limit their chances of promotion. Women managers in the retailing and book publishing industries I interviewed (Marshall, 1984) wanted to blend aspects of several approaches together into a more robust approach.

Recent research shows that some, possibly many, women are developing alternative management styles, high in attention to both task and people. In doing so they are both refuting earlier stereotypes of them as only skilled in managing relationships, and are showing their competence in terms of a new ideal – that of transformational leadership (Rosener, 1990). The latter is depicted as interactive, motivating subordinates to meet personal and corporate goals simultaneously, achieving high-quality performance and inspirational in times of change. But these findings should not be interpreted as guarantees that women are now wholly accepted as managers. Ideals keep changing. (Some commentators would suggest they often do so just as women have proved themselves able to match previously stated criteria.) Women therefore need to be aware of the standards against which they are being judged – and of their own views on these standards.

Some women managers are looking for flexible ways to fit employment into their lives, and find the standard, life-long career pattern constraining. They typically consider a wide range of factors including intrinsic job challenge, their health, relationships and their sense of personal identity in any decisions they make about work. Female values thus shape their engagement with employment (Marshall, 1989). They are simultaneously ambitious in their own distinctive ways. But being employed is one highly significant role amongst several, which they seek to balance, if not at one specific time at least during their life course.

Research suggests that women can bring a different range of viewpoints to management. Gilligan (1982), for example, distinguishes between two moral codes, one used more consistently by men and the other by women. The male moral system views the world in terms of rights and principles, which can be defended and used as the basis for decision-making. The female system perceives life as a network of social relationships, with the individual at its centre. Right and wrong become relative and pragmatic, dependent on the situation. Gilligan concludes that women 'speak in a different voice', a view that is widely held amongst linguistic analysts too (Spender, 1980). Other authors identify intuition, which involves subjective and contextual awareness, as an approach to understanding which has much to offer in organizations. But women managers' perspectives tend to go unheard if they differ from established frameworks, and this may eventually undermine women's own faith in them. Many have therefore learnt to translate between languages, to express their views in more commonly accepted terms. This is both a strain and a potential skill as they see the world simultaneously from more than one viewpoint. Overcoming silence and finding voices for their experiences are currently highly important priorities for women managers (Belenky *et al.*, 1986).

Women have until recently had few competent female role models to look to in their search for alternative approaches to management. The women who had reached middle- and senior-level jobs had mainly copied male styles. Stereotypes of hard, lonely, older women managers are still common, and the expectation that they might become like this deters some people from aspiring to top positions. Those women who have survived without copying dominant styles have mainly remained invisible, their learnings and accommodations kept private. This dearth of role models is partly because female values remain in the background of organizational life and do not impact its public face. It is also because women have tended not to identify or mix with each other at work. To gain acceptance, particularly at senior levels, they have identified with their male colleagues rather than with other women.

This situation is changing, there is now more networking and sense of alliance between some women. But there are also signs of tensions which need addressing as the increasing numbers of women in management make differences amongst them more apparent. For example, individuals have adopted particular styles to cope with the nature of employment as they see it. Some have become outwardly tough, others have presented themselves as professional before all else, others have accentuated their femininity, and so on. These differences in style can set them apart, and may lead some to feel undermined or up-staged.

Tensions are also surfacing between some older and some younger women managers at the moment. The latter are criticizing the former for having adapted to male-dominated cultures, and claim that this is certainly no longer necessary as equal opportunities are now firmly established. Older managers can feel both misunderstood – thinking that they previously had little choice given prevailing cultural norms – and cynical – doubting whether their younger colleagues really appreciate the dynamics of power they may encounter as they move up the organization.

For the various reasons above, women need opportunities to share their perspectives, experiences and ways of coping, as a process of peer support or mentoring. They also need to discuss their differences, rather than acting these out in covert contests.

The analysis of needs above reveals seven main development priorities for women. They are:

1. Developing an awareness of how organizational cultures are created and maintained, and how power is deployed to shape values and behaviour – especially those which are gender-related.
2. Creating their own management styles, drawing on a full range of potential options.
3. Developing strategies and management skills for being effective in *355*

current organizational cultures.
4. Developing strategies and skills for influencing and changing cultures.
5. Developing confidence in their internal voices, and skills to articulate their viewpoints.
6. Exploring how they manage power, both when they might be undermined by others and when they have potentially 'superior' power.
7. Reviewing what they want from employment as a continuing life process, and devising strategies for achieving quality in the portfolio of life roles they choose.

Shared development needs

This chapter concentrates on differences, and so has little to say about the many development needs which women share with men. These are particularly in the realm of specific skills or general management training such as Master in Business Administration (MBA) programmes. Women need to gain access to a wide array of training, in which they are under-represented relative to men, and to see promotion opportunities ahead of them to make their experiences meaningful. However, as social values have been so firmly male-dominated until recently, no training can currently be assumed to be gender-neutral. Any course should explore whether its roots incorporate gender-biased assumptions, for example by devaluing management skills previously stereotyped as female or treating as complete 'knowledge' frameworks derived only from studies of men in male-dominated organizations. This inquiry is best done both in course development and as an active process with participants.

In the remainder of this chapter I explore the current training and development provision for women managers. In taking this perspective I do not assume that women are deficient in some way, need to be socialized into 'normal' organizational behaviour and should necessarily adapt. This was an implicit assumption of much early development for them (taking for granted the superiority of male over female values), and lingers on covertly in some activities. Rather, I think that to achieve true equal opportunities, organizations need to grow and change as they incorporate more women. Any training and development for women managers is therefore best undertaken as part of a committed, long-term organizational change initiative.

MANAGEMENT DEVELOPMENT PROVISION

There is now a wide range of courses and other development opportunities directed at women managers. Company support for this provision fluctuates significantly with other social and economic factors. The last ten years have seen at least two major renewals of interest in women's development in the UK. The first was in response to expected skills shortages as a result of demographic trends. Some organizations introduced training for women returners and enhanced childcare provision. Interest waned, however, when recession caused rising unemployment. The potential boost for women's fortunes largely failed to materialize.

In 1991 the launch of Opportunity 2000, a Business in the Community initiative to increase the quality and quantity of women's participation in the workforce, created renewed attention to women's development. By the end of Opportunity 2000's first year 150 companies were involved, representing approximately 20 per cent of employees in the UK (Hammond, 1992). These have set their own individual agendas for change, some more robust than others. The more committed have introduced substantial training programmes for women – and some gender-awareness training for men – as part of wider cultural change initiatives.

The activities discussed below are not solely relevant to women, but do directly address their concerns. In some areas, such as assertion, men are now showing an interest in training initiated for women; in others, women's training shares a label with men's, but typically takes a different form in practice. It is important to recognize that the unequal patterning of social power which has helped shape women's development needs can also hamper appropriate attention to them. For this reason training structures are as significant as specific course topics. These aspects are dealt with separately.

Training structures

Networking

As they become more involved in the world of work and reflective about their places in it, many women are looking for people of 'their own kind' to mix with. They also often feel cut off from established channels of communication and information sharing. These various motives have led to a growth in women's networks and associations, some official (like the European Women's Management Development Network), others informal; some with a specified constituency such as women in publishing or computing, and others looser groupings of people who feel they can benefit from dialogue. Broadly-based networks offer members reference points outside their immediate work context and news on current developments. Informal networks within a company or locality serve other, more supportive, functions as well.

As these activities grow, women are exposed to possible role models as well as friends and contacts. Coaching by mentors higher up their organizations has been a major factor in many women managers' success; networking offers more lateral coaching relationships. Some organizations are deliberately creating opportunities on induction programmes for new female recruits to meet established women managers, making such relationships more possible. Advice to trainers and members on creating and fostering networks is also now available.

357

Women-only training and groups

Although we are experiencing their re-emergence in society, female values remain fragile and their development tentative. They need protection if they are not to be swamped or overridden by their robust male counterparts. Similarly, in their development, women need the comparative safety of working in women-only groups. Here participants can, to a certain extent, suspend dominant cultural stereotypes, and explore and compare experiences which either men do not share or which affect them differently. Even patterns of conversation make this more difficult to do in mixed company. Men and their opinions tend to dominate and either leave women out or assign them to supportive roles. This pattern occurs even in mixed-sex discussions of *women's* issues. Men often speak for women with a clarity which is difficult to counter, or women may be reluctant to contradict if their own ideas are more diffusely formed or grounded in socially muted values. In women-only groups, participants can concentrate on understanding and supporting each other, and finding clear expressions of their own needs, rather than on competing for attention. They are also more able to take risks.

Early initiatives in assertion and management training, and the recent impetus from Opportunity 2000, have done much to establish women-only courses as viable and valuable activities. Their number is increasing, despite debate and some criticism. Amongst other things this reflects a growing identification amongst women, and in this way too provides new models of possible working practice. There is also more attention and respect for women's diversity, reflected for example in the emergence of some training specifically for black women managers.

Women-only organizations and networks are also flourishing. These vary widely in their ways of working and the issues they address. Some act as support groups, in which members talk through attitudes, motivations, problems and choices, gaining new perspectives and sharing ways of coping. Some are organized on a company or occupational basis and have a clear objective of professional development, running seminars on management skills, inviting guest speakers and so on. Some represent women's viewpoints to their organization or industry.

Women-only activities also bring their challenges. Sometimes conflict within a group is suppressed, partly as a relief from more combative relationships outside, and harmony becomes more important than allowing a diversity of views. Managing conflict and dealing with envy, competition and betrayal are now emerging as important issues for women to work on generally. Many of them reject competitive, rivalry-based models for handling differences, and are looking for alternatives which combine mutual recognition and self-assertion.

Many men find women-only activities bewildering and threatening, and it is therefore no easy path to introduce them into organizations. (There are also, now, increasing numbers of men who understand, respect and support such initiatives.) Once a women's group is set up it is not unusual for individual men to make powerful bids to join or to find out what is being discussed. Sometimes women are subtly deterred from being members by male managers' comments. For example, some women have been asked in appraisal interviews whether they *really* need to belong to a particular industry's women's network, their managers inferring that doing so demonstrates weakness or aggression on their part. Also women can be hesitant about joining women-only activities: some are unwilling to attract attention; others think that separate development may harden stereotypes which might otherwise be shifting. Any women's group which intends to report back to and influence the rest of the organization must consider how this can be achieved without creating battle inappropriately or breaching the safety of the group. These 'safe spaces' need, then, careful management and attention.

Flexibility

A keynote of women's development needs as outlined above is exploration. Predetermined course formats are not usually sufficiently flexible to meet this requirement. Sometimes, therefore, open time is scheduled on courses during which participants can work individually or in small groups on topics of their choice, using trainers as facilitators. The diversity that women bring to training is also accommodated by attention to contracting at the start of and during a course. Participants may be asked, for example, to write down three things they want from the programme, three things which will stop them achieving these objectives and three things they have to offer. These are then displayed publicly. Contracts help participants clarify their expectations, and give trainers an opportunity to state clearly which of these the course can and cannot meet. Contracts can be reviewed part-way through the event to monitor progress. They help increase the course relevance and tailoring, and demonstrate participants' responsibility for their own learning.

Different approaches to development opportunities

Women's development activities so far have given priority to issues that men, whose choices about employment have seemed less problematic, might view as 'background'. This contributes to differences between men and women in how they approach development opportunities. From my own experience, and discussions with other trainers, it seems that women tend to bring their whole selves, their full range of life roles, to any activities and are open to being changed by them. Men more typically present themselves as organizational people, looking for relevance within a particular area of expertise, and doubt whether radical change in adult life is possible. One consequence is that women may need help to integrate employment-based learning into the other life areas it affects. Assertion training, for example, may improve their management skills but create temporary havoc in relationships at home. Trainers will need to be alert to, and prepared to work on, these wider repercussions.

359

Dispersed training

A major need identified above was for women to increase their competence in potentially inhospitable organizational cultures. Once-and-for-all training is seldom the best way to achieve this, despite its practical and financial advantages. Instead some courses meet at regular intervals for several weeks or months with opportunities for members to test out their new skills in between. This format has been especially successful for some assertion and self-development training.

Self-development groups

Opportunities for maximum flexibility are offered by self-development groups for women. A group meets at regular intervals, with a trainer acting as facilitator. Participants manage their own process, identify their individual and collective needs, and plan and run a programme of activities to address these. The emphasis is on holistic development, addressing employment in the context of other life areas, and recognizing the interdependence of thinking, feeling and doing. Such groups can be highly successful, supporting their members in significant work and personal learning. Managing the group's development and decision-making themselves gives participants valuable experience, and opportunities to experiment with varied styles and strategies.

Training topics

Assertiveness

The single most significant and impactful training topic for women so far has been assertiveness; this directly addresses their traditionally inferior social position, and offers ways to reclaim personal and organizational power. Assertion training helps women develop their personal self-confidence and their interpersonal skills, including their abilities to express and honour their own perspectives, even when these do not conform to established organizational norms and ways of thinking. Participants tend to favour styles which reflect their female grounding and reject behaviours they find too aggressive or competitive.

    The basic principles of assertion training are: respect for self and others; equality; responsibility for one's own needs; maintaining appropriate boundaries between oneself and others; and choice – including when and whether to be assertive. Typical exercises involve practising assertive techniques such as dealing with anger, accepting or giving criticism, and saying 'no'; role-plays of problem situations; explorations of non-verbal behaviour and its implicit messages; and distinguishing between assertive, passive and aggressive behaviour. Dickson (1982) provides a valuable primer.

    Some organizations recognize the benefits of assertion training and offer it

widely. Many courses, however, go on outside companies as part of women's development for themselves, but with obvious job implications. Assertiveness is a valuable first rung of management training for women. Its basic principles are being incorporated in other types of programme.

Management courses for women

Many companies, higher education establishments and training organizations now run management training courses for women, some targeted at those in senior positions. Opportunity 2000 has provided a significant boost to activities.

Courses cover an established range of skills, such as leadership, time management, negotiating, stress management and decision-making, but take on a distinctive flavour because their participants are women. In sessions on stress, for example, the pressures of working in competitive, male-dominated environments and conflicts between life roles usually figure as concerns. As identity issues are central to many participants' approaches to work, activities to explore personal values and reinforce self-confidence are typically included.

Three topics are particularly gaining prominence in management development for women. The first is power. Women managers encounter power in many overt and covert ways. Assertion training largely addresses their potential powerlessness. They need also to explore how they handle their own various sources of power, especially that of organizational status, which is relatively unfamiliar to them, and may prove initially uncomfortable for their colleagues. Many have co-operative ideals, wanting to exercise power with others rather than over them, and must develop strategies for doing this effectively, especially in organizations which are still largely hierarchic.

More women are also becoming interested in how power can be used to shape values and norms of behaviour, to define reality for people. Through such processes cultural habits become established, or may be changed. In their experiences of male-dominated organizational cultures, women managers are experiencing this form of power in action, and appreciate how resilient it is to influence. Learning about definitional power therefore has several purposes: developing their abilities to notice when such power is used against their potential interests, strengthening skills for countering such moves, and giving them access to strategies for establishing and defending their own viewpoints within the culture. However, many women reject the dominant view that organizational politics, through which such agendas are achieved, are necessary or desirable. They want to find more open ways of negotiating between differences.

Secondly, and on a related theme, increasing attention is being paid to organizational cultures, how they work and how they can be changed. Many women see culture change as the essential next step to achieving equal opportunities in practice; some are now in positions from which they can influence norms and values.

The third topic which now appears widely on training course agendas is *361* 'self-presentation'; its prominence is intriguing and gives appropriately mixed messages about women's acceptability as managers. Similar titles cover diverse offerings. Some seem to advocate adjusting to dominant cultural norms: by dressing for success, learning to make a confident first impression, maintaining a professional, unemotional, image, asserting authority and so on. Such advice could reinforce any uncertainties women have about being accepted or taken seriously as managers, and persuade them to adopt masks to gain legitimacy. Other courses, with which I have more sympathy, encourage self-expression by seeking congruity between outer and inner self-images and exploring possibilities of style. They advocate play, enjoyment and choice.

As women engage in development they often question established values and assumptions, and arrive at new formulations. Alternative perceptions of leadership, effectiveness, power and so on – ones more compatible with female values – are thus emerging. More important than potential new guidelines, however, are the freedoms individual women are being offered and are taking to explore for themselves and achieve their own uniquely appropriate blend of female and male values from which to operate.

Life-planning and career-building

An early training concern amongst women was life-planning, and this is still a major priority. The basic format of reviewing one's past history, assessing strengths and weaknesses, identifying unfulfilled ambitions and so forming plans for future development is already well-established. Women bring several distinctive concerns to these activities, and their own patterns of life phases. The early thirties are emerging as a critical time for many who then review their career progress and wonder whether to have children.

Balancing career with a home life is a continuing focus of attention, as is how to manage potentially conflicting needs in dual-career families. Whether to interrupt their career at some point is a particularly difficult decision for women. Some companies are now offering Returner Schemes to allow extended leave for parenting, with opportunities for keeping in touch through occasional training or work experience. Although such measures are helpful, the dilemmas and practical difficulties remain. Also, research in other contexts suggests that women who interrupt their careers are likely to be significantly disadvantaged in terms of pay and promotion opportunities in later working life. Improving child-care facilities, including after-school care, is an alternative approach which offers greater potential career continuity, but may encourage life overload as 'normal' for women and men.

These choices are related to how 'ambitious', in conventional terms, women want to be. Many are now setting out expecting to pursue careers continuously and with commitment; they see no need to limit their expectations. Many also want to combine involvement in a sequence of satisfying and challenging jobs with leading a balanced life and achieving

congruity between their work roles and inner senses of meaning (Marshall,

1984; 1994). Women, and their partners where appropriate, are seeking strategies and lifestyles to achieve these complex aims. They are using life-planning to explore possible options, often putting their whole lives in the balance at a particular choice point.

In their planning women have a choice between two core strategies, reflecting male- and female-based options, or can combine the two. Much career literature gives highly directive advice, telling women to be exceptionally clear about their objectives and persistent in pursuing them. This is an idealized male model of development. Some women reject its potential rigidity and point to their own success through more opportunisitc progress. They have let their lives evolve following internal voices, and have found external challenges as necessary. This, more female, strategy provides an alternative model for women and men as employment possibilities become more flexible (Handy, 1990).

Sexuality

An area which is now receiving some training attention is sexuality at work. Courses on sexual harassment are becoming available, aimed at advisers to victims and/or victims themselves. As women and men more often work together as equals, they are more exposed to dilemmas about sexual attraction. Some women are concerned about the management of sexuality in intimate working relationships, and are looking for opportunities to explore their feelings and strategies. This may well become an additional topic in assertion or management courses. Addressing such issues also means examining dominant social assumptions that sexuality is mainly heterosexual, and paying attention to the experiences of lesbian managers.

Women and men as colleagues

The initiatives covered so far have concentrated on building bridges between women and the organizations in which they work. Workshops which take 'men and women as colleagues' as their theme offer more direct opportunities to influence organizational cultures. Typically, participants work in both single- and mixed-sex groups, reporting back in full session. Attitudes to work, sex-role stereotypes, management styles and so on are both discussed and put to the test in role-plays and problem-solving activities. Training objectives are enhanced understanding of the similarities and differences between women and men, individual learning about one's own attitudes and behaviours, and awareness of how organizational structures and cultures carry and enforce norms and values about gender. When training is company-based rather than open-access, it is hoped that further development will happen on participants' return to work.

Such workshops require considerable skills from the trainers involved. Sex differences in power, language, values and emotional expression all figure prominently in the discussions themselves and need careful handling if *363* underlying assumptions about gender are to be adequately revealed and explored. The dialogue such arenas offer is a vital next step to developing women and men's relationships at work and so must be fostered, despite its challenges. Use of this kind of format for gender-related training is therefore likely to increase in the future.

CLOSING REMARKS

In this chapter I have charted women's current development needs and training provision. I have also outlined some of the issues, particularly of potentially conflicting values, which require attention in any initiative. This is an area of continuing change. Development for women still requires justification in many organizations; and often this has to be argued within dominant value frameworks which may well not appreciate women's potential talents or believe they have a legitimate right to be in management. Recent developments, such as Opportunity 2000, have created renewed interest in achieving fuller realization of equal opportunities and have given more public prominence to women's development. Also, more women now see employment as a major activity in their lives and are taking action both to maximize their individual prospects and to influence their working environments.

But there are also contrary voices. Some men resent attention being paid to women's needs, and are especially unconvinced that access needs opening to them as employment opportunities generally contract. Some women are hesitant about identifying themselves as having separate concerns lest they be seen as troublesome. We need more open expression of such views and issues so that we can manage them overtly and productively rather than negotiating round them covertly. This means being willing to engage in culture change together. If we do not establish more open dialogue we risk perpetuating current power differences and cultural patterns in any development activities we undertake, and so continuing to devalue and mute women's perspectives. To guard against this we need both separate development for women, to strengthen their voices, and joint development through dialogue between women and men.

REFERENCES

Belenky, M. F., Clinchy, B. M., Goldberger, N. R. and Tarule, J. M. (1986) *Women's Ways of Knowing: The development of self, voice and mind* (New York: Basic Books).

Capra, C. (1982) *The Turning Point: Science, Society and the Rising Culture* (Aldershot: Wildwood House).

Dickson, A. (1982) *A Woman in Your Own Right* (London: Quartet Books).

Gilligan, C. (1982) *In a Different Voice: Psychological Theory and Women's Development* (Cambridge, Mass.: Harvard University Press).

Gordon, S. (1991) *Prisoners of Men's Dreams: Striking out for a new feminine future* (Boston, Mass.: Little, Brown and Company).

Hammond, V. (1992) 'Opportunity 2000: A culture change approach to equal opportunities', *Women in Management Review*, 7(7), pp. 3–10.

Handy, C. (1990) *The Age of Unreason* (London: Arrow Books).

Loden, M. (1985) *Feminine Leadership, or How to Succeed in Business without Being One of the Boys* (London: Times Books).

Marshall, J. (1984) *Women Managers: Travellers in a Male World* (Chichester: John Wiley).

Marshall, J. (1989) 'Re-visioning career concepts', in Arthur, M. B., Hall, D. T. and Lawrence, B. S. (eds), *Handbook of Career Theory* (Cambridge: Cambridge University Press), pp. 275–91.

Marshall, J. (1994) 'Why Women Leave Senior Management Jobs: My research approach and some initial findings' in Tanton, M. (ed), *Women in Management: A developing presence* (London: Routledge Press).

Rosener, J. B. (1990) 'Ways Women Lead', *Harvard Business Review* (Nov–Dec), pp. 119–25.

Spender, D. (1980) *Man-Made Language* (London: Routledge and Kegan Paul).

24 Management development and organization development

Graham Robinson

I wrote the original version of this chapter in 1986. At that time the UK was emerging from the most significant recession since the 1930s and showing signs of the recovery and attendant optimism which preceded the disastrous boom of 1989. In writing a piece on the relationship between organization and management development, I was concerned about what I considered to be a dangerous fragmentation between increasingly specialized disciplines, each of which purported to be serving managers endeavouring to cope with an exponentially accelerating rate of change. I was writing in the heady, post-Peters and Waterman days when everything was '*excellent*' and every management text contained at least one superlative in its title.

For the third edition of this handbook I revised the chapter to take account of the significant changes which seemed to be heralded by the impact of the Management Charter Initiative (MCI) and the concept of national standards for management qualification. In my introduction to the chapter, I bemoaned the fact that, in the midst of all this change, organization development appeared to have come 'to occupy more and more of a back seat'.

Now I am writing from a perspective which has changed dramatically once again. Depending on who your favourite economic guru or political pundit happens to be, we are presently crawling out, or still in the middle, of an even deeper and longer recession than that of the 1980s. Manufacturing in the UK in general, and in the South-East of England (the garden of Yuppiedom) in particular, has been hard hit. Mobile young managers find themselves landed with the yoke of negative equity, and the name of the managerial game and that of its advisers, has moved on yet again. Organizations have '*rationalized*', '*downsized*' and '*rightsized*'. Tom Peters' exhortation to managers to create fewer, flatter, structures and bash bureaucracy has largely become a regular feature of organizational life. Not, I suspect, as a response to true believers espousing his cause, but as part of a generalized and increasingly desperate bid for survival (with a bit of encouragement from political dogma). ICI is in the midst of splitting itself into two or more separate businesses following the predatory bid from Hanson. IBM and General Motors have recorded the largest corporate losses in the history of capitalism, while Microsoft founded, managed and largely owned by Bill Gates, still under forty and dismissed as 'nerdy' by a senior executive in a competitor company, has recorded a higher turnover than the once seemingly indomitable IBM.

In this world turned upside down, organization development as a distinct discipline appears to have faded even further from view, while some of the underlying assumptions and values of management development (derived to a great extent from experiences gained in supporting the big corporate guns) have been opened up to some serious questioning, as the organizations in which they were developed vie with one another to see which can operate with the leanest corporate office of them all.

As if all this were not sufficient, the focus of attention has begun to fall increasingly upon smaller and medium sized enterprises (SMEs), encouraging the question, *'What have organization and management development ever done for them?'* While such businesses have always represented a major slice of most Western economies, it is really only the conspicuous failure of so many big organizations which has drawn their smaller fellows into the sights of management and organization development practitioners. As the Russian proverb puts it, *'When the devil is hungry, he will eat flies.'*

All of this suggested to me that I should scrap the original chapter and start all over again, reflecting the new realities. However, the distinctions described in the original chapter, between organization and management development, still have a major influence upon the mind-sets of many of us who provide advice and guidance to managers on how they might improve their own or their organization's performance. As mind-sets lead to actions which are guided by assumptions lurking somewhere below the conscious level, it is as well to have them articulated and made explicit, particularly if economic circumstances may have served to drive them even deeper below the level of surface awareness. I have, therefore, decided to leave the core of the chapter largely unchanged, even at the risk of some of it now seeming a little quaint.

If you don't know where you have come from it may be a little more difficult to see where you are going.

THE BACKGROUND

Huczynski (1987) has suggested that organization development (OD) is:

> ... now generally regarded as being concerned with helping the members of an organization to improve its total ability to manage and develop itself, so it is able to respond to the environmental pressures it faces. Development implies that the organization needs to learn how to adapt and change its culture so that it can continue to survive and achieve its core purpose.

He goes on to state that:

If an organization's members are to develop and learn how to adapt and change, they need to acquire skills additional to, or other than, those they already possess.

If this is the case, and I believe Huczynski to be right, I would argue that the connections between effective management development and effective OD must be seamless. The variations between the particular contributions to organizational learning, achievement of purpose and, ultimately, to survival made by the different disciplines are largely ones of accountability, emphasis and preference. A significant and, hopefully, beneficial outcome of the recession for the practice of management may have been to hammer a nail into the coffin of the self-indulgent inter-disciplinary rivalries between those disciplines which must now cooperate in making a concrete (i.e. measurable) contribution to organizational performance or leave the stage to those who can.

First, however, it is necessary to be clear about terms. I quoted from Huczynski by way of a first definition of the subject. In 1990 I used the following quotation from Kilmann (1989) to place OD in its current context:

> The field of organization development, as it first emerged in the 1950s, was envisaged as offering methods for systemwide change that would significantly improve the function of entire organizations. For the most part, however, this majestic vision has been lost and forgotten. . . . Today, however, as many organizations are coming to realize that 'future shock' is upon them, the need for fundamental, systemwide change is being voiced more and more frequently. Now entire organizations must be transformed into market-driven, innovative, and adaptive systems if they are to survive and prosper in the highly competitive, global environment of the next decades. Given this situation, there is an urgent need to rejuvenate the theory and practice of organization development – to supply programmes for systemwide change.

Many of the new approaches used to achieve organizational transformation, such as performance management, total quality management, and the Investor in People initiative, *do* borrow heavily and appropriately from *'the theory and practice of organization development'* but, having been tempered by economic turmoil, with somewhat less of the latter's idealism and naïveté. At the same time there has been a recognition of the requirement for managers to be able to develop and learn with less of the prescriptive arrogance that characterized many of the traditional, centralized, specialist-owned programmes of management development.

Much of the distinction between OD and management development was made possible by their mutual separation from the guts and politics of organizational and managerial performance. The debates over the distinctiveness of either reduced the effectiveness of both, leading in turn to an increased separation from the client managers for whose benefit they were both supposed to exist.

But now the situation is changing, largely as a consequence of *force majeure* as opposed to a conscious recognition of the requirement to change. Perhaps this does not matter, so long as we developers have learned along the way and, more importantly, our management clients have derived a benefit from that learning.

Let us now examine the aims and intentions of management and OD more closely.

Management development has been described as *'an attempt to increase managerial effectiveness through planned and deliberate learning processes'* (Training Agency UK, 1977).

The customers for such processes, client managers, have tended to have fairly clear views about management development within their organizations, and they have usually had few problems in making a distinction between their perceptions of management development on the one hand and management training on the other. While the latter has been perceived as a process necessary to the acquisition of skills (such as budgetary development and control), management development tends to be viewed as a broadening, educational process by means of which the individual is initiated, shaped or fitted to the attitudes, values, rites and rituals of successively higher levels within the organization. As such, management development may or may not encompass formal training, and it may be self-managed. Many organizations have attached especially high value to processes of management self-development, even to the extent of welcoming back the prodigal manager who, having resigned *'to gain experience in another environment'*, now returns to the fold with renewed vigour. Others stress the value of a broad base of experience, but tend to reward *'loyalty and long service'*. This automatically places severe constraints on the perceived benefits and wisdom of pursuing opportunities for such broadening.

To an extent, then, client managers would relate management training to a process by means of which the individual acquires the skills associated with a specific management job or level. They would tend to regard management development as having much more to do with career development and progression.

This difference in perception tends to be thrown into much sharper relief in organizations where responsibility for management training is assigned to the training function, while management development is assigned as a personnel responsibility. This distinction is further reinforced where there is real, or perceived, competition between the two functions over which is accountable for what and as to where the senior status lies.

As industry struggles to recover from the impact of two very deep recessions in little over a decade, this separation of functions has tended to be reduced as part of the slimming-down process. The single, leaner function which has succeeded separated training and personnel functions in a great many organizations, under the title of human resource management, has narrowed the gap somewhat. But, as with management development and OD, the separated mind-sets associated with skills training on the one hand, and with personal growth and development on the other, still linger on.

Whatever the situation in a specific organization, there would appear to be *369* a general consensus among client managers that both management training and development are a 'good thing' and that their organization probably has not done, or is not doing, enough in these areas.

The views of client managers towards OD are quite different. For a start it tends to be less immediately meaningful to managers outside the human resources, personnel and training functions themselves. In response to an illustration or example of a piece of OD work, client managers will tend to respond with a reference to the name of a particular consultant or academic who *once did some work with the company along those lines*, rather than indicate any familiarity with, or expectations of, OD *per se*. As a consequence, OD tends to be known in terms of what particular practitioners do, rather than as a process or discipline with which managers are naturally familiar.

I have long been intrigued by human resource specialists' use of the acronym OD in discussions relating to OD processes and practice. Unlike other management specialisms developed over the past thirty years, the acronym does not appear to have been picked up by client managers themselves. Thus, while it would be quite unremarkable to hear an experienced line manager make reference to HRD (human resource development), O & M (organization and methods), OR (operations research) or to IT (information technology), the letters OD roll rarely off the tongues of the same individuals. Similarly, personnel and training people rarely, if ever, make reference to MD (management development) or MT (management training).

The use of the label 'OD' may provide a clue to one of the significant areas of difference between management development and organization development, and this difference relates to management's sense of identification with and ownership of the two processes.

In the 1960s, operational research was perceived as having a particularly significant contribution to make to the resolution of highly complex management problems in conditions of high uncertainty and risk. It had already made dramatic contributions in the military field during the Second World War, when interdisciplinary teams of scientists had applied the scientific method to the analysis, modelling and resolution of previously intractable problems. At about the same time in the 1960s, a number of reports were circulating in the USA which were highly critical of current business school practice. Such practice was, at that time, highly dependent upon *crude, non-rigorous, highly specific descriptions of particular businesses; there was little if any generalization across many businesses to formulate a set of general principles that could apply to many situations*' (Mitroff and Kilmann, 1984). The successful application of scientific method to the resolution of complex management problems offered by the OR people contrasted strongly with the perceived inadequacies of the business schools. The latter, argued Mitroff and Kilmann, over-reacted, consciously trying to emulate the academic departments that had spawned the successful scientists and technologists. They hired newly accredited PhDs from prestigious universities who had been trained in the so-called pure (i.e. untainted by practical application) sciences and academically respectable disciplines, such as computer science, economics, industrial engineering, mathematics, political science, psychology, sociology, etc. As a result the academic respectability of the business schools went up enormously.

The expectations that organizations had of the scientists in the OR teams, both in the university departments and in their client organizations in the private and public sectors, were extremely high and many successes were achieved (for example, the development of critical path analysis and PERT). Not unnaturally, therefore, the suggestion was made that the success of the natural sciences should be capable of being emulated by the behavioural scientists. Initially, this emulation took the form of the development of human factors groups within the OR teams – in the UK for example, within the British Iron and Steel Research Association (BISRA), and the National Coal Board – and direct consultation from the universities and research institutes, such as Birkbeck College and the Tavistock Institute. In the USA, specialist behavioural science teams sprang up at the interface between business and academic institutions to examine the specific contribution that behavioural science would make to the development of these organizations, and thus OD was born.

There was a fundamental difference in the antecedents of management development and OD. Management development was always a process 'owned' by the organization itself. It may not have been done particularly well, but the manager within the organization could identify with it as a process that had specific meaning for him, within the context of the norms and values of the organization by which he was employed. Organization development, on the other hand, was more specialized, more specific and, in aspiration at least, more scientific. It tended to be the domain of the business school and the research institutes rather than incorporated into the organization itself. Although not writing specifically about organization development, Mitroff and Kilmann provide a possible insight as to why the values and concepts of organization development have rarely been incorporated into the organizations that it was meant to be serving:

> A PhD straight out of graduate school who had never in his or her life even been near a real business organization, could teach, write, and do research on business and management. While they thus achieved greater prestige in their own network, they increasingly lost touch with the business community and the world at large. Intentionally or unintentionally, they shut out from the halls of academia the very reality they were supposedly in the business of studying.

The Mitroff and Kilmann argument may tend towards the extreme and, as noted above, they are not referring to OD as such but to the relationship between the business schools and business in general. It does, however, provide a backdrop for the image of the OD practitioner as an 'outsider'. The practitioners themselves have tended to prefer this role, as facilitator and change agent, as consultant and catalyst, as opposed to that of integrated participant in the hurly-burly of the organizations which they have aspired to develop.

371

With the dramatic economic changes which commenced in the 1980s, the increase in uncertainty at all organizational levels and reduction in confidence in the ability of Cartesian logic to produce the right answers to the complex problems of organizational and business life, there began a process of challenge to the contributions offered by all the specialisms which had developed so rapidly and with such promise in the 1960s. Line managers tended to become much more suspicious of operations research, other than in those areas of complexity where it had an established track record (vehicle scheduling, stock control and reordering, life cycle forecasting, etc.). It tends to be perceived as *'esoteric, back room stuff'*, highly mathematical and largely beyond the comprehension of the managers whom it is there to serve. O & M too has lost much of the gloss that it had in the 1960s, not least because its emphasis on rationalism leads to a natural (though not always fair) association with rationalization which in turn means *'putting the squeeze on my department'*. OD has suffered in its turn from its identification with outsiders to the organization. Its emphasis on humanist values has had a rough ride in organizations forced by economic necessity to experience the massive employee shake-outs of the late 1970s, 1980s and now again in the early 1990s. At the same time there is a much greater awareness of the limitations to the skills that managers have at their disposal to enable them to tackle the challenges that the new circumstances present. Therefore, of the four specialisms mentioned (operational research, organization and methods, organization development and management development), managers might naturally be expected to identify more closely with the latter than with the others. As a manager, it is *I* who am looking for help in raising my capability to deliver against frightening levels of demand and expectation. It is *I* who need that support in order to maximize my chances of survival. It is *my* head on the block. I am apt in these circumstances to ask, very forcibly, the question, *'What's in it for me?'*, when offered support from any specialist practitioner purporting to be able to assist in the solution of my most pressing problems. By and large, the acceptable answer is more likely to come from the management developer than from the other specialists with lesser concerns for an immediate personal impact.

OD FRAMEWORKS

Before pursuing the theme of similarities and differences between OD and management development further, it would be helpful to be clear about the particular frameworks within which OD has endeavoured to operate. The word 'frameworks' is used, rather than 'definition' or 'frame of reference', because the field has become too imprecise for any one of the many attempts at definition to be entirely adequate. Bennis (1969) described OD as *'a response to change, a complex educational strategy intended to change the beliefs, attitudes, values and structure of organizations so that they can better adapt to new technologies, markets, and challenges, and the dizzying rate of change itself'*. Such a description places OD at the apex of the organizational pyramid. It is strategic, it is concerned with values, and it is concerned with structure. If OD interventions are to be effective in terms of Bennis's description, then they must be made with the full participation and commitment of top management. Beckhard (1969) wrote:

> In an organization-development effort, the top management of the system has a personal investment in the programme and its outcomes. They actively participate in the management of the effort. This does not mean that they must participate in the same activities as the others, but it does mean that they must actively support the methods used to achieve the goals.

Perhaps less elegantly, but with a shrewd eye for the realities of organizational life, Reddin (1977) wrote:

> When change agents tell me that they plan to attempt a change from the bottom up, I remind them of the military dictum that the penalty for mutiny is death.

But is this insistence on top management involvement realistic? In the current climate such involvement is usually the result of massive and usually externally induced change, such as merger, take-over or bottom-line crisis. There are a great many examples where such involvement has been the springboard for the initiation of successful OD-type interventions. But in the majority of organizations, the demands of running the operation in a difficult, but not necessarily catastrophic, environment may make the demand for such involvement unrealistic. Highly motivated teams operating just below, but with the blessing of, such top managers may provide a more realistic driving-force for organizational transformation and development (Katzenbach and Smith, 1993). Bennis himself goes on to suggest that his description of OD may be to provide *'an abstract and perhaps, useless, definition'*. In order to clarify his position, therefore, he goes on to provide four examples of OD in practice:

1. Team development.
2. Inter-group conflict resolution.
3. Confrontation meetings.
4. Feedback.

Each of these examples is concerned with 'process' issues having an impact on the effectiveness achieved by particular work-groups, either internally or at the interface between groups. Each is also concerned with the intervention of a third-party 'change agent' or facilitator. Margerison (1978), writing ten years after Bennis, picks upon this latter point to suggest a simpler framework for OD than that of the earlier writers:

> The term 'organization development' . . . means the skills and methods used by people to facilitate organizational improvement.

While Margerison's descriptions may reflect what OD has often become   *373* (and may provide an explanation as to why client managers have a hard time in recognizing the term 'organization development' at all), it has lost two key elements of the Bennis and Beckhard requirements. The first of these is strategy and the second is top-level commitment. While the earlier writers' aspirations may have been too high (reflecting Mitroff and Kilmann's concern about business schools' distance from organizational realities), Margerison's description opens the door to the cynical comment that OD is what organization developers do when it is successful. When it is not, it is what the client manager did and, therefore, is not OD.

A really useful framework would probably lie somewhere between the two and would include a reference to the areas of knowledge and the particular skills and methods the organization developer would characteristically employ. Margulies and Raia (1972) went a long way towards meeting this requirement when they stated that:

> Organization development borrows from a number of disciplines, including Anthropology, Sociology, Psychology and Economics. It generally involves the use of concepts and data from the behavioural sciences to attempt to facilitate the process of planned change.

The toolbag is specified with the references to the disciplines upon which OD practitioners draw, and the stress upon planned change goes some way to meet Bennis' emphasis upon OD as a strategic activity (though it would not be argued here that a strategy and a plan are one and the same thing). Margulies and Raia again:

> Organization development is essentially a systems approach to the total set of functional and interpersonal role relationships in organizations. An organization can be viewed as a system of coordinated human activities, a complex whole consisting of a number of interacting and interrelated elements or subsystems. A change in any one part will have an impact on one or more of the other parts . . . organization development itself can be viewed as a system of three related elements – values, process and technology.

They then provided examples of what these three elements might comprise. These examples are summarized here.

Values

1. Providing opportunities for people to function as human beings rather than as resources in the productive process.
2. Providing opportunities for each organization member, as well as for the organization itself, to develop to his or her full potential.
3. Seeking to increase the effectiveness of the organization in terms of all its goals.
4. Attempting to create an environment in which it is possible to find exciting and challenging work.
5. Providing opportunities for people in organizations to influence the way

in which they relate to work, the organization, and the environment.

6.   Treating each human being as a person with a complex set of needs, all of which are important in his or her work and in his or her life.

Process

1.   Data-gathering.
2.   Organization diagnosis.
3.   Action intervention.

Technology

1.   New ways of organizational learning.
2.   New ways of coping.
3.   New ways of problem-solving.

The set of values provided by Margulies and Raia are essentially humanist in orientation. This provides another clue to the externalization of OD from the organizations within which it is practised. The values as listed are desirable to most people, but the experience of recent life in large organizations has not done much to suggest that these values are shared within the organizations themselves. More difficult still, because organizational members can identify with them at an individual level, they are easily espoused by the organization in formalized expressions of its values: *'Our greatest asset is our people and their unswerving commitment to Company goals.'* But, to paraphrase Argyris (1974 and 1976), the values in use are demonstrably different. *'Despite the best endeavours of Senior Management the economic pressures have meant that we have had to release five hundred valued members of the workforce.'* Thus, the experience of organizational members during the 1980s and early 1990s has tended to be at odds with the stated values of organizational, functionalist or pragmatic values concerned with being clear about terms and conditions of staff (or, increasingly, subcontractors), equipment, finance and time. These values place emphasis upon effective and efficient delivery as opposed to the more general values of human potential and satisfaction.

This is not to disagree with those who argue that it is possible to have *both* sets of values represented (and, hopefully, shared) within the same organization, but to suggest that the emphasis placed by OD practitioners upon humanist values puts them in a frame of reference that is essentially external to that of their client organizations. In the 1970s, as the pressures of impending recession increasingly made themselves felt, the discussion was frequently to be heard as to whether the organization developer should remain professional and independent of the politics and in-fighting within organizations (in which individual and corporate survival were becoming dominant themes) or whether they should regard themselves as part of the process and be there in the thick of it. In the 1990s and beyond, it can no longer be a matter for debate – the value position of the practitioner will have to be   *375* made clear.

Galbraith (1977) does not start from the same, humanist, standpoint that characterizes the writers referred to so far. He is, however, very much in tune with the systems orientation espoused by Margulies and Raia, and places great emphasis upon the importance of strategy, in common with Bennis. But perhaps the most significant difference in style in Galbraith's work from those alluded to previously is the sense that he is writing for the manager who *owns* the problem rather than for the OD practitioner who can *analyse and understand* the problem. Indeed, he refers to organization design as the key issue and not to OD:

> Organization design is conceived to be a decision process to bring about a coherence between the goals or purposes for which the organization exists, the patterns of division of labour and inter-unit coordination, and the people who do the work. The notion of strategic choice suggests that there are choices of goals and purposes, choices of different organizing modes, choices of processes for integrating individuals into the organization, and finally, a choice as to whether goals, organizations, individuals or some combination of them should be changed in order to adapt to changes in the environment. Organization design is concerned with maintaining the coherence of these choices over time.

These choices are fundamental and confront the manager with increasing frequency.

Writing some time later, Galbraith (1983) developed his systems orientation further to indicate that organizations

> . . . consist of structure, processes that cut the structural lines like budgeting, planning teams, and so on, reward systems like promotions and compensation, and finally, people practices like selection and development.

This approach is considerably more in harmony with the prevailing, functionalist orientation that is characteristic of the 1990s management style, than is the humanist approach characteristic of Bennis, Margulies, Raia, etc. His emphasis upon the notion of choice and, in particular, strategic choice would also find favour with Mitroff and Kilmann (1984) who berate the business schools and their academic antecedents for their post-1960s emphasis upon training students to tackle exercises rather than to solve problems:

> It is vital as a culture that we come to appreciate that there is a vast difference between structured-bounded exercises and unstructured-unbounded problems ... In a phrase we have bred a nation of certainty-junkies. We have trained the members of our culture to expect a daily dosage of highly structured-bounded exercises. The difficulty is that the problems of organizations and society have become highly unstructured and unbounded.

Their reference to certainty-junkies will strike a chord in the hearts of management trainers who are asked so frequently to 'dispense with the theoretical stuff and give us some techniques to fix these problems once and for all'. All too often the expectation seems to be that, provided one has the analytical ability to take a problem apart and break it down into its constituent parts, it will be possible to examine it logically and resolve it with precision. Unfortunately, the resolution of organizational and managerial problems tends to be less about elegance and simplicity and a great deal more about subtlety, ambiguity and choices.

LOOKING FOR A SILVER LINING

In the 1930s the sale of comics, escapist 'penny dreadfuls', sky-rocketed. The same period saw the rise of Hollywood and the Busby Berkeley musicals. Both had as much to do with the harsh realities of an economically depressed industrial society as the 'Fame' musicals have to do with youth unemployment in the 1980s and the 'Terminator' movies had for the 1990s. These situations do require a catharsis, a discharge from the unremitting gloom of the dole queue and company insolvency. It is not surprising, then, that the studies of excellence and success from the McKinsey Group – Peters and Waterman (1982) and Deal and Kennedy (1982) – and others – Goldsmith and Clutterbuck (1984) and Kanter (1984 and 1989) – proved so successful. The intention is not to suggest that these works were, to management in the 1980s, a precise equivalent of the penny dreadfuls and Hollywood to the unemployed of the 1930s. There are, however, certain parallels. Peters and Waterman do leave the reader with a warm feeling for the anecdotes of successful organizations awash with style, shared values and champions. They do not, unfortunately, leave that same reader with any prescription for action if that reader happens to be the manager of an organization which is manifestly unsuccessful or in a declining industry (a serious omission which Peters sought to rectify in his later books, *Thriving on Chaos* (1987) and *Liberation Management* (1992)).

Nevertheless, The McKinsey 'Seven-S' model offered by Peters and Waterman in 1982 has some close affinity with the systems model offered by Galbraith:

strategy
structure
systems
staff
skills
shared values
style.

The elements of the McKinsey model are very similar to Galbraith's (for 'people' in Galbraith, read 'staff' and 'skills' in Peters and Waterman; for 'systems' read 'processes'; for part of 'shared values' read 'rewards', and add 'style'). Both emphasize the importance of strategy as a cornerstone in fostering corporate success.

But Peters and Waterman make no reference to organization development as such, though they do refer to one or two practitioners by name (including   *377*

Bennis). Writing for an audience of managers, the concepts, values (even the name) of OD do not enter the pages of the best-selling book on management practice in the last decade. Once more, this would appear in keeping with the view of OD as an externalized process as opposed to an accepted area of effective management practice to be internalized within the organization.

The key to opening the door of management practice to the processes of OD lies in the strategic focus emphasized by Bennis, reinforced by Galbraith, and central to the McKinsey 'Seven-S' model. Unless the OD process (and, indeed, the management development process) is closely related to, and in keeping with, the organization's driving strategy it cannot be effective. This may well mean that the practitioner may have to forego the lucrative assignment where the strategy espoused (or used) by the client organization is inconsistent with those humanist values referred to by Margulies and Raia. He will certainly have an obligation to make them explicit, change his values, or play Iago to his client's Othello.

STRATEGY AS THE INTEGRATING THEME

As long ago as the early 1980s Professor Phillipe de Woot (1984) sounded a loud cautionary note about the enthusiasm among European managers for the findings of the McKinsey Group and, by implication, for Goldsmith and Clutterbuck in the UK as well. He pointed out that the assumption underlying their approach is that most companies are overmanaged in what they refer to as the 'Hard S's' (strategy, structure and systems). They have developed these to an extent where the individual manager is reduced to being an administrator of a decision system rather than being required to be a decision-taker, and certainly not a risk-taker, himself. The experiences of the turbulent economy since de Woot's work was undertaken have only served to reinforce his point. But has the move to leaner, meaner and more efficient management structures made all that much difference?

The writers on corporate excellence concentrated much of their attention on reviving interest in the so-called 'Soft S's' (staff, skills, shared values and style) which, one might think, should be regarded as a shot in the arm for the humanist values of OD. But, argued de Woot, this only makes sense if the underlying assumptions of over-management and over-control were correct. In the European context he found little evidence to suggest that they were.

The results of a six-year research programme headed by de Woot suggested that very few European organizations practised the basics of strategic management which are a prerequisite for corporate success, regardless of whether the management emphasis is hard, soft, or balanced. An organization committed to these basics would demonstrate that commitment through elements such as clarity over corporate goals, systematic management development at all levels, and a range of sophisticated decision support processes and systems. In the absence of these, he argued, to jump on the 'Excellence' bandwagon may be meaningless or downright dangerous for an organization lacking in professionalism and 'tightness' (clear operating procedures, control systems, levels of authority, etc.). Such 'tightness' needs to exist not only at the centre but throughout all of its operating units. No large company can be truly innovative and entrepreneurial (let alone intrapreneurial) if it has not developed a highly professional base for its total operation. De Woot warned against interpreting this professionalism too narrowly, stating that 'tightness' based only on financial controls is totally inadequate since it gives the headquarters no ability to provide strategic direction and to communicate fruitfully with its offshoots.

Such was the state of apparent strategic backwardness in Europe in the early 1980s that de Woot found:

1. That a number of top managers did not believe in defining clear objectives, and making them explicit throughout the company. *'I am not the Pope',* he quoted one as saying. Such companies, he reported, *'suffer from "Shakespearean" intrigue and instability'.*
2. That top management frequently failed to set a strong lead.
3. That employees *'are often slaves to external social values, rather than to the organization's culture'.*

Once more the critical finger is being pointed at the negative consequences of adherence to values that are external to the organization itself, whether these external values are those of society at large, or those of the academic community, as claimed by Mitroff and Kilmann, or those humanist values claimed to be at the heart of OD by Margulies and Raia.

In the absence of a clearly expressed strategic framework and an associated and consistent organizational value system to which their contribution can relate, organization and management developers alike are likely to share a common experience of floundering around in a sea of apparently random, at best feudal, managerial behaviour. In such an environment, development, whether organizational, managerial, group, or individual employee-based, is likely to be characterized by a series of fits and starts and sudden changes of direction resulting from the importation of new techniques having all the characteristics of 'the flavour of the month'.

If de Woot was correct, and experience would suggest that at least he was on the right track, it is clear that the thrust of both management development and OD in Europe should be towards the specification, clarification and communication of organizational strategies and values. In order to be effective in this role, the developers have to earn the right to contribute. They have not always been particularly successful in so doing, not simply, as Mitroff and Kilmann argue, because they have used inappropriate models imported from inappropriate cultural and value sets, but because they have not had the corporate 'clout' to be heard. Perhaps the two things go together.

Have things changed as organizations have slimmed down in order to survive? The harsh reality is that a great many who *didn't* change *haven't* survived, and not just in Europe. Many of the problems currently being encountered by the 'Excellent' companies of the 1980s are precisely those *379* summarized by de Woot in the early 1980s. Tom Peters now argues very strongly for much fuzzier or softer structures, dedicated to the achievement of clearly articulated strategic intentions which are known by, and which have the commitment of, organizational members at every level in the organization. In such an environment the boundaries and distinction between sales, production and R&D become increasingly irrelevant. How much more must this be true of supporting disciplines such as management development and OD?

ON THE HORNS OF A DILEMMA

To summarize, for OD interventions to be effective they must be consistent with, and contribute to, the strategies and values of the organizations within which the intervention is made. However, it has been suggested that most European organizations pay scant attention to managing strategically, preferring to adopt a more reactive, seat-of-the-pants style. This unsystematic approach creates a vacuum which is filled by the importation of values and quasi-strategies from outside the organization, for example, from government statements, from business schools, from external change agents, or from internal specialist functions, such as personnel or training. But because these are imported values and do not form part of a 'tight' whole, they are fragmented and essentially ephemeral. Beckhard's response to this situation, presumably, would be that this is precisely why OD interventions should only be made with the involvement of top management. Unfortunately, experience suggests that the internal specialists rarely carry the corporate 'clout' to make effective interventions at that, top management, level. Therefore, when the need for such an intervention is recognized, it is more often than not assigned to an external adviser who owns another set of values . . . and the process is perpetuated. The resolution of the problem must lie within the organization itself, and a resolution is essential to corporate survival, for the non-European competition does not appear to share this problem to anything like the same degree. *'If we do not create a managerial revolution,'* warned de Woot, *'we will wake up one bright morning and discover that ... we have become under-developed and colonized. By then it will be too late.'*

It is interesting to note that similar concerns are expressed among management developers. For example, Critchley and Casey in Chapter 26 argue against the conventional approach to team management development. A view which would suggest that before a management group can seriously address such issues as strategy formulation or the determination of key tasks, it is first necessary for them to build a degree of openness and trust. Critchley and Casey argue that, on the contrary:

> High levels of openness and trust are only rarely needed, and management groups get most of their work done very well without them, preferring for safety and comfort to remain relatively closed, and, covertly at least, distrustful. To ask such groups to make a major cultural shift, to take such big risks with each other as to be fully open and trusting, requires some mighty cogent justification ... if

their purpose is to be of real value to their clients ... they (should) start by encouraging their clients to clarify the role and purpose of the management group in question, to identify the nature of the tasks which they need to address as a group – complex puzzles or real problems – and then to consider the appropriate modes of working, and the skills and processes that go with them. When we have reached this stage, most of us have the skills and technologies to provide what is needed. What is often left out is the diagnostic work which gets us to that stage.

CONCLUSION: RESOLVING THE DILEMMA

If management development is effective it *will* result in positive OD, with effectiveness being measured in terms of enhanced organizational capability. It has been asserted in the earlier part of this chapter that management development is more generally recognized by in-company management as a 'good thing' than is OD. This is because highly-stretched managers can usually identify a potential personal benefit to themselves from an effective management development process. This benefit may not necessarily be obtained directly: *'My boss should go on this programme'* is a statement not unfamiliar to the management trainer.

It was also asserted that expectations of management development programmes, with some notable exceptions, tend not to be very high. However, the very fact that management development as a potentially 'good thing' is a commonly shared value in a great many organizations gives the management developer a significant 'leg-up'. It is eminently sensible for the management developer to ask the question of senior management: *'Management development for what?'* Indeed, if the question is not being asked, then the organization ought to be seriously questioning the value of having management developers in any case. The answers to the question should lead, step by step, to a clarification of the role and purpose of the management group. This is the investment in the diagnostic process argued for strongly by Margulies and Raia, and so frequently neglected in practice as observed by Critchley and Casey.

Presented with the results of the diagnosis, the next step needs to be placed firmly in the hands of the management group itself, and that is a questioning of the group's contribution to the achievement of overall organizational strategy, aims and objectives. If the answer is not apparent, then, either the group has misjudged its role and purpose, or the strategy, aims and objectives are unclear. Whatever the reason for the situation in a specific instance, the group, which owns the problem, should push, and push hard, for its resolution. In this, the members of the group must be supported and encouraged by the management developer. This individual cannot afford to sit on a professional fence for, if he or she does, they will have earned the comparatively low expectations which are so often expressed about their chosen field. If, on the other hand, the management developer does get involved in the uncomfortable process of questioning and reappraisal that will result, he or she will have made a significant contribution to a genuine process of OD. Such *381* a process will not of necessity incorporate the humanist values espoused by writers such as Margulies and Raia, it may even bring about the management revolution felt by de Woot to be so vital for European economic survival. Some practitioners who go down this road will no doubt wish that they had heeded Reddin's warning that *'the penalty for mutiny is death'*. But, whatever the outcome for the management developer, going through the process should make a significant contribution to the two things that all the writers referred to in this chapter seem to be agreed upon, and that is that genuine OD is contingent upon the espousal of clearly formulated and communicated strategies on the one hand, and internally developed shared values on the other.

The pain of the recessions of the 1980s and 1990s has been shared by managers, management developers and organization developers alike. This trial by ordeal has probably, for those who have survived at least, served to break down the barriers and to develop a community of shared values which should have been there in any case. But the most powerful of necessary lessons will often only be learned as a response to a major crisis.

It is currently fashionable to describe those organizations which *do* adapt, change and, perhaps, even flourish in times of economic adversity as *'learning organizations'*. There is a risk, of course, that the embattled manager may dismiss the term as just another example of specialist, consultant-speak (like management development or OD). On the other hand, the term might just be indicative of a much needed shift in emphasis as a consequence of which managers, management developers and organization developers *all* begin to recognize and appreciate the value of their various, different contributions and to demonstrate an enthusiasm and willingness to learn, really learn, from one another to the benefit of themselves and of their organizations.

REFERENCES

Argyris, C. (1976) *Increasing Leadership Effectiveness* (New York: John Wiley).

Argyris, C. and Schon, D. A. (1974) *Theory in Practice: Increasing Professional Effectiveness* (San Francisco: Jossey-Bass).

Beckhard, R. (1969) *Organization Development: Strategies and Models* (Reading, Mass.: Addison-Wesley).

Bennis, W. (1969) *Organization Development: its Nature, Origins and Prospects* (Reading, Mass.: Addison-Wesley).

de Woot, P. (1984) 'Le Management Strategie des Groupes Industriels', *Economics* (Paris). Quoted by Lorenz, C., *Financial Times* (London), 26 November 1984.

Deal, T. E. and Kennedy, A. (1982) *Corporate Cultures: Rites and Rituals of Organizational Life* (Reading, Mass.: Addison-Wesley).

Galbraith, J. R. (1977) *Organization Design* (Reading, Mass.: Addison-Wesley).

Galbraith, J. R. (1983) 'Strategy and Organization Planning', in *Human Resource Management*, 22 (1/2).

Goldsmith, W. and Clutterbuck, D. (1984) *The Winning Streak* (London: Weidenfeld and Nicolson).

Huczynski, A. (1987) *Encyclopedia of Organizational Change Methods* (Aldershot: Gower).

Kanter, R. M. (1984) *Change Masters* (London: George Allen & Unwin).

Kanter, R. M. (1989) *When Giants Learn to Dance* (London: Simon & Schuster).

Katzenbach, J. and Smith, D. (1993) *The Wisdom of Teams: Creating the High Performance Organization* (Cambridge, Mass.: Harvard Business School Press).

Kilmann R. (1989) *Managing Beyond the Quick Fix* (London: Jossey-Bass).

Margerison, C. (1978) *Influencing Organizational Change* (London: IPM).

Margulies and Raia (1972) *Organization Development: Values, Process and Technology* (New York: McGraw-Hill).

Mitroff, I. and Kilmann, R. (1984) *Corporate Tragedies* (New York: Praeger).

Peters, T. (1987) *Thriving on Chaos* (New York: Alfred Knopf).

Peters, T. (1992) *Liberation Management* (London: Macmillan). Training Agency (1977) *Management Development* (London).

Peters, T. J. and Waterman, R. H. (1982) *In Search of Excellence* (New York: Harper & Row).

Reddin, W. J. (1977) 'Confessions of an Organizational Change Agent', *Group and Organisation Studies* (March) (International Authors BV).

25 The role of the management development specialist

Tony Pont

The 1990s will probably be a time of unprecedented change, both in scope and pace. On the back of a series of reports (Constable and McCormick, 1987; Coopers & Lybrand, 1985; Handy *et al.*, 1987), the training and development field in the UK underwent a massive expansion during the years of economic prosperity in the late 1980s. In the decade ahead, it will have to adopt accordingly and, like all functions, will have to justify its existence in what seems sure to be leaner times.

Economic, social and organizational change will require an unprecedented level of learning throughout working life, so training and development should take on an increasingly important role in facilitating this learning. The role of the developer will be a shared one amongst all members of the organization. Everyone will have a responsibility for developing self and others, and all development will require sound, economic justification.

Before discussing the role of the management development specialist in detail, we should first consider some definitions. Whilst many have seen training and development as inseparable the recently published *Developing the Developers* report by Megginson and Pedler (1991) found that many developers saw important differences between training and development, and they wanted to keep the terms separate. Two-thirds of 633 respondents to Megginson and Pedler saw themselves more as developers than trainers.

The authors defined training as 'the relatively systematic attempt to transfer knowledge or skills from one who knows or can do to one who does not know or cannot do'. Development was described as 'working with individuals or organizations to enable them to cross a threshold, which has qualitative significance to them and their life'.

The term 'development' is defined further by Margerison (1991) who distinguishes between development at the personal level and at the organizational level. At the personal level 'it is the process by which you and others gain the skills and abilities to manage yourself and others. Management development is a personal responsibility.' At the organizational level it:

> involves all the issues related on a continuum – from recruitment and selection to induction to self-development to top team development. Management development is a way of doing business… It is where management development is seen as part of the future, rather than simply solving today's problems, that the importance becomes visible to all. In such places, you will find a supportive atmosphere conducive to learning.

It is becoming increasingly accepted that everyone in the organization has a responsibility for management development, be it their own or others'. Nevertheless there must surely be a role for someone who acts as the management development specialist whose primary task must be that of a facilitator or enabler, in helping everyone (including self) develop as a person and as a manager, for the benefit both of the individual and the organization. Before we consider the role, we should look at where such a role exists in the organizational structure.

THE STRUCTURE OF ORGANIZATIONS

There are numerous models of organizational structure, but I propose to use the model (see Figure 25.1) described in great detail by Mintzberg (1983). It is not applicable to all organizations, but it can be applied to most, especially those with a manufacturing function.

1. The strategic apex

This is responsible for ensuring that the organization serves its mission and that it serves the needs of those who control it and have power over it (e.g. owners, government agencies, etc.). As a general rule, the strategic apex takes the widest and as a result the most abstract perspective of the organization. Work at this level is generally characterized by a minimum of repetition and standardization, much discretion and relatively long decision-making cycles.

2. The operating core

This includes those members – the operators – who perform the basic work related directly to the production of goods and services. Machine operators and sales people are to be found here.

3. The middle line

The strategic apex is joined by a chain of middle-line managers with formal authority. The chain runs from the senior managers to the first-line supervisors (such as shop foremen), who have direct authority over the operators. Descending the chain of authority, managerial jobs change in their   *385*

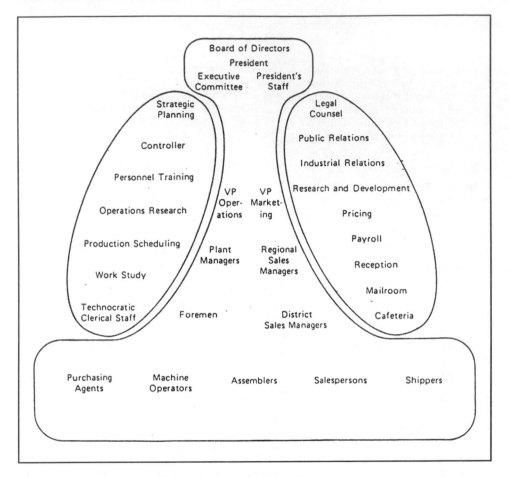

Source: H. Mintzberg, Structure in Fives: Designing Effective Organisations, 1983, p. 18. Reprinted by permission of Prentice Hall, Englewood Cliffs, New Jersey.

Figure 25.1   The organizational structure (after Mintzberg, 1983). Some members and units of the parts of the manufacturing firm

orientation, becoming more intricate and elaborated, less abstract and aggregated, and more focused on the flow of work.

4. The support staff

These are the specialized units that exist to provide support to the organization outside its operations. In a manufacturing organization, this would include legal counsel and cafeteria services.

Large organizations tend to provide their own support services instead of purchasing them externally as they want to exercise control over these services, probably to reduce the uncertainty of buying them on the open market and perhaps also to increase the certainty of outcome. By fighting its own court cases the manufacturing company closely controls the barristers it uses; and by feeding its own employees in the cafeteria, it can shorten the lunch break, as well as determining the quality of food its employees eat.

The support units are found at different levels of the hierarchy, depending on the receivers of their services. In most organizations public relations and legal counsel are located near the top, since they tend to serve the strategic apex directly, whilst at the lower levels are to be found the services with more standardized work, akin to the work of the technostructure.

5. The technostructure

In this area are to be found the analysts who serve the organization by affecting the work of others. These analysts are removed from the operating workflow, although they may design it or train others to do it. Thus the technostructure is only effective when it can use its analytical techniques to make the work of others more effective.

It is in this area of the organization that personnel analysts (including trainers and recruiters) are to be found. Among that function is the standardization of skills, sometimes set within the organization, but mostly to levels of standardization set outside the organization.

Traditionally, management development has been located within the technostructure, reporting into the personnel/human resources function to a personnel director. In this position it is peripheral to the main mission of the organization, which creates problems but also has some advantages and can create opportunities. On the one hand it can be seen as an expensive overhead fighting for limited resources with other 'cost' functions and with little access to, or influence on, senior management: on the other hand, it can stand back, take an objective view of the whole, be in tune with the organization's external environment, and make appropriate interventions in an effective, credible and cost-effective manner. The latter provides the springboard and the opportunity to consider some of the major roles of the management development specialist, which are listed below and then discussed in detail.

1. To raise the profile of management development in the organization.
2. To market and sell training and development to line management.
3. To assist in the creation of a learning organization.
4. To raise the quality of management development activities and to provide evidence of returns on investment.
5. To be aware of external developments.
6. To design and deliver a portfolio of development opportunities.
7. To develop self and the status of management development.
8. To develop consultancy and interventionist skills.

TO RAISE THE PROFILE OF MANAGEMENT DEVELOPMENT IN THE ORGANIZATION

Historically, management development has been at a disadvantage in the   *387* organizational hierarchy so that it has suffered from a low profile and a lack of political and financial clout. Some of its inherited baggage can be summarized as follows:

1. It has reported to a personnel director who may have lacked status in the organization. How often have we seen a senior line manager from another function put out to grass as head of personnel in order to lengthen his service record and increase his pension entitlement? The 'Wing Commander Retired' syndrome has been in evidence and has not helped the image of personnel. Such a situation has blinded some line managers to the excellent work that may have been taking place in management development. Fortunately, as the personnel function has become increasingly valued, this scenario is becoming less common.
2. Some UK personnel professionals learnt their trade in the adversarial years of the 1970s and early 1980s, when trade union power and influence were high and containment and control, not growth, was the order of the day. Understanding of the development process was minimal, if not non-existent, and the ability to think strategically or long-term rather than short-term was limited. There was very little risk-taking, and few were prepared to shout about people development and the benefits of strategic thinking.
3. As part of the personnel function it has enjoyed too frequently, at best, middle-management status and in a function that is viewed as a cost or expensive overhead fighting for finite resources with profit functions or with other cost functions who have been able to make their case more persuasively for a bigger slice of the cake.

Without the cash there are severe limitations on what can be achieved, however praiseworthy the cause. As Margaret Thatcher said, 'No-one would remember the Good Samaritan if he only had good intentions. He had money as well.'

Consequently, in some organizations, management development has had little, if any, input into corporate strategy or the business plan, and in extreme cases probably did not even know what they were. Access to the strategic apex and communication down from the apex were non-existent. Fortunately, as management development has gained a higher profile with consequent recognition of the need for it to be included in the strategic plan, an increasing number of developers are now working at a senior level in the organization.

The case, therefore, for a repositioning of management development to a senior level within the organizational hierarchy, is a sound one. Perhaps the personnel director should be relocated to report directly to the chief executive or to a wealth-creating function? Or perhaps the personnel function should be seen as an independent function, peripheral to the organization, which sells its services to the organization, in line with Handy's 'cloverleaf' model representing the core workforce, the contractual fringe and the flexible labour force. Perhaps personnel could be located in the latter two areas?

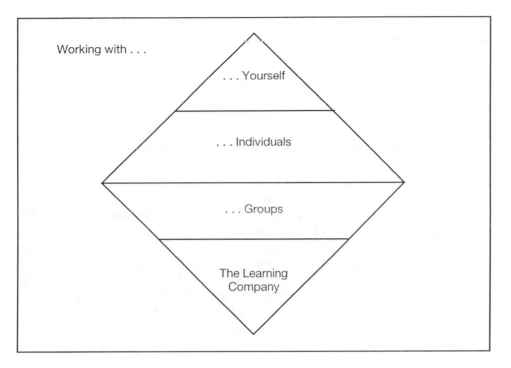

Source: D. Megginson and M. Pedler, *Self-Development: A Facilitator's Guide* © 1992 McGraw Hill. Reproduced with permission of the publisher.

Figure 25.2   Developer's diamond field

Whatever the structure, a major role for the management development specialist is to overcome of the legacy of low status, have greater access to the key organizational decision-makers, make a major input into corporate strategy, and fight for, and get, a bigger slice of the corporate cake.

TO MARKET AND SELL TRAINING AND DEVELOPMENT TO LINE MANAGEMENT

Megginson and Pedler (1992) have stated that the developer's task is to 'empower people to learn from acting and to act on the basis of learning'. This brief sentence contains a number of key approaches and concepts which will be developed later. They believe that the developer's field of work covers four main settings which are set out in Figure 25.2.

Traditionally, much of the developer's work has been with the middle two groups, who are often line managers, but in the future, the relative importance of the two outer segments should increase.

Many line managers still view training and development with suspicion. The notion that 'it's a week off work, in nice surroundings with good food whilst orienteering around the countryside in pursuit of the Holy Grail' still persists. No tangible return on money spent is evident. The usual arguments about personal growth, self-discovery, 'coming out of their shell', better motivated, etc., whilst probably true, are nevertheless difficult to prove and impossible to quantify.

Management development needs selling and, as in all selling situations, managers need to be sold the benefits, not only for their department, but also for themselves. All line managers are human and will look for the personal benefit in any situation, so it needs stressing.

Some ways therefore of selling training and development are listed here.

1. By 'adding value'. Management development activities need to do this; often it has not happened. The fictitious view outlined above contains more than a grain of truth. Often such activities do not deal with the real world, there is no follow-up or implementation and they have little bearing on the bottom line. This focus on 'inputs' rather than 'outputs' has partly helped create our fictitious image. A change of focus in which line managers see something implemented with bottom-line improvements that reflect favourably on their own performance, will certainly improve the priority that management development has in their budget allocations.

2. By creating high-quality learning experiences for the participants who feel within themselves the value and benefits of a programme. Participants in many programmes are the senior managers and decision-makers of tomorrow, and good experiences will create a favourable attitude to management development activities so that in future management development will possibly move up the organizational political agenda and gather greater resources. In short, we are creating an improved organizational attitude (and possible culture change) in the long term to management development.

3. By marketing management development more aggressively in the organization. No product or service was ever sold by taking a back seat. It needs promoting. Promotional literature should be sufficiently eye-catching to make managers open it. Why not feature photographs of some of them (a good mixture, including senior managers) on the cover of your prospectus? It will emphasize the message that management development is about people, whilst those given exposure will certainly circulate to all and sundry.

   As part of the marketing mission, never miss an opportunity to get good publicity and raise the profile. There are plenty of opportunities. Why not invite top management to course dinners, graduation ceremonies, presentation of a national award? Once they are there, use the publicity machine in the most effective way – the company newsletter, local press, local radio and, if possible, national press. It is surprising how chief executives can find the time, despite their busy schedules, to attend such high-profile functions. Some good photographs, a few well-chosen words from the chief executive about 'how we view our people as our greatest resource', helps raise the profile of management development enormously and makes the withdrawal of future resources that much more difficult.

4. All management development activities should be a partnership
    between line management, the individual and the management
    development specialist. Involvement is the name of the game and this is
    shown diagrammatically by the 'Training Triangle' (see Figure 25.3).

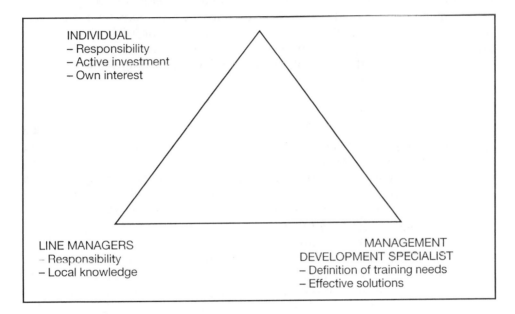

INDIVIDUAL
– Responsibility
– Active investment
– Own interest

LINE MANAGERS
– Responsibility
– Local knowledge

MANAGEMENT
DEVELOPMENT SPECIALIST
– Definition of training needs
– Effective solutions

Figure 25.3   The 'Training Triangle'

Most managers have their training and development needs regularly assessed
through a number of mechanisms – appraisal, career counselling, psychometric
testing. Whatever the mechanism, the training and development needs of the
individual are his or her responsibility, but usually emerge as a result of a
contracting process between individual and line manager. Where appropriate
the management development specialist will provide additional support
(counselling, advice, direction) to arrive at efficient solutions. Sometimes the
resources for the solutions lie within the organization, but sometimes they may
lie outside it. Part of the role of the management development specialist is to be
aware of the external options and advise and arrange accordingly.

TO ASSIST IN THE CREATION OF A LEARNING ORGANIZATION

This loosely-defined concept has gained increasing exposure in recent years.
Garratt (1987) proposed a theory of organizations as 'learning systems' in
which success depended on two key skills – learning continuously and giving
direction. Pedler, Boydell and Burgoyne (1989) defined it as 'an organization
which facilitates the learning of all its members and continuously transforms
itself'. Pedler et al., (1989) has since preferred the term 'Learning Company'
applying it not so much to a particular legal form of organization, or private   *391*

sector company, but in the more general sense of 'a company of people' who are 'companions' in an enterprise together.

Whatever the definition, the concept has some key implications for both individuals and organizations. At the individual level, learning and development are crucial to personal growth and occupational competence, in accordance with many of the theories expounded by the humanistic school of psychology. At the organizational level, the formula popularized by Revans (1982) – that for an organization to survive, its rate of learning must be equal to or greater than the rate of change in its external environment – is fundamental. This is expressed:

$$L \geqslant C$$

The role of top management is to ensure that this is so. If the organization's rate of learning in relation to the rate of environmental change is not being monitored and learning is slow, then the organization will decay and may eventually die. One role, therefore, of the management development specialist is to monitor this and report it to senior management for appropriate action.

The creation of a learning organization is not an instant one. There is no quick fix. It is a long-term creation. It is influenced by a number of nebulous, but nonetheless very real factors such as cultures, values and attitudes and by a number of realities of organizational life which reflect the psychological state of its members and mitigate against the process of self and organizational development.

Hofstede (1980) defined culture as:

> the collective mental programming of the people in an environment. Culture is not characteristic of individuals; it encompasses a number of people who were conditioned by the same education and life experience. The collective mental programming is different from other groups.
>
> Culture in this sense is often very difficult to change; if it does so at all, it changes slowly. This is not only because it exists in the minds of the people, but, if it is shared by a number of people, because it has become crystallized in the institutions these people have built together.

It is not my intention here to describe and discuss culture in great detail. Clearly it has an important effect on learning and development and a favourable culture must exist in creating a learning organization. Culture change is slow, and therefore the creation of a learning culture is not something that is achieved overnight. But, as we have argued, management development must be viewed as long-term rather than short-term.

A feature of a culture in which continual learning is valued must be placing a large emphasis on self-development. Peter Drucker (1982) has written 'development is always self-development... the responsibilities rest with the individual, his/her abilities and efforts'. In some organizations such personal responsibility will be hard for employees to accept. It is not uncommon for people to project their own fear of the unknown onto a third party and blame the organization to cover up their own reluctance or inability to risk themselves. Any form of personal responsibility is rejected. How often have we heard the use of the word 'they' by employees: 'They wouldn't let me go,' 'They didn't move quickly enough,' as a way of off-loading responsibility away from self onto others?

Conversely, in many organizations the culture does not encourage self-directed effort by individuals, as the work of both Argyris and Morgan has demonstrated.

Argyris (1985) states that 'it is my hypothesis that the present organization strategies developed and used by administrators (be they industrial, educational, governmental or trade union) lead to human and organizational decay. It is also my hypothesis that this need not be so.'

This suggestion that in organizations individual development is stunted and potential is not achieved is attributed to the way organizations are run. Argyris suggests the main problem is that the typical approach to the management of organizations and the lack of interpersonal competence in them prevents people becoming mature in outlook and fails to arouse their full psychological energy. People are short-sighted in their actions in doing the job, concerned with present advantage and unable to see future consequences; they shirk responsibility and are uninterested in opportunities.

Additionally, defensive behaviours and protection of territory are widespread. People display a superficial 'pseudo health' in which there is no overt dissatisfaction, but each individual performs his or her task in accordance with the procedures and routines established for their position in the hierarchy. Keeping one's nose clean becomes the order of the day. In such organizations individuals rarely progress. They think short-term and only in relation to their own limited area. They are reactive, not pro-active. They accept a passive and dependent position without initiative. Their behaviour reinforces the *status quo* and the hierarchical pyramid.

Argyris distinguishes between single and double loop learning, the former being a kind of self-sealing process in which operating norms are rarely questioned or changed. Double loop learning involves the process of questioning whether operating norms are appropriate and then initiating appropriate action. Clearly the task of getting managers to double-loop learning is an on-going and long-term one, reinforcing the view expressed earlier that all management development needs to be viewed long-term.

Another reality of organizational life has been described by Gareth Morgan (1986). He traces relations between our conscious and unconscious life and how managers act out their own neuroses at work for a whole range of reasons, ranging from Freudian repressed sexuality to transitional objects, to Jung's theories on repressed opposites of rationality. From our early conditioning some of these factors and our perception of the world become embedded in our unconscious, affecting our behaviour at work and how we relate to reality. The range of reasons can provide an explanation of how aggression, envy, anger, resentment, sexual sublimation and many other dimensions of our hidden life may be built into work and organization. They lie at the centre of many issues associated with group dynamics, innovation and change.

The role of the unconscious in organization life has been viewed by Delahanty and Gemill (1982) as a kind of 'black hole' in that the energies of people in the organization are swallowed and trapped and channelled into unproductive effort. But it is possible to release trapped organizational energy in a way to promote positive and creative transformation and change at both the individual and organization level and create more positive and harmonious relationships among individuals, groups, the organization and its environment.

It is not the suggestion here that management development specialists become specialist psychoanalysts; however, an understanding of the contribution psychology can make is important. Similarly, the whole field of behavioural sciences has relevance to understanding behaviour at work so that when interventions are made they are made on the basis of greater objectivity and empathy and thereby become much more effective. A search for greater knowledge and understanding of the emerging field of behavioural sciences is developmental for the management development specialist and, if nothing else, highlights the challenge of developing individuals to fulfil potential. As Argyris has stated, only a fraction of this potential is utilized, so the challenge is very firmly in evidence.

Central to the goal of realizing human potential is the empowerment concept, which is about giving individuals the inner resources to change and develop themselves. This is a change of focus from the thinking of yesteryear when it was viewed as the role of the organization to take such responsibility. For many, empowerment will be difficult if not impossible: for others, who possess the self-directed drive and inner resources, it may also be difficult because of constraints imposed by the organization and its individual managers. As Morgan has outlined, human characteristics such as resentment, envy, insensitivity, threat, etc., can cause a line manager to block an aspiring subordinate, making progress difficult. One way around such a dilemma is the use of a third party (possibly the management development specialist?) to enable the blocked individual to achieve the desired outcome. Third parties are among the most effective ways to remove blockages, be they organizational or cognitive, and the skills of empathy and counselling, allied to a deep understanding of behavioural science theory and political acumen, can enable effective solutions to be skilfully achieved.

TO RAISE THE QUALITY OF MANAGEMENT DEVELOPMENT ACTIVITIES AND TO PROVIDE EVIDENCE OF RETURNS ON INVESTMENT

The best source of business is your existing clients. One can certainly take the view that line managers are clients and therefore it is important to deliver a quality service that meets their needs and makes them satisfied customers. There are a number of ways in which this can be achieved:

1. All training and development activities are delivered in a form that provides customer satisfaction. On training courses participative methodology rather than 'chalk and talk' has increased widely over recent years and has many potential benefits. The trainer's role changes from that of teacher/tutor to facilitator. Some organizations are now using line managers in a training role and have sent them on 'Training the Trainer' courses. My own book, *Developing Effective Training Skills* (1991/1994), was written for this very purpose and has been used widely throughout the world as a basis for such training and getting new recruits to training to adopt a learner-centred, not a teacher-centred, approach.

2. Some of the lessons of the Peters and Waterman book *In Search of Excellence* (1982) should not be lost on the management development specialist, especially the advice of 'staying close to the customer'. Our customers are our line managers and the importance of regular contact, credible options and quality solutions should not be forgotten. The quality philosophy stresses that our internal customers are just as important as our external customers and management development specialists are no exception.

3. All management development activities need to be evaluated not only as a learning experience in themselves, but evaluated in terms of how they have benefited the organization. Evaluation of activity is vital in order to obtain feedback on quality, how far provision meets need and whether the organization is obtaining a return on its investment.

   An example of how a management development programme can offer a return on investment is a programme that I assisted in designing and delivering with the retailer, Marshell Group Ltd (MGL).

MGL is a national multiple retailer in the UK covering some 700 retail outlets under various names, with an annual turnover of some £450 million. It employs almost 3 000 people, from assistants in the retailing units through to area management through to the main board. MGL is a subsidiary of Gallaher UK Ltd, which is a major overseas subsidiary of American Brands Inc.

In the early 1990s, the newly appointed chairman and chief executive, George Carpenter, realized the importance of developing a pro-active role for senior management in the future strategic planning of the company in the 1990s and beyond. It was recognized that a number of opportunities would arise in the market-place where MGL should seek to expand and build upon current expertise; and secondly, a change in culture and management style would be required in the management of staff in order to optimize performance.

A programme was therefore designed to develop the strategic thinking and planning processes of MGL's senior management. Participants on the programme were split into three main groups or sets, each charged with the responsibility of producing a clearly specified strategic project in the context of the future direction of MGL.

An action learning approach was used based upon:

- A questioning approach to the important business issues
- Getting the main concerns about the present and the future into good managerial focus
- Developing additional personnel and managerial skills
- Using specialist inputs from outside the company to shape up strategic options and to make the right choice about future direction.

As with all action learning approaches the programme (see Figure 25.4) was a blend of specialist external input and utilization of group resources. It was recognized that all participants have an important contribution to make and it is the responsibility of the set to ensure that everyone gets a full opportunity to do this (i.e. use set resources to their full extent in finding solutions to company issues).

At the end of the programme three projects were presented on the specified company strategic issues to an audience of course participants, external consultants, chief executive and members of the board of the parent company, giving an in-depth assessment and outline of the strategic direction the company should take in the years ahead. Since the programme was presented, MGL profits have shown substantial and continual improvement.

By utilizing real-life projects and senior personnel within the company, MGL had determined its future strategic direction for the next decade and at the same time undertaken a valuable and worthwhile management development activity. Costs have been recouped several times over, thus proving that management development can be a valuable investment and that it can be a

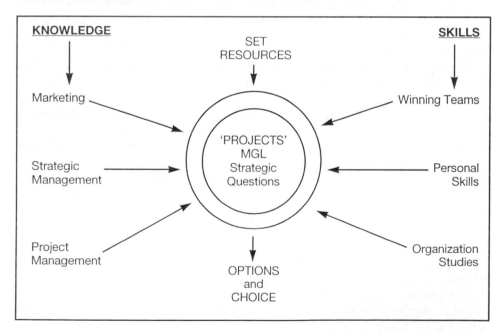

Figure 25.4   The MGL strategic thinking and planning programme

worthwhile vehicle for improving company profitability.

TO BE AWARE OF EXTERNAL DEVELOPMENTS

All organizations must display a sensitivity to their external environment. Inward-looking organizations can perish if they are not alert to new developments and market opportunities. History is littered with examples of organizations or industrial sectors who paid the ultimate price for being unaware of the market, new developments and customer needs. (The British motor-cycle industry in the 1960s and the American automobile industry in the 1970s ignored the Japanese threat and suffered accordingly.)

The same lessons need to be learned for the management development function. In recent years in the UK there has been a plethora of developments. Initiatives usually referred to by acronyms have mushroomed regularly: Accreditation of Prior Learning (APL); National Vocational Qualifications (NVQ); Business Growth Training (BGT); Investors in People (IPP); Management Charter Initiative (MCI); all have helped raise the profile of training and development and, more importantly, sometimes provided funding for new initiatives.

In the management education world there have been significant developments and currently the consumer is spoilt for choice. Qualification programmes abound, each with different methods of study. In the case of the MBA degree which experienced great popularity and expansion in the UK in the late 1980s, the route may vary from full-time to part-time, diploma to MBA enhancement. Methods of study vary from traditional lectures to distance learning to action learning to self-development packages. A role for the management development specialist is to be aware of these developments and tailor them to individual and organizational needs. This is one area where line management usually welcomes advice and direction.

TO DESIGN AND DELIVER A PORTFOLIO OF DEVELOPMENT OPPORTUNITIES

We have moved on from the notion that development only takes place when someone goes on a course. There is no doubt that a well-designed and -delivered management development course can be enormously stimulating and beneficial to participants, but there are a host of other opportunities. These include distance learning, job share, swap or rotation, self-development packages, self-development groups, community service, secondment and exchange.

Some of these opportunities do not necessarily have to be directly connected with work. Much of what we do in our leisure time is a learning opportunity. Membership of a local club, sports club or voluntary organization, especially if one takes a leadership or executive role, offers the opportunity to learn and apply sound management principles. Organizations should encourage their employees to develop such activities (provided it does

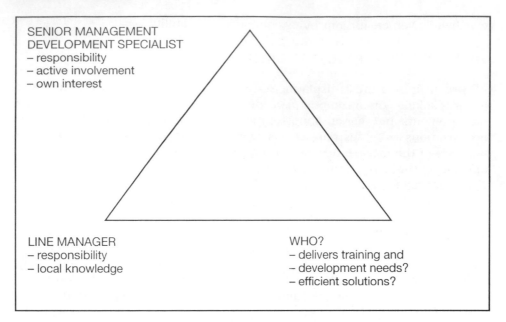

SENIOR MANAGEMENT
DEVELOPMENT SPECIALIST
– responsibility
– active involvement
– own interest

LINE MANAGER
– responsibility
– local knowledge

WHO?
– delivers training and
– development needs?
– efficient solutions?

Figure 25.5   Management development dilemma

not interfere with their work duties!) and support them where appropriate.

The key point with many of these opportunities is that they have to be appropriate to the individual concerned and they need to be processed and evaluated by both the individual and the organization. Alan Mumford (1993) lists many development learning opportunities and how they can give added value to the individual and the organization. Crucial to their value is how these opportunities are processed. The key on many occasions is the sharing of experience. Often this does not happen and valuable lessons are lost.

TO DEVELOP SELF AND THE STATUS OF MANAGEMENT DEVELOPMENT

As outlined earlier, for reasons of history and position in the organization hierarchy, management development, and therefore the position of the developer, has lacked status. As a result management development specialists, whilst dedicating much of their time to facilitating the learning and development of others, often at great expense to the company, neglect their own needs. In the role of nurturing parents they take a vicarious satisfaction in the achievement of others. They need to take more for themselves. Development of the developer is as important as developing others.

How can this be brought about? It is my belief that the solution lies in a continuation of internal and external resourcing. Internally, the case needs to be made for time off, cash, etc., in much the same way as it is made for line management. But how can objectivity be brought to bear on the situation, especially in the case of the most senior management development professional in the organization? The dilemma is shown by the use of the training triangle that was shown in Figure 25.3.

In this situation, who takes the counselling and enabling role to define the training and development needs and provide efficient solutions? For a junior trainer it may be a peer or senior member of the human resources function, but in the case of the senior person, who fulfils this role?

One solution would be the formation of a self-development group, a network of management development specialists. Such a group formed 'Club Management Development', which I directed on behalf of the International Management Centres. The latter was a forum for those people engaged in management development where the profession could share, compare and advise one another on the challenges and issues they faced. The Club met bi-monthly at the premises of its members but informal networking was encouraged. It offered the following benefits to members.

1. The opportunity to belong to a support group of like-minded individuals and to keep up-to-date with developments elsewhere.
2. The opportunity to keep abreast of leading-edge developments in other organizations and take from them what was appropriate to one's own organization.
3. The opportunity to receive feedback and critique on work and developments in one's own organization so that each member could become even more professional in their work.
4. For those who wanted, the opportunity to submit for a qualification such as M.Phil. by Explication and Portfolio, the portfolio relating to members' own experience, publications and achievements.
5. The opportunity to publish work in journals or other publications. Here the support and critique of members was vital before publication.
6. Links with the Club CEOs (Chief Executive Officers) at their annual conference to improve the dialogue and understanding with top decision-makers, whilst at the same time furthering the course and improving the profile of management development.

    A reciprocal invitation to Club MD's Annual Conference was extended to CEOs to improve the CEOs' understanding of the management development function.
7. A forum to address the needs of individual members and their companies as they arose. It also in some cases offered the solution to the problem posed earlier (see Figure 25.5) in that the support group of respected peers sometimes helped provide tailored solutions to training needs.

Empowering the management development specialist to develop themselves can only benefit the organization and its employees. How can developers preach empowerment and development if they do not practise what they preach?

TO DEVELOP CONSULTANCY AND INTERVENTIONIST SKILLS

One advantage of being in a support role to the organization is that one can often apply an external perspective by not being too close to the situation. Distance lends itself to objectivity. Developing consultancy skills is a key area for management development specialists, but also important is knowing when to bring in external consultants. For numerous reasons it may not be appropriate to resource the situation internally, and external resources must be used. Selection, briefing and managing external consultants are skills that need to be developed.

The guiding principle on interventionist tactics is 'appropriateness'. When to intervene, what type of intervention to make and whom to involve are decisions that are crucial and are skills that can only be developed with experience.

Whatever resource is used, the ultimate responsibility for development rests with the individual and his or her line manager. It was stated earlier that the developer's task is to 'empower people to learn from acting and to act on the basis of learning'. A key role for the management development specialist is to empower line managers to take responsibility for themselves and their subordinates, and to encourage an organization climate in which this is so. Facilitating the development of the line manager as a developer is crucial.

A good example in which organizations have fostered self-development groups is the use of Action Learning Sets. Action learning was developed by Revans and deals with the reality of the work situation. Managers with real-life problems work in sets, support and learn from each other and take responsibility for ensuring implementation and therefore a return on investment. It aims to develop the questioning abilities of all levels of staff so that action to overcome problems can be identified and the solutions implemented. The solutions need to be consistent with the vision of senior management, and for real success that vision must contain commitment from the top to make the best use of those in the organization to implement the solutions.

Action Learning Sets may be organized using internal staff or external consultants. The management developer can action any role the set deems appropriate. Once the process is launched in a sizeable organization it can be self-sustaining if line managers are prepared to act as set advisers for groups of their subordinates or peers. It is essentially about applying skills of analysis and logic to problems, sharing skills and then meeting peer expectations. Learning occurs through taking action and also from group processes. Based on the equation:

$$L = P + Q \text{ where}$$
$$P = \text{Programmed knowledge and}$$
$$Q = \text{Ability to ask probing questions}$$

the set can ask for any input of 'P' relevant to its particular situation.

Increasingly, in recent years, Action Learning Sets have addressed issues of a strategic or cross-functional nature.

Key decisions therefore, for the management development specialist, are to identify when Action Learning Sets are appropriate, decide whether to act as a facilitator, whether to use external facilitation, or whether to develop facilitation skills in line managers. My own view is that the long-term goal is to develop facilitation or set adviser skills among line management, but selection of the right individuals is crucial. Such a process is developmental, individually and organizationally, and it involves greater numbers of managers addressing problems or issues related to their own reality in the organization.

CONCLUSION

Management development has enjoyed an increasingly high profile in the last decade. Increasing realization that learning is a life-long process and that people are the key resource of the organization have contributed, and awareness has been translated into commitment with greater financial investment. The economic boom of the late 1980s in the UK helped ensure increased financial resources, but in the leaner times of the 1990s management development will have to fight hard to maintain its share of the cake, let alone increase it. That is both a challenge and an opportunity, and it is vital that the head of steam that has been generated is not allowed to dissipate. Furthermore management development must not be allowed to suffer from 'stop-go' activity linked to the economic cycle. Even during recessionary times companies must be encouraged to train and develop, to think beyond the present in order to gain competitive advantage for when good times follow.

Like Martin Luther King, I too have a dream. It is that one day:

1. Training and development will no longer be the poor cousin of the organization, and that investment in people will be seen as the most important investment that can be made.
2. People will take more and more responsibility for their own development and will view, if not demand, training and development opportunities as an important part of their employment package.

    A key role in this vision will be played by line management supported in the appropriate way by training and development specialists. Top management, aware of the importance of development, will see it as a major vehicle in the achievement of corporate objectives, and therefore training and development plans will be closely integrated with business plans. Such commitment from top to bottom of the organization will be a good start in the creation of a learning organization which will be a reality and not just a vague concept.
3. Management development specialists will become acutely aware of the relationship between development and profit. They must strive to prove to key decision-makers that training and development achieves tangible bottom-line results. In the recessionary times of the 1990s this is a

401

challenge worldwide. I firmly believe that it is possible to integrate sound humanistic principles with the financial pragmatism demanded by the economic climate of the 1990s.

As the pace of change accelerates, the tasks people do, the way they do them and their importance to the business will all change rapidly. People must adapt accordingly. They will need to empower themselves to adapt and change. Continuous retraining, updating and development will be the order of the day to cope with change both within and between organizations. The empowerment process is crucial and yet another powerful argument for making training and development adopt a learner-centred approach rather than a teacher-centred approach. In the final analysis, responsibility for learning and associated behavioural change must rest with the individual and with the organization facilitating the process and acting as an enabler. The management development specialist should be the most important enabler in this analysis.

REFERENCES

Argyris, C. (1985) *Strategy, Change and Defensive Routines* (London: Pitman).

Constable, J. and McCormick, R. (1987) *The Making of British Managers* (London: BIM with CBI).

Coopers and Lybrand Associates (1985) *Challenge to Complacency* (London: MSC).

Delahanty, F. and Gemill, G. (1982) 'The Black Hole in Group Development'. Presented to the Academy of Management Meetings, New York 1982.

Drucker, P. (1982) *The Adventures of a Bystander* (London: Heinemann).

Garratt, B. (1987) *The Learning Organisation* (London: Fontana/Collins).

Handy, C. (1990) *Inside Organisations* (London: BBC Publications).

Handy, C. *et al.* (1987) *The Making of Managers: A Report on Management Education, Training and Development in USA, W. Germany, France, Japan and UK* (London: NEDO, MSC and BIM).

Hofstede, G. (1980) 'Motivation, Leadership and Organisation: Do American Theories Apply Abroad?' *Organisational Dynamics* (Summer), pp. 42–63.

Margerison, C. J. (1991) *Making Management Development Work: Achieving Success in the Nineties* (Maidenhead: McGraw-Hill).

Megginson, D. and Pedler, M. (1991) *Developing the Developers* (London: AMED).

Megginson, D. and Pedler, M. (1992) *Self-Development: A Facilitator's Guide* (Maidenhead: McGraw-Hill).

Mintzberg, H. (1983) *Structure in Fives: Designing Effective Organisations* (Englewood Cliffs, N.J.: Prentice-Hall).

Morgan, G. (1986) *Images of Organisation* (Beverley Hills, Calif.: Sage Publications).

Mumford, A. C. (1993) *Management Development: Strategies for Action*, 2nd edn (London: IPM).

Pedler, M., Boydell, T., and Burgoyne, J. (1989) 'Towards the Learning Company', *Management Education and Development*, 20(1) (Spring).

Peters, T. J. and Waterman, R. H. (1982) *In Search of Excellence: Lessons from America's Best Run Companies* (London: Harper & Row).

Pont, A. T. M. (1991) *Developing Effective Training Skills*, 2nd edn (Maidenhead: McGraw Hill).

Revans, R. (1982) *The Origins and Growth of Action Learning* (Bromley: Chartwell-Bratt).

26 Team-building*

Bill Critchley and David Casey

It all started during one of those midnight conversations between consultants in a residential workshop. We were running a team-building session with a top management group and something very odd began to appear. Our disturbing (but also exciting) discovery was that for most of their time this group of people had absolutely no need to work as a team; indeed, the attempt to do so was causing more puzzlement and scepticism than motivation and commitment. In our midnight reflections we were honest enough to confess to each other that this was not the first time our team-building efforts had cast doubts on the very validity of teamwork itself, within our client groups.

We admitted that we had both been working from some implicit assumptions that good teamwork is a characteristic of healthy, effectively functioning organizations. Now we started to question those assumptions. First, we flushed out what our assumptions actually were. In essence it came down to something like the following.

We had been assuming that the top group in any organization (be it the board of directors or the local authority management committee or whatever the top group is called) *should be a team* and ought to *work as a team*. Teamwork at the top is crucial to organizational success, we assumed. We further assumed that a properly functioning team is one in which:

- People care for each other
- People are open and truthful
- There is a high level of trust
- Decisions are made by consensus
- There is strong team commitment
- Conflict is faced up to and worked through

 * First published in *Management Education and Development*, 15 (2) 1984.

- People really listen to ideas and to feelings
- Feelings are expressed freely
- Process issues (task and feelings) are dealt with.

Finally, it had always seemed logical to us that a team-building catalyst could always help any team to function better – and so help any organization perform better as an organization; better functioning would lead the organization to achieve its purposes more effectively.

The harsh reality we now came up against was at odds with this cosy view of teams, teamwork and team-building. In truth, the director of education has little need to work in harness with his fellow chief officers in a county council; he or she might need the support of the chief executive and the chair of the elected members' education committee, but the other chief officers in that local authority have neither the expertise nor the interest, nor indeed the time, to contribute to what is essentially very specialized work.

Even in industry, whilst it is clear that the marketing and production directors of a company must work closely together to ensure that the production schedule is synchronized with sales forecasts, and the finance director needs to be involved – to look at the cash flow implications of varying stock levels – they do not need to involve the *whole* team; and they certainly do not need to develop high levels of trust and openness to work through those kinds of business issues.

On the other hand, most people would agree that *strategic* decisions, concerned with the future direction of the whole enterprise, should involve all those at the top; strategy should demand an input from every member of the top group, and for strategic discussion and strategic decision-making, teamwork at the top is essential. But how much time do most top management groups actually spend discussing strategy? Our experiences, in a wide variety of organizations, suggest that 10 per cent is a high figure for most organizations – often 5 per cent would be nearer the mark. This means that 90–95 per cent of decisions in organizations are essentially operational – that is, decisions made within departments based usually on a fair amount of information and expertise. In those conditions, high levels of trust and openness may be nice, but are not necessary; consensus is strictly not an issue and in any case would take up far too much time. There is therefore no need for high levels of interpersonal skills.

Why, then, is so much time and money invested in team-building, we asked ourselves? At this stage in our discussions we began to face a rather disturbing possibility. Perhaps the spread of team-building has more to do with team-builders and *their* needs and values, rather than a careful analysis of what is appropriate and necessary for the organization. To test out this alarming hypothesis we each wrote down an honest and frank list of reasons why we ourselves engaged in team-building. We recommend this as an enlightening activity for other team-builders – perhaps, like us, they will arrive at this kind of conclusion: team-builders work as catalysts to help management groups function better as open teams for a variety of reasons, including the following: *405*

1. They like it – enjoy the risks.
2. Because they are good at it.
3. It is flattering to be asked.
4. They receive rewarding personal feedback.
5. Professional kudos – not many people do team-building with top teams.
6. There is money in it.
7. It accords with their values: for instance, democracy is preferred to autocracy.
8. They gain power; process interventions are powerful in business settings whereas the client is on home ground and can bamboozle the consultant in business discussions.

All these reasons are concerned with the needs, skills and values of the *team-builder* rather than the management group being 'helped'. This could explain why many team-building exercises leave the so-called 'management team' excited and stimulated by the experience, only to find they are spending an unnecessary amount of time together discussing other people's departmental issues. Later on, because they cannot see the benefit of working together on such issues, they abandon 'teamwork' altogether. Such a management group has been accidentally led to disillusionment with the whole idea of teamwork and the value of team-building.

We began to see, as our discussions went on through the small hours, that there is a very *large* proportion of most managers' work where teamwork is not needed (and to attempt to inculcate teamwork is dysfunctional). There is, at the same time, a very *small* proportion of their work where teamwork is absolutely vital (and to ignore team-working skills is to invite disaster). This latter work, which demands a team approach, is typified by strategic work but not limited to strategic work. It is any work characterized by a high level of *choice* and by the condition of *maximum uncertainty.*

Most people find choice and uncertainty uncomfortable. Many senior managers attempt to deny the choice element by the employment of complex models and techniques. We do not think most people's management experience teaches them to make choices about the future, for instance – it puts the main emphasis on establishing as many facts as possible and reviewing options in the light of past experience. That is why models like, for example, the Boston portfolio model and the General Electric matrix are so popular; they provide comforting analytic frameworks for looking at strategic options, but they are appealing really to our operational mentality. The hope often is that they will somehow come up with a solution to the strategic question; but of course they cannot make choices for people and they do not throw any light on the future.

The top team of an organization, if it is to achieve quality and commitment in its decisions about future directions, will need to pool the full extent of each individual's wisdom and experience. That means something quite different from reacting to a problem in terms of their own functional knowledge and experience; it means exposing fully their *uncertainties,* taking *unaccustomed risks* by airing their own subjective view of the world and struggling to build some *common perceptions and possibilities.* This is where that much abused word 'sharing' really comes into its own. In this context, it is not merely a value-laden exhortation, it is vital to the future of the organization. Ideas and opinions are all we have to inform our view of the future, but if we are to take a risk with a fragile idea or opinion, unsubstantiated by facts, we will take it only if the climate is right. Conversely, if we take the risk and the sheer airiness and vulnerability of the idea attracts a volley of ridicule and abuse, then it will die quickly and be lost forever.

Most functional executives, brought up in the turbulence of politics and interfunctional warfare, find the transition from functional to strategic mode very difficult to make; they do not always see the difference – and if they do, they are reluctant to leave their mountain-top, the summit of knowledge, experience and hence power, for the equality and shared uncertainty of strategic decision-making. And yet this is one area where real teamwork is not only necessary but vital.

We had by now got ourselves thoroughly confused. We seemed to be forcing team-building on groups which had no need to be a team and missing the one area where teamwork is essential – because choice and uncertainty were at a maximum and for this very reason managers were shying away from the work – work which can be done only by a team. We resorted to diagrams to help clear our minds, and these new diagrams form the basis of the next section of this chapter.

THEORETICAL CONSIDERATIONS CONCERNING MANAGEMENT GROUPS

We found these kinds of discussion taking us farther and farther away from team-building and closer and closer to an understanding of why management groups work (or do not work) in the ways they do. In the end, we developed two basic diagrams, showing the relationships between a number of variables which operate in management groups:

1. The degree of *uncertainty* in the management task.
2. The need for *sharing* in the groups.
3. *Modes* of working.
4. Different kinds of *internal group process.*
5. Different levels of *interpersonal skills.*
6. The role of the *leader.*

We would now like to present these two framework diagrams as diagnostic tools, which general management groups have found very useful in coming to terms with how they work, and why. These simple diagrams are helping groups see *what kind of groups they are*, and when (and if) they want to be a team, rather than jumping to the conclusion that all groups need team-building.

Throughout the discussion, we will be talking about the management group   *407*

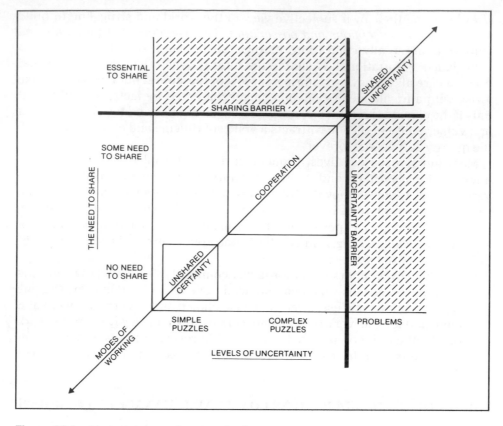

Figure 26.1 Uncertainty and group sharing

– that is, the leader plus those immediately responsible to him or her, perhaps five to ten people in all, at the top of their organization or their part of the organization. The first diagram (Figure 26.1) shows the relationship between the level of uncertainty inherent in any group task and the need for members of that group to share with each other. Expressed simply: 'The more uncertainty – the more need to share'. Everyday examples of this truism are children holding hands for comfort in the dark or NASA research scientists brainstorming for fresh ideas on the frontiers of man's knowledge: any uncertainty – emotional, physical or intellectual – can best be coped with by sharing.

However, the converse is also true – where there is less uncertainty, there is less need to share. The same children will feel no need to hold hands round the breakfast table where all is secure; the NASA scientists during the final launch will each get on with their own well-rehearsed part of the launch programme in relative isolation from each other. Only if something goes wrong (uncertainty floods back) will they need to share, quickly and fully. It took us a long time to realize the full significance of this in terms of the need to share in

a management group.

We are dealing here only with the top group of the organization where *task* is the dominant imperative; there are other situations in which other objectives demand sharing – for instance, if one is dealing with the whole fabric of a complete organization and attempting a global shift in attitudes, then *culture-building* may become the dominant imperative and sharing at all levels in that organization may become necessary. But that is a different situation – we are looking here at the top management group where task must be the dominant imperative.

In Figure 26.1 we have used Revans' powerful distinction between problems (no answer is known to exist) and puzzles (the answer exists somewhere – just find it) to describe different levels of uncertainty (see also Chapter 14 above): deciding about capital punishment is a problem for society; tracking down a murderer is a puzzle for the police.

Work-groups dealing with genuine problems (of which strategy is only one example) would be well advised to share as much as possible with each other. They should share feelings to gain support, as well as ideas to penetrate the unknown. Figure 26.1 shows two shaded areas. These shaded areas must be avoided. The shaded area on the right indicates the futility of tackling real problems unless people are prepared to share; the shaded area at the top indicates that there is no point in sharing to solve mere puzzles.

Two 'barriers' appear on our model; they indicate that a positive effort must be made if a breakthrough to a new level of working is to be accomplished. For instance, the uncertainty barrier represents a step into the unknown – a deliberate attempt to work in areas of ambiguity, uncertainty and ambivalence. To avoid the shaded areas and arrive in the top right-hand corner, the group must break through *both* barriers at the *same* time. This is the *only* way to solve genuine problems. Most management groups stay behind both barriers in Figure 26.1 and handle work which is in the nature of a puzzle – and to achieve this they *cooperate,* rather than share, with each other. As long as they continue to limit their work to solving puzzles, they are quite right to stay within the sharing and uncertainty barriers of Figure 26.1.

As team-builders, we now see that we must spend time identifying in which *modes of working* any management group operates. The three modes of working come out in Figure 26.1 as the diagonal, and we would like to describe each mode, by working up the diagonal of Figure 26.1 from left to right.

Mode of unshared certainty

The proper mode for simple puzzles of a technical nature in everyday work, where every member of the group is *relatively competent within his or her field* and speaks from the authority of his or her specialism: ideal when the work issues are independent of each other – as they often are. A healthy attitude is: 'I will pull my weight and see that my part is done well.' Attitudes can become unhealthy if they move towards 'my interests must come first'.

Mode of cooperation

The appropriate mode for complex puzzles which impinge on the work of several members of the management group. In this mode (very common in local authorities) group members recognize the need for give-and-take, cooperation, negotiation and passing of information on a need-to-know basis. The attitude is: 'I'll cooperate for the good of the whole and because other members of this group have their rights and problems too.' Sharing is restricted to *what is necessary* and each group member still works from the security (certainty) of his or her own professional base, recognizing the professional bases of his or her colleagues.

Mode of shared uncertainty

A rare mode; partly because it is appropriate only for genuine problems (such as strategy) where *nobody knows what to do*, uncertainty is rife and full sharing between members is the only way out; partly because, even when it is the appropriate mode, many management groups never reach these professional heights. The attitude of members has to be: 'The good of the whole outweighs any one member's interest – including mine. I carry an equal responsibility with my colleagues for the whole, and for this particular work I am not able to rely on my specialism, because my functional expertise is, for this problem we all face, irrelevant.'

Clearly, this top mode of 'shared uncertainty' is extremely demanding, and it is not surprising that many management groups try hard to avoid it. We know several boards of directors, and even more local authority management 'teams', who have devised a brilliant trick to avoid handling genuine problems requiring genuine sharing in the top mode. Quite simply – they turn all *strategic* problems into *operational* puzzles! How? There are very many variations of this trick available; for example:

- Appoint a working party
- Ask a consultant to recommend
- Recruit a corporate planner
- Set up a think-tank; etc.

To make sure the trick works, the terms of reference are: 'Your recommendation must be short and must ask us to decide between option *A* or option *B*.' Choosing between *A* and *B* is an operational puzzle they *can* solve and it leaves them with the comfortable illusion that they have actually been engaging in strategic problem-resolution work, whereas the truth is they have avoided uncertainty, avoided sharing their fears and ideas, avoided their real work, by converting frightening problems into management puzzles. And who can blame them! We do not feel we have the right to censure top groups for not working in the top mode of shared uncertainty. We do feel we have the obligation to analyse quite rigorously how top groups actually work, before we plunge in with our team-building help.

In Figure 26.1, the size of the box for each mode indicates very roughly how frequently each mode might be needed by most management groups. Sadly, we see many management groups working in modes which are inappropriate to the work being done; it is not just that many top groups fail to push through to the top mode; many management groups get stuck in the bottom box quite a lot of the time, when they should be working in the middle mode. On the other hand, other groups go through a pantomime of sitting round a table trying to work in the middle mode, but in truth feeling bored and uninterested because the middle mode is inappropriate and each member of the group could carry on separately with his or her own work, without pretending to share it with colleagues, who do not need to know anyway. In other words, their appropriate mode is unshared certainty, and attempts at sharing are boring or frustrating facades.

Our diagram shows an arrow on both ends of the diagonal, to illustrate that all three modes of working are necessary at different times, and effective work-groups can (and should) slide up and down the diagonal. We do not see any management group working in one mode all the time – the really effective group is able to move from mode to mode as the *task* requires. Although it may think of itself as a management 'team', a top group will be truly functioning as a *team* only when it is operating in the *top mode*.

We use the word 'team' here in the sense used in the first part of this chapter, which we believe is the sense used by most team-builders in team-building work. Because we now believe that working in the top mode of shared uncertainty is called for infrequently – by the nature of the work – and is actually practised even less frequently, we now doubt the value of team-building work with most management groups, when there is so much more urgent work to be done with these groups. We found in Figure 26.1 that when we plotted the level of uncertainty in the work against the need to share, we discovered three modes of working, on the diagonal of the diagram. These three modes of working were:

1. Unshared certainty.
2. Cooperation.
3. Shared uncertainty.

We now want to go on to answer the question: 'How does a management group work in each of these modes? What *processes* are needed, what *skills* are required, and how does the *leader* function?'

The format of Figure 26.2 is the same as Figure 26.1; only the variables are different. The vertical axis of Figure 26.2 is the diagonal lifted from Figure 26.1 (modes), and two new variables are introduced – *processes* on the horizontal axis, while *interpersonal skills* become the new diagonal.

Processes

To start with the horizontal axis – processes. We distinguish three levels of process in any group. At the most perfunctory there are *polite social processes*, very important to sustain the social lubrication of a healthy group, but not focused on the work itself. The work is accomplished largely via *task processes* – the way work is organized, distributed, ideas generated and shared, decisions made, and so forth. The third level of process concerns people's feelings (*feelings processes*) and how these are handled by themselves and by others.

Reference to Figure 26.2 will make it clear that as the mode of working becomes more difficult, ascending the vertical axis, from unshared certainty towards shared uncertainty, so the processes needed to accomplish this more difficult work also become more difficult, as the group moves along the horizontal axis from simple basic social processes, through task processes, towards the much more difficult processes of working with people's deeper feelings.

Many groups never reach the top mode of shared uncertainty, where people's feelings are actually *part of the work* and all is uncertainty, excitement and trust.

The shaded areas are to be avoided (as in Figure 26.1). The right-hand shaded area indicates that it is absurd to indulge in work with people's feelings if the group is working only in the two lower modes of unshared certainty and cooperation – to engage in soul-searching to accomplish this kind of work is ridiculous and brings team-building into disrepute; the top shaded area indicates similarly that there is no need to share deeply when only the two lower levels of processes (basic social processes and task processes) are operating.

However, a management group faced with the need to tackle uncertainty can either 'funk' the whole thing, by staying safely behind the barriers (which is what most management groups appear to do), or it can have the courage to break through both barriers simultaneously, arriving (breathlessly) in the top righthand corner, where the mode of working is shared uncertainty and the necessary processes are task *and* feelings processes together. Those few management groups which accomplish this become *teams*.

Interpersonal skills

The final variable is the diagonal of Figure 26.2, *interpersonal skills*, and, clearly, there is an ascending order of skill from the lowest (but *not* least important) level of polite social skills to the highest possible level of interpersonal skills required in the rarified atmosphere of highest uncertainty and real teamwork. But, for the middle mode, a solid raft of straightforward interpersonal skills is needed by all managers – empathy, cooperation, communication, listening, negotiating, and many more. We have come to believe that here is the greatest area of need.

412

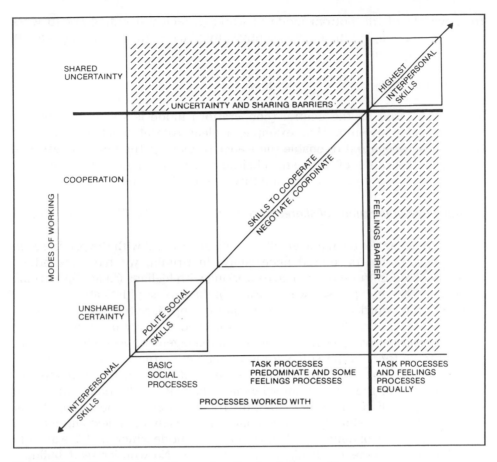

Figure 26.2 Modes of working and methods of cooperation

The leader's role

The group leader and group leadership have not been mentioned so far, in an attempt to keep things simple. The whole question of 'leadership' is fundamental to the operation of all management groups, and we would like to make some observations now.

Leader's role in the mode of unshared certainty

The leader is hardly needed at all in the unshared certainty mode and, indeed, the social lubrication process of a group working in this mode may well be carried out much better by an informal leader – there is nothing so embarrassing as the formal group leader bravely trying to lead the group through its Christmas lunch in the canteen! Some local authority chief executives (so-called) suffer an even worse fate – they cannot find a role at all, because the members of their management team (so-called) steadfastly refuse *413* to move out of the bottom mode of working, tacitly deciding *not* to work together and denying the chief executive any place in the organization at all! This is not uncommon.

Leader's role in the mode of cooperation

The leader's role in the central (cooperation) mode is well-established in management convention. For example, a clear role at meetings has been universally recognized to enable the leader to manage the task processes in particular; this role is of course the chairperson. Coordination of the task is at its core, and most group leaders find this role relatively clear.

Leader's role in the mode of shared uncertainty

No such role has yet been universally recognized to deal with the processes in the highest mode, of shared uncertainty. In Britain, we have the added difficulty of our cultural resistance to working with feelings (in action learning language, 'No sets please, we're British'). In this sophisticated mode of working, the word 'catalyst' seems more appropriate than the word 'chairperson', and often a team-builder is invited to carry out this role. But where does this leave the group leader? All management group leaders have learned to be the chairperson, very few have yet learned to be the catalyst. And in any case, to be the catalyst and the leader at the same time is to attempt the north face of the Eiger of interpersonal skills. It can be done, but not in carpet slippers. If, on the other hand, the role of catalyst is performed by an outsider, the leadership dynamic becomes immensely complex, and adds a significant overlay of difficulty when working in a mode which we have already shown to be extremely difficult in the first place. No wonder team-building often fails.

CONCLUSIONS

Many team-builders are unaware of the shaded 'no-go' areas and dreamily assume that any progress towards open attitudes, free expression of feelings and genuine sharing in any management group is beneficial. This is not so – to be of benefit there needs to be a very delicate and deliberate balance between what *work* the group has decided to pursue (what level of *uncertainty*), and the degree of sharing and expression of feelings the group is prepared for, to accomplish that work. Only if the balance is right will the management group be able to aim accurately at the top righthand corner of Figures 26.1 and 26.2 and succeed in breaking through all the barriers at the same time to experience *real teamwork*. Attempts to push through only *one* barrier (trying to handle uncertainty without sharing; sharing for the sake of sharing; being open for the sake of being open) will fail, and in failing will probably make things worse for that management group.

Strategic planners are often guilty of pushing management groups towards handling uncertainty without the concomitant abilities to share and work with feelings. Team-builders are often guilty of the converse sin – pushing management groups to be open and share their feelings, when the group has no intention whatever of getting into work where the level of uncertainty is high. Neither will succeed. It is no coincidence that both strategic planning and team-building can fall quickly into disrepute; it may be too late to save strategic planning from the management scrapheap – it is not too late to save team-building.

FURTHER READING

Adair, John (1986) *Effective Teambuilding* (Aldershot: Gower).

Belbin, R. M. (1981) *Management Teams: Why they Succeed or Fail* (London: Heinemann).

Hastings, C., Bixby, P. and Chaudhry-Lawton, R. (1986) *The Superteam Solution* (Aldershot: Gower).

Woodcock, M. (1989) *Team Development Manual*, 2nd edn (Aldershot: Gower).

27 Evaluation

Peter Bramley

The idea of the training department as a passive provider of a menu of courses appears to be giving way to the concept of training as a *management function* which contributes to the growth and development of the organization. As a result, the role of the training manager is changing and the skills of *boundary management* (e.g. acquiring resources, building relationships and coordinating activities with other functions) are becoming even more crucial to the survival of training departments as the latter become more exposed.

There is a growing trend for all institutions, political, educational or even medical, to be required to provide evidence of their effectiveness. With training departments this evidence has usually been provided by established reputation – of the trainers, the training manager, and repeat business – and not by indices of changed participant behaviour or of increases in organizational effectiveness. When it becomes necessary to compete for resources, established reputations do not offer such a strong case as evaluated contributions to effectiveness.

Evaluation can provide this sort of information and thus be used to build up a sound track record. The act of following up training and developmental activities also helps to improve relationships with line managers, and these can become crucial to the decision of whether to expand or cut the training department. There are also obvious benefits for the trainers in that the information collected provides a more accurate appreciation of the training need as well as indicating strengths and weaknesses of various parts of the programme and any problems in transferring back to the workplace.

Why is it, then, that so few training departments evaluate their work? It is certainly difficult and time-consuming to do so, but that is probably not the main problem. My opinion is that the philosophy of evaluation requires a reappraisal of what the purpose of training is; a change from conceptualizing it as meeting training needs to thinking of it as an attempt to improve organizational effectiveness. This chapter is based upon that philosophy.

EVALUATING THE TRAINING PROCESS

The process by which training is delivered and the model on which this is based can be evaluated against examples of good practice. Some models assume that useful learning takes place as a result of interaction with others. Some are based on the principle that, as job performance is judged by the assessment of skills, the function of training should be to improve these. Other models focus on improved effectiveness in the job context. It is surely worth considering whether the model on which a training activity is based is consistent with the purpose, but my experience is that this is not often done.

Individual training models

Training of individuals has its origin in craft apprenticeships where a young person learned, over a period of some years, to imitate the skills of his master. Technical training has been greatly influenced by this tradition of teaching skills to individuals in the belief that they will later find a use for them (Figure 27.1).

The focus is on individuals, and the process is one of encouraging them to learn something said to be useful and then expecting them to find uses for the learning. In attempting to evaluate training based on this model, it is sometimes very difficult to identify changes in work performance. With many forms of technical training, where the equipment used in training is very similar to that in the workplace, the changes in skills levels achieved during training will usually transfer quite easily into the job (provided there is an opportunity to practise them there). The model is, however, being used for other forms of training. With most supervisory and management training, the work situation does not closely resemble that simulated in the training, and the changes achieved in the training programme often do not result in changes in work performance. The latter will often mean changing the ways in which things are done within the organization, and the model shown (Figure 27.1) is inappropriate for that purpose.

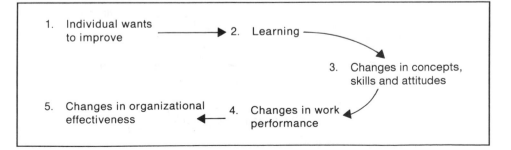

Figure 27.1   Individual training model

As Katz and Kahn (1978) point out, attempts to change parts of organizations by using models like this have a 'long history of theoretical inadequacy and practical failure'. The logic of the approach is that, as organizations are made up of individuals, it must be possible to change the organization by changing the members. This is, however, a great simplification of organizational reality. An organization will have objectives, priorities and policies. It will also have a structure and accepted ways of doing things. All of these situational factors will have some effect on shaping the behaviour of members of the organization within their work. Often the 'changed' individual is not able to change these situational factors.

It is worthwhile investigating this further as it is crucial to an understanding of why training sometimes fails to have any effect. The work context can be represented as an interaction between the situation and the people in it. If this interaction is not as effective as it might be, then changing the people by training might be considered as a way of improving things. However, this will only be successful if the people are sufficiently autonomous to change the interaction and thus the work situation. This might be true where people are trained to use a piece of equipment like a keyboard or a lathe, but there is no reason to assume that it is the case with a supervisory problem. Other things affect the situation, and they may have more influence over the way in which the work is done than the skills of the supervisor (see Figure 27.1).

Such matters as the *structure* of the organization (who reports to whom, how many levels and whether people can communicate horizontally), the *culture* (in what spirit people relate to each other, to what extent individuality is valued), the *design of the work* (the extent to which this is frustrating or stress-inducing), and whether good performance is actually *rewarded* (by recognition, praise, and promotion, as well as financially) will all affect the job situation. It will often be necessary to change some of these as well as to train

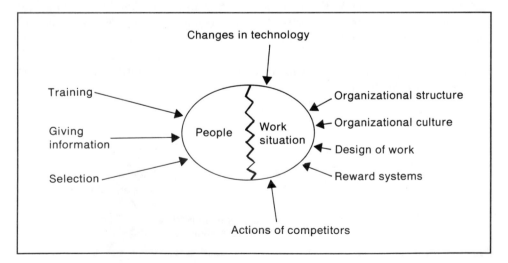

Figure 27.2   Changing the way the work is done

the people, as their effect on the interaction may be more powerful than the ability of the individuals to innovate in the job (Figure 27.2).

Increased effectiveness model

We can see that changing the performance of people in the job is rather more complicated than Figure 27.1 would suggest. In order to think this through we need to consider a model which is based on changing effectiveness rather than on educating individuals. A possible model is offered in Figure 27.3. The process starts in a part of the organization with a decision about what level of effectiveness is desirable. The second stage is to define criteria by which changes towards the more desirable state can be measured (i.e. 'How will we know if we are getting there?'). In defining the resources necessary (Stage 3 of the model), aspects of the job situation other than the skills of the people will be considered, and it may be that changing some of these will achieve the desired improvements without training. If training or development activities are thought to be necessary they are organized, and the extent to which any learning is useful will be monitored by changes in *job performance* not, as is usually the case with the model in Figure 27.1, by changes measured during training. This model is much more appropriate for the kind of work where people have some discretion about what they do or the ability to negotiate priorities.

Training as organizational change

A rather different cycle is suggested by considering training as a way of enhancing organizational effectiveness. The process starts with an analysis of the existing situation as suggested in Figure 27.3. The needs identified will be phrased in terms of new work practices which will enhance the effectiveness of the particular part of the organization. The senior management of that part of the organization must be involved at all stages and be committed to

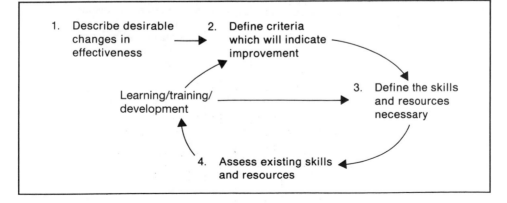

Figure 27.3 Increased effectiveness model

changing organizational structures or practices which conflict with the new practices which are being introduced. In almost every case this will imply that these managers are involved in the design and delivery of the developmental activities, whether on- or off-job. They will also be responsible for encouraging the new behaviours in the workplace by appraising performance and coaching or supervising as necessary to ensure that the learning becomes incorporated in standard work practices.

The model is cyclical and Stage 1 often becomes a Stage 5, 'analyse the changed situation' and so on.

It should be noted that this model is profoundly different to that shown in Figure 27.1. The intention is the same – to change the way that individuals work – but now the new behaviours are embedded in the organizational context. In the earlier model they were encouraged in a training context and it was hoped that individuals would apply them in their work.

Consider these two models as possible ways of changing part of the organizational culture, say, trying to achieve a more participative management style. Would training individual managers and supervisors off-job and returning them to an unsuspecting workplace as suggested by the model in Figure 27.1 be likely to succeed? Would the procedure suggested by Figure 27.4, carried out in the workplace, be more likely to succeed or less? (The evaluation of the process by which training is delivered is more fully discussed in Bramley, 1990.)

EVALUATING CHANGES DUE TO TRAINING

Changes in organizations occur at many levels and take many forms. Consequently, developing criteria by which changes can be evaluated may result in a range of indices. A good place to start is by establishing that learning has taken place at the individual level. This is one of the necessary

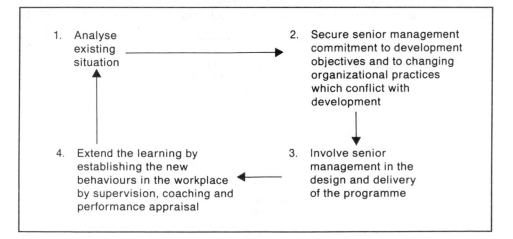

1. Analyse existing situation

2. Secure senior management commitment to development objectives and to changing organizational practices which conflict with development

4. Extend the learning by establishing the new behaviours in the workplace by supervision, coaching and performance appraisal

3. Involve senior management in the design and delivery of the programme

Figure 27.4   Training/development as organizational change

conditions of those strategies of organizational change which focus on people. It cannot be assumed, however, that individual changes will lead to a change in effectiveness, and this will need to be evaluated in its own right.

Changes in levels of knowledge

All jobs require the holder to have some knowledge. What type of knowledge is required? How can this be analysed? It is helpful, in attempting to answer these questions, to have some framework in which to carry out the analysis. One which has proved to be useful is to describe the sort of knowledge required at three levels (this is developed from Bloom, 1956).

1. The basic level is that of *isolated pieces of information* – ability to recall simple lists or state simple rules, knowing a range of simple facts about the job area.
2. A higher level is to be able to arrange a good many of the pieces into *procedures*, how to do things, how to order sets of actions (e.g. starting up a processing plant involves a series of actions which must be done in a certain sequence).
3. Higher still is the knowledge with which to *analyse* any particular situation for its key elements and thus to make a decision about whether procedure 'A' is more likely to be successful than (say) procedure 'D'. This is essentially the skill to be able to select the most appropriate procedure or method of doing something, given the nature of the problem, the organizational context, etc.

This is an hierarchical set and it is not possible to achieve the higher levels without knowledge at the lower levels. The function of training could, therefore, be seen as:

- Analysing what is required at each of the three levels for satisfactory job performance
- Discovering what the trainees know at each level before they attend the training
- Trying to close that gap
- Communicating to the supervisor or manager to what extent they are below satisfactory job performance levels at the end of training.

The three levels of knowledge have quite different implications for the learning process. Isolated pieces of information can be quite easily transferred by lectures to large groups, or by paper-based texts or by programmed packages. All of these methods are relatively inexpensive. Procedures too can be learned fairly cheaply by using checklists and prompts plus, perhaps, some supervised practice.

The implications of the third (analytic) level are quite different. If this is to be achieved the learners will have to practise in realistic situations and make *421* decisions about how to handle them. As this is actually a simulation of some aspects of the job, it will be much more expensive to design and run off-job than the work at the lower levels. It may well be more appropriate to try to develop at this level by on-job tasking, supervising or mentoring.

Knowledge is usually taught in the belief that it is necessary in the job, and evaluation can take the form of following-up to discover if the learning has been useful. A simple questionnaire may well be sufficient for this:

- How useful is knowledge of this for your job?
- Have you used knowledge of this in the last six months?
- Was the reference material given out sufficient?

Such questions should be asked for each of the topics covered on an off-job programme. Following-up by using interviews will improve the quality of the information gathered, but it is an expensive procedure. A more appropriate method for on-job development is the use of learning objectives, learning contracts and action plans.

Attitude change versus behaviour change

When thinking about how training and development activities might be structured in order to increase the likelihood of achieving their purpose, it is necessary to distinguish skills from attitudes. The distinction is an important one. Indeed, failure to clarify the difference between skills training and attitude change can often result in confusion. This is not to suggest that the two are incompatible, but rather that it is necessary to decide which aspects of programmes are addressed to skills and which to attitudes. In this way the process of evaluation can be designed to look at one aspect separately from the other and to give appropriate feedback. Let us consider a working definition which will clarify this important distinction. An *attitude* is a tendency or a predisposition to behave in certain ways in particular situations, whereas a *skill* is an ability to do something well. Attitudes can be measured directly but are usually inferred from the things which people say or are seen to do. Changing someone's attitude to something may well change what they say or do, but this will not necessarily follow. People behave in ways which they believe to be appropriate to the situation in which they find themselves, so that other variables in the present situation may be more powerful in selecting behaviour than attitudes previously held.

Attitudes can be measured or discussed early in a developmental programme, and it is possible to reassess them towards the end and thus show changes in the expected direction. Often this is done in an informal way as an end-of-course discussion of 'What were the most important things for me?' It is possible to make this more formal by developing action plans – 'What will I do more of and what will I do less of when I return to work?' There are also inventories which can be used early and late in the programme. Useful sources of these can be found in Henerson, Morris and Fitzgibbon (1978) and also Cook *et al* (1981). The inventories will seldom be exactly what is required but the formats can be used to build up something specific for a particular programme. An alternative method of assessing changes in attitude is by the use of a simple repertory grid technique. Honey (1979) provides a detailed example of how to do this.

Following up attitude-changing activities to discover whether the changes are maintained in the workplace is quite difficult to do, and it is doubtful whether this is actually worthwhile. It is more helpful to observe the actual behaviour to discover if it has changed. It will usually be necessary to enlist the help of line managers or supervisors or, even better, subordinates in order to do this.

Changes in individual effectiveness

Behaviour scales for assessing change can be designed to make explicit what changes are likely. It might also be possible to integrate these with annual performance appraisal categories. If this can be done then the employing managers will be able to provide evidence of whether changes have taken place and, if so, whether increased effectiveness is the result. For instance, a study by Latham and Saari (1979) assessed increased performance by an improvement in ratings on the annual appraisal; they also measured productivity in the sections for which the supervisors were responsible, and were able to show an increase after developmental activities designed to improve interpersonal skills.

Another way of facilitating the transfer of learning back to work, or from one work activity to another, is by the use of action planning. At intervals during the learning, the managers are asked to focus on the *utility* of what has been discussed. Towards the end of the programme they cluster the items into areas and then arrange them in some order of priority. The action plan for (say) the next six months is then drafted by putting some time-frame on each area to be tackled. It will also be necessary to write down against each area likely countervailing forces and how these are to be overcome. The questions which need to be addressed will include the following:

- Will this action affect other people? How will they react to it?
- Whose authority will be necessary to implement this action? How do I ensure that this will be available?
- What organizational constraints are likely to prevent this action? What can be done to ease them?

The action plan is a piece of positive management. It forms a set of goals to be achieved and gives a time-frame and rationale for each of them. If it has been produced off-job, the plan should be discussed with the employing manager, before or after return to work. It is necessary to review progress on action plans, and some months later questions can be asked, for example:

- How much of your action plan have you been able to implement?
- Which actions have been shelved, and why?
- What positive benefits in terms of effectiveness in your part of the organization have resulted from carrying out your action plan?

A specific form of action planning is through the use of action learning with an organizational project as the focus for the learning. This project often has, as a focus, the increased effectiveness of a part of the company and can show a good return for the investment in whatever training input is necessary. An example of this was described by Woodward (1975). (The programme investigated was for supervisors and led to a National Examinations Board in Supervisory Studies qualification.) There was formal course work, mainly on theories of management, which was examined. There was also a work-based project which was intended to show the advantages of good supervisory practice. Woodward was unable to show any differences in ways of working as a result of the theoretical part of the course. This ought not to surprise us, we have considered good examples of the processes which are needed in order to change the ways in which people do things at work. Theoretical input on the nature of management, without role-play or work-based practice, is not one of them. Woodward was able to estimate the benefits of the project work and six of the twelve projects showed positive benefits. Averaged over the twelve, the return on training investment (course fee, travel, subsistence, equipment costs, pay of trainees, and covering costs) was 2.9:1,

Changes in the effectiveness of teams

Team development is intended to improve the effectiveness of a group of people whose jobs require that they work together. It assumes:

- That the group has some reason for existing, some common goals and problems
- That interdependent action is required to achieve the goals or solve the problems
- That it is valuable to spend time in trying to understand and improve the way in which group members work together to achieve their tasks.

Team development activities may focus on working relationships or on action planning. There are three main models: problem-solving, interpersonal, and role-identification.

The problem-solving model

Encourages the group to identify problem areas which are affecting the achievement of group goals. Action planning is then used as a method of tackling the problems. Quality circles offer the best known example of problem-solving groups and can give a good return on training investment.

424

Robson (1982) quotes the average return as being between 5:1 and 8:1.

The interpersonal model

Attempts to improve decision-making and problem-solving by increasing communication and cooperation on the assumption that improving interpersonal skills increases the effectiveness of the team. In evaluations of this kind of approach, groups regularly report improvements in agreeing goals, increasing cooperation and reducing conflict. There is not so much evidence that these improvements can be linked to higher levels of organizational effectiveness.

The role-identification model

Attempts to increase effectiveness by increasing understanding of the interacting roles within the group. Belbin (1981) describes ways in which this can be done and some criteria for evaluation.

It is, of course, possible to combine the different models. For instance, the Blake and Mouton (1969) Managerial Grid is a combination of problem-solving and interpersonal approaches.

Changes in organizational effectiveness

Organizational effectiveness is not a simple concept, with only the balance sheet at the end of the year as the criterion to be assessed. There are many ways in which one can look at it and many writers have offered sets of criteria. One of the early attempts was that of Georgeopolos and Tannenbaum (1957) who evaluated effectiveness in terms of productivity, flexibility and the absence of organizational strain. More familiar is the approach of Blake and Mouton (1964), which seeks the simultaneous achievement of high production-centred and high people-centred methods of management. Katz and Kahn (1978) argue for growth, survival and control over the environment.

A more recent classification has been offered by Cameron (1980), who considers that almost all views on organizational effectiveness can be summarized under four headings – goal-directed, resource-acquiring, satisfying customers, and internal processes.

Goal-directed

Product goals Many organizations have basic measurements of work output, for instance:

- *Quantity*: produced, completed, processed, sold, turnover, etc.
- *Quality*: rejects, scrap, error rates, etc.
- *Variety*: diversity of products, etc.

It is sometimes possible to evaluate developmental activities against this sort of criterion (for instance, Latham and Saari, 1979), but it is necessary to control for variations in organizational performance which have nothing to do with the intervention. This means that the output of a comparable part of the organization, where there has been no attempt at developmental activity, is monitored on the same time series of measurements as the part under examination.

System goals Most organizations have system goals like:

● Growth in assets, sales, manpower
● Deadline rates, percentage of quota achieved, on-time shipments
● Reduction of stoppages, machine down-time, overtime worked.

Provided techniques for assessing these have been developed within the organizations, they can be used as criteria against which to assess management learning. Once again, however, some sort of control will be necessary to isolate the effect of the learning from the peaks and troughs of organizational performance. If the techniques of assessing system goals do not already exist, it is doubtful whether the evaluator will be able to develop them within a reasonable cost. One way of trying to achieve system goals (and also product goals) through learning is to adopt a problem-solving or project-based approach. What little is known about motivation in adults suggests that they are eager to solve what they regard as important problems. It would thus seem likely that learning experiences which enable them to tackle current problems would be well received (see Chapter 15). This may account for the growing popularity of on-the-job development and action-learning approaches to management learning.

Resource-acquiring

Effectiveness can be assessed by the extent to which the organization acquires needed resources, the emphasis being on inputs to increase competitiveness rather than outputs. The criteria for evaluation are usually long-term comparisons and it is difficult to isolate the effects of learning activities. However, aspects of resource acquisition which can easily be related to on- and off-job developmental activities include:

● Increasing the pool of trained staff
● Increasing employment flexibility
● Developing skills and abilities for future job requirements.

Satisfying customers

Many organizations survey customer satisfaction in some way, and it may be possible to relate this to learning activities. However, care must be taken to control for variations in image which have nothing to do with training.

If the 'organization' is defined as the work-group or department, then how well this satisfies those who contact it can be more directly related to training or developmental activities. Surveys of things like 'confidence in', 'loyalty to' and 'what they do which obstructs things which we want to do' can be carried out before and after training. A good example is the systems analysis carried out by Ford Europe. The heads of the various functions were asked to write down what the other functions did which *helped* them, and what they did which *hindered*. These lists were assembled into wall displays and, for the first time, the top few managers in each function were able to see how each of the other functions valued their contribution. The training input was a facilitation of group problem-solving so that functions could draw up plans for how to improve their 'image' and thus improve the transfer of work and information across functional boundaries. Organizational change initiatives based upon Total Quality Management also use this criterion of 'satisfying customers' as a category of effectiveness. Quite explicit measures are used to assess the extent to which each of the sections 'delight their customers', and many of these can be used in evaluation of training input.

Internal processes

Effectiveness can also be defined in terms of smooth information flows, lack of internal strain, clear definition of roles, clear statements of mission and targets integrated into the business plans, good cooperation between departments, or effective teamwork. Efforts to improve indices of these might be related to hard data like grievances, disciplinary actions, absenteeism, sick rates or turnover, but are more likely to be assessed by use of subjective opinions of 'how we were' or 'how we would like to be'. A whole range of survey instruments to measure attitudes in this area has been produced within the organizational development movement. A useful source of such instruments is Cook *et al.* (1981).

I have found this classification of Cameron's to be very useful when discussing evaluation of training events with line managers. It is possible to consider effectiveness at levels lower than that of the whole organization and thus to build up a matrix (see Figure 27.5).

The matrix can be used to discuss desirable changes in effectiveness which might accrue from off-job training or on-job development events. These should be identified by the type of effectiveness and the level at which they will be measured. You might like to try to use the matrix by mapping onto it the changes in effectiveness which you might expect from a particular programme. These can be at the level of the individual, the group or one of the higher levels (the higher the better). The changes might be expected in more than one category of effectiveness.

I have also found this matrix to be useful when discussing with line managers exactly what is supposed to change as a result of a training programme and how this change is to be measured. This is likely to be one of   *427*

	Individual (my work)	Work group (my section)	Function (my dept)	Regional level	Organizational level
Goal-directed					
Resource acquiring					
Satisfying constituencies					
Internal processes					

Figure 27.5   The organizational effectiveness matrix

the problems in trying to use the training model which is shown in Figure 27.3. It is also interesting, as a theoretical exercise, to attempt some mapping of possible changes for courses which are already running. I suggest that you try it for yourselves with a programme which is designed for individuals at a certain level in the organization – say, 'Principles of Management' for junior managers, and then again with an on-job programme which is 'tailor-made' for improving the effectiveness of a particular individual or group at work. What criteria can you measure? Which kind of programme do you find easier to evaluate?

PURPOSES FOR EVALUATION

The discussion so far has been about how to evaluate the learning process and how to measure the changes which are expected to result from it. Now we turn to the more 'political' aspects of evaluation, the various purposes which it can serve and the approaches through which these purposes can be met. Before we become too deeply involved in this, it would be worthwhile for you to consider what your views are with respect to evaluation. What sort of process do you think that it should be? Figure 27.6 offers a set of five-point scales with anchors at each end. I suggest that you select a point on each scale line which represents your position with regard to the process of evaluation.

The left-hand side of these scales represents a view that the main purpose of evaluation is to assess the worth of training to the organization, and that this is best done by quantitative methods. The right-hand side is quite close to research on methods of learning, where the quality of the experience, as reported by those involved, is the main focus. Many trainers oscillate between these two positions and hope that evaluation will satisfy both purposes. As we shall see, this is difficult to achieve. Particular forms of evaluation can be designed to meet particular purposes, but it is necessary to be clear about what the purpose is before embarking on the process.

Evaluation of training should be:						
Helping the manage- ment to inspect training	1	2	3	4	5	Helping the trainers to develop activities
An assessment process which leads to recom- mendations	1	2	3	4	5	Non-judgemental and therefore likely to pose questions
Statistical and scientific, as its primary concern is with objective mea- surement	1	2	3	4	5	Anecdotal and descrip- tive, as its primary concern is with subjec- tive interpretation
A carefully planned pro- cess with a set agenda	1	2	3	4	5	Changing throughout as the focus changes during the process
Estimating the worth of training activities to the organization	1	2	3	4	5	Providing feedback to the training department
Based on large samples and asking quite simple questions	1	2	3	4	5	Based on small samples and using in-depth questioning
Part of the process for all training activities	1	2	3	4	5	Carried out only when there is some doubt about a programme

Figure 27.6 Evaluation of training (Adapted from an idea by Len Gill of Merseyside Police)

Purposes for evaluation

Goldstein (1986) defines evaluation as 'the systematic collection of descriptive and judgemental information necessary to make effective decisions related to the selection, adoption, value and modification of various instructional activities'. I think this definition sound and would argue that it implies that evaluation is a set of information-gathering techniques. Further, that the selection of a particular strategy or technique, or of the particular aspect of the learning process which is examined, will vary with the purpose for which the evaluation is intended. Various purposes have been proposed by different authors. I prefer to group them into five main categories – feedback, control, research, intervention, and power games.

Feedback

Feedback evaluation provides quality control over the design and delivery of learning activities. Feedback to the participants will be an essential part of the learning process. Timely feedback, to those organizing the learning, about the effectiveness of particular methods and about the achievement of the objectives set will help in the development of the programme currently being run and those planned for future occasions. The information which needs to be collected for feedback evaluation is:

429

- *Before and after measures* of levels of knowledge, concepts used, skills, attitudes and behaviour
- Sufficient detail to be able to *review each topic* covered during the learning event and each learning situation
- Evidence of *transfer of learning* to the workplace.

The main purpose of what we are calling feedback evaluation is the development of learning situations and training programmes, improving what is being offered. There is a secondary aspect, as identifying what is good and what is not so good improves the professional ability of members of the training department.

Control

Control evaluation relates training policy and practice to organizational goals. There could also be a concern for the value to the organization of the contribution of the training function, as well as its costs. Careful control evaluation might also answer questions like, 'Will a main focus on training give a better solution to the problem than restructuring the department or re-designing some of the jobs?' The information required for control evaluation is therefore:

- That required for *feedback* (and listed above)
- Some measures of the *worth* of the output of the training to the organization
- Some measures of *cost*
- Some attempt at a *competitive study* of different mixes of methods for tackling the problem.

Control evaluation is quite close to to the lefthand side of the scales in Figure 27.6. It is something that an organization might require of a training manager or might impose through the creation of a group of people responsible for evaluation.

Research

Research evaluation seeks to add to knowledge of training principles and practice in a way which will have more general application than feedback evaluation. Studies of ways in which people learn or studies of factors which facilitate transfer would be examples. Research evaluation can also serve to improve the techniques available for other purposes, like feedback, control and intervention. Research evaluation requires some form of experimental design to counteract threats to internal validity – the confidence with which conclusions can be drawn from the data, and the extent to which alternative explanations can be ruled out (i.e. be attributed to the procedure described rather than to some variables which have not been controlled). It also needs some external validity – the extent to which the findings can be generalized to other situations. Research evaluation of training within organizations is difficult as there is seldom the opportunity to set up true control groups and time series of observations. There are not many examples in the literature, but a notable exception is the study by Latham and Saari (1979) which was referred to above.

Intervention

It is a mistake to believe that the process of evaluation is one of applying some objective measuring instrument external to and independent of the programme being evaluated. The evaluation is actually likely to affect the way in which the programme is viewed, and can be used to redefine the sharing of responsibility for the learning between the facilitators, learners and employing managers. Planned intervention through evaluation can involve the line managers and strengthen the liaison role between the training department and other functions within the organization. It can thus be a powerful method of intervening into the human resource procedures within an organization.

Power games

Perhaps all information is powerful, but certainly evaluative information about training events can be used within the organizational political games. It is not possible to avoid this, and perhaps it is not desirable to do so. It does, however, place a burden on the evaluator to make sure that the evidence which is being used is based upon a sound study. People often make up their minds on anecdotal evidence. For instance, much of the bad press which sensitivity training received was at the level of, 'Did you hear about what happened on the . . . programme last week?'

APPROACHES TO EVALUATION

Having decided on a purpose (or set of purposes) for the evaluation, the next phase is to select a suitable approach. Most authors describing evaluations appear to suggest that the approach they are advocating is unique. In a sense this is true – no one ever exactly replicates an evaluation – but it is possible to classify approaches into four main types – goal-based, systems, responsive evaluation and quasi-legal.

Goal-based

Goal-based evaluation starts from the position that training activities are cyclic. First, needs are identified and then precise (and preferably behavioural) objectives are set. The cycle ends with assessment of the extent to which the objectives have been attained, of the relationship between amounts of learning and methods employed, and of the extent to which the   *431* objectives achieved contribute to meeting the need identified. This approach is almost universally recommended by trainers for trainers, and there have been numbers of attempts to describe the various levels at which the objectives should be set. A typical framework is that of Hamblin (1974). The five levels for evaluation are said to be linked by a cause-and-effect chain:

	training
leads to	reactions
which lead to	learning
which leads to	changes in behaviour
which lead to	changes in the organization

This chain can break between any of the levels and one function of the evaluation might be to discover why the breakdown occurred.

Most evaluation of training is done at the reactions level. In the USA, Ralphs and Stephan (1986) found that 86 per cent of the Fortune 500 companies 'usually' evaluated their courses by means of evaluation forms filled in by learners at the end of the course, whereas only 12 per cent 'usually' used business data records. The study *Training in Britain* (1989) carried out for the Training Agency, surveyed a large number of organizations, responsible for some 80 per cent of the employed workforce in the UK. The results showed that, in 1986/87, 90 per cent of the organizations used the reaction level of evaluation, but only 19 per cent attempted any evaluation in terms of benefits to the organization. Only half of this 19 per cent were using before-and-after comparisons of behaviour and only 3 per cent were attempting to relate benefits to cost.

Perhaps an assumption is being made that favourable reactions imply useful learning or will predict changes in behaviour or higher levels of effectiveness. There is not much evidence to support this view. The survey carried out by Alliger and Janak (1989) found only twelve articles in which attempts had been made to correlate the various levels – there was no relationship between reaction measures and the other three levels of criteria and *good reactions did not predict learning or behaviour or organizational results any better than poor reactions*. The mean correlation between learning and behaviour was found to be +0.13 and that between behaviour and organizational results was +0.9. This implies that the prediction of the higher level from the lower one will, on average, not account for more than 4 per cent of the variance. I would argue that these results mean that, if it is necessary to carry out an evaluation, this should be done at all four levels because the different levels are providing different kinds of evidence.

The setting of learning objectives is also to be recommended for on-job development and developmental activities other than off-job training courses. The developing manager and the supervisor (perhaps assisted by a member of the training department) analyse the possibilities for learning within the tasks set for (say) the next six months. A learning contract is then drawn up which specifies some four to six objectives to be achieved during the period. A simple format for the contract can be constructed (see Figure 27.7). The process of developing this contract and evaluating the achievement of the

Objectives set	Strategy for achieving the objectives	Criteria and means of evaluating progress
Objective 1	How you intend to do it	How you intend to measure achievement
Objective 2	"	"
Objective 3	"	"
etc.		
		Date: Signed:

Figure 27.7 Format for the contract

objectives set is one way of encouraging the Type 2 learning described by Mumford (see Chapter 1).

There is a clear bias in the methods discussed above towards the idea that successful training activities are based upon a fairly precise specification of aims and objectives. This does not imply that 'development' is not worthwhile, rather that there should be some clarity in the expectations of the parties involved in the process. For instance, some management programmes are habitually justified by managers and trainers as providing a 'broadening experience'. When pressed to explain the concept of 'broadening', most responses can be classified into two areas:

1. Improving contacts across functional boundaries.
2. Learning to work in teams rather than as an individual.

At this level of conceptualization, it is possible to write objectives. What is being suggested is that facilitators of learning have to tread a path between setting aims so vague that no one can tell whether they have been achieved, and setting behavioural objectives so tightly drawn that no room is left for unintended outcomes and the complexity and subtlety of human behaviour.

Systems

Systems evaluation sets out to answer questions, such as:

- Is the programme reaching the target population?
- Is it effective?
- Is it cost-effective?

These sorts of questions are posed by policy-makers looking for 'hard' data   *433* and they largely exclude the gathering of opinions. The main difficulty in applying this approach (which is widely recommended for evaluating social and educational programmes) to training is to decide on criteria of effectiveness. Effectiveness criteria which satisfy accountants are usually quantitative measures, and often these are trivial. For instance, much of the work in the public sector seems now to be judged in terms of 'how many' (patients per year, arrests per month, GCSE passes, etc.) rather than by the quality of what is being done.

This variety of the systems approach is used in some organizations, and training departments must take some responsibility for it. Many of them are producing statistics each year which represent the 'business' that they are doing in terms of numbers on courses. This may be the only format in which senior management can understand the contribution of training, but using this 'head count' as the sole form of evaluation is tantamount to abdicating and leaving the field to accountants.

A more productive way of thinking about a systems approach is to consider the training department as an organizational sub-system and to look at the relationship between the work it is doing and the business plan for the organization. A simple matrix like that described by Pepper (1984) will help with this (see Figure 27.8).

The categories of people across the top of this matrix will vary from organization to organization, but the reasons for training or developing which are listed on the left of the matrix should cover most situations. The matrix can be drawn as a wall chart and learning opportunities offered at present or in the near future mapped onto it. Any specific activity may be represented in more than one box. For instance, introduction of new desk-top technology could include training in how to use it and also discussions on the effects of it on existing relationships and procedures.

	Senior managers	Middle managers	1st line managers	Operating core	Admin staff
New recruits					
Promotions					
New equipment					
New procedures					
Maintenance of capabilities					
New standards					
New legislation					

434   Figure 27.8   The training opportunity matrix (adapted from Pepper, 1984)

Looking closely at the matrix gives a good feel for what is being provided, and also what is *not* being provided. Questions can then be formulated to investigate the logic underlying this provision. For instance, how does the provision correlate with the goals in the annual business plan? What proportion of the budget is being spent on maintenance of the skills pools, and how much on the development of new procedures? If the organization concerned is large, the matrix may become too confused and it may be better to produce a separate matrix for each function. These matrices can be compared with statements of what are considered to be key aspects of organizational effectiveness (achieving goals, satisfying constituencies and so on) for each of the functions.

Responsive evaluation

The term 'responsive evaluation' was first used by Stake (1975) to describe a strategy in which the evaluator is less concerned with the objectives of the programme than with its effects in relation to the concerns of interested parties – the 'stakeholders'.

In conducting a responsive evaluation, the evaluator first talks to the main clients, the staff organizing the programme, and to a sample of those who will be affected by the programme, both trainees and line managers, to gain a sense of their posture with regard to the programme and the purposes for the evaluation. The evaluator then makes personal observations of the programme to get a direct sense of what it is about. He or she has then begun to discover the purpose of the programme, both stated and real, and also the concerns that various stakeholders may have and is in a position to conceptualize the issues and problems which the evaluation should address.

The design of the evaluation takes place next, and it should be noted that this is well into the process of evaluation. It cannot be designed before the evaluator can specify the kinds of data and information which will be needed to satisfy the various issues and concerns. The evaluator selects whatever methods and instruments are most appropriate and collects data. The information collected is organized into themes, and the evaluator matches issues and concerns to audiences in deciding what form the report will take (as there may be different reports for different audiences). It is worth noting the interactions implicit in this process; at any stage the evaluator may reformulate what is being done, and there is no certain way of predicting the outcome of the evaluation.

Parlett and Hamilton (1977) describe a form of evaluation which has some similarities to responsive evaluation, and recommend it for educational research. The primary concern of 'illuminative evaluation' is with description and interpretation rather than with measurement and prediction. The suggested method by which to achieve this is 'progressive focusing', which means the systematic reduction of the breadth of the enquiry to give more concentrated attention to the emerging issues. A key value which is apparent in the work of Parlett and Hamilton is that they reject the classical evaluator's   *435* stance of seeking an objective truth that is equally relevant to all of the parties, in favour of acknowledging the diversity of questions posed by different interest groups.

Legge (1984) also arrives at a position which is quite close to that of responsive evaluation from a quite different route. She discusses the research on evaluation of planned organizational change and criticizes it on two main grounds. The first of these is that evaluation research which is rigorous enough to be acceptable to an academic is almost always too trivial to be useful to decision-makers, as the designs are so restrictive that most of the things which are of interest are controlled out. The second is that most of the research is so badly designed that it is unacceptable to an academic because threats to internal validity have not been controlled and there is little confidence in the conclusions drawn. Legge suggests that, rather than attempting evaluation as rigorously controlled research, a 'contingent approach' be adopted. This essentially consists of asking the major stakeholders four major questions:

1. Do you want the proposed change programme to be evaluated?
2. What functions do you wish the evaluation to serve?
3. Which (of a number of possible alternatives) approach best matches the functional requirements of the evaluation exercise?
4. To what extent are constraints on the planning and implementation of the change programme, which will be necessary because of this approach to evaluation, acceptable?

The general perspective of responsive evaluation is very different to those (like objectives-based and systems approaches) which are essentially based upon scientific enquiry. Evaluators are subjective partners with stakeholders in the creation of the data and 'truth' is a matter of consensus among informed people; it does not correspond with an objective reality. The evaluation is a joint collaborative process which results in something being constructed rather than revealed by the investigation. The responsive approach also involves protracted negotiations with a wide range of stakeholders in constructing the report. It is thus more likely to reflect their reality and be useful for them than those prepared by more scientific approaches.

Responsive evaluation is gaining ground as the most favoured method for evaluating educational and social programmes in the USA. It has obvious strengths as a procedure for evaluating management training and development activities within organizations, because it attempts to take into account the interests of various groups rather than just the sponsors of the programme. It also has a rationale for collecting information – the needs of the various stakeholders.

Quasi-legal evaluation

436   To adopt this approach, a tribunal is set up, and witnesses are called to testify

and submit evidence. Great care is taken to hear a wide range of 'evidence' (opinions, value and beliefs) from the organizers of the programme and the 'users', as well as accountants. Such an approach has been used to evaluate social programmes but not, to my knowledge, for learning activities sponsored by organizations. It might, however, be suitable for something wide-ranging, for instance, a full review of the purpose, strategy and value of management training and development within the company.

OBJECTIVITY OF EVALUATION

It should be obvious, from a consideration of the various strategies available, that evaluation will never produce an absolute truth. The objectives and systems approaches lead to the collection of 'hard' facts which can be reliably measured, but the evaluators hold values which determine which pieces of information are collected. The other approaches are subjective in their methods of collecting information, but attempt to get at a wider 'truth'.

The evidence produced in an evaluation report should be both credible (i.e. have some reliability of measurement) and useful. The objectivity comes from a certainty that if someone else had carried out the evaluation he or she would have come to similar conclusions.

PRESENTING AN EVALUATION REPORT

The final stage of most evaluations will be the presentation of the report. The extent to which this will be accepted and acted upon will depend to a large extent on what took place at the beginning of the study. It is crucial to identify the major stakeholders and to try to discover what agendas they have. Many of those who have a long-term interest in the programme will have strong views on the desired outcomes of the study. It is essential to keep such people informed during the evaluation and to involve them in key decisions, if they are to 'own', and therefore act on, the results. This is not to imply that the evaluator must produce the findings which they are expecting, rather that their views must be incorporated and they must be kept informed. It is, of course, also essential to establish that the people receiving the report have the power to implement the changes being suggested. One way of overcoming some of the problems in presenting the report is to discover what kind of report the major stakeholders expect. In Figure 27.6 you were asked to decide what it was that you meant by 'evaluation'. Making a decision on each of the scales makes explicit what kind of process evaluation is thought to be. Before embarking on an evaluation, you might consider asking the senior stakeholders to fill in a set of attitude scales like those in Figure 27.6. You will then know what kind of data they think that you ought to collect and something about how they expect you to present it. That should at least alert you to some of the problems if their views are very different from your own.

The way in which the findings are communicated during the study will depend upon organizational style. Some organizations prefer written   *437* memoranda, but in many the important decisions are actually made in face-to-face discussions. The presentation of the report itself is not the time to 'defend', if there is some bad news; those concerned should be aware of it before the presentation. This area, of the problems of presenting evaluative reports, has been rather neglected in the literature, but interesting discussions may be found in Patton (1978) and Easterby-Smith (1994).

DO YOU REALLY WANT TO EVALUATE YOUR TRAINING?

If it is to become the integral part of training and development activities which has been suggested in this chapter, evaluation requires the expenditure of energy and time. The costs can be heavy and, if the evaluation is to be justified as an investment, some selection of programmes seems to be indicated. Some training events are essentially social (for example, the one-day get-together where people from different functions meet and hear a series of briefings on the work of other parts of the organization). Evaluation of such events would hardly be worth the cost involved.

The importance of the programme is a further criterion for consideration. Usually evaluation of one-off programmes would not be considered worthwhile. However, if the programme is intended to help with the solution of some important problem then evaluation is indicated. Similarly, if the consequences of not ensuring that the training has been effective (for instance with safety training) are important, then evaluation should be considered.

The data produced in an evaluation study is likely to be a source of power. This will certainly be the case where the primary purpose of evaluation is that of control, for example central evaluation of decentralized training, or management-commissioned evaluation. Most evaluative data should be useful rather than threatening, but training can never be evaluated without some judgements being made about the trainers responsible. This could account for the widespread defensiveness among practitioners when faced with proposals for evaluation. My reply would be that there are important benefits in increasing the quality of the training and thus the effectiveness of the training department.

Evaluation can also improve the relationship between the training department and the rest of the organization by producing evidence of real worth to the organization, by linking training events to improved organizational effectiveness, and by changing the relationship with line managers. Training departments have largely avoided the challenge of evaluating their activities. The consequence may be that, by default, they will be assessed only in terms of their cost to the organization.

REFERENCES

Alliger, G. M. and Janak, E. A. (1989) 'Kirkpatrick's levels of training criteria: Thirty years later', *Personnel Psychology*, 42, pp. 331–42.

Belbin, R. M. (1981) *Management Teams: Why they Succeed or Fail* (London: Heinemann).

Blake, R. R. and Mouton, J. S. (1964) *The Managerial Grid* (Houston, Tx.: Gulf).

Blake, R. R. and Mouton, J. S. (1969) *Building a Dynamic Corporation through Grid Organization* (Reading, Mass.: Addison-Wesley).

Bloom, B. S. (1956) *Taxonomy of Educational Objectives* (New York: Macmillan).

Bramley, P. (1990) *Evaluating Training Effectiveness: Translating Theory into Practice* (Maidenhead: McGraw-Hill).

Cameron, K. (1980) 'Critical questions in assessing organisational effectiveness', *Organisational Dynamics* (Autumn) pp. 66–80.

Cook, J. D., Hepworth, S. J., Wall, T. D. and Warr, P. B. (1981) *The Experience of Work* (London: Academic Press).

Davies, I. K. (1971) *The Management of Learning* (London: McGraw-Hill).

Department of Employment (1971) *Glossary of Training Terms* (London: HMSO).

Easterby-Smith, M. (1994) *Evaluating Management Development, Training and Education*, 2nd edn (Aldershot: Gower).

Georgeopolos, B. S. and Tannenbaum, A. S. (1957) 'The study of organizational effectiveness', *American Sociological Review,* 22, pp. 534–40.

Goldstein, A. P. and Sorcher, M. (1974) *Changing Supervisor Behaviour* (New York: Pergamon Press).

Goldstein, I. L. (1986) *Training in Organizations*, 2nd edn (Calif.: Brooks/Cole).

Hamblin, A. C. (1974) *Evaluation and Control of Training* (London: McGraw-Hill).

Henerson, M. E., Morris, L. L. and Fitzgibbon, C. T. (1978) *How to Measure Attitudes* (Beverley Hills, Calif.: Sage).

Honey, P. (1979) 'The Repertory Grid in Action', *Industrial and Commercial Training* (September).

Katz, D. and Kahn, R. L. (1978) *The Social Psychology of Organizations*, 2nd edn (New York: Wiley).

Kirkpatrick, D. L. (1967) 'Evaluation of Training', in Craig, R. L. and Bittel, L. R. (eds) *Training and Development Handbook* (New York: McGraw-Hill).

Latham, E. P. and Saari, L. M. (1979) 'The Application of Social Learning Theory to Training Supervisors through Behavioural Modelling', *Journal of Applied Psychology*, 64, pp. 239–46.

Legge, K. (1984) *Evaluating Planned Organizational Change* (London: Academic Press).

Parlett, M. and Hamilton, D. (1977) 'Evaluation as a new approach to the study of innovative programmes', in Hamilton, D., Jenkins, D., King, C., MacDonald, B. and Parlett, M. (eds) *Beyond the Numbers Game* (London: Macmillan).

Patton, M. C. E. (1978) *Utilization-focused Evaluation* (Beverley Hills, Calif.: Sage).

Pepper, A. D. (1984) *Managing the Training and Development Function* (Aldershot: Gower).

Rackham, N. and Morgan, T. (1977) *Behavioural Analysis in Training* (Maidenhead: McGraw-Hill).

Ralphs, L. T. and Stephan, E. (1986) 'HRD in the Fortune 500', *Training and Development Journal*, 40, pp. 69–76.

Robson, M. (1982) *Quality Circles: A Practical Guide* (Aldershot: Gower).

Rossi, P. H., Freeman, H. E. and Wright, S. R. (1979) *Evaluation: A Systematic Approach* (Beverley Hills, Calif.: Sage).

Stake, R. E. (ed.) (1975) *Evaluating the Arts in Education: A Responsive Approach* (Columbus, Ohio: Merrill).

Training Agency (1989) *Training in Britain: A Study of Funding, Activity and Attitudes* (London: HMSO).

Woodward, N. (1975) 'Cost-Benefit Analysis of Supervisor Training', *Industrial Relations Journal*, 6(2), pp. 41–7.

28 Choosing resources

Michael Abrahams

It is more important than ever that training and development budgets are used in the most cost-effective way. Some years ago many newly-appointed management development specialists (MDSs) were expected to learn on-the-job. A portion of their budget was spent on 'mistakes'; it was part of the learning experience. Today, that luxury is rarely available. As value for money is uppermost in the minds of the board, and more time is expended monitoring the effectiveness of training, the choice of a supplier of development activities must be the right one.

This chapter outlines resources available to an MDS, and some methods which I have found to be practical in making a choice of suitable development suppliers. It will cover:

- Management consultants
- Management consultancies
- Business schools
- Management colleges
- Public training courses
- Consortium programmes
- Training packages.

LOOKING FOR EVIDENCE

The comments made in this chapter presume that a careful analysis of needs has been undertaken as described by Andrew Stewart in Chapter 3. Choosing a course or other development activity for reasons other than need is unlikely to prove useful, but it does happen. The decision to use external resources to address training or development needs is usually taken after discussions have led to the realization that the organization does not have sufficient trained or

441

qualified personnel capable of providing the knowledge and skills required for their management. The care taken in arriving at the decision to use external resources is often in direct contrast to the random way in which the resources are finally chosen.

There is a plethora of claims contained in mailshots from individuals, consultancies and prestigious business schools; words such as new, unique, tried, tested, etc., are part and parcel of their marketing pitch. It is of little use to initiate discussions with consultants, academic institutions or others in response to the number of colours used in their brochures or their geographical proximity. Equally, to choose to use a resource simply because the chief executive had some 'good experiences' with it in the past may be politic, but it will not be a decision based on up-to-date knowledge.

In the human psyche there is a deep desire to codify, categorize and label behaviour. The work done by psychologists to encapsulate characteristics of behaviour and personality using psychometric tests, and the willingness of organizations to buy the latest thinking in order to improve their selection or development processes, are tributes to hope rather than reality. Similarly, if the MDS administers a test to a putative supplier to check their chances of success, there is unlikely to be much correlation between forecast and outcome. Evidence of past successes, provided by the use of written material, references and observation, are more likely to be accurate.

The following sections of this chapter aim to provide guidance on how to obtain this evidence and to suggest ways in which the information can be used to make the best choices. Sometimes the material gathered will be unclear and it will be difficult to make a decision. The choice will then be decided by the 'chemistry' that exists between the MDS and supplier, and maybe by comparative costs – a factor which has become more important in recent years.

The availability and quality of management consultants and academics has increased during the last ten years. Institutions of management teaching are far more rigorous than they were in the past, and the growth of large training and OD consultancies have gone a long way to ensure a measure of integrity. Nevertheless, it pays to be choosy and the first step should be to contact organizations who can give advice about suppliers of training and development.

The organizations listed below will supply information. Those marked † are not without interest in supplying consultants or courses themselves, but they maintain a professional distance when asked for advice.

The Association of Management Education & Development
21 Catherine Street
London
WC2B 5JS

†The Institute of Management
Management House
Cottingham Road,
Corby

Northants
NN17 1TT.

†The Institute of Personnel Management
IPM House
Camp Road
Wimbledon
London
SW19 4UW.

Information concerning *individual* consultants is obtainable from the Brind Register but information is supplied to member organizations only.

Brind Register
11 Firs Avenue
Muswell Hill
London
N10 3LY

The following provide data on a variety of courses in the UK, Europe and the USA.

Brickers Executive Education Service
425A Family Farm Road
Woodside
California 94026, USA

Directory of Management Training
Hoskyns Education
Hoskyns Group plc
5 Kerley Road
Bournemouth
BH2 5DR

The Management Courses Index
7 Princes Street
London
W1R 7RB

The experience of other MDSs or management trainers within the public and private sectors is invaluable. Networks of MDSs exist, and their knowledge and skills in choosing suppliers can be useful to an individual in the early stages. It is worthwhile making contact and tapping into various professional groups, possibly by joining an organization such as the Institute of Personnel and Development. Initially, there may be a tendency to accept the judgement of others; it must be remembered, however, that a consultant who is successful in one organization could be a disaster in another.

443

CONSULTANTS

Robert Townsend (1971) described consultants as: 'People who borrow your watch to tell you what time it is and then walk off with it.'

The consultants dealt with in this section are not those who collate the collective wisdom of employees, feed it to the board in a large report and then walk away after making a number of recommendations that everyone knew they would make. Human resource development consultants do speak to the people within the organization, but usually they stay to carry out their recommendations.

Consultants can be private individuals who work on their own or occasionally with other consultants; or they can be part of a consultancy group. Sometimes they are people who are encouraged to act as consultants as part of their contract at a business school, management college, or in some cases their company.

The decision to employ an external consultant is often made because an organization's own specialists are fully engaged or they do not have the expertise. A consultant can be an advantage, because he or she will be seen as neutral and have no involvement in the internal politics of the organization. At the same time, the external consultant is likely to have greater credibility and experience to draw upon than many internal consultants. (It is well known that 'a prophet is not without honour save in his own land').

Before contracting to employ an external consultant, try to evaluate their work either by seeing them in operation, if they conduct courses, or by talking with the MDSs of those organizations where they have worked. A consultant will always refer an enquiring MDS to an organization where they have been successful; the secret is to tease out where success has *not* been achieved. No one likes to advertise their failures but if a consultant is experienced, assured and successful, he/she will not wish to appear omnipotent and may, if questioned, volunteer information about a number of experiences they would not wish to repeat.

Before making a choice, an MDS should arrange to meet a number of consultants and, using a similar format, should evaluate the response of each consultant. The MDS should then reflect on their personal reaction to each consultant as they are likely to be working closely with him/her. Another criterion is whether the consultant will be acceptable within the culture of the organization. A training consultant who uses Neuro-Linguistic Programming or Gestalt may not be suitable for an organization whose managers expect training to be conducted in a more cognitive mode. Similarly, an individual presenting him/herself wearing a bandanna and sandals to carry out research in a bank will be regarded with scepticism. It is also necessary to know what methods the consultants favour and how flexible they are within their repertoire.

Any discussions should be concerned with contracting an *individual*, and not a consultancy. Problems can occur if the MDS has built a rapport with a consultant only to find that he or she then sub-contracts to someone who may not be as experienced or as acceptable to the organization.

Final points to be clarified before employing a consultant are – how much time will the consultant be able to devote to the assignment and how much will it cost?

Time

A useful measure is to check how many projects a consultant has on his/her books at any one time – three would appear to be the maximum that an individual can handle effectively.

Cost

At the present time nearly all consultants are open to negotiation about their daily rate. As a guide, the average price for a consultant working at middle and senior level is about £800 per day (£1 000–£1 200 if they are paid a salary by an employing consultancy). Academics or senior consultants working in an area such as Business Strategy will charge up to £2 500 per day. For a management 'Guru' (mostly American), expect to pay anything up to $35 000 per day.

After initial discussions, the consultant should be asked to define what he/she understands to be the issue/problem in question, and outline the proposed course of action; if the consultant has understood the situation, it should be evident from the clarity of the proposal. If the outline is acceptable, with only some 'fine tuning' required, then it is likely that a working arrangement will succeed.

CONSULTANCIES

I have found that the relationship with an individual consultant is more likely to prove successful than the relationship with a group of consultants. There is no guarantee that good working relationships will ensue simply because the consultancy has 'a good name'. There has been a growth in recent years of consultancies seeing themselves more as 'corporations' in their own right. This is manifested by the increasing size of this type of organization and the fact that many of the old established management accountancy consultancies have merged. For the MDS it will mean less choice of consultancies, but possibly a greater chance of finding good people within one consultancy. An exception can be demonstrated in advertisements (Figures 28.1 and 28.2) which reveal the calibre of consultants required by some consultancies and underline the necessity of checking the CVs of people being used.

When an independent trainer joins a consultancy his/her daily fee can increase considerably – often by as much as 50 per cent.

<u>OUTPLACEMENT & CAREER COUNSELLING</u>

THE growth business opportunity of the decade. Badly needed. Recession-driven and with tremendous growth potential. THIS is NOT a franchise. Your once-only investment of £3 750 purchases expert coaching, training manuals, local business database, videos and all starting and supporting material – your new business will become self-financing and cash-positive very quickly.

For full details, Contact:–

The XXX Group
Recruitment and Training Consultants

Figure 28.1   This advertisement appeared in a reputable international news journal

---

Ms X has moved from education where she had considerable experience working with pupils with special educational needs and in developing in-service training courses for teachers. She is a partner in a consultancy specializing in organizational change, training and recruitment. Her particular strengths are in communication skills, creativity, problem-solving, stress management and team-building.

Figure 28.2   This advertisement, which appeared in a professional journal, demonstrates the still prevalent state of 'unconscious incompetence' present in a surprising number of 'would-be' consultants

Questions to a consultant or consultancies

1. Do you have experience of my type of organization or sector?
2. What experience have you had with the type of contract I have outlined?
3. Have you had experience working at the level of management we have in mind, and with the volume we are expecting?
4. Can you give me evidence of the results of your work in other organizations?
5. Who else in the consultancy might be working on the assignment? What evidence is there of their competence and suitability?
6. Are you willing to make modifications to the work as we proceed?
7. What method of evaluation do you recommend, and will you be involved with it?
8. How many projects/assignments are you working on at the moment?
9. How much will it cost my company – broken down by consultant days and an outline of expenses charged?
10. What would the potential cancellation costs be?

BUSINESS SCHOOLS

For a given level of management, business school programmes can look similar. The objectives are almost interchangeable and the core content which accounts for something like 70 per cent of the offering, is predictable. Each institution will claim that its faculty, and visiting faculty, is excellent. In fact excellence, in terms of genuinely wishing to provide a worthwhile educative experience, is maintained throughout a wide spectrum of business schools.

The problem for a MDS lies in choosing the best programme to fit the objectives of a prospective participant and their organization. For example, a business school programme with a strong bias towards industrial marketing will not necessarily benefit an individual from a service industry such as insurance. It will be of interest, and it may be filed away for future reference, but any application of technique or knowledge may never take place because the fields of endeavour are so divergent. An appropriate programme would show that one or more members of the faculty has experience with marketing services such as banking, or preferably, in this instance, insurance.

Another example of a possible mismatch between participant and programme is that of a programme showing a distinct leaning towards the behavioural sciences, with elements of personal exposure implicit in the objectives, and an individual whose expectations are geared towards improving his/her financial knowledge, decision-making skills, or powers of business analysis.

Before choosing to use a business school programme, an MDS could ask the following questions:

1. What does the organization require of its managers in the next five to ten years that a business school programme might help to fulfil?
2. What will managers need for their development?
3. Have we undertaken a proper analysis of their individual needs?
4. Do they require an intensive educational programme or a skills programme?
5. When is the best time – this year or next?
6. How does their experience shape the type of programme to be used – are they specialists who need to know more about their specialization, or about another one?
7. Are they managers whose experience has been in a limited number of functional areas, and who therefore need exposure to a range of issues facing the organization?
8. Do any of the managers require exposure to an international faculty or participant group?

An important factor is to engage the manager with the choice of their programmes. This reduces the risk of the manager feeling he/she was 'sent on this course . . . ', etc.

The most important aspect associated with any senior management business school/management college programme is the need to ensure that the attending managers have either a different job on their return, or that their present job requires restructuring in such a way that they can use at least some of the ideas learnt during the programme. I have known of a considerable number of senior *447* managers who, having been on a management programme, leave their nominating companies, not because they were badly briefed, de-briefed or had no briefing at all, but because no allowance had been made for their 'growth'.

HOW TO CHOOSE A BUSINESS SCHOOL

Having determined the specific educational requirement for an individual and decided to use a business school, the MDS may find the following series of actions and questions useful.

Collecting data by post

Brochures outlining courses are the marketing and public relations side of a business school. Their function is to sell and to give outline information; the more prestigious the school the more emphasis there is on the quality and experience of the faculty, and on course structure and content, to ensure applications are from suitably high-calibre managers. Less prestigious business schools may stress uniqueness and novelty, and it is not unusual for some institutions to promote the setting of their colleges or the age of the buildings in order to establish an aura of tradition and learning.

Objectives

The course objectives will indicate whether the level of managers targeted is correct; if objectives outline strategic thinking, macro-economics, and international takeovers, but suggest that the course is aimed at middle management, then the course is patently misdirected.

The brochure should indicate the interrelationship between the various levels of courses offered, thereby giving clues on the thinking and 'house style' of the school.

Content

The course content (or programme overview) will indicate the time allocated to the operational and corporate level of business and should match the objectives. Any programme which suggests, for example, that the objectives are to increase an individual's capacity to comprehend strategic decisions but apportions 80 per cent of its time to finance and management accounting, is unlikely to meet its objectives.

Faculty

A list of faculty members should feature somewhere in the brochure. The list may indicate whether the faculty is full-time, part-time, visiting, etc., and the mix of faculty nationalities. Brief study will also show the Alma Mater of each member of the faculty and whether there is a preponderance of US-trained professors and lecturers, or a balance between New World-trained and the European- or Asian-educated faculty. A balance is particularly useful if the school is European and the intending participant is to be based in Europe. Many American managers posted to Europe bemoan the over-emphasis placed on US-trained faculty in European business schools and the over-use of US case study material. However, many European business schools, particularly INSEAD and IMD, have built up an impressive number of cases based on European and Pacific Basin organizations.

The faculty list should also indicate the strategic thrust of the school. For example, Durham is strong on small business development, Chicago concentrates much of its activity on quantitative analysis, and at Darden the focus is on manufacturing.

Teaching methods

The brochure should be informative regarding teaching methods. Some schools use case study only, following the lead given by Harvard. It has been suggested that this method is designed to teach people to analyse business problems and make theoretical decisions whilst divorcing them from reality. It must be said that the method does not suit all managers. The reading workload of sometimes two to three cases a day for between 14 and 70 days, depending on the length of the course, can be onerous and could therefore make learning more difficult. Equally some schools use a high number of lectures, say three to four per day. (This method can be numbing both to mind and rear end!) Some schools have finally accepted that teaching methods need to be varied, and use case study, lectures, real-life consultancy, computers, simulation, role-play and advanced audio-visual presentation techniques to make their teaching points.

Participants

A list of recent participants will enable the MDS to assess the levels and background of those managers who have attended programmes at the school in question. It should be noted if a high proportion of the participants hail from one sector of endeavour – perhaps merchant banking. If this is obvious and the MDS is employed by a plastic container producer, then the course is likely to be less than fruitful for the production manager. Similarly, if the majority of participants came from one geographical area, e.g. Scandinavia or Nigeria, then the benefit of a mixed international flavour would be diluted. The level of managers attending programmes can usually be gauged by the job titles given, but it is worth remembering that vice-presidents abound in American companies and that there appear to be a large number of senior executives in merchant banking who are disarmingly young and inexperienced! Contacting the MDS in a company shown to have had a manager as a participant on a course, or contacting the manager him/herself in order to discuss their view of the programme, will be time well spent.

449

Publications

It is useful to obtain a list of recent research publications and articles. This will give the MDS an idea of the research strengths of the school and whether some of the published material might be applicable to his or her own organization. Such a list, too, will indicate if members of the faculty have interests which the MDS will see as useful in his/her organization.

MBA programme

If the school has an MBA programme it is useful to get information on the curriculum, the number of students, the programme demands, the average age, conditions of entry, breakdown of nationalities, drop-out rate, etc. These can form the basis of discussion on a subsequent visit to the school. Information of the type outlined above can be obtained by post.

Timing

It is not unusual for the ideal programme to be run at a less than ideal time for the prospective participant! In fact it is probably a truism that most managers/executives who attend business school programmes find it difficult to release themselves from their responsibilities. The organization may also find that its manpower planning has been less than effective, as it is unable to replace the individual even on a temporary basis! Detailed knowledge of the course and its likely benefits are essential for the MDS in these circumstances and can help to persuade the manager of the opportunity being offered. The MDS could also suggest that one manager's absence is an opportunity to develop the person acting as a temporary replacement.

Geography/cost

The geographical location of a business school is a strong factor in determining its acceptability. Proximity can be a positive factor, but a programme held an appreciable distance from the prospective candidates' workplace can also be seen as a bonus. It has been said that, for organizations based in the UK, a business school programme increases in its perceived value in direct proportion to its distance south of Calais or west of Cork! Hence the popularity of programmes in the USA or Europe. The cost of a programme is not inconsiderable, and the closer to the home base, the less the overall bill.

VISITING A SCHOOL

The most effective method of choosing a business school is to visit a number in order to build up a picture and to get an understanding of the methods and quality offered at each. Here are some questions which can be asked of
directors, staff faculty and participants, and also some suggested areas to

observe.

Management structure

- Where are the decisions made?
- Is there an Advisory Board?
- What is its function?
- Who are represented?
- How is it structured?
- What is the level of independence of the faculty?
- Can they match their material to the needs of the companies represented on a particular programme?

Short courses

- What is the percentage of standard programmes (i.e. 'off the shelf') to 'in company' programmes?
- What changes in the profile of courses has taken place over the past five years?
- What is/are the most supported course[s] and the least supported course[s]?
- What are the candidates' 'entry qualifications' for a particular course?
- How many applications does a school refuse?
- What is the average number of people on courses compared to the targeted number?

The last is an important question. Some schools accept too many people for a programme either because they do not wish to disappoint or because they wish to maintain income. Other courses have too few people on them and should have been cancelled.

MBAs

- What percentage leave for immediate employment?
- What is the percentage of 'funded' students?
- How many 'drop out' or are asked to 'drop out' during a programme?
- Is there a counsellor for the students?
- What is the pass rate?
- Is there an alumni of MBAs? How does it support the school?
- Do any of the faculty teach solely on MBA programmes?

General

- Which teaching disciplines are particularly strong?
- Which research area is particularly strong?
- What is the academic turnover rate?

- What proportion of an academic's time is given over to consultancy?
- Do any of the faculty hold directorial appointments in business?

Observation points

1. Sit in on a class and observe the level of participation. If the class is being conducted in English, note if the participants have difficulty with the language. If this is so, the question to the directing staff could be, 'What steps do you take to ensure that a candidate who has English as a second or third language is fluent?' (There are tests available. e.g. TOEFL – Test of English as a Foreign Language.)
2. Are there any 'clowns' or 'sleepers' on the course? This could indicate disaffection with either the subject or the teacher, or it might mean that the individual should not be on the programme and that the admission committee was lax.
3. Are the teaching methods appropriate to the subject? For example, to give a lecture with no visual aids or participation on the subject of Capital Evaluation Techniques does not bear thinking about, but it happens.
4. What 'energy level' do the participants display for the subject? Talk to a cross-section of participants and get views on the course and faculty and, where possible, comparisons with other courses that individuals have attended in their career.
5. How many participants turn up late for class? This is often a measure of disaffection with the tutor or the programme.
6. Who does most of the talking in a case study class? If it is the tutor, then the class has not done enough work on the case or has not understood it.
7. How often does the programme director appear to have contact with participants? Little is gained if the director introduces the programme, disappears for its duration and then turns up only to take brickbats or plaudits at the end.
8. Is there a confusion between working hard and learning well? They are not necessarily one and the same thing.
9. Have the faculty talked to each other before the programme? Sometimes, unnecessary overlaps/gaps occur because some tutors have failed to discuss content.

The principal

It is worthwhile meeting the head of the school and, if possible, posing the question, 'What are, in your view, the critical problems facing management education and how will the school respond?' Responses can indicate whether any actions being considered are innovative and responsive. The principal of a school can have great or little influence on the institution, and it is useful to check out their record in innovation and steering by having discussions with experienced MDSs.

Business schools are usually amenable to visits from MDSs. It is significant that, for all the organizations represented on the 'rolls of honour' as having sent participants to programmes, very few MDSs from those organizations visit programmes and talk with the faculty or directing staff. To make an investment of up to £35 000 for a senior manager to undertake a business school programme, without a specialist visiting and undertaking some of the questioning and observations shown on the checklist, does not serve the interest of either the nominators or the business schools.

MANAGEMENT COLLEGES

The management college is mainly a UK/European phenomenon. In the USA there is far more emphasis on post-graduate/pre-experience education, and therefore accreditation is more in evidence in that country. The situation in the UK is changing somewhat, and more emphasis is being placed on the middle management MBA, possibly to the detriment of its British equivalent, the accountancy degree.

Colleges provide short courses in general management, specific discipline and management skills, essentially for post-experience managers. The work is usually sound but needs to be approached with caution if senior managers are being considered for placement. The faculty will usually have had previous management experience and/or have been management consultants. The approach recommended for business schools (i.e. the questions and observation notes) apply equally to management colleges such as Ashridge or Henley.

The question about directorial appointments is particularly apposite for anyone considering a management college MBA. It is not unheard of for faculty members of some of the 'lower order' management colleges to be attending MBA programmes at business schools (as participants!) and then teaching their students directly on their return.

Management colleges in the UK have been active in linking up with their European mainland equivalents to provide an international perspective. This may be due to a lack of international faculty in the respective institutions but the idea is positive and will do much to benefit the choice available to the MDS.

PUBLIC TRAINING COURSES

Courses associated with technical expertise, computers, textile technology, engineering, etc., where individuals are being technically trained or updated on the 'state of the art', are not the subject of this section.

Public courses and training packages are offered by profit-making organizations to participants wishing to gain expertise in a number of areas such as: Training Skills, Stress Management, Time Management, etc. Such courses abound with 'the elixir effect' – the claim to have the ultimate solution to all human resource development problems. There is no standard by which these courses can be assessed. That is not to say that there should not be a standard, or that it would be difficult to institute. It would make the job of   *453* choosing a suitable course very much easier and may rid the market of some less than professional operators.

CHOOSING A COURSE

Some course providers produce timetables covering a wide variety of subjects. It is enlightening to count the number of times a particular trainer's name appears as the subject course leader or tutor. In some instances a name appears so often that it stretches credulity that any individual is so skilled and knowledgeable that they can teach such a wide range of subjects. An area of even greater concern is course providers who fail to give any information at all about their tutors. It is not unknown for jobbing trainers to be called in to run public programmes that have been over-subscribed, in order that two programmes can be run in parallel, thus increasing income for the training company at the expense of any quality control.

Course objectives

What are the course objectives? What knowledge will participants gain, and/or what skills will they develop? If answers to these questions prove unsatisfactory, then it is likely that the course content will be equally woolly.

What methods are employed? The methods should recognize that learning is not entirely a listening process but a talking, doing, practising activity as well.

Course objectives, content and methods must be in harmony.

Objectives should be limited to achievable, quantifiable behavioural or knowledge targets. Content must be adequate to cover the objectives but should not be a huge list of words and phrases designed to demonstrate the erudition of the trainer. The methods should be appropriate to the subject – i.e. behaviour modification is not achieved by lecture, and marketing strategy analysis is unlikely to be learnt using interpersonal process recall.

The quality of the course tutor is critical. There are some very charismatic seminar leaders, particularly in the marketing field, where bravura performances are applauded, but they are not necessarily good at facilitating learning. On the latter subject, the MDS grapevine could be consulted. The problem is, as ever, one person's evaluation of an individual can be widely different from another and there are no agreed criteria. Price is no guide. A more expensive course means only that the course is more expensive. There are courses available, often mounted by the 'newer' universities, which are professionally tutored, well-run and inexpensive.

The final check on a public course is either to send a suitable candidate whose judgement can be trusted or for the MDS to attend the course him/herself. If the candidate or MDS is satisfied that the objectives of the programme are met, that the content is appropriate and that the course leader is able, then the course should prove worthwhile.

CONSORTIUM PROGRAMMES

The advantages of consortium programmes can best be described by an examination of the relative merits and demerits of internally run programmes and those of business schools, management colleges or public training programmes.

Internal programmes

The advantages of programmes mounted by an individual organization are:

1. Programme objectives will be in line with company aims.
2. Content can be carefully scrutinized to ensure suitability and relevance.
3. Faculty can be individually chosen for their match and skill in delivering what is required. The level is therefore more likely to be of uniform excellence.
4. By negotiating with the potential faculty, and perhaps making the course non-residential, a company-focused programme will cost less.

The disadvantages are:

1. The participants will not be able to match themselves against similar-level managers from a variety of other organizations.
2. There may be a 'cross-fertilization of self-ignorance'.

External programmes

The advantages of an external business school/management college/public course are:

1. The participants will usually be drawn from a wide range of enterprises, both national and international, which increases the value of a programme.
2. Managers/executives have time to reflect on their job, careers and the totality of their lives when they take structured time off the job and often return refreshed and energized.

The disadvantages of this type of programme are:

1. The MDS has little control over the aims and objectives of the programme.
2. The faculty can vary in excellence from brilliant to awful.
3. The participants can be wrongly selected, including the individual chosen by the MDS.

455

The consortium programme

The consortium programme eliminates most of the disadvantages and capitalizes on the advantages of external and internal programmes. This is done by agreeing with a variety of organizations on the objective of a programme, choosing a disinterested 'chairman', picking an ideal faculty and ensuring that the level of participants guarantees a high level of commitment and intellectual stimulation.

The first programme in the UK was the one I set up for Marks & Spencer. It included IBM, the Cabinet Office, Barclays Bank, Rothschilds Bank, Pilkingtons and a number of others. It is still operating at senior and middle management level.

TRAINING PACKAGES

Often advertised as offering 'all a trainer needs to conduct effective training at every level', training packages are attractive as they can be a useful adjunct to development activities already in operation. Indeed, they can form the basis of a whole range of associated activities. However, their ease can be their failing if an MDS is not concerned or knowledgeable about the underlying theoretical framework. Participants on any such programme soon see through hollow trainers who mouth words from the course manual and who are not able to answer questions, think on their feet, read the group and respond to it.

Some organizations who promote training packages offer to train trainers in their use, but what they often fail to do is check whether the packages are appropriate to the organization. They may claim that their training package can easily be assimilated within any current training or development activities, but this needs careful analysis for the following reasons:

1. Many packages originate in the USA and changing 'sidewalk' to 'pavement', or dubbing a Home Counties voice on a videotape, does not bridge the culture gap.
2. 'Ra, Ra' training may suit the marketing department of a floor polish company but not a firm of accountants, and there is no way that the style can be altered.
3. Packages which provide all materials down to flipchart pages and notes, and which do not allow the buyer any chance to 'personalize' or 'customize' them, are inflexible and show that they are not sensitive to the needs of the purchasing organization.

Computer-aided training and multi-media packages are becoming increasingly sophisticated and, with the advent of reasonably priced expert systems, this form of training and development will grow. (see Chapter 12.) It may not be possible for the MDS to check with previous users on the effectiveness of the offered systems as they may be completely new. If budgets will stretch, the best way to use this medium is to have it 'built' to the organization's own

456

specification rather than buying a package off the shelf.

SUMMARY

In these days, when training and development budgets are closely scrutinized – and yes, cut – and when a new management development manager is wary of trying out new approaches for fear of wasting the organization's money, it is more important than ever to be sure that the supplier of a development activity is the right one. Deciding who will supply consultancy or training/development services is often a matter of using the tried and tested, or is the whim of the chief executive, or the proximity of the seeking organization to a business school, or even shared experiences between the MDS and the supplier.

What I have endeavoured to outline in this chapter are some techniques and guidelines to ensure the choice of development suppliers is made in a professional manner. In the final analysis the question to be asked is: Will the development activity achieve positive results for the organization? If the results achieved are positive, and observable or quantifiable by whatever means deemed appropriate, then the supplier will have been effective.

FURTHER READING

Huczynski, Andrzej (1983) *Encyclopedia of Management Development Methods* (Aldershot: Gower).

Moulton, Harper (Annually) *The CER Evaluation Guide to Executive Programmes* (New York: Corporate Education Resources Inc.).

Oliver, Judy (1990) *Developing Managers. A Guide to Executive Programmes in Europe and the USA* (London: *Economist* Publications).

Rogers, Jane (1988) *MBA: The Best Business Tool? A Guide to British and European Business Schools* (London: *Economist* Publications).

Steverink, Leo (Annually) *European Management Education Guide* (Netherlands: IMEX).

Townsend, R. (1971) *Up the Organization* (London: Coronet).

Index